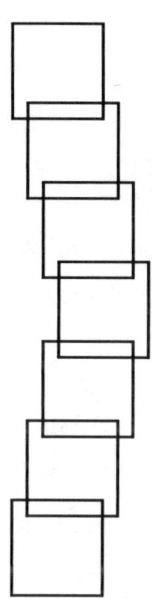

MANAGEMENT IN TRANSITION

Transforming Managerial Practices
and Organizational Strategies
for a New Work Culture

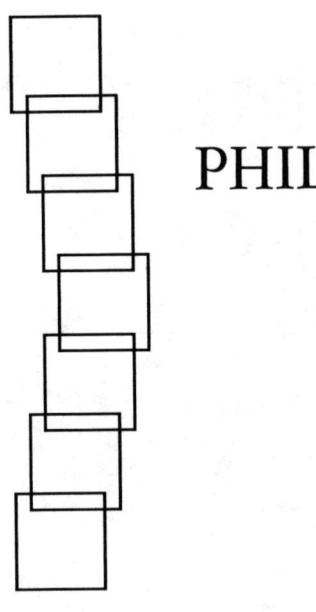

PHILIP R. HARRIS

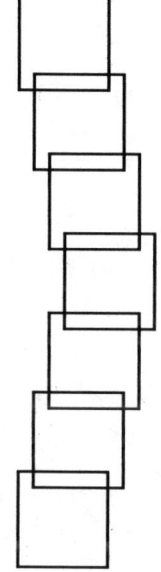

MANAGEMENT IN TRANSITION

Jossey-Bass Publishers

San Francisco • London • 1985

MANAGEMENT IN TRANSITION
Transforming Managerial Practices and Organizational Strategies for a New Work Culture
by Philip R. Harris

Copyright © 1985 by: Jossey-Bass Inc., Publishers
433 California Street
San Francisco, California 94104

Jossey-Bass Limited
28 Banner Street
London EC1Y 8QE

Philip R. Harris

Copyright under International, Pan American, and Universal Copyright Conventions. All rights reserved. No part of this book may be reproduced in any form—except for brief quotation (not to exceed 1,000 words) in a review or professional work—without permission in writing from the publishers.

Library of Congress Cataloging-in-Publication Data

Harris, Philip R. (Philip Robert) (date)
   Management in transition.

   (The Jossey-Bass management series) (The Jossey-Bass social and behavioral science series)
   Bibliography: p. 369
   Includes index.
   1. Corporate culture. 2. Leadership. 3. Organizational change. I. Title. II. Series. III. Series: Jossey-Bass social and behavioral science series.
HD58.7.H3695   1985   658.4   85-45055
ISBN 0-87589-660-X (alk. paper)

Manufactured in the United States of America

The paper in this book meets the guidelines for permanence and durability of the Committee on Production Guidelines for Book Longevity of the Council on Library Resources.

JACKET DESIGN BY WILLI BAUM

FIRST EDITION

Code 8532

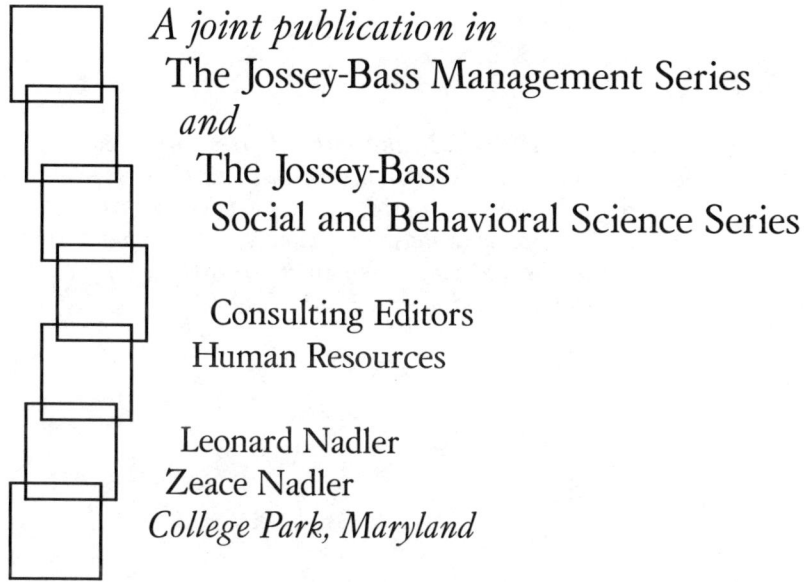

A joint publication in
The Jossey-Bass Management Series
and
The Jossey-Bass
Social and Behavioral Science Series

Consulting Editors
Human Resources

Leonard Nadler
Zeace Nadler
College Park, Maryland

To all creative deviants and risk takers in organizations, who exercise leadership in moving their systems beyond the status quo, but especially to three outstanding professionals who successfully experienced transitional management: Dorothy Lipp Harris, Joseph Ferreira, and Hank Koehn.

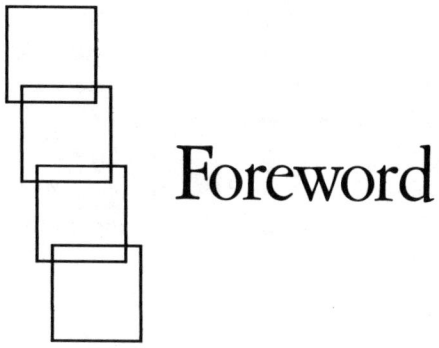

Foreword

This volume examines the themes of how new technologies are impacting work, reshaping its nature and scope, and requiring new forms of management adaptation. *Management in Transition* will be most useful to any manager seeking to adjust to the impact of new technology on the work culture he or she manages, any manager seeking to apply proactive thinking to decisions, any manager seeking to build excellence in organizational culture, and any manager wanting to analyze the adaptations of fast growth enterprises. It is an eclectic collection of insights and analyses about the present transitional dislocations. This book provides thoughtful managers with useful visions of our future destiny.

These Turbulent Times Are Different

A few years ago, in the course of a conversation with three other company presidents, many questions were asked. Are interest rates going up or down? Should we reorganize our work force now, or not at all? Should we diversify or not? After careful consideration, and to make a point, I replied to each "A versus B" question, "Yes!" Success in turbulent times requires us to plan both ways and to make the best decisions we can as we lead forward.

The plethora of business books of the 1980s verifies what we already know: We are suffering through future shocks and turbulent times; we are witnessing nine lifestyles in megatrends, while seeking the path toward excellence and high performance/high output management. Such works carry a message: The American economy has caught a cold and the whole world is reaching for Kleenex while various doctors exhort their favorite prescriptions. Contemporary business volumes are an indication that we have not yet fully arranged the final picture. The most perspicacious doctors, such as organizational psychologist Philip Harris, have acutely discerned the whole upheaval as symptoms of the transition. The American economy has been moving slowly from being the world's major smokestack industry center, the fast growing "caterpillar of the past," into the "chrysalis for the present." What is only dimly perceived are the features of the "beautiful butterfly of the future." Enough has been seen to give the fast track leaders and doers a basis for effective actions now. Thoughtful managers are in this frenetic chrysalis, acting to create their future, even if the butterfly will not emerge in its full splendor for twenty-five or more years.

Our author gives us perspective here as we move between the industrial past and the information/technology future. He concludes that four forces of change deserve special attention:

1. new technologies altering the work culture;
2. proactive vanguard thinking;
3. excellence in organizational culture;
4. adaptations of fast-growth enterprises.

Profile of Future Successes

Adapting successfully to these forces requires a critical strategy of changing the manager's functions into a profile of success. This book recommends a managerial orientation toward professional competence and self-actualization; talent utilization; participation and wellness; meaningful and personalized work experiences; an informal work environment; management by negotiation; the model of high performance that transforms

Foreword

the organization's culture; networks, continuous learning, and computer skills as priorities; intense working for fun and profit; corporate social responsibility; and the practice of synergy, collaborativeness, circular communication, risk taking, and innovation. As examples of the transformational management strategies, the author specifically discusses office automation, robotics, entrepreneurialism (and intrapreneurialism), and models of past and future work cultures.

Harris's thesis in this, his twenty-ninth major book on management and education, is that managers are in transition to the new work culture described in this text.

The author has reviewed the cutting-edge volumes in business and management and shares his analysis with us. Applying insights from cultural anthropology and psychology, this renowned management consultant provides practical examples of companies that have achieved superior results through adaptation, and he offers them as possible models for emulation.

The many organizations that, due to internal hardening of their arteries, fail to adapt, or that respond too slowly to the rapid changes in their environment, may do a major disservice to their work force and stockholders. Developing trends or shifts in what customers want need not leave the customers stranded. To prevent a market vacuum from developing, the author sees hope in activities of the entrepreneur—that lonely, gutsy, visionary who risks life, limb, family, security, and comfort to start a new business. Within the confines of the United States, at least 2,000 entrepreneurs everyday will make the decision to leave their secure jobs, while striving to implement their visions of creating new companies that satisfy many happy new customers. If entrepreneurialism had not already existed, today's economy would have to invent it to assure progress.

Doing the Right Things

Sounds good, we say, but how do we get down to specifics? If this is what is happening, what should we as managers of the existing, troubled, or uneasy companies start doing about it right now? The essence of the message here proposes:

1. Emphasize adult education. Reeducate our existing work force, especially managers to see employees as human capital to be developed, enhanced, and better utilized. Use the new technology to foster this human resource development.

2. Improve performance and productivity by linking compensation to performance and results. Then sustain a high performing corporate culture by adding fun, stimulating innovation, fostering participation, encouraging competence and communication, and offering adequate compensation. Our special attention is directed in this book to the strategies of building teams and networks. Successful team dynamics are seen as the key to high output and fast-growth management.

3. Cope successfully with the stresses of our turbulent times by (a) managing for wellness, (b) cultivating stimulating work challenges, (c) rewarding commitment, and (d) building influence and control to enhance the quality of work life.

4. Develop new models of management to cope with the rapid adaptations of the transition to the metaindustrial culture.

To ensure a successful transition, future organizations must emerge more humanized and technological, more focused and flexible, more cohesive and integrated, more creative and entrepreneurial, and led by managers who facilitate planned changes. Thus, effective new management transforms organizations to deal with these realities: a diversified work force; a type of work oriented toward information, technology, and service; a market economy that is global, volatile, competitive, and qualitative; an organizational structure that is multidimensional, encouraging more autonomy and entrepreneurship; and a society that is more pluralistic, global, and in constant change.

Adroit managers lead by example in planning for cultural changes while continually asking "What business *should* we be in?"

Making the Right Choices

I believe companies and organizations in transition have several options: They can focus on the past, present, or future. If they are overwhelmed, they will seek the nostalgia of the past

Foreword

and wither. If they act in the present, they will survive and adapt, presuming their environment changes slowly enough. If they perceive the future as opportunity, to be seized instead of just something with which they have to cope, they will grab the initiative, and see the butterfly emerge.

Should the work force perceive themselves as members of teams focusing on output and results, they will survive and even prosper. If they feel empowered to adventurous innovation and prudent risk, they can become the emergent butterfly. If they believe results bring certain reward, much can be accomplished. If they are motivated because they really want to contribute to "our success" and to accept this challenge, they can initiate the emergence of elegant butterflies.

It is up to organizational leadership to encourage such an outlook with high vitality and challenge. It is up to the new management to coach effectively and provide purpose and meaning to our colleagues at work. Leadership is a matter of taking the right actions, not merely a matter of our position or tactics. Reading this volume is certainly a step in the right direction. May each reader soar on the wings of butterflies and help his or her people to do the same!

Mountain View, California Martin Apple
July 1985 Chief Executive Officer
  Adytum, Inc., High Tech
  Business Development

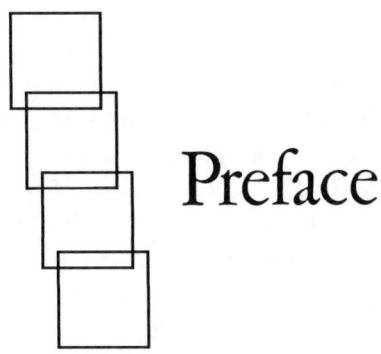

Preface

Have you ever experienced a profound personal transition that changed your attitudes, thinking, and life-style? If so, then you have insight into the turbulence and trauma that managers worldwide are going through as they struggle to redefine their roles and redirect their efforts. While a Fulbright professor in India, I went through a transitional experience, reflected in this book, that made me conscious of the need to change our outlook and approach to leadership. Since then my research, writing, and consulting have focused on the management of change and its relationship to the concepts of culture and communication. From that cross-cultural learning and what followed eventually emerged my two latest books on the new work culture. *Management in Transition* is the climax of those previous efforts.

As this book was being completed, two events occurred that confirm my course and insights. In 1983, the Graduate School of Business at the University of Southern California issued a journal entitled *New Management*. The meaning of the term is discussed in the opening chapter of this book, but the contents of that inaugural issue summarized what I had sensed for two decades: Major alterations were under way in managerial role and style, from the executive to supervisory levels. Then, in December 1984, *The Economist* reported on its survey of "the new corporate manager." Essentially, both publications reinforced my own position and writings about the global shift from the production of goods by machines to knowledge-intensive, often highly technical, work dominated by information processing. In advanced industrial societies this shift is a formidable force for change in the way we conduct business and manage people. It also alters the way in which we create wealth. As I revise these pages prior to publication, another work has appeared to further confirm my thesis. In *The Information Payoff: The Transformation of Work in the Electronic Age,* Strassman (1985) suggests that the explosion in information and in the use of information technologies fundamentally transforms our society and is comparable to the transition those in the past experienced in the movement from an agricultural to an industrial age.

This transition may explain why books on management have suddenly begun to make the best seller lists. People who have responsibility for managing resources—whether human, material, or natural—are searching for better ways of coping with rapid changes in society and the world of work. They seek to adapt their own management styles and their organizations to better fit people, and to be more effective and profitable.

Increasingly, the public looks to professional managers, whether in corporations, government, or other institutions, to exercise leadership in the ongoing cultural transformation. They have high expectations that those in management can help solve problems, not only within their own companies and agencies, but within the communities in which these organizations operate. With greater frequency, especially in newly industrialized countries, global managers are taking on the new roles of problem solver, shaper of culture, and even educator. The unfolding "information society" offers immense challenges and opportunities to the new manager and executive, particularly with reference to the use of the new technologies and controlling their impacts on people. *The Economist*'s Hugh Sandeman (December 22, 1984) emphasizes that the transformation of business and industry goes beyond changes in management methods to alteration of organizational patterns and to creation of a corpo-

Preface xvii

rate "high technology" culture that motivates both knowledge and service workers.

This book has been written with two audiences in mind. First, it is for the thinking executive and manager in the midst of role transition. It will prove valuable for professional development, either through personal reading and cogitation, or through formal human resource development.

The ideas in this book have been tested successfully in Managing the New Work Culture seminars sponsored by the National Training Laboratories (NTL) Institute. Thus, trainers and consultants will also find the volume a helpful resource in their management and executive development efforts.

However, the chapters have special value for informal management discussions and staff development. Groups of thinking managers might gather weekly for lunch, using one chapter a week as the springboard for sharing ideas and analyzing their own transitional experience with organizational renewal or with fast-growth enterprises.

The second audience for which this book is written is future managers—people who now are aspiring to management positions. They may already be in the job market as specialists, technicians, or professionals who seek administrative responsibility. Or they may be students in schools of business and management throughout the world.

Lester B. Korn, a leading executive search specialist, maintains that tomorrow's top managers should be increasingly futuristic, humanistic, cross-culturally oriented, and able to deal with technological change. For that to happen, he recommends that today's business schools develop broader interdisciplinary materials for their students. I hope that *Management in Transition* may contribute to these changes and, through the examples it offers of critical incidents and the descriptions it contains that are drawn from the real world of management, assist the business graduate to improve the human side of enterprise.

Peter Drucker (1985) is recognized as the prophet and philosopher of professional management as a discipline of exercising responsibility—something more than an art or science. His thinking has provided us with a transitional bridge into the twenty-first century business and management. In the midst of a management revolution, Drucker calmly focused our attention on the values of decentralization, management by objectives, and the need to concentrate on customers and market forces. *Management in Transition* reaffirms his message about the importance of risk taking, strategic decisions, integrated teams, managing by measurable results, and being able to relate business activities to the larger realities of the organization and the external environment. This book also underscores his pregnant insights about capitalization upon people's individual differences and natural talents, about diversity in viewpoints and solutions, about developing organizations that are learning environments, about providing roles where performance competence is possible and viewing the worker as a resource, not just a cost. In fact, most of the themes I identify as characteristic of the new work culture—be it the importance of information technologies, participatory management, or entrepreneurship and innovation—were first articulated by this lone scholar whom many academics rejected. My goal here is to contribute to the creation of future-oriented leaders, like Peter Drucker, who dare to be different by looking beyond present horizons and influencing tomorrow.

Overview of the Contents

The twelve chapters of this volume are designed to further the process of adaptation for contemporary executives and managers. Part One, "New Priorities and Roles for Management," contains six chapters that deal with various crucial dimensions of the new work culture. This section of the book is intended to help readers cope with immediate managerial and organizational renewal as well as with long-range planning and forecasting. Each chapter begins with an executive summary of main themes. Chapter One provides insights into how work is being transformed by technology and the resultant need to cultivate change in organizations and in management. It discusses transition in social systems and describes general strategies that

Preface

can further planned changes in organizational markets, structures, and attitudes. The chapter ends with an examination of futuristic organizational models and management styles.

Having considered some of the major developments in the work environment, Chapter Two goes on to concentrate on the new work culture, beginning with an in-depth definition of the term. From an examination of past work cultures, including the agricultural and industrial ages, the reader is directed to current trends and finally to projections of what is likely to happen in the future work environment. Insights are offered on today's and tomorrow's organizational cultures, with emphasis on how the practice of synergy can advance management effectiveness.

An increasingly significant aspect of the new work culture is entrepreneurialism, especially technological venturing. Chapter Three considers this phenomenon in terms of start-up enterprises, intrapreneurialism within existing organizations, and its relation to innovative management. The importance of entrepreneurialism to women is given special attention. The case study on entrepreneurialism reflects my experience as a consultant to key executives in a high-tech, start-up firm, and offers practical insights that may have application in other entrepreneurial settings. For example, there are ten guidelines, which range from the business plan to cash flow.

Chapter Four discusses human resource development for managers in the new work culture, focusing not only on how the new technologies affect people at work but also on how they can be the means to advance employees' education and training.

Chapter Five explores a central force changing our work environment and roles—automation, especially computerized operations. A case study directs special attention to the impact of office automation on a large corporation. The case study offers insights that may facilitate the introduction of new technologies into the reader's organization. The chapter goes on to consider how such automation alters the manager's role by opening new dimensions for obtaining and using information resources.

Chapter Six expands on the theme of automation but focuses on robotics—another technical development transforming both office and plant. This chapter describes how robotics are affecting jobs and people as well as productivity and profitability. Finally, the discussion centers on the future of robotics and manufacturing, and further alteration of managerial positions and relationships.

The second half of *Management in Transition* considers specific strategies for coping with organizational change. Chapter Seven analyzes ways to sustain and improve high performance, especially with a diversified staff that includes workers who are not necessarily full-time employees. Since a major characteristic of the new work culture is greater personnel involvement, Chapter Eight probes how we may manage more effectively through teams. Processes, activities, skills, roles, and building practices for improved team management are reviewed for the reader's benefit.

The new work environment calls for increasing information exchange among people, and Chapter Nine investigates how this can be done through networking. The reader is given the opportunity to compare how this may be accomplished either through personal or electronic networks, so as to stay on the cutting edge in his or her field.

Coping with myriad changes may cause stress and tension. Thus, Chapter Ten takes up the matter of managing for personal wellness as well as for corporate health. Stress management strategies and health maintenance resources are considered along with ways executive and employee lifestyles can be geared to maintaining wellness.

The concluding chapters in Part Two confront the twin issues of transition and transformation. Chapter Eleven focuses on the transitional experience and how it can be managed more effectively. The various manifestations of culture shock are described and strategies are offered for coping with change on a personal and professional basis. Specific consideration is given to role transformation, using examples of modern women and the manager as cases for consideration. Chapter Twelve focuses on the leadership tools necessary to meet the challenge of transformational management in the new work culture: specifically,

Preface

strategies for coping with organizational change as well as for capitalizing on the opportunities that emerge in this metaindustrial era.

A variety of resources for thoughtful managers are appended at the back of this book. They are primarily instruments intended to facilitate human factor data gathering for individual, group, and organizational analysis. Three of these are specifically aimed at assessment of transformational management skills, organizational roles and relationships, and quality of life. Two are for use in group situations relative to team synergy and maturity. All five instruments are supplemental to information provided in the text and offer the reader a chance for personal application of the theory presented there. The References constitute a bibliography of works, most published in the last ten years, that will help readers expand their awareness of changing management thought and practice.

Management in Transition combines contemporary theory and practical ideas drawn from my own applied research and my experience as a manager, administrator, and entrepreneur over the past forty years. It is a synthesis that includes my perspectives as university and corporate executive as well as lecturer, but especially as a behavioral science management consultant to over 170 human systems worldwide. It is the twenty-ninth book that I have written or edited on the subjects of education and management. My 1983 text, *New Worlds, New Ways, New Management,* provides an introduction to my analysis of the transformation to a metaindustrial work culture.

Acknowledgments

Management in Transition is the result of the contributions of many people, some in the organizations and publications about which I have written or that I have cited in the references, others who have provided support or inspiration in special ways. First and foremost, my wife, Dorothy Lipp Harris, professor of management at United States International University, graciously and judiciously provided editorial as well as professional advice throughout the writing of this book, and tested portions of it in her graduate courses. Second, Martin A. Apple, founder of Adytum and other high-tech firms, critiqued the manuscript and provided its foreword. As both client and friend, he has given me insight into high technology management and its challenges.

I am grateful, also, to Leonard Nadler, an esteemed colleague, who assumed the role of consulting editor for the fourth time on a book of mine, and his astute spouse, Zeace, who also consulted on this book. A special word of acknowledgment is due to George Kozmetsky, of the Institute for Constructive Capitalism at the University of Texas at Austin; his enthusiasm for entrepreneurialism inspired my approach to this topic in Chapter Three. I also wish to express profound gratitude to the thousands of managers and executives who have participated in my many leadership and management development programs. They have taught this management and organizational psychologist a great deal that is reflected in these pages.

La Jolla, California Philip R. Harris
July 1985

Contents

Foreword ix

Preface xv

The Author xxv

Part I: New Priorities and Roles for Management

1. Transforming Work, Organizations, and Management   1

2. Creating a New Work Culture   30

3. Venturing in Entrepreneurialism and Innovation   69

4. Advancing Human Resource Development Through New Technologies   99

5. Remaking Roles in Automated Enterprises   135

6. Realizing the Potential of Robotics   170

Part II: New Management and Leadership Strategies

7. Managing for High Performance — 203

8. Managing Effectively Through Teams — 227

9. Managing Effectively by Networking — 249

10. Promoting Employee and Executive Wellness — 269

11. Succeeding in Work, Role, and Personal Transitions — 299

12. Succeeding Through Transformational Management — 323

Resources: Instruments for Assessing Managerial and Organizational Performance

A. Inventory of Transformational Management Skills — 353

B. Team Synergy Analysis Inventory — 357

C. Group Maturity Analysis — 360

D. Organizational Roles and Relationships Inventory — 362

E. Quality-of-Life Index: A Manager's Health and Wellness Inventory — 365

References — 369

Index — 385

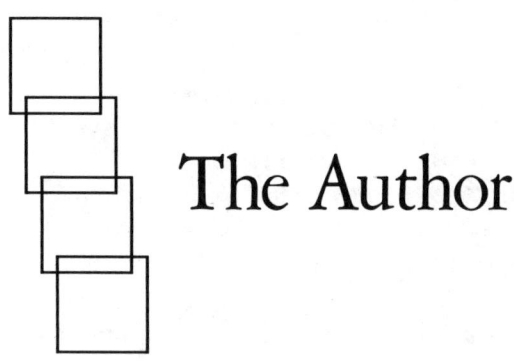

The Author

Philip R. Harris is president of Harris International, Ltd., in La Jolla, California. He received his B.A. degree (1949) in business administration from St. John's University, and his M.S. (1952) and Ph.D. (1956) degrees in counseling psychology from Fordham University. He was first licensed as a psychologist in 1959 by the University of the State of New York, Education Department.

For over twenty years, Harris has been engaged in action research as a management and organizational psychologist. In the field of behavioral science management, his research focus has been on leadership and human behavior in organizations, with particular emphasis on culture, communication, and the impact of change. Currently, Harris is investigating high-technology executive networking, high-performing employees, and the changing role of information professionals. He is engaged in research on space industrialization, and has received a faculty fellowship for a National Aeronautics and Space Administration (NASA) Summer Study at the University of California, San Diego (1984).

Awards Harris has received include New York City Young Man of the Year, from the Junior Chamber of Commerce (1959); Fulbright Professor to India, from the United States

State Department (1962); and the Torch Award for outstanding contributions to human resource development, from the American Society for Training and Development (1975).

Harris has written or edited more than 29 books and more than 160 journal articles. His recent management books include *New Worlds, New Ways, New Management* (1983), *Managing Cultural Synergy* (1982, with R. T. Moran); *Managing Cultural Differences* (1979, with R. T. Moran); *Improving Management Communication Skills* (1978, with D. L. Harris); and *Effective Management of Change* (1976). As an editor, he recently produced *Global Strategies for Human Resource Development* (1984) for the American Society for Training and Development, and *Innovations in Global Consultation* for the International Consultants Foundation (1980). Two of his books have been translated into Japanese. For several years, he wrote a column on training for *Successful Meetings* (1974-1978).

As a consultant with a global practice, Harris has served over 170 human systems, concentrating on executive, management, and organization development. His clients include multinational corporations (IBM, Control Data, N. V. Philips, General Motors), government agencies (NASA, United States Forest Service, U.S. Department of Labor, U.S. Department of Education); military services (U.S. Navy, U.S. Marine Corps, Army Corps of Engineers); consulting organizations (The Diebold Group, American Management Associations, Young Presidents Organization); and trade and professional associations (American Institute of Banking, American Association of Museums, Association of Venezuelan Executives). On international assignments, Harris frequently works with his wife, psychologist Dorothy Lipp Harris.

A school and higher education administrator from 1952 to 1964, Harris served last as vice-president of development for St. Francis College in Brooklyn, New York (1959-1964). He has been a visiting professor and lecturer in many universities worldwide, including Pennsylvania State University, Temple University, and Sophia University in Tokyo. He also has served as a senior associate for Leadership Resources, Inc.

(1966-1969), a fellow of the National Training Laboratory (NTL) (1968-1984), and as vice-president for management and organization development at Copley International Corporation (1970-1971).

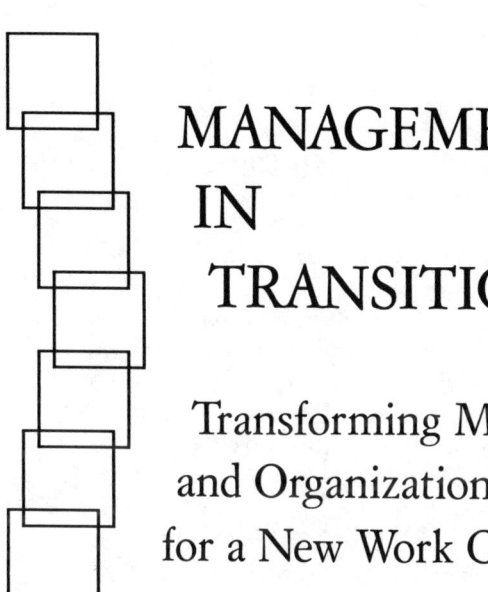

MANAGEMENT IN TRANSITION

Transforming Managerial Practices
and Organizational Strategies
for a New Work Culture

The corporate world that we have grown up in is changing radically. Gone is the grey flannel "organization man" safe in a bureaucratic hierarchy. Here to stay are the entrepreneurs, the innovators, the "hands on" shirtsleeves risk takers who are pointing us in the direction of a global economy.

We need these "changemasters" to get us through these diverse and increasingly competitive times. And we ourselves must adapt and change, too. Because it is our responsibility to lead our evolving organizations, and to do so effectively will require new knowledge and more finely tuned management skills.

Thomas R. Horton
President and Chief
Executive Officer
American Management
Associations

ONE

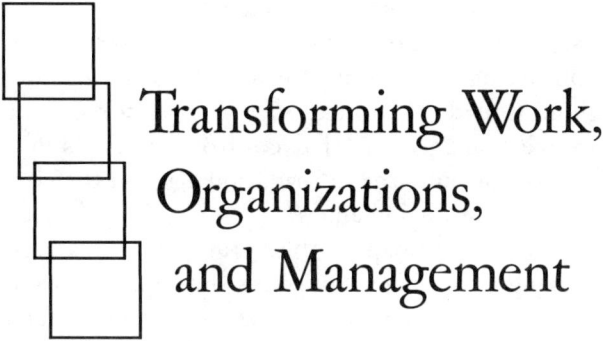

Transforming Work, Organizations, and Management

Executive Summary. Today's managers function between two worlds of work—industrial and postindustrial. Thus, in a sense, contemporary management is cross-cultural and requires a transition from the traditional way of operating to experimentation with new styles of managing. Thinking managers not only are aware of the changes underway in the emerging information society and work environment but are innovative and futuristic in their coping strategies.

This chapter provides an overview of four major developments deserving the attention of "metaindustrial management": these are trends toward (1) the adoption of new technologies, (2) vanguard management thinking and planning, (3) excellence in organizations, and (4) fast-growth enterprises. In view of these trends, it becomes clear that we must rejuvenate our images of the organization and of management: The outcome will be a new management and work culture characterized by organizational changes in terms of markets, structures, and attitudes. As a result, leaders will be better able to facilitate the transition of people and human systems into the twenty-first century.

The Transformation of Work

What is the common theme in each of the following critical incidents recently reported in various media?

- Britain's Marks & Spencer, the retail group, does not manufacture anything and administers as little as possible. It contracts its entire computer bureau and is now considering contracting for its entire personnel department.
- The U.S. Department of Agriculture's forest service has inaugurated a continuing exercise in "futuring" for its Pacific/Southwest Region. Called "Vision-1995," it is a forecasting strategy for resource management that confronts with its new technology the transition into the information age and the consequent need for organizational changes.
- Sears, Roebuck is reshaping the nature of its business. Formerly emphasizing providing retail goods through stores and catalogues, it now is offering diverse personal services, many through subsidiaries or contractors, that range from finances to eye care.
- As a result of deregulation, AT&T is struggling to transform itself from Ma Bell, the telephone company, into an aggressive and diversified telecommunication-information conglomerate. In the process, it is reducing its national work force by 11,000 and moving toward building a full-scale communication network to connect with the personal computers it now markets.
- In response to competition, IBM has acquired the Rolm Corporation in Santa Clara, California, so as to obtain networking capabilities for the linking of customer communications and computing. The people at the smaller Silicon Valley firms are uneasy about being swallowed up by the computer giant. What will it do to their driving entrepreneurial spirit? Some Rolm employees are experiencing symptoms of stress as a result of the takeover—stomachaches, headaches, and backaches.
- Federal Express, the fast-growth delivery company, can adjust its work schedule from twenty to thirty-two hours a week to match changes in market demand. This is because one third of its work force is part-time; to protect its core of full-time employees, the company varies its reliance on subcontractors.

What is evident in the previous situations is that business, be it in the public or private sector, is not being conducted as usual. All of the organizations cited are in transition from traditional operations, experimenting with a new style of managing. All are coping with rapid change and, in the process, they are literally revamping the work culture. Most managers caught in the middle of this profound social shift function on two planes —one is the way we have always done things, and the other is the way we are going to do them from now on into the twenty-first century.

Thus, in a way, all management has become cross-cultural. We used to think of cross-cultural management as occurring when one left his or her homeland to engage in business or professional activity in an alien culture. Now, organizational leaders are involved in crossing over from old, familiar work environments into a strange, sometimes uncomfortable, exciting business scene. The only certainty about the future is that we will be dealing with uncertainty and impermanence as we shape the new work culture.

There was a time when the term *technology transfer* referred to the movement of advanced technology from the First World to the less developed Third World countries. Now, the term can mean the replacement or supplementing of low tech with high tech. It is no wonder managers are bewildered by the scope and speed of new technologies, as well as by the way commercial activity is being altered. In the office, for instance, managers cope simultaneously with the introduction of automation, communication networks, computer graphics, data base management, information centers, performance modeling, and configuration management. What, then, is happening in the work arena, and how did it begin?

For about 125 years, the United States has been in the industrial stage of human development. This industrialization stimulated a way of life that influenced our history and culture; it made its presence known in everything from legislation to occupations, but most of all in the economy. Such industrialization was experienced by many Western nations, as well as by Japan. Regardless of where this phenomenon took place, it created a work culture centered around urbanization, factories, and machines. It replaced the agricultural stage of development, with its emphasis on a rural way of life largely focused on farming and ranching. In some nations, such as England, this process of industrialization was spread over several hundred years, while in the United States the transition occurred in just over a century.

During the first eighty years of the twentieth century in most advanced economies, the industrial culture dominated both family and work life. The shift is away from merely producing things, to the processing of information and the providing of services. Currently, we are at a major turning point in our way of living and working that is postindustrial. The difference now is that the transition is taking place in decades, not centuries, and the new technologies are doubling the amount of information available to us in the metaindustrial work culture almost every twenty-five years. Figure 1 depicts this acceleration in terms of our changing work environment and information.

Figure 1. Perspective of Human Development and Work Culture.

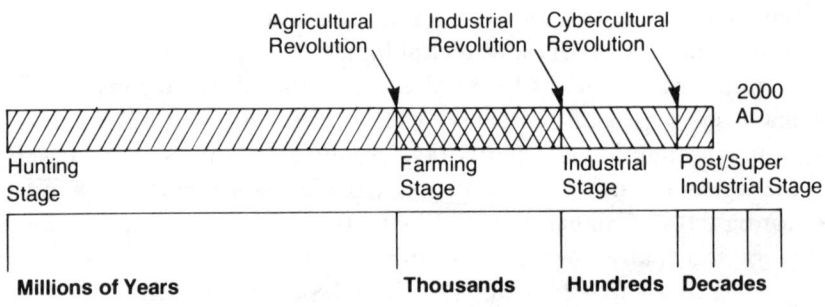

1 million = 1,000 thousands = 10,000 hundreds = 100,000 tens (decades)

Some executives and managers heeded the early warnings of scholars, researchers, and futurists predicting the impact of such technological change upon business and organizations. They undertook strategic planning and management to alter their corporate processes, products, and services. However, many leaders failed to prepare themselves and their colleagues for entry into the turbulent new work life. Thus, we hear of turmoil and trauma in the business world and among human systems, often accompanied by future shock in individuals and organization shock in institutions. Among traditional factory and craft workers, the media has labeled it "blue-collar blues." For some personnel, the transition to a technological work culture has been marked by economic hardship and disillusionment, as chaotic changes take place in the classic organizational missions, structures, and production, causing many occupations to become obsolete, some industries to become archaic, and some institutions or agencies to question their very purpose of existence.

National media accentuate the problems and pain of this transfer when reporting the increasing business bankruptcies, plant closures, and massive reductions in work force. In the early 1980s, for instance, press stories reported that 19 percent of the autoworkers would be on indefinite lay-off, while 119,000 steelworkers would be idle because their industry was operating at only 42 percent of capacity. Organization shock was evident in 1982 when 25,346 American businesses went bankrupt, but positive effects of the on-going transition were evident: In that same year, 566,942 new companies came into being, many of them in high-tech fields and many owned by women. From 1983 to 1984, the American economy generated 4.2 million new jobs. The phenomenon of changes in the economy and organizational transitions even made a national magazine cover story. In an editorial on the upheavals, the job market was described aptly as a shifting mosaic of dead ends and bright prospects. The introduction to this feature symbolized the transition in one New England factory: "Near the corner of Main and Walnut streets in the small town of Maynard, Massachusetts, stands a massive complex of aged red brick buildings. Within those walls, workers toiled amid clanging, churning machinery to produce carpets in the 1850s and Army blankets during two World Wars. But today the sturdy, old facade houses an entirely different enterprise. The noisy machines and the grease-stained factory have given way to offices where engineers huddle over glowing oscilloscopes and secretaries peck quietly at word processors. The woolen mill has been reborn as the headquarters of the Digital Equipment Corporation, the second largest computer manufacturer in the world!" ("The New Economy," 1983).

Such a transformation is indicative of the emerging new economy, which is surging ahead under the cataclysm of innovative, high-tech activities. The transition of the old New England factory into a high-technology headquarters epitomizes the metamorphosis underway and the opportunities being created. Yet, Lester Thurow of the M.I.T. Sloan School of Management, warns that we must also endeavor to prevent the decline of industrial America. He maintains that while manufacturing is on the edge of an economy recovery, the smokestack industries and even high-tech growth are being threatened because of their inability to compete against lower prices in the international marketplace. This economist suggests that part of the problem is caused by driving up the costs of our products in the private sector through bureaucracies which add too much managerial and support staff instead of reducing them by intelligent use of new technologies. If the free enterprise system and its market economy are to function in a healthy and growing manner, then transformational management becomes essential.

Thinking managers are conscious of the deeper implications behind such major social and economic changes. They have vision and the ability to project ahead, anticipate, and plan strategy. Thoughtful managers analyze and act globally, and they are not locked into old mind sets and obsolete business procedures. Thus, they are able to influence the future and lead their people into the new age that is upon us. Jonas Salk (1983) reminds us that evolution is a process of changing relationships and suggests that we now live in a time of metabiological evolution—that is, a period when ideas are as important as genes and wisdom is becoming a new criterion for fitness. By that Salk meant the ability to look into the future, to consider the consequences of decisions and judgments made today, to learn from the past and from failures, and to live between two epochs. If we are to use both the present and the past as a trajectory into the future, thinking managers must be aware of

Transforming Work, Organizations, and Management   7

significant trends and be able to capitalize on them. John Naisbitt (1982, 1983) highlighted some of these "megatrends":

- the transformation from an industrial to an information society (refer to Figure 1);
- the simultaneous growth of high touch with high technology, as people seek to aggregate to make up for any technological dehumanization;
- the shift from a national to a global economy, in which economic efforts are interdependent;
- the passage from short-term to long-term perspective in thinking and planning;
- the movement away from centralized structures and concentrations to decentralized or more localized responsibility;
- the inclination away from institutional to self-help, whether in terms of education, health, or welfare;
- the turning from representative to participatory democracy, so that people can be more involved in influencing their own life space;
- the demographic shift from north to south, from frostbelt to sunbelt, with its implications for new infrastructures and political representation;
- the shift in personal choice from either/or to multiple options; and
- the transition in America from a male-dominated society to a more androgynous one in which the male/female contribution is more balanced.

Such social trends have their counterparts in business or organizational trends, such as the democratization of management and the demands of women for salary equality and management responsibility. Here, it is appropriate to focus on four related developments.

The Trend Toward New Technologies. Just as the invention of the steam engine was the benchmark of the industrial revolution, so the creation of the computer may be said to be the catalyst of the cybercultural, microelectronic, or information revolution (Forester, 1985). *Cybernetics* was the term invented by the late M.I.T. physicist, Norbert Wiener, to describe the science of communication and control in man and machines; through cybernation or advanced automation, the computer and/or robots become extensions of the human brain, capable of directing and supervising machines. With such new technologies, a super- or supraindustrial work culture is coming into being.

AT&T used the designation *metaindustrial* in one of its emerging issues studies to explain that we have moved beyond the industrial way of thinking and acting (Coleman, 1980). Metaindustrial management may have come into being in the late 1950s when the U.S.S.R. and the United States began to launch space satellites. The complexity of space missions to successfully send unmanned and manned spacecraft into orbit called for another kind of management. Seamans and Ordway (1977, p. 270) said it best when commenting on this space heritage: "The Apollo project which landed a team of American astronauts on the Moon is generally considered as one of the greatest technological endeavors in the history of mankind." But, to achieve this, a managerial effort no less prodigious than the technological one was required.

In other words, large-scale enterprises like these required leadership practices that went beyond the traditional, and the innovations that resulted may very well be the prototypes of what is called new management. Thus, NASA and its contracting partners in the aerospace industry created matrix and team management and used Planned Program Evaluation and Review Technique (PERT) and computer systems to track decision implementation. The effective management of space macroprojects meant integrating diverse disciplines, talents, technologies, and resources around the globe (Levine, 1982). Unique goal achievement and penetration of the high frontier were accomplished when Armstrong and Aldrin reached the lunar surface and left this message: "Here Men from the Planet Earth first set foot upon the Moon, July 1969, A.D. We came in peace for all mankind!" The new space management now had opened the way for *new* space markets and industrialization.

But, for the moment, let us concentrate on the technological spinoffs of outer space endeavors that contributed so much to the emergence of high-technology industry. What are some of these new technologies that are a driving force in the metaindustrial work culture? Finkelstein and Newman (1984) provided this synthesis:

- *Microprocessors:* low-cost and complete desk-top computer systems with peripherals, which extend the powers of all managers. Their availability has led to the emergence of managerial work stations and decentralized information systems and, consequently, less dependence by managers on secretaries and support staff. Microprocessors' spreading use is undermining traditional structures and styles, roles and relationships.

- *Computer-aided design/manufacturing* (CAD/CAM)—which is both a technique and an art. This capability is abetting reindustrialization, shortening the life cycle of design and manufacturing, and contributing to computerized production. It changes tooling, ordering, scheduling, and inspection; coupled with robotics, it lowers production costs.

- *Fiber optics and telecommunications*—new communications breakthroughs that can be used by management. Fiber optics employs photons of light on logic chips and expands the number of messages that can be handled simultaneously. Telecommunications by means of satellite permits the quick transfer of messages and materials over vast distances, such as through facsimile transmission, videotext, teletext, and cellular telephones.

- *Biogenetics/bioagriculture:* The bioengineering of plants, animals, and humans. DNA deciphering has led to the synthetic production of interferon and insulin, programmed bacteria, protein production, plant cloning, and a new genealogy of plants. It has resulted in the "green revolution" and the spawning of new businesses in "biotech," "agtech," or "gentech" areas.

- *Lasers/holography:* versatile and powerful tools using light beams or three-dimensional photography. Lasers can weld together a detached retina, bore a tunnel, or be used as a weapon. Holography can produce high-volume images in microscopy or advertising, as well as create optimal memories for storing large amounts of binary data. It has been used for everything from mapping salt domes and oil prospecting to enhancing radar/sonar capability.

The preceding five categories are the principal driving technologies altering our society and work culture. Every day more inventions and patents expand the list of these high technologies, which causes rapid technological obsolescence while doubling knowledge every five to seven years. John Zysman, codirector of the Berkeley Round Table on the International Economy at the University of California, believes that the new technologies are transforming the whole economy as well as backward industries considered labor intensive. He maintains that these advanced technologies must be applied not only to textiles and apparel making but also to the making of pens, washing machines, and other consumer goods. Zysman advocates both government investment incentives in this regard and the establishment of "extension services" to help high technologies spread—such as those that helped make American farms the most efficient in the world ("The High-Tech Challenge," 1984). The outcome of such innovations are fresh business activities altering conventional products, marketing, management, personnel, and resource allocation strategies.

The Trend Toward Vanguard Management Thinking and Planning. Two types of organizations and executives coexist today, according to James O'Toole (1983), a professor at the University of Southern California's Center for Futures Research. The "old guard" consists of those clinging to industrial-age mind sets and management practices, ever mindful of immediate profit and stock market response to their corporate practice. This kind of thinking probably prevailed in the forty companies no longer on the list of "*Fortune* 100" corporations that dominated industry fifty years ago, in contrast to the sixty on the list that are still succeeding in business.

The "vanguard" group, on the other hand, is abuzz with change and is more visionary, concerned with long-range performance and strong, shared cultural characteristics in the organization. Members of this group operate on a corporate philosophy of multiple responsibility: "When you visit the vanguard corporations, they say 'The purpose of this corporation is to provide goods and services that society needs and to provide employment.' The way that is done is to satisfy the interests of various stakeholders. The stakeholders include the shareholders, but also the employees, consumers, communities they serve, broader society, and future generations" (Fleming, 1983, p. 2).

Corporate philosophy that is straightforward and inspirational is essential for stimulating excellence in organizational culture. For example, IBM's philosophy is simply: Respect the individual, provide the best service in the world, and excel in execution. The founder of Johnson & Johnson established a philosophy consisting of four priorities: first, the customer; second, the employees; third, the community; fourth, the shareholders. The vanguard corporations are learning organizations, because their executives assume that there is always something they do not know, and they are willing to change. In the *Los Angeles Times,* O'Toole cites some examples of companies with such cultural characteristics: Atlantic Richfield, Control Data, Dayton Hudson, John Deere, Honeywell, Kodak, Motorola, and Weyerhaeuser.

O'Toole's research (see O'Toole, 1982), part of a twenty-year forecast study, may indicate why he and his colleagues at the University of Southern California Graduate School of Business Administration launched a magazine, *New Management,* for executives who want to be in the vanguard (available from Wilson Learning Corporation, 6950 Washington Ave. South, Eden Prairie, Minn. 55344). In the first editorial, O'Toole (1983, p. 3) encapsulated the theme of this book as follows:

New management organizations are:

- oriented toward tomorrow, constantly attuned to the long-term future;
- oriented toward people, dedicated to the fullest development and utilization of human resources;
- oriented toward product, more committed to the consumer market than to the stock market;
- oriented toward technology, determined to develop and employ the most advanced tools available;

- oriented toward quality, concerned with excellence, service, and competence;
- oriented toward external environment, actively exerting leadership in meeting concerns of stakeholders from the local community, to the nation, to the world community;
- oriented toward free market competition, imbued with the innovative spirit of risk-taking capitalism;
- oriented toward continuing examination and revision of corporate values, compensation, reward, and incentive systems;
- oriented toward basic management concerns, such as the making and selling of things or the providing of services;
- oriented toward innovation and openness to new ideas, nurturing and encouraging those who question the oldest corporate assumptions and who propose the boldest changes.

Interestingly, *New Management* is now into its second volume and devoted an issue (1985, no. 3) to discussion of the ideas of the "father of new management," Peter Drucker, who provided the seminal thoughts for the above managerial orientations.

The Trend Toward Excellence in Organizational Structure. Such vanguard thinking and planning becomes internalized through the culture of metaindustrial organizations. The Federal Reserve Bank of Atlanta, for example, asked Wall Street analysts and branch directors for their choices of the top companies in the Southeast. Among the well-respected 100 companies that emerged were 22 high performers (such firms as Charter Medical, Coca-Cola, Delta Airlines, Federal Express, Flowers Industries, Home Depot, Nucor, and Sonoco Products). Common threads among these excellent companies correlate somewhat with O'Toole's stated characteristics—namely, commitment to technology, highly motivated workers, decentralized decision making, generally informed management, a corporate sense of mission, and encouragement of employee stock ownership. Basically, these high-achieving organizations are people oriented, so they motivate the rank and file, as well as management ("Top Companies . . . ," 1984).

After writing the best selling book *In Search of Excellence* with Robert Waterman in 1982, Thomas Peters rechecked

Transforming Work, Organizations, and Management

conclusions of that study (1983b). He subsequently found in working with 200 groups of executives that his earlier conclusions not only were confirmed but were underestimated. On the basis of his research, Peters offered the following suggestions for those who would renew their corporate or agency culture:

- Cultivate a bias for action rather than being overly analytical—"do it, fix it, try it."
- Stay close to the customers by seeking product ideas from them, listen intently and regularly, and then provide superior, tailored service of quality and reliability.
- Foster autonomy and entrepreneurship by encouraging innovation, creativity, practical risk taking, and support of "good tries"—innovations do not usually occur according to plan.
- Obtain productivity through people, treating them as adults with dignity and respect; regard employees as a capital investment and avoid we/they labor attitudes.
- Use approaches to management that are hands-on, value driven—walk the plant floors, visit the stores, meet personally employees and customers (MBWA = managing by wandering around).
- "Stick to the knitting" means stay with what one does best and avoid acquisitions of businesses about which one knows nothing.
- Maintain simple staffs and lean form in terms of both structure and numbers.
- Balance control simultaneously with loose/tight properties—that is, be both centralized and decentralized, push autonomy down to the product development team or shop floor while supporting central, core values. Now Peters (1985) has further expounded on these themes in a new book, *A Passion for Excellence: The Leadership Difference.*

Notice how the themes of such researchers as O'Toole and Peters confirm and supplement one another. They even corroborate one another's findings in many selections of vanguard/ excellent companies. They note the importance of encouraging a volume of small experimental groups, of having a common culture and technological background, of intangibles that contribute to successful achievement—such as quality service, championing people and their ideas, and small-scale control. The fundamental message of such scholars is that excellence in organizational culture can be achieved through emphasizing customer service, open communications, and improved community relations while deemphasizing rules, regulations, and excessive reliance on numbers and papers. The soundness of such observations is not diminished by critics who point to some of the "excellent companies" that subsequently get into difficulty because of changes in the economy or the market. Such choices are relative to conditions at the time of identification. For instance, in a 1985 television interview, Peters still defended forty-two of his forty-three choices for excellent companies, regretting only the nomination of Atari. Meanwhile, his research with Waterman has spawned a growth industry of books, films, videos, and documentaries on excellence in management.

Are there other aspects of organizational culture and managerial know-how that contribute to excellence? My research into successful macromanagement may provide metaindustrial managers with additional insights for improving performance. The very thinking, style, and skills that make for effective leadership in large-scale enterprises have transfer applications to other management situations (Harris, 1984):

- *synergy*—the capacity to facilitate cooperation and collaboration in bringing together diverse elements so as to produce more than the sum of their parts;
- *intercultural skill*—the competency to overcome differences in people and cultures through cross-cultural communication and negotiation;
- *managing interfaces*—the capability to bring together on time various resources required to achieve project or mission goals (such as human, information, technology, material, and financial resources);
- *political savvy*—the ability to identify, then gain support and agreement from, various constituencies or governmental actors/entities so vital to program success;
- *financial astuteness*—knowledge of economic realities and constraints and the ability to put together the necessary

funding to undertake and complete a project while controlling excessive expenditures;

• *cosmopolitanism*—sensitivity to global issues affecting a program or project, such as legal, ecological, environmental, or human issues, the capacity to cope with them effectively, and the consequent interdependence of decisions and actions. These are additional leadership qualities to be cultivated in the new work culture. They may not be present in any one person but can be possessed by a team that is carefully put together and supported (Brown, 1982).

The Trend Toward Fast-Growth Enterprises. The acceleration of change and the rapid advances of the last half century are rolling back the frontiers of the mind, as well as telescoping our sense of time: What would have taken a hundred years to accomplish in the industrial age now can be done in ten. Those managers and entrepreneurs that anticipated these changes and rode the wave of innovation now prosper. For instance, among the early winners in the new work situation is high-tech-minded Michael Boone. As a twenty-one-year-old Stanford University student, he started a computer software company in his dormitory room; before he graduated, he was president of a million-dollar corporation. But this wave of innovation is an uneven wave, bringing uneven benefits to different people, regions, and companies. At the moment, Adam Osborne and his company, Osborne Computers, are down but attempting a comeback, while Steven Jobs and Apple still ride the crest. The losers, in any event, are those who do not master the new technological tools and languages or understand their implications—such as why automation is hastening the disappearance of skilled craftspeople, draftspeople, and middle managers. Or inquire, why statistics is not taught in American elementary schools, as it is in Japan.

In less than a generation, advanced, technically oriented countries have raced toward a radically different economy. What are the new businesses that have resulted like? The companies spawned are called "fast growth," and their managers are on the "fast track." They are more likely to be found in magazines for entrepreneurs, such as *Inc.* or *Venture,* than in *For-*

tune or *Forbes. Venture* publishes an annual "Fast Track 100" directory of the 100 largest businesses that were started in the last decade and are still run by their founders (Weber, 1983). For 1982, the range was from number 1, Apple Computer, Inc., with $583 million in sales, to number 100, Intertec Data Systems Corporations, with $20.7 million in sales. Careful examination of such rankings may indicate where the American economy is going and where the looming growth industries and jobs may be. Analysis reveals that two thirds of these enterprises are in the sunbelt states and that 47 of them are high-tech firms while 39 are service companies. It is obvious that the new economy will be oriented toward both information processing and services businesses—the latter already account for 87 percent of the gross national product and employ 70 percent of the United States work force. The high-growth service companies tend to be run by management groups with centralized support services and are concentrated in health care, transportation, retailing, restaurants, and consulting (Kozmetsky, Gill, and Smilor, 1985).

For thinking managers attempting to get a sense of the future, other characteristics of the fast-growth, high-performing companies also are worthy of note:

- They utilize capital-intensive concepts, such as software programming, franchising, discounting, and lean organizations.
- They favor an economy of scale toward a smaller rather than a larger company.
- They are capable of swiftly meeting foreign competition by real innovation that is not easily copied.
- They employ educated, often technically oriented, knowledge workers, training them in-house for more sophisticated positions.
- They operate with a small management team with technical, marketing, and survival skills necessary for the high-tech or fast-growth environment.
- They seek growth areas for business expansion, such as leisure activities, computer hard- and software, biotechnology, and robotics.
- They attract executives with a mind set that is differ-

ent from the conventional, whose slogan is, "How much better it could be; let's go out and make it happen."

What do the fast-growth organizations look like and how do people work in them? The new economy companies do not put great emphasis on appearances and hierarchy or on such trappings as expensive offices, prestigious titles, and special executive privileges. The entrepreneurs seek low-cost facilities, and they thrive on informality and risk taking. Further, they can experience spectacular growth rates—from 25 percent to 400 percent per year. Apple Computers, for instance, went from start-up in the garage of two college dropouts to the *"Fortune 500"* list in just six years. The pace of the fast-growth firm is exciting and may generate fabulous wealth and new roles and careers, as well as new perils. For managers and technicians, the stimulating work life is also conducive to rapid burnout, especially among key executives, and preventive measures for stress management are essential (see Chapter Ten). The Pulitzer-prize-winning best seller, *The Soul of the New Machine,* graphically describes life in one such computer entity (Kidder, 1981).

Overnight, these high-growth companies seem to spread across the land as they create new high-tech industrial parks and then "valleys of the chips" while expanding into the international marketplace. We can see prototypes of tomorrow's organizations in the silicon valleys of both northern and southern California, along Massachusetts's Route 128 strip, and in North Carolina's Research Triangle Park. They spawn out of North America even into the Third World. Depressed cities, states, and nations offer a variety of incentives to attract the new industry —from tax breaks, seed money, and venture capital to buildings, laboratories, and research centers. For relocation, the fledgling firms, such as MCC of Austin, favor areas with high-quality university resources and research facilities, as well as localities that offer personnel the best quality of life, including reasonably priced housing.

The fast-growth/high-technology corporations are catalysts in the creation of the new information society (Masuda, 1981). The implications are global, whether in England, the mother of the industrial revolution, or in Japan, the beneficiary of postwar revitalization of its industries. What the latter's prime minister, Yasushi Nakasone, pointed out to his countrymen is valid for the entire planet's citizenry: "Japan has reached the stage at which we must create with our own wisdom and effort an unexplored society which no country in the world has yet experienced.... Complete rethinking of attitudes and policies which characterized economic management until now will be necessary" ("Nakasone Urges Technology Focus," 1983, p. 2).

New Images of Organizations and Management

The transformation underway is prodding us to alter the way we look at human institutions and their leaders. After all, an organization is simply a collection of people mobilized to action by common objectives, expectations, and obligations. But, today, we also envision an organization as an energy exchange system: The input of psychic, physical, or material energy is converted and channeled into constructive output. An organization also has a life cycle as it grows, develops, expands, stabilizes, declines, and disappears—unless it is revitalized and continues in altered form (Kimberly, Miles, and Associates, 1980). Within the macroculture of society, the organization is a microculture with its own unique system for communication and language, dress and appearance, food and feeding habits, time and time consciousness, rewards and recognitions, relationships and sexuality, values and norms, senses of self and space, processes and learning, beliefs and attitudes, and habits and customs (Harris and Moran, 1979).

Since the organization is a dynamic human system, it experiences the need for renewal and may go through transitions that result in transformations. Such changes may occur because of new people, new technology, or new circumstances. When reorganization takes place, it involves the severing of existing relationships, the dissolution of existing roles, structures, and arrangements—transformation through planned renewal or change is the ideal. With high-growth companies, the organizational life cycle from birth to death or to retrenchment may be compressed. Their way of coping with the reality of impermanence is open-ended innovation in every aspect of their business.

As organizations change, so must their managers; during periods of such instability, managers with vision have rare opportunities to influence organizational directions, to exercise more leverage and power, to carve out new roles, and to create new life forms or structures. Whatever the role of executive or manager may evolve to, society is already expressing greater expectations of such persons in this postindustrial period. For example, my wife, Dorothy L. Harris, a management professor and consultant, once startled an audience of multinational executives by reminding them that they were the new priests, the new educators, and the new creators of culture, especially in developing economies.

The practice of professional management has always been conceived of as both a science and an art. Thus, it was refreshing to read in *The Tarrytown Letter* this description of the business leader as the ultimate artist (Clarke, 1983, p. 3): "When the Renaissance and the Reformation split off high art for the elect, and folk art for the commoner, the bourgeois businessman, already in the middle, arrived at the threshold of the modern era with little or no artistic heritage. High art above him, folk art beneath him, he simply moved out to pioneer in the unseen and unknown. There he designed and built modern civilization, the most stupendous creation yet in the history of man, with headquarters in the U.S.A. As Eric Hoffer once noted, the great artists of America were the well known figures who created railroads, sewing machines, air brakes, barbed wire, automobiles, telephones, and on and on. The Westinghouses, the Bells, the Deeres, the Singers, and the Fords not only established America's Middle Class, they established America as the middle itself, the most powerful option in Western history against the narrow alternative of lord or serf, rich or poor."

What is the image that business schools give their graduates of management? Narrow-minded M.B.A. types who think only in quantifiable terms and are driven solely by the "bottom line" will not be able to transform society, much less their own organizations. Fortunately, many universities are broadening their curricula to match the new image of a manager's role. Tomorrow's managers will represent a convergence of study between science and commerce, between technology and the humanities. They will be equally comfortable in solving global housing shortages, in protecting the environment, in managing human services, or in industrializing space.

Today's managers still operate in flux and uncertainty in a time marked by economic recession and growth contradictions. With multiple options available, we realize that there is no one best way and that the past can offer us little guidance about a drastically altered future. So managers will learn to rely more on imagination and intuition, creatively balancing obsolete and cutting-edge technology. In *Redefining the Manager's Job,* Kastens (1980) proposes that future managers will have to exact rigorous personal responsibility before accountability is extended to others. In a resource-limited economy, he believes that deploying and employing those resources toward a predetermined objective will be the benchmark for measuring managerial effectiveness. Essentially, analysis of the right side of Table 1 indicates that the metaindustrial manager is more informal, enthusiastic, and adroit (defined as expert, nimble, skillful, resourceful, and adept) than the traditional manager. Today, we should be comfortable with team management, especially with entrepreneurial groups. When top management is equally competent, but in different areas, the concept of the multiple executive proves worthwhile to practice, for it shares talent.

Other characteristics should also be cultivated if we are to be successful as transformational managers. Besides being futuristically oriented, broad minded, and collaborative, the manager in transition must be able to cope with ambiguity. The new breed of leaders is intrinsically motivated and continually learning. Thus, such managers are open to lateral transfers in more participative work systems, because additional skills are then acquired. This type of manager values quality—of working life, as well as of product and service. In life-style, such persons seek balance and flexibility. Although we may walk a transitional tightrope, it is still possible to develop a creative work environment in which people are enthused about superb performance

Table 1. Contrasting Attitudes and Styles of Managers.

Traditional Manager of the Disappearing Industrial Work Culture	Transformational Manager of the Emerging Metaindustrial Work Culture
• Stodgy/Rigid: staid, slow to act; closed-minded to new ideas and approaches	• Dynamic/Flexible: forcefully acts in response to people/situations/markets; open-minded
• Past Oriented: concerned for "how we always did it" and maintenance of status quo	• Anticipative/Future Oriented: concerned for planning change, forecasting tomorrow
• Short-term Oriented: considers immediate impact, profits, markets, and issues	• Long-term Oriented: considers down-the-line implications of present actions and strategies
• Quantity/Product Oriented: culture-bound to "our way and what's good for us" in terms of numbers, goods, and things that produce profits; meets the bottom-line considerations only	• Quality/Service Oriented: culture-sensitive to customer/consumer needs that results in profitable performance; exercises corporate social responsibility
• Institutional/Hierarchical Oriented: loyal to organization, accomplishment of tasks, and following chain of command or orders	• Individual/Team Oriented: concerned for people, group loyalties, and process, using informal networks and relationships; participative
• Competitive/Combatative: plays fiercely as in sports for game's sake and winning only; sometimes arrogant and manipulative in pursuit of the prize	• Cooperative/Facilitative: seeks synergy and enjoyment in business/professional life; consults and collaborates with others for win/win experiences
• Pack Thinking: plays it safe and goes along with the crowd; blends in like the organization man; does what everybody else does	• Vanguard Thinking: stays informed and on the cutting edge; innovates and takes responsible risks even if it means being a creative deviant
• Conformity/Re-enforces Dependency: big daddy knows best; does what he's told; believes in power for the few elite at top, being an organization man	• Initiative/Autonomy: encourages creative thought and action; interdependence; self-help, awareness, and responsibility; power sharing and networking
• Pragmatic/Mechanistic: concerned for the practical and quantifiable; for getting things done at any cost; number counter/cruncher	• Conceptualizer/Synthesizer: concerned for concepts, models, and paradigms that fit ideas and things together for action purposes; links together pieces and parts into a whole
• Environmentally Amoral: exploitative and conquering approach toward nature; concern is for economic security and welfare only	• Environmentally/Ecologically Sensitive: partner with nature on Spaceship Earth; preserves and conserves where feasible; enhances quality of life on planet earth
• Average Performance: concerned for unit production and organizational standards or for quantity called for in union contracts	• Competent Performance: sets high personal and professional standards for self and others; concerned with self-development and actualization

and obtain genuine enjoyment from accomplishment. Obviously, these observations imply a need for a total revision of our image of the manager's role.

McGill University professor Henry Mintzberg (1983) maintains that managers will manifest and practice a combination of ten interwining roles. He groups these into three major categories: (1) interpersonal roles—as figurehead, leader, liaison; (2) informational roles—as monitor, disseminator, and communicator; (3) decisional roles—as entrepreneur, disturbance handler, resource allocator, and negotiator. One conclusion from his Canadian studies with chief executives was that it is in the integration of these roles that management is effective. Perhaps success lies in the sharing of the roles with other members of the management team. (Appendix A provides an inventory of transformational management skills, which the reader may use for self-assessment in this regard.)

Before managers can transform their organizations, it is vital that we first transform our vision of the manager's role. The industrial work culture has conditioned us to envision the managerial function in a way that becomes increasingly inappropriate. In the emerging information society, knowledge is both power and a resource; the manager's information role and base assume critical importance. Metaindustrial managers not only give information resources high priority but master the tools from personal computers to teleconferencing.

Organization Transition Strategies

Transition has been defined as movement or passage from one position, state, stage, subject, or concept to another. *Strategy* is a means for coping with such transitions, be they personal or organizational. Strategy is using planning, methods, or maneuvers to obtain a specific goal or result (Ansoff, 1984). Developing strategies that will help organizations bridge the gap between the industrial and metaindustrial work cultures calls for input and insight. Sage business and government leaders can heed certain indicators in developing effective organizational strategies. The chapters of this book, especially Part Two, encapsulate some of these indicators to assist us in repositioning ourselves and our enterprises. We know that automation is a key strategy toward increasing productivity growth—producing more goods with less labor and cost. Therefore, the introduction of programmable robots into a manufacturing plant may make sense when they enable five employees to do in sixteen hours what it formerly took seventy workers sixteen days to accomplish. But, as was found in renewing a General Electric plant with such a strategy, robotization also demands transitional planning with the work force to be reduced in number. The remaining work may have to be spread out by shortening work hours or by promoting job sharing, or it may involve education for new roles.

Thinking managers cultivate foresight by learning to scan the social and economic environment, sensing new directions, and seeking the best prospects for concentrating human energy. There is a variety of resources to help one stay well informed and on the cutting edge of one's industry or field. They range from newsletters and reports of technological forecasting to subscription to an electronic network and data source. However, there is one very simple but profitable way to stay professionally alert—the "bag lunch." In this strategy, a group of colleagues agrees to meet weekly for lunch. Beforehand, they also decide to read some agreed-upon material related to their work —a chapter in a new management book, an article in a technical or business journal, a company report, or whatever. One person accepts responsibility each time for leading the analysis of the author's message. Some of the volumes cited in the reference section, such as Lawrence and Dyer's (1983) *Renewing American Industry* or Sears's (1983) *Back in Working Order,* might make good subjects for such discussions. The technique is both mind stretching and informal managerial development that fosters peer relationships. Some companies have turned it into a "brown bag university," in which academic credit is gained for participation in the weekly "seminar."

One reason for adopting such an approach is that information and knowledge are the new currency. Know-how is a value-creating activity. Productivity in the emerging twenty-first century is equivalent to the know-how of finding, keeping, and building know-how and of combining know-hows in flexibly effective ways (Finkelstein and Newman, 1984). Any human resource development, formal or not, is an enhancement of human assets.

To illustrate how an information scan may result in managerial insights, consider three changes affecting organizations and what a literature search might reveal:

Market Changes. The market for new goods and services is becoming increasingly global, fragmented, and customized. Since the world is becoming a single marketplace, goods are being produced wherever they can be manufactured at the lowest cost, regardless of national boundaries—often in Third World nations. For managers, this implies planning to move beyond domestic markets and removing provincial perceptual blinders about where workers and customers are to be found. Then, adoption of strategies for international business is required, which may include cross-cultural training of marketing, sales, and technical personnel.

Market changes mean preparing for an altered work force. The International Labour Office estimates that, by the year 2,000, thirty-six million people will enter the global labor pool, and 85 percent of them will be from developing nations. In addition, these market trends will cause a shift from centralized to decentralized marketing and distribution to meet the worldwide demand for more customized products and services. In the industrial age, it was efficient to mass produce standardized products, but in the postindustrial age the market may dictate otherwise. That was what Toffler was trying to alert us to in his *Future Shock* (1970) and *The Third Wave* (1980) messages about "de-massification" of both markets and media and the erosion of distinction between producer and consumer. One response from managers, for instance, would be to use computers to integrate consumers into the production process or to integrate more functions into fewer parts by overspecialization, substituting wholes for many discrete components.

Structural Changes. At the end of the 1970s, the American economy began to shift from high-volume standardized production—characteristic of the industrial age and dependent on capital-intensive, traditionally manufactured products (Reich, 1983); the high-volume industries, such as basic steel, textile, automobile production, consumer electronics, rubber, and petrochemicals, require primarily skilled labor, and thus such technological processes can be replicated anywhere in the world. The significant development for manufacturing managers is a move toward flexible systems of production for use with emerging metaindustrial processes based on precision engineering, complex testing, sophisticated maintenance, custom tailoring to consumer needs, and rapid technological changes. These work activities are also resistant to low-wage competition. Rather than separating business functions as in the past, new systems are based on integration of design, engineering, purchasing, manufacturing, distribution, marketing, and sales. Synergy extends beyond manufacturing to team management. Flexible-system production is designed to uncover and solve new problems and to use a system geared to change, adaptability, and ultrastability.

Factories of the future are already employing these new production strategies. For example, Sara Lee Bakeries in Deerfield, Illinois, was among the pioneers in cybernation. Another prototype of the epochal structural change is John Deere and Company in Waterloo, Iowa. Its flexible manufacturing process includes computer-controlled tools that can perform a variety of drilling, boring, threading, and milling tasks. This permits more personalized product diversity, eliminates many traditional production jobs, and allows for quick product change. Today, with more automation, Deere provides twenty-one models of its tractors versus four under the old assembly line system; and with machines capable of a wider variety of functions, Deere can meet customer needs for different transmissions and clutches. Changes are also reflected in the fact that marketing and sales divisions now have a greater influence on production, based on customer requests, and the role of engineering has been altered. For managers in manufacturing, this means a total transition from the conventional operations and culture of the organization.

Attitudinal Changes. The preceding illustrations of market and manufacturing changes mandate more fundamental alterations in managerial attitudes—that is, a change in one's psychological construct, or the way a person puts meaning into life or work space. Industrial thinking has conditioned us to perceive, behave, and act in prescribed ways about work and workers, but the new metaindustrial culture requires a revision of traditional work concepts, habits, roles, and relationships.

Management is indeed a "whole new ball game"; yet some managers persist in playing in the old ballpark, thinking that the same players and rules still function. Frederick Taylor's classic dictum of "scientific management" no longer applies—namely, that each worker performs a definite task in a definite manner and a definite time. Operating like the systems of a human body, flexible production mechanisms are more related to preindustrial activities—a small, informal, loosely organized conglomeration of skilled craftspersons working together to make one finished product. But now the product is being made with the help of automated machines and robots.

Thus, managers are being challenged to change their attitudes not only about production but also about conventional assumptions regarding hierarchical corporate superstructures, standard operating procedures and performance, and tried-and-true engineering and manufacturing practices. To meet these challenges, transformational management depends on reeducation and retraining of both attitudes and competencies and on developing a metaindustrial philosophy toward changing markets, manufacturing, and human resource concepts. The new work systems require fewer layers of management, realigning organizational power toward lower levels of supervision. They blur functional distinctions, titles, and lines of authority. They demand more intimate communication and cooperation among organizational units (Adams, 1984).

Organizations will have to employ many other strategies to lessen the trauma of transition and to further economic and career growth. The authors of *Supermanaging* (Brown and Weiner, 1984) warned that knowing the environment is only the first step in mastering change; knowledge of how to respond and awareness of what priorities to assign are also critical. Per-

Transforming Work, Organizations, and Management

haps the reader might seek answers to the following questions from the standpoint of his or her own organization:

- If new technology and automation are used to improve productivity, how do we reorganize management so it is more lean and flexible?
- Are there markets we have overlooked in the low- or no-technology industries, such as multiple services fields, fitness and recreation, media and software production, education and training?
- Do we need to provide personnel with continuing education in science and technology, including the high-tech workers who must run to catch up with developments in their own fields?
- Can we renew older facilities and convert them to new uses rather than relocate plants?
- Can we reduce traditional high wage and benefit costs through participation in profit-sharing plans, equity ownership, creative compensation (such as sabbaticals, incentive travel, uncompensated leave time), or contracting services?
- Can we cooperate with local school districts, community colleges, and universities in curriculum renewal, internships, employee exchanges, and technology transfer so that educational offerings will be more relevant and qualified graduates more available in terms of market and management needs?

It is time to think previously unthinkable thoughts and to take risks doing previously unthinkable things. William Thurston, president of Gen Rad, a Concord, Massachusetts, electronics firm, said it best relative to management strategies: "The first thing managers have to do is to take responsibility for their own destiny. They should stop complaining about the changes and get busy. They should keep up to date in technology, and be responsive to the marketplace" ("The New Economy," 1983, p. 70).

Conclusion

Perhaps the best way to conclude this overview is to draw a profile of tomorrow's metaindustrial management. These are the qualities such managers are likely to display and the activities in which these leaders will probably, whether in the private or public sector, engage. Regardless of sex, race, or culture, expect global managers to:

- be more professionally competent and self-actualized;
- be oriented toward talent utilization, participation, collaboration, wellness, and enhanced quality of life;
- seek meaningful and personalized work experiences, allowing for more control over life and work space as well as a more relaxed and informal work environment;
- desire opportunities to exercise more creativity and responsibility while expecting generous entitlements;
- engage in negotiations as leaders of semi-autonomous units for managerial and economic arrangements within a corporate context concerned about mutual interests of both colleagues and the firm;
- transmit organizational culture to teams or work units in which their function is to be both facilitator and model of high-performance behavior;
- work intensely for profit while also pursuing diverse leisure and fitness activity that is recreative;
- place high priority on career development, colleagueship, networking, research and computer skills, and continuous learning;
- believe in corporate social responsibility, environmental and consumer protections, earned equality, and quality service that is profitable;
- practice synergy and collaborativeness, circular organizational communications, risk taking, and especially innovation.

According to the late Herman Kahn, the inhabitants of Earth are in the midst of the 400-year "Great Transition." During this transition, occurring during the years 1800 to 2200, almost every country will find its way along an economic progression from preindustrial to industrial to postindustrial. The result will be that, whereas 200 years ago humankind was everywhere scarce and poor, 200 years hence people will be everywhere numerous, rich, and in control of their environment. What will have made this most dramatic revolution possible is the art of manufacturing (Koehn and Selbert, 1984, p. 2).

The challenge for transformational leadership in these transitional times is best put by Roger B. Smith, the chairman of General Motors: "Let's not just go two steps, let's go into the twenty-first century. You don't just stumble into the future. You create your own future" (*Time,* June 17, 1985, p. 59).

TWO

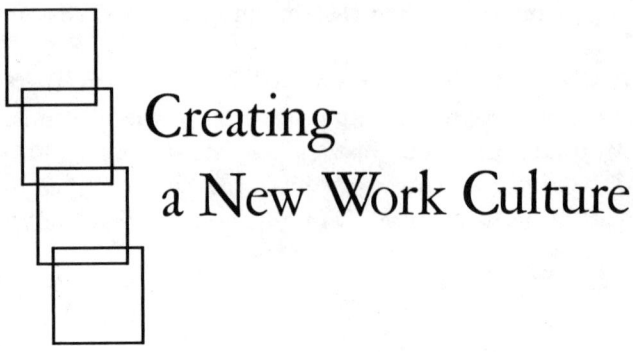

Creating a New Work Culture

Executive Summary. Culture is a dynamic mechanism for human coping and achievement. It influences all facets of human life. Some aspects of culture are universal, while others differ in terms of people, places, and times. Culture is a learned adaptation that is transmitted to contemporary and future generations, although such wisdom is relative and in need of continuing reassessment.

Whether we view this concept in the context of a nation and its people or an organization and its personnel, culture develops slowly, affecting our identity, behavior, and performance. The models and tools of cultural anthropology also can be applied to the analysis of work and how it is performed. Thus, in the past, work cultures have developed around the life-styles of hunter, farmer, and factory worker. Presently, we are in transition to a work environment centered around the knowledge or information worker. Within that classification, there is an emerging subculture of global management, so a rationale is provided as to why modern managers need both cultural awareness and skills.

The new work culture that is both information oriented and flexible is characterized by personnel who seek greater autonomy and control over their work space, more organizational communication and information, participation and involvement in the enterprise, meaningful and synergistic organizational relationships, creative and demanding norms and standards, improved productivity through new technologies, and emphasis on enhanced quality of work life and entrepreneurialism. Since it is more technically oriented, this emerging culture devotes more efforts and expenditures to research and development. To best comprehend these changes and their meaning for the new management, we examine here their implications for both current and future organizational cultures. Special attention is directed to the need for synergistic strategies when altering corporate culture through diversifications, break-ups, buy-ins, and joint ventures.

Manager's Guide to Culture

Culture is a fascinating concept that helps managers understand much about other countries and people, as well as about human systems and work environments. More specifically, culture helps us comprehend a little better our behavior, as well as that of customers, employees, and suppliers. Thanks to the research shared with us by cultural anthropologists, we may even gain better understanding of ourselves and of the groups to which we belong.

Each of us, to a greater or lesser degree, is a product of our culture. Our behavior is influenced by our heritage, the national culture of our origin, which we can call our "macroculture," whether it is American, British, French, Japanese, or whatever. Within a society, this is the mainstream culture for the majority of citizens of that country. We are further affected by the many subgroups (or "microcultures") of which we are a part—such as ethnic, sexual, or religious groups. Each of our affiliations—be it the military, a corporation, or a profession, such as medicine or engineering; an industry, such as construction or petroleum, a trade association, or a union—has its own unique microculture.

These cultural inputs alter our perceptions, the way we read meaning into our life space and daily experiences. Culture influences us to form basic assumptions about human nature, reality, truth, relationships, and the myriad activities or events that occur in our lives. As members of cultural groups, we formulate these assumptions into a pattern that determines "normal" behavior for each person. Culture affects how we think and feel and what we perceive as right and wrong or appropriate and inappropriate. For example, how do we define management or leadership? Those raised in a Western country have a culturally conditioned set of assumptions and perceptions that is far different from that of someone raised in some Eastern culture.

Our culture affects how we view the nature of work and the worker, what we consider satisfactory performance and productivity, what we see as adequate education and training of employees, and the like. However, it is only in recent years that business operations have discovered the significance of culture and only in this decade that most universities have begun to offer cross-cultural management courses to business administration students. If the global manager is to be effective in the international marketplace, cultural awareness and skills are essential. Furthermore, a worldwide subculture of management is emerging, and one needs to know how to function effectively in it.

So, once again, what is culture? Culture is the way people, as a group, learn to cope under a peculiar set of circumstances. Geography, climate, stages of human and economic development, and related factors prompt unique cultural adaptations. Consciously or unconsciously, these adaptations become assumptions, habits, customs, and traditions about our world and how it "is." There may be good reasons for some of these formulations and practices, but some may be irrational. Rites, rituals, myths, and heroes are created to solidify and carry on this special data base and to socialize new members. These coping skills are developed and transmitted to the next generations. Thus, a body of communicable knowledge, beliefs, values, norms, art, artifacts, and laws perpetuates the culture through social structures, institutions, or systems.

The diversity of culture can be seen in the various systems people establish to carry on their unique way of life. To understand any culture, we can examine such systems relative to kinship, education, economics, politics, health, security, recreation, or religion. For instance, in the United States, there is a cultural proclivity to organize, so, as a people, we have a wide network of social groupings. Anthropologists would categorize this as the "associative system"; when analyzing a particular culture, they would analyze under this classification fraternal and secret societies, trade and professional associations, and hobby or athletic organizations. Such methods for studying a culture can be helpful to a confused manager who has been sent overseas to do business in an alien environment or who must cope with minorities in the work place or try to influence company culture.

Just as our biological inheritance influences behavior, so does culture. Literally, humans are culture-bearing animals who communicate culture in manifold ways by transmitting and receiving messages within a particular cultural context. Some cultural traits and procedures are shared by all humankind and are designated cultural "universals." That is, this common expression of human nature can be found, in one form or another, in most cultures. The list is lengthy, so let us just say that they range from age grading, sports, and bodily adornments to marriage, weaning, trade, or even status differences.

Some people become locked into their cultural viewpoints and thus become provincial or ethnocentric. Global managers, however, should be cosmopolitan in their cultural perspectives. That is, we do not deny our heritage or primary culture and its contributions to us; but the process of maturation involves growing in skills of acculturation—the integration of insights from other cultures into one's own construct. In the classic work *Beyond Culture,* anthropologist Edward Hall (1976) points out that culture is an extension of self but that we can get so caught up in its web as to repress our true nature, deny our talents, and punish ourselves for imagined failures. He advocates that we stop blaming ourselves for perceived inadequacies and embark on the difficult journey of moving *beyond* culture.

Culture gives both individuals and groups a sense of identity, a point of reference for answering the age-old question,

"Who am I?" But, as people mature, they must revise their self-concepts from time to time. The same may be said for their role and organizational images. Yes, we often experience crises as we make this reevaluation and go through this transition to a new life-style and a new way of looking at life. Because culture is a process of formation and change, it involves continuing adaptation to the surrounding circumstances. It is this very quality of culture that has ensured our survival as human beings. Now humankind is in the process of a universal reassessment and cultural change in our concept of the species. For example, we thought we knew when life began and ended, but genetic engineering and its potential for life control are altering those traditional beliefs.

More importantly, we thought we were earthbound, despite the thousands of years during which poets, novelists, and artists told us about man on the moon and life beyond Earth. Then, in the last quarter century, we began to go into space, to explore the high frontier, and not only to put humans on the moon (Apollo 11) but to leave them in space stations up to 237 days (Salyut 7). Life in zero or near-zero gravity is quite different, and it is opening up new potential and opportunities for us. Such space activities are altering global earth culture—we are not earthbound any longer, and maybe our real home is "out there." We are in the process of creating a new space-based culture (Harris, 1985). We have seen this cultural change in space spinoffs that result in new high technologies, new ways of communicating with satellites, new views of our land masses and oceans, new means of transportation and war, new food and dress, and new habitats and work habits. Literally, the new view from space not only changes our perspectives of Earth but is forcing us to transform our very image of ourselves as a species.

In 1984, I was engaged in a NASA summer study on "Technological Springboards into the Twenty-First Century," the proceedings of which have been published by the Johnson Space Center (McKay, 1985). The primary purpose of the program was to engage in strategic planning for the next step beyond an American space station in the 1990s—namely a lunar

Creating a New Work Culture

base to be established around the year 2010. Part of my research was on space management and culture. I was intrigued with the realization that the very procedures developed in systems to deploy managers and technicians from their home to a host culture overseas can be adapted to "space deployment systems" to transfer personnel from this planet into space.

The same models we use to analyze an unfamiliar culture here, whether a country or a corporation, can be transposed to the situation in space. Figure 2 illustrates this in terms of ten classifications for examining a foreign culture when we travel or work abroad (Harris and Moran, 1979). But this diagram is of the moon, and it shows the same characteristics in the context of the emerging space culture we are in the process of creating on the lunar surface. Culture, for example, affects our understanding of time and space. Project ahead twenty-five years and imagine astronauts and technauts working at a lunar outpost. Imagine their sense of time when they operate in two weeks of light and two weeks of darkness; imagine their sense of space when they can freely float around and look back at us with a view of the universe! With these ideas in mind, we begin to gain feeble appreciation of the transition underway for all of us, managers and others alike. We are all, in a sense, pioneers of the new work culture whether as a knowledge worker in a high-tech operation here on Earth, or a technician working at a lunar outpost.

A strong case can be made as to why thinking managers should learn more about culture and how it affects business and behavior on the job. The following twelve reasons summarize the rationale for managers to increase their cultural awareness and skills:

1. Culture provides a sense of identity to both individuals and organizations, especially in terms of the value system transmitted.

2. Cultural knowledge provides insight into people and their behavior. Understanding both a culture's generalities and its specifics can facilitate intercultural communication and customer relations, as well as increase productivity and profitability. Based on this, business protocol can be developed that is

36   Management in Transition

Figure 2. Characteristics of Space Culture or Any Culture on Earth.

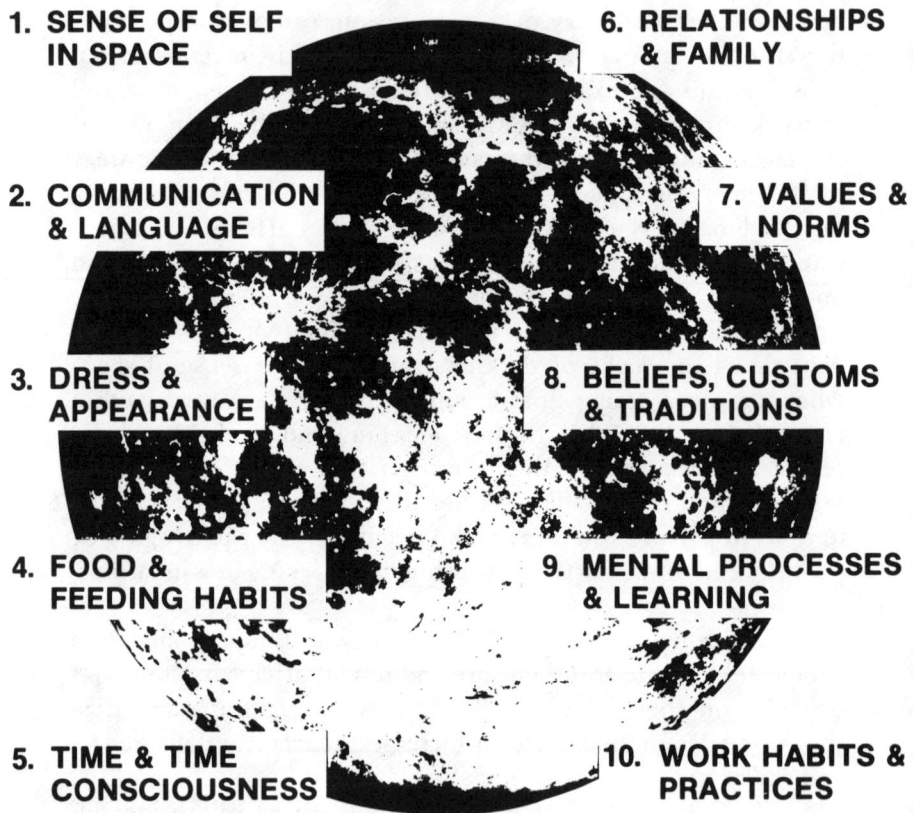

Note: Reprinted with permission of aerospace illustrator Dennis M. Davidson of University of California at San Diego Medical School.

in tune with the character of locals, their codes of commonly approved practices, their ideologies and standards.

3. Cultural knowledge and skills can be helpful in understanding and influencing one's corporate culture. Organizational culture affects human performance and productivity on the job. Various specializations, departments, and divisions within human systems develop unique subcultures that can become barriers to communication with the larger enterprise.

4. Cultural concepts are useful for analyses of work cultures and for contrasting the disappearing industrial work environment with the emerging metaindustrial work culture.

5. Cultural insights and conceptual tools are vital in the study of comparative management and thus in helping one become less culture bound in one's approach to management and leadership. This will enable one to work more effectively in the universal subculture of global management while being sensitive to the differences in local culture's approaches to administration.

6. Cultural competencies are essential to those in international business and trade. They not only help us cope with indigenous social conventions and thus avoid social blunders, but these skills enable representatives of multinational corporations to build cultural synergy with local peoples and institutions, especially customers.

7. Cultural knowledge is applicable to all relocation experiences, whether domestic or international. This is true for the individual manager or technician facing a transfer as well as for subordinates and their families involved in geographic and cultural change.

8. Cultural components should be built into all management development and foreign deployment systems. Acculturation to alien environments abroad can be fostered in order to improve the overseas experience and productivity. Furthermore, it can be applied to lessen reentry shock and aid in reintegration into the home and organizational culture.

9. Cultural understanding of the diversity in markets can improve organizational strategies with minorities and ethnic groups at home as well as the penetration of overseas markets, particularly in the Third World countries.

10. Cultural capabilities enhance one's participation in international organizations, which range from UNESCO and quasi-governmental entities to global trade and professional associations to transnational enterprises within the private sector.

11. Cultural competencies are valuable within regional economic associations, such as the EEC, ASEAN, and other cooperative efforts by governments within a geographic region. The Pacific Basin is an example of a regional economic arena in which such skills are vital.

12. Cultural understanding will have great implications for space industrialization as we create a new space culture in the high frontier.

Past Work Cultures

Through the prism of culture, we can better analyze people in teams, corporations, professions, nations, and even stages of human development. Let us begin with some specific applications of cultural insights in terms of work. The hunting stage of work culture still exists in the remote interiors of Third World economies, just as the agricultural work culture continues to function in some preindustrial nations. But in most economically advanced countries, inhabitants are either in or coming out of the industrial stage of development.

Europeans, North Americans, and the Japanese, for instance, are products of the industrial work culture. It dominated the European life-style for over two hundred years, the American scene for over a century, and Japan for just over fifty years. To meet the needs of smokestack industries and their factory workers, organizational models were developed, management practices inaugurated, and trade unions organized. In the beginning of that transition to industrialization, this happened gradually and, in fact, simultaneously with the diminution of the agricultural way of life. In the United States and Canada, for example, there was a population shift in the last part of the nineteenth and early twentieth centuries from rural to urban areas in search of new employment; whereas at the beginning of this period nine out of ten earned their livelihoods in an agriculturally related occupation, the ratio would become one in twenty by 1970. Towns developed around the great factories, such as occurred in England and New England. Production no longer was dependent on village artisans, craftspersons, and household workers but stemmed from factory systems that emphasized interchangeable parts, standardization, duplication, replication, mass production, and wide distribution of products. The new machines not only changed the way we lived and worked, but they even transformed the farm.

In the United States, as in other industrialized countries, national and state legislation was passed to cope with the new situation, to protect both employer and employees. These laws regulated labor relations, unionization, compensation, social security, retirement, health and safety, child labor, equal employment opportunity, and eventually environmental protection. Various other social systems adapted to the realities of this industrialization, from education and health to recreation and religion (largely a product of the agricultural work culture). Work specialization, for instance, led to the formation of new industrial trade and professional associations, to journals and reports, and to research and development counseling.

Management came into its own as both an art and a science during this industrial stage. Until then, our notions of leadership had come largely from the monasteries, the military, and the great trading companies. The factory system was the catalyst to a management approach based on division of labor, for manufacturing initially was divided into small distinct stages and tasks so that workers could be specialized. The assembly line was the efficient outcome—where the hands were often engaged in mostly mindless activities and drudgery. Machine power replaced the brawn of the agricultural period and became more sophisticated and complex in the struggle to contain operational costs. In the process, people became more educated and affluent; they had more opportunity for recreation and travel—the middle class expanded (Koehn and Selbert, 1984).

Thus, in an industrialized country, society—its institutions and thinking—were centered around this mechanized way of working and doing business. A whole life-style emerged that might be called the industrial work culture. Here is a profile of this disappearing bureaucracy, which still continues in many places (Harris and Moran, 1979, p. 109):

> [It is] an industrial system characterized by division of labor, hierarchy, and some stability or permanence. ... Workers are in sharply defined slots or roles, operating within a chain of command from top down or vertical power distribution. ... [It involves] somewhat intractable structures, static operations [and is] slow to change in a society in which things are largely stable, routine and predictable. Decisions are made at the top and organizational communications are vertical, slow, and with some delay. Staff/line arrangements exist between support and operative units. [With its] emphasis on efficiency, profitability, plant/equipment maintenance, and capital expansion ... this culture required a mass of moderately educated workers.
> 'The Organization Man' best described the industrial worker who applied 'his' skills for the good of the corporation or agency. Managers are considered the 'brains,' and laborers the 'hands' who are conditioned somewhat to subservience and dependence—they look to the organization for rewards and recognition, and are paid to conform. This was a white-male dominated work environment, in which minorities and women until recently were banned, ignored or in lower paying positions. The corporate culture focused on competition, winning at all costs, achieving quantity production, status in the organization, economic security, and maintaining the status quo. ... Creative deviants were usually driven out of such organizations for lack of conformity. They became the exceptions, often the free-swinging entrepreneurs and rugged individualists who built the vast enterprises in which others served.

Notice the use of the past tense in the previous description. That is the way it was, but the culture is changing. We are in the midst of a profound social and vocational transition that

Creating a New Work Culture

is causing crisis in human systems. Many of the traditions, practices, regulations, and laws developed for an industrial way of life now handicap people in more technically advanced societies. Today, management is experiencing the trauma of trying to undo archaic institutions and their trappings in terms of contracts and procedures or to renew industries and businesses capable of being salvaged and fit into a new form. A case in point is the issue of deregulation in banking, utilities, and transportation industries. Rather than bewailing the protectionism that is passing, managers in such corporations should welcome the resultant opportunities and the liberation of their enterprises. Management then can realign itself with a free market economy, along with the new directions in organizations and in the work performed.

The Work Culture of the Future

As we seek to cope with the new work environment and its management by information, we are creating a new culture. We literally are redefining the nature of work, the role of the worker, and the relationships required by the new situation brought on by the microelectronics revolution. Our work customs, traditions, habits, practices, institutions, and legislations are being transformed. Take, as a case in point, trade and professional associations—some are going out of business because the trade is disappearing or because association membership is dropping drastically. For those that are continuing to survive, attendance at conventions and meetings typically is declining; but their information exchange and professional growth efforts are partially accomplished through new mechanisms—networking, either in person or electronically. New interest groups are formed to deal with new realities, such as biotechnology. Teleconferencing and videoconferencing by satellite replace old meeting formats.

For a better understanding of this new work culture, let us begin by examining work itself as a concept. What is happening to our notions about it? Work has been defined in the past as exertion or effort directed to produce or accomplish something. We have used a variety of words to describe it, such as labor, toil, undertaking, employment, and enterprise. Regarding the term *work*, a host of related designations has come to be used, such as occupation, vocation, job, profession, operation, task, project, and industry. In the past, we made clear distinctions between work and play, but such separations are eroding. We also have placed emphasis on work that is effective, productive, useful, and profitable. Perhaps the transformation in the concept of work can best be appreciated in terms of energy.

In the past, work required expenditure of much physical energy; present and future work requires less of that and more psychic energy or brain power. The driving force that is changing the nature of work is new technology—so much so that craft workers and their union leaders are alarmed at the prospect of being thrown on the "trash heap." The same force is altering relationships between and among workers, disciplines, and professions. Not only is it changing the relationship between the supervisor and the supervised, but it is eliminating whole levels of management. Industrial-age approaches, systems, and legislation are becoming increasingly obsolete; they must undergo renewal, or they will disappear. They simply do not meet human need at this time. They are not relevant for life and work in the rapidly approaching twenty-first century.

The media has alerted us all to the problems of the traditional manufacturing industries, and employee lay-offs on a mass basis have dramatically brought occupational changes to our attention. One example of such an industrial problem is the culture shock being experienced by trade unions worldwide. Originally formed to protect workers from exploitation in the factory system, the trade unions made great gains in this century by raising the levels of their members' incomes as well as by ensuring their vacation and fringe benefits, health, safety, and welfare. But these international unions grew affluent, bureaucratic, inefficient, and sometimes corrupt. At a time when some union leaders were exploiting their own membership, management was becoming more enlightened, automatically providing for many of the workers' needs and providing a more creative work environment.

Two trends currently are contributing to a drastic drop in union membership: new plant programs are being inaugurated that cause workers to vote in favor of nonunionization, and many traditional occupations around which unions were organized are becoming archaic—they are being replaced by new careers not covered by classic union contracts. In the industrial age, machines replaced brawn; in the postindustrial age, computers and cybernated systems are replacing human brain power and supervision, taking over the control of machines. How does one unionize a robot? Further, rank-and-file union adherents are rejecting the union leadership, especially on matters of contract negotiations. While trade union leaders of the old school seek to take care of hygiene needs, modern workers are more concerned about issues related to job security, retraining, education, and quality of work life. The impact of the new work culture on trade unions may be their gradual disappearance in the next century—unless they can create a new mediating role for themselves, a synergy between labor (increasingly knowledge workers) and management to replace past adversarial relations. In fact, the very role of management is being transformed as more employees share in those possibilities.

To gain some insight into the future of work and organizations, we would do well to study what is happening in high-technology firms, in fast-growth companies, and in venture capital enterprises. These undertakings are the laboratories of the new work culture that will prevail in the decades ahead; there they are developing tomorrow's metaindustrial work styles and practices and new management strategies are being painfully forged, whether in a newly formed space technology business or an entrepreneurial business unit within a *Fortune* 500" corporation. (As proof that leadership styles are adapting to this emerging work culture, a computer search on the subject—a review of the Dow Jones data base from 1983 back to 1979—revealed 64,184 entries or key word counts for "new management." Incidentally, there were 13,050 references for biotechnology management alone!)

For some, work has only economic meaning—a means for producing goods and services, for acquiring purchasing power through income and profits. For others, work activity is fundamental to the way we live and express ourselves, be it in arts, crafts, or technology. Our very identity, for many people, is defined in terms of work roles. Hans Selye, an international authority on stress, reminds us that work is a basic biological human need. He is concerned that this means for normal functioning may become redundant because of automation and that people have not been prepared for the constructive use of increased leisure. Yoneji Masuda (1981), a distinguished Japanese scholar, is optimistic about such technological developments and their impact on work. He believes that humankind will be freed from being forced to work for subsistence and that the free time thus created can be used for learning, personal development, rest, and play. Willis Harman (Villoldo and Dychtman, 1981), a Stanford social scientist and engineer, points out that outdated conceptions of work cause many problems and dilemmas. In discussing the future of work, he analyzes such issues as overpopulation, cybernation, and chronic unemployment; underemployment and the way it hampers the development of human potential; alternative work styles and the transformation of society. Hank Koehn (1984), the Los Angeles bank futurist, feels that work and our attitudes toward it are bound up in our moral and religious outlook on life. Many see work as more than merely earning a salary and conceive it as something that is necessary for living; some maintain that it is morally and ethically good to work.

One thing is certain: namely, that not only the way in which we work but also our very notions about work are changing. Tomorrow's work not only will be different but will be constantly changing. The notion of work as productive human activity is shifting from material to nonmaterial goals. This implies more than the development of a service economy; the increasing priority we place on higher needs will change both the products and the conditions of work (Best, 1973). There is already a strong trend toward enhancing the quality of work activity and thus making it a more positive and valued part of the human experience. Our culture has always prized the work ethic, but Americans now want that work to be more

Creating a New Work Culture

meaningful. Some consensus exists concerning having a guaranteed right to work as well as equal employment opportunity for all citizens. Other trends regarding work are:

- Information orientation: The organization of work increasingly involves the systematic gathering and structuring of information. Its processing includes storage, examination, assemblage, translation, and distribution by people or machines and its transmission to the proper user in a timely and relevant manner.
- Work time flexibility: The work week is constantly being reduced for people. By 1990, the American standard probably will change from forty to thirty-six hours of work per week. The work time schedule is becoming more flexible (in 1980, ten million American workers were using some kind of flexible work schedule or compressed work week).
- Part-time work and work sharing: The voluntary holding of permanent but part-time jobs is on the increase (presently, this involves 11.8 million American workers, mainly women). Regular work assignments are being shared with other employees or volunteers, including husband-wife teams (28 percent of American workers now job share).

The pertinence of this topic can be seen in the many conferences being organized on work or its productivity. For example, in 1983 The World Future Society sponsored one on "Working Now and in the Future" (Didsbury, 1983). Some futurists forecast that with the widespread adoption of automation, work for income will become a privilege in the next century, and that a guaranteed annual income may become the norm in technological societies.

Since we perceive the future dimly, we cannot predict absolutely the outcome of the ongoing transformation in the work culture. Organizational innovators are experimenting with what we consider new, and some of their efforts will become standard practice in the decades ahead. However, my research has identified ten probable characteristics of tomorrow's work culture:

1. more autonomy
2. more communications/information

3. more participation
4. more informal/synergistic relationships
5. more creative/high-performing norms
6. more performance/productivity with automation
7. more enhanced quality of work life
8. more technically oriented
9. more research and development
10. more entrepreneurial spirit

These key developments in the work place are discussed briefly in following sections.

Autonomy and Control over Work Space. People seek more control over both their work and their work space. They wish more freedom of choice, more self-responsibility, and more authority (especially at lower levels of the organization). They want more ownership in the work, psychologically and/or literally. They want to transcend the traditional boundaries that constrict, separate, or regulate work. They also expect the freedom to be human at work, including the freedom to err when taking risks and to learn from failure. The drive for autonomy may even extend into the ownership of businesses, either directly as stockholders or through profit sharing. Or, when large corporations set out to close down operations, employees (such as in the Weirtown Steel Company) may combine resources and buy out the company; sixty companies in the United States were purchased by their workers in the past year.

Among the many illustrations of this trend are industrial democracy, worker ownership, and contract work. By contract work, I mean situations in which expensive full-time workers are turned into cheaper independent subcontractors to their former employers. By "turfing" them out and signing contracts, companies not only cut costs but retain relationships with personnel they trust. Rank-Xerox, for example, sold its computer terminals to twenty employees and gave them contracts to work from their homes in Britain (for a maximum of 100 days). ICI, a British chemical giant, seconded their former employees into their own businesses and initially guaranteed their income. Many European firms are doing the same. British government agencies and the European Common Market are funding consultants to train unemployed managers in how to raise venture capital and get their own enterprises going. Five thousand American companies have some form of employee ownership plan, and limited federal financial assistance for such programs is available, according to the National Council on Employee Ownership.

Participation and Involvement in the Enterprise. People seek more involvement and democratization in the enterprises they serve. For knowledge workers, this may mean sharing in management problem solving, planning, and decision making. For management, it means efforts to obtain consensus or to negotiate power sharing and compromises. The trend is manifested in team, project, and product management, as well as in various attempts at collegiality, such as networking. Chapters Eight and Nine discuss this further.

Sweden has pioneered in labor safety through a worker participation system for protection purposes. It features a worker safety ombudsman in every plant, a safety committee made up of employees and employers, worker risk education programs, and consensual decision making. Westinghouse instituted a participatory management approach that featured extensive use of quality circles. Ford Motor Company involved employees in discussions improving productivity and quality of performance.

Communications and Information Orientation. People seek more open, authentic, and circular communications at work. They wish to have input and to give feedback, so they are willing to respond to work and attitudinal surveys through such means as interviews or such instruments as questionnaires, inventories, and opinion polls. They expect to use a variety of media in transmitting messages at work, including electronic devices. Technological advances in business communications have gone from the telegraph and the telephone in the nineteenth century to radio, television, computer, microwave, satellite, computerized PBX, media integration, and fiber optics in the twentieth century. Management information systems are now both centralized and distributed. But the abundant electronically generated data must be managed and translated into useful information. These data are critical to the effective economic functioning of the organization and its profitability. Because these data also must be transformed into knowledge that can be applied for organizational effectiveness, information management will be the principal concern of all management levels in metaindustrial organizations. Communication planning and coordination should become a senior management function.

New telecommunication technology is now being used to link an organization's facilities, its subsidiaries, and its total work force, which may be widely scattered over a diverse geographic area. Lincoln National Life Insurance in Fort Wayne, Indiana, for example, unified its telephone system through a large modular installation using private microwave pathways. This innovation brought about dramatic improvements in productivity and customer relations while decreasing operating costs by 15 percent. Increased microwave capability enables the company to accommodate computer terminals, high-speed facsimile transmissions, and videoconferencing. As another example, Atlantic Richfield Company (ARCO) has completed the first phase of a private internal satellite communication network that will permit videoconferencing among its many domestic locations in the United States. ARCO will use this technology to discuss and review exploration and drilling progress in its oil endeavors. Meanwhile, AETNA has completed 5,000 videoconferences since mid-1981 between two remote sites and plans to link thirteen more sites throughout the country. And many companies, such as Ford Motor Company and IBM, use public videoconferencing to introduce new products ("Business Communications," 1983; Lazer and others, 1983; Pope, 1983).

Informal and Synergistic Relationships. People seek work relations that are cooperative, meaningful, caring, and respectful. Knowledge workers resist hierarchical or status relations and prefer those that are more informal and interdependent, marked by equality and integrity. Such organizational relations may be intense but temporary, as in ad hoc task forces, and pluralistic (including women and minorities). With reference to man-machine relationships brought on by the new technology, many people welcome robots and computerization and are comfortable with them. Others suffer from either cyberphobia (fear of technology) or cyberphrenia (addiction to technology). The complexities of metaindustrial organizations and their missions call for more synergistic relations that feature collaboration among people and with their technologies (Corning, 1983; Moran and Harris, 1982).

The matrix organization is more adaptive, cross-functional, and task oriented. It features temporary work groups and relationships instead of permanent departments; decentralized authority; decision making dominated by technical concerns; complexity; and reporting to two or more supervisors or project managers. It thrives in the smaller entrepreneurial, innovation-oriented culture but often encounters difficulties and turf battling when the company grows larger, such as happened at Intel and Texas Instruments. In a sprawling organization, matrix can only work and counter uncertainty when people really understand their professional relationships.

Enhanced Quality of Work Life. People today seek work that is fulfilling, meaningful, and psychologically rewarding. Knowledge workers want a creative corporate environment that energizes them both mentally and physically. They have high expectations regarding entitlements, such as wellness program opportunities and sabbatical leaves, as well as their physical work surroundings, such as plant facilities being more like college campuses and concern for ecology on the part of management. Often, they prefer more leave time or incentive travel to increased pay; they are more concerned about the corporate support services and fringe benefits that permit them to function effectively on and off the job. Chapters Ten and Eleven discuss this development further.

As middle management shrinks, the role of first-line supervisor is enhanced by computer-based technology and a participatory managerial style. The change is illustrated in the new supervisor type on automobile assembly lines. For instance, Ford Motor Company and the United Auto Workers have inaugurated a worker participation program to improve product quality and production, as well as worker environment. Called Employee Involvement (EI), at Ford's Edison (New Jersey) plant such persons in authority chat with employees, solicit their ideas, and encourage them to stop assembly lines when defects are spotted. A first-line manager now has an enabling function rather than a control function, thanks to the introduction of the computer. This means that the supervisor facilitates worker problem solving and job analysis, tests employee suggestions, and fosters self-management teams. The new management representative is more human than was the case in the past—he or she smiles and jokes with workers, helps workers analyze what went wrong when they make mistakes, and promotes a family-like harmony. As a result, quality of work life has improved for everybody, hostility toward bosses and absenteeism have been reduced, discipline now is constructive, and disciplinary hearings are held less frequently and are more helpful. People maintenance is the primary activity of the new supervisor; as a result, personnel are happier on the job.

Creative Organizational Norms. People are supporting new work standards that emphasize competence, high performance, entrepreneurship, risk taking, venturesomeness, audaciousness, and creativity. Knowledge workers prefer managers open to change, who are more flexible and tentative. Standards of work behavior and performance must reflect such sentiments, whether they appear in personnel manuals, union contracts, work conventions, or management pronouncements. Metaindustrial organizations avoid publishing too many standards that constrain innovation and rigidly set out expectations. Chapter Seven provides further insight into this characteristic.

New norms encourage flexibility, ultrastability, and management by exception. In high-technology, rapid-growth firms, accommodations are made for those on the "fast track." For instance, Intel grew rapidly when it cultivated an environment of innovation that excited and energized its technical personnel. As it became more established and attempted to meet economic changes, Intel now faces crises, and some of its best talent is "jumping ship"—many to start up their own companies and threaten Intel's technical prowess. At Xerox Corporation, executives had to fight their own entrenched system to become more competitive. Managers, conditioned by the older norms, were reluctant to use their new-found authority for fear of being second guessed. In one widely reported instance, executive vice-president William Glavin found some managers vacillating because of concerns of reprisal if they failed in their new use of authority and risk taking. As a result, the corporate culture change at Xerox has been tremendous.

High Performance and Productivity. People in meta-industrial organizations are achievement oriented and develop a new work ethic of professionalism. Knowledge workers use technology, such as automation and robots, to become more productive. Their sense of time is different, and they are not confined by the nine-to-five syndrome. They work more than an eight-hour day if project deadlines demand it; they work weekends if a tight schedule requires it. Then they take time off to compensate for their extra effort to get the job done well and on time. Such concepts as "excellence," "quality," and "service" motivate their high performance in what is a career, not merely a job. They seek self-approval for top performance, not just organizational recognition.

In conducting performance management workshop research, Harris International of La Jolla, California, a consulting firm, discovered that top performers confirmed the preceding observations. By videotaping these outstanding employees or supervisors in a two-day problem-solving conference, the consultants found that not only could the results of recorded insights be used as powerful feedback to top management, but also the videotapes could be used as a training tool with average performers. New norms can be set by the high achievers who become behavior models. R. D. Zickelfoose, training manager for General Telephone in Marion, Ohio, holds that human resource development should not be used to maintain existing work practices. He recommends that we train toward maximum performance and use top performers in developing job criteria (Harris, 1980).

Entrepreneurial Orientation. People in the new work culture value pluralism, competent performance, and innovation.

As a result, and in accordance with the first characteristic of greater autonomy, they are espousing entrepreneurial or intrapreneurial endeavors. This is in harmony with North American culture and parallel to the growth of the venture capital industry. Entrepreneurial types focus on where opportunities are going to be, then create concepts, processes, products, or structures to capitalize on them. These promoters match people and resources with opportunities for greater choice, self-expression, and profit. This spirit energizes people to create and take responsibility for their own futures by making the most of knowledge, talent, and change. Chapter Three discusses this in more depth.

Already involved in a successful career as a corporate lawyer and vice-president of the Kern County Land Company, Tommy Davis (see "What Makes Tommy Davis Run?", 1983) became fascinated with new technology developments. He took night courses in electronics and sought entrepreneurial opportunities to make a fortune out of what came from people's minds. He began by convincing his own employer to back his first venture in military electronics, then formed his own company with a Wall Street financier, Arthur Rock. Together, they raised a venture capital fund of $3.2 million. Their first effort was to finance an entrepreneur named Max Palevsky, who started a computer company, Scientific Data Systems; eight years later it was sold to Xerox for $940 million. Peter Farley is a physician who decided to get an M.B.A. at Stanford University's business school. While there, he gathered together some faculty talent and funds to found a new enterprise, Cetus Corporation, a pioneer in genetic engineering. He sold the firm for a profitable $45 million or more and now is developing another company dealing with computer diagnostics.

In the United States, it is estimated that roughly thirty million new jobs are being created by fast-growth entrepreneurial enterprises. Sixty percent of them usually have fewer than twenty employees, some as a result of franchising. Although a third of the 600,000 American company start-ups may fail, the high-growth pattern continues in those that make it.

In large and complex corporations, the intrapreneurial

revolution is extending the concept of small, high-risk work place ventures. At Baker International, participants in new department or division ventures receive incentives in the form of shares that are later convertible to regular corporate stock at a lush price if the venture profits. Multinational corporations, such as General Electric, are setting up such corporate entrepreneurial teams. James Meehan (Pinchot, 1984b) heads up one such venture group in robotics and believes that they give employees a sense of owning the business. That means they spend a lot less time worrying about treading on toes and much more time thinking about how to move this new business forward.

Technological Orientation. People are engaged in work of a more technical nature, often related to information processing. Technology and its tools are artifacts of culture, but in the new work culture the use of such not only is increasing but is being miniaturized (Cornish, 1985). The trend is toward microfabrication and microelectronics—developing smaller, faster, more energy-efficient machines. It is manifested in microchips, lasers, and miniwonders of all types. George Kozmetsky (1981, p. 11), at the University of Texas's Institute of Constructive Capitalism, maintains that, "The technologies for the 1980s must be viewed as a national and a world resource, as a generator of wealth, as a means to increase productivity and international trade, as an area for assessment of public and private risk-taking, and last as an influencing factor for changes in the organization, education, and training of the workforce." (See Chapters Five and Six for discussion of the major manifestations of the new technologies, automation, and robotics.)

By the year 2,000, one third of the work force in industrialized countries will be teleworking, using telecommunications rather than transportation to link themselves to central work sites, while half of the management will be using electronic work stations. That was the prediction of a panel of experts in July 1982 at the Fourth General Assembly of the World Future Society. In the information society, a computer-literate population increasingly will use electronic devices to conduct both business and personal activities, according to these futurists. They also maintain that a third of the work force will experience significant disruptions of their jobs because of robotics (Didsbury, 1984).

Research and Development (R&D) Orientation. People in metaindustrial organizations will have a greater R&D orientation. Research will be used to identify people, products, processes, and markets; it will maintain both technological innovation and advantage. It will affect the "bottom-line" mentality and balance short-term returns against long-term pay-offs. Knowledge workers will employ research skills for human factor data gathering to improve organizational effectiveness, for enhancing risk analysis systems, in responding to user and customer needs, for exploring space opportunities. Management by information will require technological forecasting and futures research and greater use of both internal and external research resources. This means not only utilization of outside research groups but also establishing research consortiums among companies in an industry, for example, or synergistic relationship between corporations and universities (Corning, 1983).

The federal government is parceling out $43 billion in research and development funds to aid small businesses. The Small Business Innovation Research (SBIR) program stipulates that each of the eighteen federal departments must give 1.25 percent of its total R&D funds to qualifying small businesses. The aim is to promote research projects that can lead to the development of commercial products. The first phase of grants is up to $50,000 to determine feasibility, while the second grant may be up to $300,000 to assist in prototype development and market penetration. The premise is that small and entrepreneurial companies are producing much of the high-technology innovation leading to the computerization of American industry. In 1984, the United States spent a record $97 billion on R&D, of which industry was spending 51 percent; the National Academy of Engineering reported that all major corporations were putting more money into R&D than ever before.

These ten major thrusts in the emerging work culture are epitomized in the contemporary corporate leadership. *Business Week* devoted a whole issue (April 25, 1983) to the "New Era for Management." In that issue, two executives were cited as

Creating a New Work Culture

examples of the new breed of leaders. John E. Welch, Jr., was chosen chairman of the board for General Electric because he demonstrated both technical and entrepreneurial skills. Similarly, F. James McDonald, president of General Motors, was selected because of his ability to use both engineering and managerial competencies to improve the quality of car manufacturing. The common element in both management backgrounds and value systems was successful operating experience and performance in a high-technology work environment. These new corporate "heroes" are performance oriented, seek personnel who are better than the best, and maintain lean staffs. Chapter Twelve offers further input in this subject.

Insights for Tomorrow's Organizational Cultures

The work macroculture is expressed within the context of a corporation or agency's microculture. Thus, to understand the new management and worker attitudes, values, and practices, it is best to view them in terms of an organization's culture.

An organization is people—a collection of human objectives, expectations, and obligations; a structuring of roles and relationships. Organizations, as noted previously, are best envisioned as energy exchange systems that transform natural, machine-produced, and human energy into products and services. In the new, creative work environment, organizational cultures energize people, both individually and in groups. Then the culture becomes a powerful force for directing the efforts of personnel toward achieving the company or association's goals. This type of cultural support system gives employees a sense of identity, pride, and loyalty. It also serves to set this enterprise apart from others in its industry or arena and to differentiate its boundaries. There are many dimensions to organizational and work culture, as Figure 3 illustrates.

M.I.T. behavioral scientist Edgar Schein (1985) confirms my vision of the key elements to transform in human systems. Thinking managers within their own corporations, agencies, or associations should monitor and plan changes in these twelve aspects of their work culture:

Figure 3. Some Dimensions of Organizational and Work Culture.

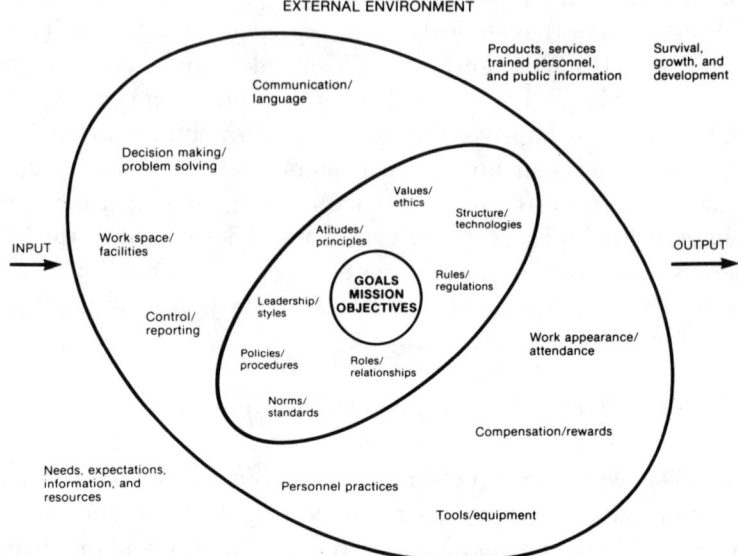

Note: Reprinted with permission of aerospace illustrator Dennis M. Davidson of University of California at San Diego Medical School.

1. goals, missions, and objectives as expressed in the creeds, charters, and other statements of corporate purpose;
2. attitudes, beliefs, principles, and philosophies;
3. priorities, values, ethics, status, and reward systems;
4. norms, standards, rules, and regulations;
5. design, structure, organization, and technology;
6. policies, procedures, and processes;
7. communication systems, languages, and terminologies;
8. control, reporting, and personnel practices;
9. decision making, problem solving, conflict resolution;
10. compensations, recognitions, and promotions;
11. work environment in terms of appearances of people and physical space;
12. leadership in terms of behavior modeling and emphasis, teaching, and coaching.

Creating a New Work Culture 57

Organizational culture can affect more than work or dress styles; it affects the bottom line. One United States global conglomerate, IBM, knows that fact better than many of its competitors—it has been called one of the best-run corporations in American history. Its unique competitive spirit and culture have led to its preeminence in the information industry and brought "Big Blue" to successful penetration of 130 countries (the nickname came from the color of its product line.) Its corporate culture is an extension of its charismatic founder; personnel share Tom Watson's beliefs and principles. Even when employees leave this computer colossus, they carry with them IBM's standards and codes—these may extend from a neat, conservative appearance to high business ethics. IBM actively tries to retain personnel for a lifetime, gives them generous fringe benefits, and promotes a "100% Club," which rewards those who achieve sales goals. IBM is a prototype of the high-tech corporate culture, with its emphasis on R&D ($3 billion in 1982), on filing patents for inventions (11,000 over the past twenty-five years), on directing great care to evaluating buyers' needs, and on major investment in human resource development ($500 million last year) (*Time,* July 11, 1983, pp. 44-54, and Oct. 8, 1984, p. 59).

Organizational cultures are dynamic and need continuing renewal. Reorganization may lead to a severing of existing relationships, a dissolution of existing structures. For example, IBM, under its current CEO, John Opel, is going through a transformation of its corporate culture. Instead of being a big battleship in mothballs, one observer described IBM today as a fleet of killer submarines. The rethinking going on in changing IBM corporate culture has resulted in new business strategies, such as partial acquisitions of high-tech firms related to its mission (such as 12 percent of Intel and 15 percent of Rolm). Furthermore, to meet new competition in the field of communication technology (such as a deregulated AT&T), IBM has improved for market analysis its worldwide intelligence-gathering network. It is pushing for greater decentralized decision making, including the establishment of independent business units, which operate like small companies on their own. Its aggressive new policies have startled the computer industry and countered even those who would steal its business secrets. It is now a global enterprise in which international operations account for 45 percent of gross income; these international operations are run by foreign nationals who may rise to senior corporate positions. In reshaping its organizational image, IBM is developing a raft of exotic technologies, many of which are related to office automation and telecommunications. The results of these corporate culture alterations are a 25 percent rise in profits for the company in 1983's second quarter alone. Each of the ten characteristics of the new work culture discussed earlier in this chapter can be traced in these descriptions of IBM's renewal.

By revitalizing organizational culture from time to time, an enterprise responds to the internal and external forces of change, adapts to meet contemporary needs, and ensures that its activities have relevance. It is a process for organizational survival and development that delimits the impact of organization shock and crises. According to Leonard Nadler (1982), professor at George Washington University, this revitalization is what people in an organization do to themselves and their system—changing the habits and customs developed to cope with new circumstances.

Let us take one trend cited for the emerging work culture —new technologies—and examine it briefly in terms of another new direction—increased communication and information. The automation of office and plant causes a significant alteration of the organizational culture. The new information systems put more knowledge into the hands of more people, and power within a company or agency begins to shift. The traditional hierarchical pyramid takes on new form—it flattens. Computers and other automated technology permit executives to bypass middle managers, classic distinctions begin to blur, and feedback from the marketplace flows more readily at all levels. The advent of the personal computer on the manager's desktop radically alters relations with corporate information specialists and improves decision making, response time, and long-range planning. Giant companies, including Ford, Weyerhaeuser, Goodyear, and others, are discovering that the new technologies are helping create a leaner, more responsive management. A case study in Chapter Five goes into this issue in greater depth.

Corporate culture is being transformed primarily because of automation and robots. Consider this in just these six dimensions of organizational culture.

1. *Communication and Language.* As indicated in Chapter Five, computers and related technology are having a great impact on organizational communications. Desktop computers and terminals are linking managers at all levels in the enterprise and giving them direct access to MIS reports and data processing (DP) information. Most do not have to learn computer languages, but they are discovering new terminology and capabilities through the varied software now available to them, such as BASIC. In addition to having greater access to more diverse information through electronic means, managers can be connected to far-flung entities within a global enterprise. The new technology permits managers to express themselves through computer graphics, spreadsheets, networks, and a myriad of other devices.

2. *Time and Time Consciousness.* Business now can operate twenty-four hours a day through new information technology. Electronic mail, teleconferencing, and flex time are but a few of the innovations by which the computer is altering our sense of time, enabling global corporations to cope better with time zone differences.

3. *Rewards and Recognition.* Promotions and choice assignments are being granted to managers, technicians, and professionals who are computer literate. Computers are becoming organizational status symbols, and PCs are being granted as a reward to the favored few for use in the office or at home. For some of these, the real privilege is to be allowed to work at home and be electronically connected to the office.

4. *Relationships and Equal Opportunity.* We have already indicated how the computer is permitting people at all levels in the organization to establish electronic connections, as well as to link up with their counterparts in other companies

and industries. Information technology cuts across racial, sexual, and national boundaries—computer literacy and competency become the only criteria for exercising this new power.

5. *Values and Norms.* Knowledge is the new currency so highly valued in the information society. A new global culture is emerging that gives high regard to relevant, rapid, and resourceful processing of information. Competence, particularly in the new technologies, increasingly is the organizational norm.

6. *Organizational Processes and Learning.* Automated processes are becoming an economic necessity in most businesses, cutting back the size of the work force. For many organizations, their business is information processing. More frequently, training and other educational efforts are accomplished through computers and communication technologies, especially with the use of computer simulations and self-learning packages. Chapter Four expands on this theme.

These are but some dimensions of organizational culture being transformed by an information technology whose pervasive influence on the corporate environment will only grow. We are just beginning to appreciate its value in improving decision making, long-range planning, marketing, customer-need analysis, and a host of other business activities.

Synergistic Alterations of Organizational Cultures

One sage observed that to live is to change but to grow is to change often. If this is true, then it must be planned, not haphazard, change, and it applies to institutions as well as to individuals. Organizations, be they corporations, associations, or government agencies, periodically need restructuring. Every time this occurs, there is an accompanying alteration in the organizational culture. Thinking managers are wise to consider such factors in their strategic planning. If organizational energies are to be redirected constructively, then synergy not only should be a goal but should be incorporated into the change process. If executives think only in financial and legal terms in changing organizational structure and culture, the human energies are likely to be misdirected. The results may be not only not synergistic but quite frustrating, wasteful, and unprofitable.

This was particularly problematic during the industrial age, when the buying and selling of corporate assets became a latter-day phenomenon. Sometimes it was an indication of dynamic economic growth, but at other times it meant disaster. Too often, corporate planners thought narrowly of the firm's financial and material assets, totally ignoring the enterprise's human assets—in terms of either the company or agency doing the acquiring or the entity being acquired. In other words, will the two corporate cultures fit and what will the impact be on personnel in both entities? The multinational corporate giant, Schlumbergers, Ltd., for example, has this synergistic strategy: Acquire only enterprises that relate to one's basic business, either to strengthen or supplement it; try to make friendly acquisitions and avoid hostile takeovers.

Synergy is defined as cooperative and combined actions to achieve common goals. When attempting to merge organizational cultures, the transition can be facilitated for the people involved by collaborative or synergistic relationship. In the following sections, four alteration strategies are discussed that mutually benefit the parties involved. A viable synthesis can occur when executives and personnel in both entities cooperate to achieve integration and planned change. Otherwise, institutional crises and shock may deepen and people may become impaired in the reorganization endeavors (Moran and Harris, 1982).

Diversification. If we stick to the original idea of diversification into related, manageable product lines, such moves can be synergistic. Alfred Chandler, a Harvard Business School professor, notes that it has been characteristic of modern enterprises to bring many units under their control, to operate in different locations, to carry on different types of economic activities, and to handle different lines of goods and services. This system reaped some benefits, of course. For example, Swift made food cheaper by eliminating middlemen in the distribution of meat; DuPont went from producing rayon to nylon and then dacron; General Motors went on to supplement auto production with diesel locomotives. Chandler believes that what went wrong is that diversification became a corporate mania and too many firms got involved in too many other businesses. They became overextended and lost knowledge of the special characteristics of their manufacturing, markets, technology, customers, and personnel.

Too often, toward the end of the industrial age, top management lost touch with products and based decisions largely on money and management abstractions. Unfortunately, the business schools themselves contributed to this unhealthy situation, because acquisitions were sought by trained M.B.A. types looking for cash generation only ("cash cows" in the parlance of management consulting). When financial analysis alone told American management to give up a market, overseas competition stepped in to fill the gap, such as the Japanese with reference to consumer electronics. Today, the situation is slowly being reversed in the push for industrial renewal. The call is again out for hands-on management with knowledge of manufacturing and product innovation. Thus, for example, General Electric sold its coal mines and is investing the proceeds in its own high technologies.

Dresser Industries is a good example of a company learning painfully how to be more synergistic in its diversifications. When John James became chief executive, the firm had acquired a hodgepodge of product lines, some top-notch but many mediocre or less. Although Dresser basically is in the oil services business, a raft of diverse acquisitions left the corporation with everything from refractories to industrial abrasives, from earthmovers to hand tools. James developed tight financial controls and lofty targets in his acquisitions policy. He took into consideration more than financial matters and clues so that when he steps down as CEO he will leave the company with a solid financial foundation. But his intended successor, John J. Murphy, is left with the problem of trying to remodel the diversification policy—it is hoped that he will apply the principle of synergy and take into account compatible organizational cultures. Despite a tidy balance sheet and only 21 percent of capitalization in long-term debt, the new chief executive could learn something about acquisitions from his nearest competitor, Schlumbergers, Ltd.—Dresser has only 10 percent of the world market in wireline business as against Schlumberger's 70 percent, a near monopoly (Auletta, 1984).

Corporate Break-Ups. Desperate partners often have to dissolve a business relationship. Usually, this leads to disillusionment, frustration, trauma, and even organizational depression. But all such negative experiences can be delimited and countered, for all things in life are relative and no joint undertaking is permanent. Marsha Sinetar (1983) compared a corporate break-up to a marriage break-up—the promise was unfulfilled, the sense of loss and failure, and the nagging "if only" type of feelings are evident among the corporate leadership. Through Sinetar & Associates in El Segundo, California, she tries to ease the pain of corporate break-ups involving such clients as Continental Airlines, Norris Industries, and United Airlines. When a partnership, merger, or acquisition falls apart, Sinetar employs her skills as an organizational psychologist to manage the emotional upheaval that can result. According to Sinetar, maps and blueprints from the industrial age that told us how to live, work, and be a success in business are fast disappearing. By opening lines of communication and confronting problems related to a failed enterprise, rumors can be curtailed and morale restored, and growth can result from the change. Sometimes, the break-up is best for the parties involved. Organizational psychologists can help both top management and the rank and file to cope more effectively with realignment of corporate structures and processes. This is especially true relative to preparing for a break-up, as well as for a merger, by training workers to deal with differences, uncertainty, and unfamiliar situations. The only thing certain about the future is change: Once a major department, division, subsidiary, or partner is removed from the corporate culture, that environment is altered and something new must be developed in its place—an opportunity is created.

The classic case of corporate break-up may well be the court-ordered divestiture of AT&T. Quietly, its corporate HRD specialists, along with select organization development consultants, tried to prepare employees for the psychological impact of such an organizational divorce. At one point in the process, a costly strike erupted, partially due to fear of job loss because of both the break-up and more automation. In the settlement negotiations, the Communications Workers of America forced the giant utility to provide more counseling and retraining of workers for the changeovers. Apparently, all such endeavors to ready personnel for Ma Bell's break-up proved inadequate; many AT&T workers have not endured well the trauma of transition.

A feature in the *Los Angeles Times* ("The Bell Breakup: A Year Later," 1984) reported the wrenching transitional problems as being more severe than anticipated. Thousands of veteran utility people enrolled in stress management courses. Many complained of various coping problems as the work environment was transformed from that of having a paternalistic employer to one of unnerving competitive pressures. Not only have there been disruptive reductions in the work force, but also those that managed to survive are questioning themselves and their careers. Internal restructuring has led to massive job switching and transfers. The monolith's culture shock is most acute in Bell Laboratories, where reorganization is designed to make research more responsive to product development. A century-old career development pattern is being revamped—the service ethic must now include productivity and results. In retrospect, AT&T executives admit that they invested too heavily in the legal aspects and divestiture studies and not heavily enough in helping their employees acculturate to the new work environment. Such would have been a synergistic break-up strategy. Yet the renewed corporation is adapting to its changed circumstances in the information age. The new Bell system culture is more innovative, entrepreneurial, and competitive—its strategic management is oriented to the market and to success.

Buy-Ins, Not Buy-Outs. A quiet trend has been growing in both international and domestic business expansion. Instead of questionable, even hostile, takeovers, enlightened management is setting a new pattern befitting these times of changing technology and entrepreneurial fervor. IBM, again, is the best illustration of the emerging buy-in mentality. In 1983, the computer colossus purchased 15 percent of Rolm Corporation, a Santa Clara-based manufacturer of business telephone switching systems, and 12 percent of Intel Corporation, also based in Santa Clara but a manufacturer of semiconductors and microprocessors. IBM is a customer of both companies and never contemplated a complete takeover; it appreciated the corporate accomplishments and cultures of its new partners and did not interfere with their independence. Rolm's CEO, Ken Oshman, assured his employees that IBM recognized the need to preserve Rolm's culture and informal style ("The Colossus that Works," 1983; "Big Blue . . . Bigger," 1984).

These two acquisitions are examples of synergy at its best. Takeovers might have ruined two bright, promising companies, but buy-ins provided the smaller firms with needed capital for research. For IBM, Rolm's computer-controlled switchboards are the key to the automated office; Intel provides an independent source of innovative technology. Through this strategy, Rolm's and Intel's talented people remain, the entrepreneurial spirit is preserved, with its urges for achievement and self-fulfillment, the pioneering companies remain in the competitive marketplace, and the key executives head up their independent corporations, not just IBM divisions.

The approach of buy-in to related businesses is similar to the previously discussed entrepreneurial independent business units at IBM, which are themselves like start-up companies. There are now twelve such enterprises taking IBM into fields such as medical electronics and robotics. But, remember, such efforts alter corporate culture!

International Joint Ventures. In this era of fast-growth companies, the joint venture offers a unique opportunity for synergy and win/win for the organizations involved. When a corporation moves out of its own national culture into the international marketplace for such an arrangement, it involves coping with cultural differences to produce cooperation. Armco, Inc., and Mitsubishi Rayon Co. provide a demonstration of such cultural synergy. They signed a joint venture enabling Armco to sell lightweight composites in Japan; eventually a manufacturing operation may be opened. For the American firm, the venture opened the seemingly impenetrable Japanese market. For the Japanese partner, the venture gave access to Armco's materials technology. For both companies, it is a means for sharing capital and risk while sharing each other's strengths—and that is what joint ventures are all about. Too often, management fails to capitalize on another dimension: the strengths of both corporate cultures being merged in the new enterprise. It is more than merely linking American product innovation with Japanese manufacturing technology.

There are numerous other examples of international joint ventures that permit participants to draw on the best in Eastern and Western cultures. General Motors, for instance, has joint ventures not only with Toyota Motors to produce automobiles but also with Fujitsu Fanu, a low-cost machine tool and robot maker in Japan. The latter Japanese company will be able to take advantage of the robot technology General Motors originally developed for internal use. General Motors benefits in both cases by learning more about low-cost manufacturing. Low-cost manufacturing and marketing knowledge prompted IBM to form a venture in Japan to sell office automation equipment with Kanematsu-Gosho. Overseas joint ventures also can provide the American company with more control than just licensing and greater influence over the way its technology is used, especially with reference to domestic markets.

International joint ventures not only help countries readdress trade imbalances but also help them direct energies together toward constructive, mutual goals. One Boeing official wisely noted that it is better to find a way to join forces than to exhaust your energies trying to beat a competitor from another country. For example, as other nations become interested in developing their own aerospace industries, American companies are beginning to explore the possibilities of collaboration with future competitors. A consortium of American, European, and Japanese companies is being formed to develop a jet engine for a new 150-passenger plane. Airbus Industry in Europe is an exceptional illustration of how synergistic efforts can overcome corporate, cultural, and national rivalries. Successful wide-body jets have been produced by this combined enterprise of France and Germany, which own 38 percent of the venture, and Britain, which has 20 percent; other participants include Spain. If an organization does not have the material, finances, or human resources to undertake a business venture on its own, the consortium combines partners, talents, and capital. It may be the only way leaders in space commerce may open the high frontier market, as McDonnell Douglas and Johnson & Johnson have already discovered!

In contrast to the above examples of wholesome synergistic developments in the alteration of organizational structure and cultures, we have also heard numerous horror stories of destructive takeovers. They are illustrative of the industrial-age mind set and one-dimensional (financial) executive thinking. What did buy-outs, such as the DuPont-Seagram-Conoco battle and the Bendix-Marietta-Allied circus, do except rearrange their "*Fortune* 500" rankings? In the dying industrial work culture, mergers and acquisitions, often hostile, produced only worry and stress for executives and personnel instead of long-term benefits. Think of the energies and resources dissipated in Continental Airlines' bitter loss to the Texas International takeover or even Western Airlines' successful elusion of the talons of Air Florida.

Board directors that have fended off unwelcome corporate overtures for acquisition describe the experience as extremely intense, terribly time consuming, and unsettling. In a recent survey of such directors by Spencer, Stuart & Associates, 40 percent reported that the most pressing issue facing corporate directors is taking defensive measures against takeovers. No amount of warning or planning sufficiently prepared them as the crisis situation developed over such actions. They admitted that their lives and business schedules were disrupted by such acquisition attempts and that important management problems were neglected during the fray. In such situations, all the worst aspects of American competitive sports seem to get transferred from the playing fields to the board rooms. The situation becomes win/lose. Some executives and board members benefit from "golden parachutes," for which shareholders pay; some shareholders may go unharmed, but the company, its employees, and, often, the community, suffer from the corporate war. Is it any wonder that in the work environment the trend is toward synergistic mergers, divestitures, buy-ins, and joint ventures?

Conclusion

The conclusions to be drawn from this chapter by thoughtful managers are: (1) Culture is a powerful concept to be considered in terms of changing both the work environment and the organization; the strategy should be directed toward creation of a work culture in harmony with the trends of our times and people's needs during this transition. (2) Finally, synergy is to be cultivated when attempting to integrate the cultures of two or more work units or corporations.

THREE

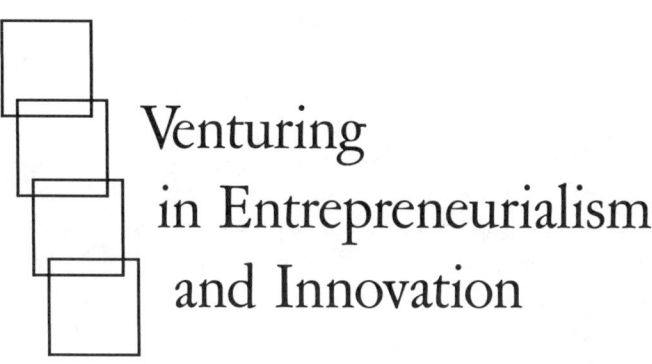

Venturing
in Entrepreneurialism
and Innovation

Executive Summary. A distinctive feature of the new work culture is the resurgence of entrepreneurialism. The expression takes many forms, from founding a new business enterprise to undertaking a technological venture of some scope to being an intrapreneur within an existing organization. However manifested, the entrepreneurial spirit involves total commitment and high performance, moderate risk taking and the exercise of creativity, effective management of change and resources, anticipation of people's needs and business opportunities, avoidance of bureaucracy and excessive expenditures, and much self-confidence and optimism. Through free enterprise, the successful application of this spirit ensures that the entrepreneur has more control over his or her own destiny, more influence and power, more freedom and compensation, more self-actualization and fulfillment.

For women in the midst of role transition, entrepreneurial activity becomes a means for accomplishment while bypassing the traditional barriers faced by females in business. Research indicates that women entrepreneurs have special qualities that ensure successful enterprises. By being entrepreneurial, women, as well as men, take advantage of opportunities by searching for profitable concepts. It is a learning and develop-

mental experience to formulate a business plan, obtain financial sponsors, recruit competent personnel, build management teams, operate by controlling costs and producing results. But real entrepreneurial growth occurs with the creation of corporate systems and culture, seeking personal and group wellness, and continuing the practice of tested procedures for organizational excellence and success.

Entrepreneurialism, whether in start-up activities or in intrapreneurialism within established enterprises, can be a means for managing innovation. Innovation translates new ideas or inventions into practical use in the form of products or processes, markets or services, concepts or systems. Innovative management requires continuing openness, an incentive system that rewards entrepreneurial-like high performance, as well as collaboration among people resources.

New managers practicing entrepreneurialism and innovation have the vision to think big and project ahead. They also know how to create synergy, particularly in the use of local resources, such as universities. They appreciate that technology venturing, especially in large-scale enterprises, such as the renewing of the earth's infrastructure or space industrialization, demands a form of macromanagement that integrates systems and resources.

Entrepreneurialism—A Timely Concept

Judging by the spate of recent books on the subject, entrepreneurialism is an idea whose time has come. In fact, Peter Drucker (1985) has now devoted a whole volume to innovation and entrepreneurship, which he rightly insists are disciplines that should be incorporated into the executive's job. Furthermore, a resurgence of interest in the phenomenon of start-up enterprises, whether within small business or larger technology ventures, occurs at a major turning point in the American economy. As we enter the information age fueled by the microelectronics revolution, the renewed emphasis on entrepreneurialism is appropriate. It is flourishing in both fast-growth, take-off companies and subsidiaries, whether through the efforts of individual business founders or of entrepreneurial groups within giant corporations. President Ronald Reagan declared in 1984 that this is the "age of the entrepreneur"; that 600,000 new businesses were incorporated that year—double the number of a decade earlier—seems to substantiate his optimism ("Those People Who Dare," 1985). The resultant new technologies are the driving forces in the creation of a new work culture and management that is more fitting for our turbulent times and changed circumstances. When the quality of entrepreneurialism is balanced with innovative management, successful technology venturing becomes possible.

Several factors are contributing to the revival of entrepreneurialism in our society:

- The process is in harmony with the American culture and dream. We value individualism, achievement, independence, pragmatism, and action; we believe in solving problems, fixing things, do-it-yourself thinking, and turning adversity into success. The entrepreneurial spirit expresses that credo.
- The renewing economy favors entrepreneurialism, particularly regarding small new businesses of service, information processing, or high-technology types. As we recently were reminded in the *Harvard Business Review* (Drucker, 1984), job growth is being generated and accelerated by such start-up enterprises. The knowledge revolution, demographic trends, venture capital growth, and incorporation of entrepreneurialism within American industries are among the forces contributing to this trend.
- National policy and programs are beginning to favor some kind of government support for entrepreneurial efforts, whether in the form of grants to minority business persons, Small Business Administration loans and management consultation, or tax advantages. Others advocate the elimination for start-up businesses of capital gains taxes on investments and even argue for government equity holdings in new ventures (Vesper, 1983). A recent Dallas conference of the Institute of Constructive Capitalism highlighted another possibility—the commercialization in the private sector of defense-related research through technology venturing (Kuhn, 1984).

- The business schools are now recognizing the timeliness of entrepreneurial research and programs. Universities have introduced more than 150 centers or courses on the subject. Obviously, the traditional idea that entrepreneurs are born, not made, is being replaced by education for entrepreneurialism as a part of effective strategy for innovative management.

For these reasons and more, a dynamic, open society and economy in the midst of changes demands more high-growth commerce, and this requires the nurturing of entrepreneurialism. As we transcend the old ways of doing business, the new system favors entrepreneurs and technology venturers, whether within established corporations or in new enterprises. For these are the creative deviants who move beyond the established boundaries and ways of commerce to innovate in their attempts to be responsive to customer and employee needs. In the process, many of them also delight in the entrepreneurial experience. As the founder of several publishing houses remarked, "The challenge for me is in the fun of the start-up. What excites me is knowing what you want to do and then doing it." It is bureaucracy at its worst that would thwart that spirit within its management and workers. When Robert E. Levinson left his post as CEO of an American Standard division to start a new hotel business, he wrote a book (1983) on the value of decentralization in big business. He sees decentralization as a means for restoring the sense of the entrepreneurial, with its accompanying excitement and fun of leadership, as well as exercising more responsibility, accountability, and authority. He would remove the layers of management insulation and expose executives to the panic of failure and the triumph of producing profit.

What exactly is this entrepreneurial spirit? The brochure of the American Association of Entrepreneurs expresses this credo: "I do not choose to be common; it is my right to be uncommon. I seek opportunity, not security. I want to take calculated risk, to dream and to build, to fail and to succeed." At the Harvard Business School, Professor Howard H. Stevenson (1985a), himself an entrepreneur, has begun a systematic inquiry into dynamic entrepreneurial performance. He describes entrepreneurs he has known who hate risk, who start up often without profit as a goal, and who may not even be innovative managers. Some of them are competent academics or professional managers who woke up one day and discovered that they were on their way to becoming entrepreneurs. Stevenson suspects that being "entrepreneurial involves a set of behaviors and choices which are fostered or deterred by environmental settings. It can be encouraged or discouraged" (Stevenson, 1983, p. 50). Table 2 summarizes Stevenson's ideas in terms of a range of behaviors exhibited in two types of managers: promoters and trustees.

Table 2. The Entrepreneurial Mind Set and Management Style.

The Promotor	The Trustee
• Perceives opportunity.	• Controls current resources.
• Has short-term orientation.	• Has evolutionary outlook.
• Makes minimal commitment of resources when decisions are made to pursue business opportunities.	• Makes maximal commitment of resources when decisions are made to pursue business opportunities.
• Prefers minimal overhead, seeking to borrow, barter, or lease.	• Prefers to own or control contractually.
• Is comfortable with a flat, lean organization that emphasizes team management and networking—knows whom to call upon.	• Is comfortable with organized hierarchy, levels of responsibility, and position management—dependent on staff.
• Creates high potential ventures to meet human needs, using varied management systems/styles—manages for ultrastability.	• Manages for stability and steady growth, seeking bottom-line profitability annually and quantifiable results.

Source: Adapted from Stevenson, 1983.

Perhaps entrepreneurialism is one expression of the innate human sense of discovery that characterizes us. Historian Daniel Boorstin (1984) reminds us that professions are organized to maintain traditional approaches to knowledge and tend to be concerned with classic controversies rather than with breaking new ground. He expresses admiration for the amateur willing to try something new: "Every true discoverer or inventor was doing something for the first time. By contrast, the maxim of both the bureaucrat and the traditionalist in the profession is, 'Never do anything for the first time.' The amateur spirit, in its original sense, is a fertile element of creativity that we are in danger of losing if we allow ourselves to be fenced in by the requirements of professionalism" (Boorstin, 1984, p. 10).

The author of *Back in Working Order,* Woodrow H. Sears (1983), maintains that there are basically three types of managers: start-up, continuity, and turnaround. In recent years, there have been widespread entrepreneurial successes in the high-technology arena, such as Apple Computer and Commodore International, as well as spectacular failures, such as Victor Technologies and Osborne Computers (now getting ready for a resurrection). Even among the successes, entrepreneurial founders sometimes have been forced to step aside and bring in "professional" management. According to Eric Flamholtz, a professor in the UCLA School of Business, that is because a different set of managerial skills and behaviors is involved. His position is that entrepreneurship requires the ability to recognize a market need and then to move quickly to develop or supply the required product or service. When the take-off company begins to experience growing pains, the founder should recognize the symptoms. At this point, the start-up firms supposedly need to go through a transformation to more formal management systems. If the entrepreneur can practice or acquire that next set of skills, he or she may have a place as the organization moves to the next stage of development. If not, the founder may have to change his or her role by moving up to chairperson, as Steven Jobs did at Apple, or by resigning or selling out. The conventional wisdom has been that the "professional" manager is what is then needed.

There is another school of thought that says professional management as we have traditionally conceived and taught it should be changed so that it becomes more entrepreneurial. The customers and employees of both today and tomorrow are literally the "children of change." Entrepreneurial, innovative leadership appeals to their needs, for it implies creative matching of individuals and resources with new opportunities and processes. University of Texas professor Eugene Konecci thinks that in our complex society the entrepreneurial spirit can best be captured in the entrepreneurial team. It is expressed in a management team that has the required talent and experience so vital in fledgling enterprises that are technology based (Kuhn, 1984).

With an eye on markets for now and the future, innovators who wish to be entrepreneurial follow two procedures to ensure success: (1) Develop and document a business concept and plan that is both technically and economically feasible. (2) Access adequate amounts of capital in forms such as credit from suppliers, loans from relatives, friends, or banks, equity funds from venture capitalists, and investments by corporate sponsors (Welsh and White, 1983). The venture capitalist is the counterpart of the entrepreneur—such a person acts like an entrepreneur in the investing of capital or in the gathering of financial supporters for the new enterprises, often in high-technology industries. There is a symbiotic relationship between venture capitalist and entrepreneur (Smilor, 1982). Each has to respect the other while playing distinctive roles—the former should not try to run the business but should be helpful and realistic.

The synergy between the two is evident in this illustration: "The clever entrepreneur knows how to not only spot socioeconomic trends but also to turn them into dynamic business opportunities. For example, in 1983 there were nearly 1.5 million first-born children in the U.S.A., 500,000 more than in 1960. With no hand-me-downs from older siblings, increased spending on children's items is indicated" (Kemp, 1984, p. 32). The entrepreneur may have good ideas on how to meet this need, develop a business plan, and organize necessary resources. But then there is the need for financing to capitalize on this strategy. If venture capital appears to be the best source for such funding, the entrepreneur may consult a directory to identify a resource, make inquiry of the association of venture capitalists, or seek a connection through an accounting or legal firm. Assuming linkage is established with a compatible venture capitalist, this is where the synergy begins. The latter can review business plans, offer useful counsel, and provide helpful monitoring of the project, in addition to supplying the start-up capital. As long as this does not become an imposition or interference, the business relationship between the two parties can be mutually supportive and profitable.

Nourishing the Entrepreneurial Spirit

If education and training can encourage development of the entrepreneurial spirit and result in more innovative management, what characteristics should we then cultivate in both business students and managers? From working with start-up company founders, I have concluded that we should foster the same qualities sought in change agents:

- openness—willingness to consider new ideas and differing opinions, to test alternative solutions to one's own;
- flexibility—adaptability to new people, information, and developments and ability to handle the unexpected and to manage by exception;
- sensitivity—empathy and consciousness of what is happening to others, as well as oneself, in the course of interactions; awareness of the feeling level of communication so as to pick up on these indicators;
- creativeness—responding with resourcefulness to new people and situations, avoiding stereotyped answers and solutions; exercise of imagination and initiative;
- achievement orientation—setting goals, objectives, and targets and energizing self toward their accomplishment;
- communicativeness—capability of establishing business relationships and exchanges with others; promotion of open, circular interaction and the ability to energize others;
- people skills—ability to be both person and task centered; ability to function effectively in groups, teams, and networks; understanding of how to involve others.

All of these are qualities that can be learned and developed in would-be entrepreneurs, especially by educators and human resource development practitioners.

To counteract the loneliness and stress of the start-up situation, founders need peer support. Sometimes this can be found within the new company, as when a multiple executive model is adopted among cofounders who not only share power and responsibility but provide both organizational and personal support to one another. Sometimes it can be gained externally by joining a CEO network, such as The Executive Committee (Vedax Sciences Corporation) or the Southern California Technology Executives Network or the similar networks that are cropping up in Seattle, San Diego, and other cities around the country. These voluntary associations usually divide into small groups so as to provide not only connection and information exchanges but also ego support and mutual assistance in problem solving. They not only facilitate executive development but contribute to the stabilization of company growth.

There is as yet no clear-cut consensus from the research as to what constitutes the entrepreneurial personality. For example, A. David Silver conducted a survey of fifty-four business owners who have accumulated personal wealth of at least $20 million through the entrepreneurial process. Based on his limited findings, Silver facetiously concluded that most of the respondents were deprived as children, felt guilty because they had let down someone important to them, had strong mothers and absent fathers, and attributed success to the creative solution of a large problem (Silver, 1983). A review of the research literature by M. Kirk Crocker, a professor at the University of Texas College of Business Administration, revealed a number of other entrepreneurial traits worth noting if we are to foster this spirit in others. In addition to a high need for achievement, they include: a drive for freedom or independence, higher thresholds for coping with stress, higher-than-average degrees of self-confidence, and risk sensitivity or awareness to anticipate difficulties (Smilor, 1982).

One of my clients, responsible for several major start-up activities, was impressed by the validity of this profile of a successful entrepreneur and shared the statement with his colleagues (White, 1977). According to White, the entrepreneur is a person who:

1. is physically resilient and able to work extended periods of time;

2. has a need to control and direct because of the conviction that he or she can do the job better;
3. has a never-ending sense of urgency and thus tackles problems immediately and persists until objectives are achieved;
4. is confident of outcomes;
5. maintains distant vision but devotes energy to the next step;
6. wants to know the status of everything while dealing with things as they are;
7. has superior conceptual ability focused on problem solving;
8. wants the business praised but is embarrassed by praise to self, so avoids status symbols;
9. is more concerned with people's accomplishments than with their feelings;
10. is capable of considerable self-control and ability to handle anxiety;
11. is attracted to challenge and plays for high stakes;
12. talks to one selected supportive person, even if that person is outside the business;
13. will not accept "it can't be done" and reacts with "why not?" in frustrating situations;
14. insists on gathering customer information firsthand;
15. starts with one product or service and builds it first to profitability;
16. perceives growth opportunities and uses his or her own and others' experience to expand it significantly;
17. seeks areas of high entry barriers and low exit barriers to achieve high margins of return;
18. aims at distinctive perceived customer values that make for purchase decisions.

In a recent AT&T newsletter, Arthur Levitt and Jack Albertine of the American Business Conference have reduced the entrepreneurial characteristics to these six:

1. unwilling to be frustrated by corporate bureaucracy;
2. inveterate salespeople who radiate self-confidence;

3. fanatically devoted to business fundamentals, such as finance;
4. uncanny ability to think like their customers;
5. persevering;
6. risk taking.

The dean of American venture capitalists, according to *Forbes* ("What Makes Tommy Davis Run?", 1983) is Tommy Davis, who helped create silicon valley in his middle years. His lofty vision is that the fortunes of the future will come out of people's minds. He demonstrates a capacity to link together ideas and talent, as he did with Scientific Data Systems and the Mayfield Funds. In looking beyond the horizon, Davis sees a new culture of management emerging that provides fulfillment to bright, hard-working young people while restoring dignity to the average job. At seventy-one years of age, Davis is convinced that people are the most important element in business and that big companies are usually inept. His entrepreneurial spirit is expressed in his innovative ideas. For instance, if he had his way, he would split companies up—bust them wide open—when sales reach the $200 million level. He also feels that venture capital companies must have super growth. This is a necessity, for it is the only way to get and keep the superachievers.

Encouraging the Female Entrepreneur

One growing alteration in this profile is worthy of note—women are increasingly moving into entrepreneurial enterprises and technology venturing. Overcoming the financial discrimination of both the venture capital and banking communities, they are beginning start-up businesses in such traditionally male fields as high technology and manufacturing, as well as services. These well-educated, competent women executives add another dimension to the emerging entrepreneurial personality, and research indicates that they differ significantly from businesswomen in general.

North American experience demonstrates that women entrepreneurs as a group have realistic expectations and low debt ratio and that they listen to advice and plow profits back into fledgling companies ("Canada's New Capitalists," 1982, p. 50). One Queen's University study in 1982 of 275 Ontario women proprietors found that they primarily strike out into their own businesses because of the challenge and desire to be their own boss. As one observed succinctly: "You learn a lot about your capabilities by putting yourself on the line. I get great satisfaction from having dared, done it, and been successful." Another Canadian study by the Thomas Riddell accounting firm revealed further insight about these women capitalists: Their businesses have a higher survival rate than the businesses of male counterparts (47 percent to 25 percent, respectively); they tend to seek help without embarrassment and to use networking intelligently; and they make more realistic projections of business without apologies than do men in similar positions. The penchant of these females for business risk taking was confirmed by Revenue Canada's Taxation Statistics, which showed women in the last decade becoming business owners in Canada at three times the rate of men.

In the United States, the story is similar for women entrepreneurs. The Small Business Administration reports that the number of self-employed females increased from 1.7 million in 1977 to 2.3 million in 1982. At this writing, over 2.5 million businesses are owned by women in this country, and these gross over $40 billion in receipts annually—almost a third of all new United States businesses are started by women. Why this growth and concentration of one gender in entrepreneurialism?

The research of Sandy Kemp (1984) into the female entrepreneurship boom indicates several interesting factors:

• Women have what it takes for successful start-up enterprises—tenacity, common sense, intelligence, decision-making skills, leadership and management skills, creativity, and, most especially, intuition.

• Women entrepreneurs are highly motivated achievers. They need to be independent, to control their destiny, to experience job satisfaction, especially by succeeding; they want to overcome the obstacles and limitations confronting women in the business world—male corporate cultures and chauvinism, un-

Venturing in Entrepreneurialism and Innovation

equal pay for comparable work, "pink-collar jobs" or "women's work" stereotyping with inadequate compensation, and inaccessibility to upper levels of management positions within large organizations.

• Compared to women not in business, women who run their own enterprises seemingly experience more personal fulfillment and self-esteem, contribute more meaningfully and productively to society, have more creative expression and control over their future, and open up more career options for proving abilities and gaining recognition.

With the encouragement of male financial leaders, female personalities continue to enrich the entrepreneurial profile. Perhaps it is women who will enable organizations to attain the fine balance we seek between entrepreneurialism and innovative management. Indications of this come from a research study on the personality of entrepreneurs conducted at the University of Texas at Austin (Smilor, 1982, pp. 111-113). Whereas too much competitiveness may impede business success, the investigators found that sensitiveness and responsiveness to others get better results—up to a 20 percent variance in gross profits; these are the very qualities that most women entrepreneurs have in abundance in contrast to their male counterparts. Thus, women's intuition, perceptiveness, and skills in human relations are significant contributors to business accomplishment.

When female and male entrepreneurs team up, we may have the right combination for success according to the research of split-brain researchers. Thus, the right hemisphere of the brain, with its emphasis on creativity, visual imagery, motor control, artistic talent, and sensing, is then coupled with the left-brain capability of logical and abstract thinking to provide unique insight into business problem solving and decision making.

Women who would be entrepreneurs can benefit from studying the business lives and strategies of female success models. How can one not be encouraged by the profile of Sandra Kurtsig, founder of ASK Computers? When she started this part-time business in her apartment in 1972, little did she realize that by 1980, when it went public, her company would be worth $8.8 million (Kemp, 1984, p. 21). As an owner of 62 percent of its stock, her personal holdings increased to $34 million. Who would not be inspired by this ambitious executive's track record of performance and her plans for $100 million in sales by mid-1986?

Sandy Kemp, already a successful entrepreneur, pursued an M.B.A. at the University of Texas. She has written of other business heroines in her book, *Women's Entrepreneurial Spirit* (1984). She believes that would-be women entrepreneurs likely will have to reorder their priorities. That may mean making such a deep commitment that one's business takes precedence over other relationships and activities. It means learning to cope with insecurity and accepting responsibility for oneself. It implies maintaining emotional balance, being organized and goal oriented, and cultivating the capacity for listening and learning.

Entrepreneurialism for women especially requires competence in whatever one undertakes and, where this is lacking, knowing how to acquire it. The latter may involve bringing together complementary human resources, forming a team, engaging in networking—all talents that many females have in abundance. However, the usual demands of entrepreneurship—designing an effective business plan, marketing it, operating an enterprise for profitable growth—apply equally to both sexes.

An Entrepreneurial Case Study

As a management psychologist, it is natural for me to focus on the human side of the start-up enterprise. Through hands-on consultation with one silicon valley high-tech take-off company during the past three years, I have reached tentative conclusions about the entrepreneurial process. These observations deal directly with such issues as founder control and ownership, impact of funding search and rapid growth on decision making, and management styles that will ensure stable growth. Essentially, this is an encapsulation of the steps that seem to be involved in building a new organization while trying to manage innovatively as they were experienced in our case study company:

1. Search for profitable concepts around which to de-

velop a successful business. This vital first step took the principal founder of the case study company almost twelve months and was the outgrowth of previous entrepreneurial experience. It involved exhaustive market research and trying out ideas on numerous knowledgeable advisers.

2. Formulate a business plan. This is a dynamic process that requires continuing testing and revision. It has to be not only market oriented and realistic but also composed in such a way that it will fly with investors. This document must appeal to typical venture capital industry attitudes, such as having a single-page summary and a pay-back period to consumers of new products (Pratt and others, 1982). Wise entrepreneurs would be well advised to go through simulated interviews with trusted and respected colleagues before actually meeting with venture capitalists or bankers to make their presentation of that plan.

3. Select carefully personnel for roles on the executive team and the board and to act as consultants. This is a critical factor that can enhance the plan and its presentation. It is debatable whether this should be done before or after venture capital is first sought. While these individuals are chosen on the basis of their reputations and track records, their initial and potential contribution to the take-off company is the principal criterion for selection. Attracting such talented people to the pregnant enterprise requires that the entrepreneur come to grips with such issues as who is to be considered founders, what expectations exist as to their financial investment and influence in the new undertaking, and how much stock and power are to be shared. The earlier these roles, relationships, and expectations are adequately clarified, the more energies will be directed toward mission accomplishment.

Particular care should be taken in choosing key professional advisers who are compensated either directly from cash income or through equity in the business. The attorney, accountant, and financial planner or insurance agent can play critical roles in the legal and financial future of the enterprise, especially regarding computerized record keeping, tax liabilities, and compensation or benefits.

4. Research and search for financial sponsors, not only for the first stage of organizational development but also for the other initial phases before the company becomes profitable. Founders should be sure to distinguish between promised and actual assets to be contributed by investors. Real, up-front money is necessary to get the enterprise functioning (although this is contrary to the view that if everyone who started a business waited until he or she had sufficient capitalization, nobody would ever start a business) (Smith, 1982). Much anguish and stress can be avoided by ensuring start-up funding before beginning operations. If the founders cannot or will not invest personal funds sufficient for this purpose, then a number of alternatives are feasible. These, as previously mentioned, range from outright loans and Eurodollar arrangements to corporate funding of a new entity or venture capital investment. For example, Elie Shneour, president of Biosystems Institute, has been involved in negotiations for numerous new enterprises in the health and biotechnology fields. In conversation with the author, this distinguished La Jolla scientist observed that many entrepreneurs would be better off finding a very reputable investment banker and then giving that person 10 percent of the stock ownership in return for locating the right investors. Even when the new business is functioning and beginning to produce profits, expansion funding will occupy much more of the entrepreneur's time and talent than is usually anticipated. That is why it is desirable for founders to think big and project ahead ten years in staging out their case for investment.

5. Control stock and cash flow if the enterprise is to be established on a sound financial footing. The entrepreneur, especially one with limited resources, can use nonvoting stock in the new venture as a means of obtaining both investment and high-priced talent, either as advisers or as executives. While the entrepreneur may wish to retain ownership and control largely for him- or herself and family, reality may dictate compromises in that regard, as when executive colleagues take on a co-founder role. Furthermore, the entrepreneur must guard against sharp or unscrupulous types whose goal is a company takeover—those who serve as financial or legal advisers or board members

solely to position themselves in time to usurp ownership. By controlling costs and limiting expenses during organizational infancy, the enterprise may survive to its next developmental stage. But, as the company begins to take off and experience fast growth, the regulation of established financial policies and systems for expenditures can have significant pay-offs while preventing undue crises in income flow.

6. *Recruit competence and build teams for certain managerial success.* Careful attention from the start-up period on to issues of human resource selection, development, and management can be the factor that not only impresses investors but guarantees corporate accomplishment. Obtaining high-performing personnel may require offering compensation greater than expected, including incentive bonuses, profit sharing, and even some equity. To retain such knowledge workers and prevent high turnover, team building and management are essential. Metaindustrial organizations will flourish under a more participative management style; I have already made the case for such changes in leadership (Harris, 1983). When two or more founders are involved in the start-up, team development to integrate goals, expectations, and management styles becomes a crucial matter. Sessions with a trained facilitator can deal with issues of trust, human relations, role clarification, power sharing, and even leadership. The process then should continue to the next level of technical or professional personnel so that synergy for success can be ensured among those coming on board from diverse backgrounds. (For further information, see Part Two, especially Chapter Eight.)

7. *Create corporate culture and systems to provide for long-term stable growth.* Founders should be aware that their behavior, leadership, and styles are helping to create an organizational culture that possibly will live on beyond them and that very well may determine the success of the new enterprise. M.I.T. professor Edgar Schein (1983) reminds us that organizational culture begins in the head of the founder and springs from that person's ideas about truth, reality, and the way the world works. He defines organizational culture as the basic assumptions the new group invents, discovers, and develops in

learning to cope with its problems of external adaptation and internal integration. Since it affects the corporate environment and productivity so profoundly and eventually affects profitability, the entrepreneur should consider early on the ramifications of corporate culture and plan for a cooperative company environment. Related to this endeavor is the installation of sound internal management systems for controlled growth. Rather than "management-by-whim" of the founder, a systems approach to finances, information, resources, processes, and services can be established modestly at the beginning and then gradually expanded for greater stability. (See Chapter Two.)

8. Produce results that ensure the survival and development of the new enterprise. "Nothing succeeds like success" may be an old adage, but it is more than true for take-off companies. The reputation of an entity as winner or loser not only affects immediate profitability—it can help or haunt the entrepreneur in later attempts to start new businesses. Venture capitalists are very particular in their investigations of a founder's previous track record. It behooves the entrepreneur not only to be results oriented but to build the organizational and business relationships that will speak well of that person in the future.

9. Ensure personal and family wellness so as to maximize one's entrepreneurial energies. The neglect of a founder's physical and psychological well-being not only can undermine one's health and business but can spill over into one's family life. There is growing evidence that entrepreneurs can become so obsessed with the fledgling enterprise that they end up workaholics, alcoholics, drug abusers, or with a "demolished home life" (Baty, 1981). To delimit the prospects of emotional breakdown, divorce from a spouse or business partner, and other such tribulations, it is wise for the executive team to build a "wellness program" as part of the corporate culture. Not only will this lower insurance rates for policies on key executives, but commitment to improved diet, exercise, and other means of stress management will likely result in improved performance and decision making.

Although owning one's own business can provide both psychological and financial returns, the costs of high achievement and success can be great. A recent study of 450 entrepreneurs confirmed the personal price entrepreneurs pay for such satisfaction (Boyd and Gumpert, 1983). Although 90 percent of those studied headed profitable companies, they were also suffering in alarming numbers from stress-related ailments and loneliness—which might have been prevented or reduced by a wellness strategy that enhanced the joys of entrepreneurialism while curbing its negative effects on the founder, as well as on his or her personal and business families. (See Chapter Ten for further information on this theme.)

10. Make use of community resources for support services, problem solving, and public relations. Goodwill is produced by providing a quality product or service at a fair price; it is also cultivated by participation in community affairs, sensitivity to the environmental or ecological concerns of one's neighbors, and sensible marketing or advertising. Once marketing strategy has begun to identify target audiences, public relations can generate a positive image for the enterprise and its people. The entrepreneur should keep computer files on all local resources in the community that can aid or abet the business, from universities to chambers of commerce or better business bureaus.

Although this has not been a case study in the usual sense, these ten guidelines do result from an actual and ongoing consulting experience with a take-off company and its founding entrepreneurs. To these insights, add those of John Lee, the founding CEO of Lee Data Corporation, a company whose sales in 1983 rocketed to $53 million and profits to $11.4 million since it opened its doors four years previously. Lee observed that almost every new company that stalled out either ran out of product, spent too much trying to keep old products alive, or did not fill in the management team before growth occurred ("It's About Time," 1983).

Entrepreneurialism is endemic to the American culture, so it is to be expected that it would manifest itself again in the ongoing transformation of the work culture. The term, coined by the French economist Jean Baptise Say, originally meant putting existing resources to new and more productive uses.

Entrepreneurs, whether acting on their own or within existing firms, shake up traditional patterns by managing more creatively. In large, complex, or bureaucratic organizations, attempts are varied in cultivating the new entrepreneurial spirit. The pursuit of such innovation may lead to decentralization, acquisition of entrepreneurial subsidiaries, or the creating of an organizational culture that favors intrapreneurialism.

Innovative Management Through Entre/Intrapreneurship

Entrepreneurialism as a means of managing innovation takes many forms. We are all aware of recent success stories about fast-growth companies in high technology. Less attention has been paid to innovators in low-technology or service businesses, such as:

- craftspersons, word processors, and professionals of all types who increasingly prefer to work independently;
- skilled white- or blue-collar workers who are being encouraged and assisted by former employers to become subcontractors to their companies;
- unemployed technicians, teachers, engineers, and other qualified personnel who have suffered from reductions in the work force and so go into business for themselves;
- American Indians, who were raised on a reservation welfare state under the Bureau of Indian Affairs (BIA) and now are being encouraged into a more entrepreneurial economy by a new presidential commission. (By deregulating the BIA, they hope to create half of the 100,000 additional jobs needed on the reservations by using tribal resources as seed capital for economic development by Indian entrepreneurs.)

However, the most encouraging trend in large, complex organizations is the fostering of intrapreneurship. This people-based approach to innovative management has been defined by Gifford Pinchot III, head of the Tarrytown Consulting Group and president of New Directions Group, Inc., as allowing "entrepreneurs ... freedom and incentive to do their best in small

Venturing in Entrepreneurialism and Innovation 89

groups within large corporations" (1984a, pp. 82-83). Called a major social invention, this strategy fosters innovation and independent thinking, especially in research and development activity. Pinchot describes intrapreneurship as having these characteristics:

• The intrapreneur gives up or risks something of value to self, such as 10 percent of the cost of the project or 20 percent of salary.

• The intrapreneur and the sponsoring corporation define their shares in the rewards of success in an equitable way.

• The intrapreneur has the opportunity to build up something akin to capital, such as intracapital for obtaining a definite amount of research and design (R&D) funds, in addition to bonus.

• The intrapreneur earns independence and autonomy and is freed from bureaucratic pressure and punishment.

• The intrapreneur who has not already built up intracapital must submit and defend the business plan for a new start-up before a corporate venture capital group, whose members also can act as advisers when no funds are involved.

• The intrapreneur with a record of successful take-off enterprises that have built up intracapital may become a venture capitalist, investing in projects of other personnel or employee syndicates.

• The intrapreneur with a new product or service that cannot be used advantageously by the corporation may have two options—organize a new division or a wholly owned subsidiary company.

Pinchot elaborates on his comparisons in "The Entrepreneurial Grid" (see Figure 4). The entre/intrapreneur within an organization is at the upper right quadrant, where vision and action intertwine.

The types of entrepreneurial activities being sponsored by transnational corporations are varied. For instance, California's Shugart Corporation organized its engineers, researchers, and sales persons into young venture capital firms, resulting in $300 million sales last year in its disc drive business. Although its intrapreneurs give up participation in cash incentive

Figure 4. The Entrepreneurial Grid and Characteristics of Reward.

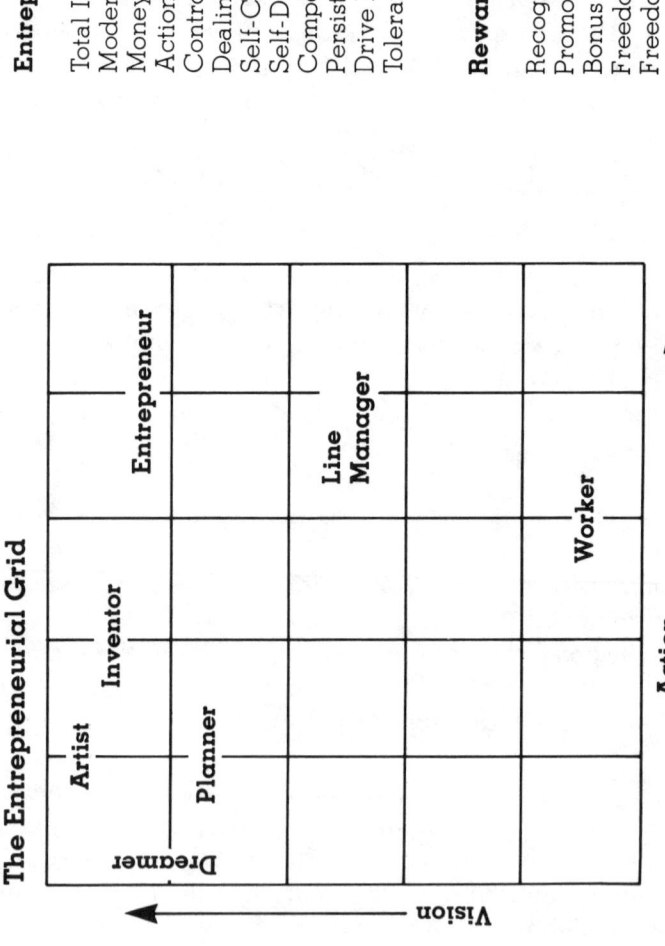

Source: By Gifford Pinchot III. Reprinted by permission from the Diebold Group 59th Plenary Meeting Summary, April 1983, p. 3.

plans, they keep other company benefits and share in the bigger pay-off. The groups are free to work where they wish and to hire outside experts, but they must sell 10,000 of their new products before any pay-off by Shugart begins. Each venture has its own board of directors; managers get a share of revenues in the first year and part of profits in the following two years. Rewards are made on the basis of "shares" received during start-up (claims on revenue and profits). The risks for participants include giving up the company's cash incentive plan, although all fringe benefits are kept if the venture fails ("World Business," 1983).

Austin's own Microelectronic and Computer Technology Corporation (MCC) is another form of intrapreneurialism on the part of a consortium of American electronics and computer companies; MCC is multicompany technology venturing aimed at innovating in the field of artificial intelligence. The leadership came from Control Data Corporation, the same company that formulated that other intrapreneurial design, ETA Systems, which benefits from its parent's cash, scientists, and facilities in its quest to dominate the supercomputer market.

Even supermarket giants faced with changing management of labor costs and incentives, as well as growing competition from more entrepreneurial independent grocery chains, are beginning to utilize intrapreneurial concepts. For example, A & P, having closed 83 stores in the Philadelphia area, which cost the unions 1,500 dues-paying members, started a new, free-standing subsidiary. Called the Super Fresh chain, management worked cooperatively with the United Food and Commercial Workers (UFCW) union to modify union contract terms (such as work rules and pay) in return for employee privileges—opening of the store's books, departmental meetings to solicit employee suggestions, and other personnel participation in risk/reward equation—just like owners of independent stores. Thus, the incentive was that if labor costs fell below 12 percent of sales, employees would begin accumulating a sliding-scale bonus paid out at year-end. By restricting union seniority privileges to a single store site, employees in a successful store no longer feared being bumped by UFCW members from a losing store in the chain. In store locations that once failed under the traditional A & P format, Super Fresh is now profiting by giving its employees a "piece of the action" through more innovative management. In the last fiscal year (1984), personnel in fifty-two of fifty-seven Super Fresh stores qualified for bonuses, both employee and shareholder earnings were restored, and an additional 700 jobs were created. Sales went up, store managers were able to manage like the independents and control their own stock, and productivity increased because employees became more involved. The message is clear: Let people mind the store who know the customer best, and give them a chance to fail or succeed on their own, plus a share in the profits or losses; then watch the positive results that follow.

Intrapreneurship captures the entrepreneurial spirit within established organizations. It is an example of innovative management in that regard, because this action-oriented strategy rewards creativity and high performance by offering freedom and incentive, self-determined goal setting and control, and moderate risk taking while encouraging start-up businesses.

Balancing entrepreneurship, in any of its manifestations, with innovation in management requires a delicate equilibrium. At the University of Southern California (USC), a study by the Center for Futures Research on declining innovation defined the term *innovation* as follows: "Innovation is the process by which a new idea or invention is translated into use. The concept of innovation includes the development and successful exploitation of new products, markets, processes, and managerial systems" (O'Toole, 1982, p. iv). In their investigations, the USC futurists discovered that among the major impediments to innovation in business were the national tax policy and the culture of an organization. These researchers concluded that the second problem might be remedied by developing new processes for analyzing the operating assumptions of a company and by reintroducing specific entrepreneurial attitudes. Since Congress has already begun the tax reform to deal with the first problem, the distinguished experts who provided input to this investigation blamed business schools for putting up the biggest barriers to innovative management through outmoded curricula, overspecialization, and short-term orientation of business education. Corporations then compound the problem by making mistaken assumptions about their competitive, social, and political environment based on past or recent experience. To succeed, management, according to these scholars, requires future-oriented behavior such as is epitomized in entrepreneurial activities. Thus, for innovative management, this USC study recommends a willingness to rethink continuously the basic assumptions of corporate culture; a reward system that provides incentives for risk taking, long-term thinking, and individual entrepreneurial performance; a climate that is people oriented and provides a sense of ownership; a CEO who so gains stockholders' trust as to convince them of a plan and philosophy that is long term as opposed to profit maximization each and every quarter; and a quality production orientation.

Perhaps this sound advice will make more sense in terms of a recent entrepreneurial activity using a franchise system to promote a new business called Mail Box Etc. ("The New Entrepreneurs," 1983). Each store in this business has up to 1,000 feet of usable space and provides mail boxes for rental, along with such ancillary services as copying and shipping. Four years after its founding, it had 140 franchises in twenty-two states; fiscal 1984 revenues doubled to $2.2 million. Although the enterprise began because there was a shortage of United States Postal Service mail boxes, Tony De Sio, its founder, says the main income flow now is from expanding and related services, such as telexes, mailgrams, copying, and packaging. Why did the government post office lose this fast-growing business? The first three points in the previous list seem to apply: Basically, there was no incentive for the civil service management and their employees to be both innovative and intrapreneurial.

Further guidance on the subject was provided by the author of *The Change Masters* (Kanter, 1983). She studied fifty major companies and discovered this new management style to be among the most innovative and successful: (1) Combine innovation with management discipline to focus initiative toward common goals. (2) Encourage collaboration, a small-company atmosphere, organization social relationships, and planned microchanges. (3) Preserve an integrated, inventive, team-oriented atmosphere with growth and stability, while avoiding segmentation.

Assuming that there is rapid growth in a take-off company implies that the founding entrepreneur must strive to keep up with changing market, customer, production, and personnel demands. Innovative management at that time means seeking creative ways to work in a smarter fashion and more effectively. One needs to make use, within budgetary constraints, of automated work stations, matrix management, and other managerial tools that will expedite the business. Thus, innovation must extend beyond product or service technology and be integrated into management and marketing. (Riggs, 1984). One illustration of such innovation is moving into the arena of international trade. Too many founders think provincially instead of globally, thus missing the chance for growth in the overseas market. Innovative executives are quite aware of the major trade shift underway from the Atlantic to the Pacific; they know and take advantage of the fact that in 1983 the United States did more trade with East Asia than with Europe (Hofheinz and Calder, 1982). The entrepreneurial spirit also flourishes in the Pacific Basin, and sales or joint ventures await the American entrepreneur there.

Start-up companies should attempt to make more effective use of their local resources, from government agencies to educational systems. In an information society, universities as knowledge centers offer a variety of services entrepreneurs can tap into for assistance. Such university assistance goes far beyond professional, technical, and extension education for executives or even part-time consultants from among the faculty. Entrepreneurs need to cultivate a synergistic relationship with universities that benefits both the growing corporation and the institution of higher education.

Obviously, this is what MCC is trying to do with the University of Texas at Austin and what a group of "*Fortune* 500" companies is doing at the University of California at San Diego through the $12 million Magnetic Recording Research Center.

Some universities are willing to provide an "incubator" role and program that fosters the development of high-technology firms on or near their campuses. The results are mutually beneficial and provide for a knowledge interchange between academia and business. Rensselaer Polytechnic Institute (RPI), for example, is using an old building on its Troy (New York) campus to house four high-tech companies. RPI not only provides the start-up firms with cheap office space but also gives them access to such university resources as faculty, library, and computer time, as well as management and financial guidance. But the university hothouse benefits more than just the entrepreneur; the start-up companies' engineers and other specialists also can contribute to improvements in curriculum and instruction. Furthermore, the incubator companies become potential tenants for RPI's 1,200-acre industrial park, which eventually provides employment to graduates and contributes to the economic base of three surrounding cities. The companies involved in the project maintain that the university is invaluable to their new ventures, especially in terms of moral support. This cooperative environment is also attractive to venture capital and for technological as well as management innovations. The model is already being replicated by other academic sponsors.

Lately, universities have become breeding grounds for entrepreneurs from among their own faculties, especially those in science, engineering, or business. A specific example of the symbiosis that can exist between a university and an entrepreneur can be found in the matter of patents. Many institutions have a policy that if faculty and researchers invent or discover something while using university time and resources, the patents or copyrights must be assigned to the university. An agreement is then entered into so that the institution and the inventor or discoverer share in the royalties or other form of income produced by the staff person's discovery. The University of Wisconsin (among others) encourages its professors to commercialize their research and established a mechanism for this in the Wisconsin Alumni Research Foundation. Unfortunately, too many universities sit on these patents and do not utilize them for public benefit because their administration is not entrepreneurially oriented. Martin Apple, adjunct professor at the University of California at San Francisco and an entrepreneur, sensed the need for university technology transfer to the world of business (personal communication with the author). Among the high-tech business development activities of his Oakland, California, company, Adytum, Inc., is the promotion of university/business forums that bring together those who hold university patents with entrepreneurs and venture capitalists interested in the commercialization of the invention or process. This is helping to reduce the time gap in university technology transfer.

Similarly, entrepreneurs are discovering another arena for development in the government laboratory. Kenneth Freese is responsible for industrial and international initiatives at one such federal facility, Los Alamos National Laboratory (LANL). At this New Mexico installation, innovative administrators have fostered an adjoining industrial park and incubator program (personal communication with the author). There, LANL scientists can become entrepreneurs or team up with entrepreneurs to apply research findings for public benefit and profit. This innovation offers a new income stream for the laboratory when federal budgets are being reduced and provides extra income to hold scientists at this remote location. It also improves morale, community relations, and public service. The country and its people benefit if public investment in research at federal or defense installations can be enhanced by technology transfer of that knowledge into the private sector.

The creative process in fast-growth management can be cultivated in numerous ways to foster problem solving and take advantage of opportunity. The entrepreneurial spirit, whether it is functioning in a small business or in a larger undertaking, should be characterized by thinking big and ahead. To transform society and management, technology venturing would seem to be the ideal entrepreneurial approach. In a new work titled *Financing and Managing Fast-Growth Companies,* technology venturing is described as a driving force in the American entrepreneurial culture (Kozmetsky, Gill, and Smilor, 1985, p. 79): "Technology venturing is a process by which major institutions take and share risk in integrating and commercializing scientific research and various technologies. It is a primary means of generating innovative products and services of economic value, particularly through a vibrant venture capital industry." Large-scale, global and interplanetary, technological venturing links public-sector initiatives with a variety of private-sector investments. It is in the high frontier, where technology venturing and commercialization are already taking place and will continue to expand. Space industrialization requires macroproject management that goes beyond the capabilities of any one country, industry, or space agency (O'Leary, 1983). It demands a space transportation system, of which the shuttle is only the initial component. It necessitates the creation of habitats and factories, of which the space station is a mere beginning, followed by a lunar base over the next twenty-five years. In 1984, the president of the United States signed an executive order authorizing the U.S. Department of Transportation to coordinate a program that would enable private corporations to launch their own satellites into space. Thus, that department has now opened a Commercial Space Transportation Office, directed by Jennifer Dorn. The president also announced a policy endorsing the establishment of a space station within a decade, and NASA already is inviting other countries, such as Japan, to invest both financial and human resources in the venture. A number of entrepreneurs, sensing the vast opportunities in the markets of space, have formed companies or organized limited partnerships to take advantage of the new high road. Other corporations have entered into joint agreements with NASA to carry on industrial or pharmaceutical research activities using the shuttle facilities or Spacelab, developed by the European Space Agency (Osborne, 1979).

But the technological venturing needed to capitalize on the commercial space market is almost beyond the capacity of a single entity, be it company or country. The only way to go up there is to create synergy among institutions and systems. Recognizing this reality for large-scale undertakings, whether on this planet or beyond, a group of universities has formed a consortium to deal with macromanagement issues. Under the leadership of Frank Davidson of M.I.T., George Kozmetsky of the

University of Texas at Austin, and Stewart Nozette of the University of California at San Diego, the first of the Large Scale Program Institutes is emerging to coordinate research and resources for such macroengineering enterprises as space development (Davidson and Cox, 1983). To be headquartered at the University of Texas at Austin in the Institute of Constructive Capitalism, the new institute is attracting the participation and support of major corporations. This is an example of the kind of government-university-industry cooperation that can foster entrepreneurialism with macroprojects. Innovative management can facilitate technology venturing in the national interest, such as through the renewal of the United States infrastructure or the commercialization of space or of defense-related technological research. If our image of an organization is that of an energy exchange system, our concern for excellence and effectiveness in operations can be achieved only when human energy is properly channeled toward mission goals. Entrepreneurialism and technology venturing are manifestations of innovative management for such purposes (see Figure 14, p. 348).

Conclusion

Our society and economy have been described by *The Economist* ("Into Intrapreneurial Britain," 1985) as "postmanagerial," where business no longer can be run by energetic bureaucrats but by a confederation of entrepreneurs. Contemporary experience in the United States seems to confirm this conclusion and underscores the need to redesign the work culture with entrepreneurialism a principal norm in a market-driven economy.

FOUR

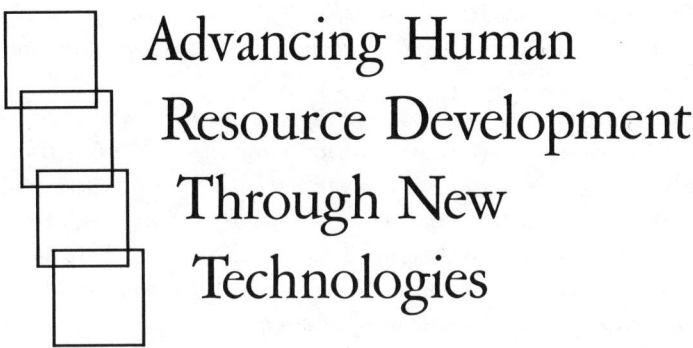

Advancing Human Resource Development Through New Technologies

Executive Summary. An organization can be viewed and managed in different ways. One way most suitable for the new work culture is the human resource approach (Bolman and Deal, 1984). In this perspective, management considers people as the key factor ensuring productivity and profitability, so strategy is directed toward enhancing and capitalizing on human assets. That is exactly what People Express is doing today, and it is the secret of that airline's success as a start-up enterprise.

The transition to a more technological work environment obviously calls for massive reeducation of the existing work force, as well as preparation for new occupations resulting from advances in microelectronics, biotechnology, and communications. But for contemporary leaders, there will also have to be a parallel new education as to the role and function of management—one that emphasizes commitment to human resource development (HRD). It is likely that metaindustrial managers will focus on resource management—human and information—as well as natural and material resources.

Human resource management and development in tomorrow's organizations probably will be more decentralized, more performance oriented and computer based, and more personalized through electronic means. To improve organizational effec-

tiveness through better utilization of human energy and creativity, the new technologies can be used not only to expand workers' output and potential but to update their knowledge and skills. In this process, HRD professional resources can be valuable for development of personnel in the new competencies needed.

In the new work culture, management thinks about optimization of all employees, including women and minorities, especially for new career and service activities. For those who cannot fit comfortably into the changed work situation, training should center more on helping such individuals operate their own small businesses or cope with the enforced leisure brought on by automation and reduction of the work force.

The spread of new technologies will revolutionize not only how we manage but also how and what we learn. Education and training will be transformed by communication technologies that are global in scope and miniaturized in use. Thinking managers study how to make the most of these new HRD capabilities, which range from computer-based instruction to videoconferencing. In an information society, the aim is to create a learning culture at work that contributes to continuing personal and professional development. In developing an organization's human assets, metaindustrial leaders search for alternative ways of educating people beyond the traditional and formal systems, such as by offering at-work academic credit and degrees. Mechanisms for innovative learning range from courses obtained via an electronic university to cooperative programs designed jointly by industry and institutions of higher education. Those who are entrepreneurially inclined will seize market opportunities for new ventures in media instruction as well as in the production and sale of learning hardware and software.

Management and executive development will increasingly focus on cross-cultural and cross-disciplinary education of business and professional leaders. That is, managers will have to be educated in scientific and technological concepts, while scientists and engineers will be trained in management and administration. Tomorrow's management will have multifaceted competencies not only in communication technologies and human resource development but also in strategic planning and forecasting, as well as in global meeting management. Just as general managers will possess broader understandings, such as in social and environmental matters, so, too, the human resource professional will become more of a generalist and consultant.

In the metaindustrial work culture, human information and technology resources take center stage. Thus, wide-ranging issues will be addressed by organizations, from the use of technology to update the work force to human-machine interface; from new learnings about occupations and organizational relations to coping with a diversified and decentralized work force. A metamorphosis is underway in our approach to people and their development within human systems.

Learning for the New Work Culture

"People are our most important product!" Do you recall that General Electric corporate slogan? Unfortunately, it was not a widely adopted theme in the disappearing industrial work environment. Too often, the factory system, dominated by machines, had a mechanistic approach to employees—for a while, they were referred to as "hands" and industrial engineering operated on the premise of workers as "interchangeable parts." The emphasis then was more on plant, not people, maintenance. Gradually, under the impact of behavioral science management research and input, managers have been changing their attitudes about personnel. Struck by declining productivity and profitability, as well as by rising labor costs, management has altered its leadership style with employees, as well as sought less labor-intensive means of production. Quality circles and participative management are "in" for those still privileged to work; so are automation and robotics as means to contain production costs involving people.

In the emerging work culture there are fewer people on the job, but they are usually better qualified and more competent than was true in the past. The majority of them are called "knowledge workers," because their efforts are mostly directed toward collecting and massaging data then shaping and processing it into information, which is transformed into knowledge for improved strategic planning, decision making, and problem solving. Thus, the metaindustrial executive is concerned about managing critical resources, especially human and information resources. Thinking managers seek ways to improve profitability and effectiveness by enhancing their organization or community's human potential. That implies an active search for means to utilize our colleagues' brain power and creativity. Since managing human resources is a primary concern, the new technology is employed to advance people's personal and professional growth. This will further their integration into the metaindustrial work scene. Management now becomes directly involved in the process of human resource development (HRD) and wisely uses the best resource consultants and information in this professional field.

Perhaps it is appropriate to clarify some terms here before proceeding. In a letter to the author, Leonard Nadler, professor at George Washington University and one of the leaders in the HRD field, suggests this definition: "Human resource development is a series of organized activities, conducted within a specified time and designed to produce behavioral change. . . . HRD's most common activities are training (learning for the present job) and education (learning for the future job). . . . Human resource management includes those other dimensions of personnel activities, such as health and safety, benefits and incentives, performance evaluation, etc." Other management experts confirm this position. For instance, the author of *Strategic Management of Human Resources* (Odiorne, 1984) indicated that traditionally management has tended to view labor in terms of supply and demand, with employees considered as short-term expenses to be minimized. His view is that employees can be considered as assets, value can be placed on them, and they can be managed as a portfolio of stocks is managed, to maintain or increase their value to the organization.

Several professional associations are available to assist thinking managers in developing new human resource strategies. Increasingly, these relate HRD to the bottom line concerns. For example, in 1985, the Human Resource Planning Society held its annual conference around the theme "Adding Value: The Accountability of Human Resources to Impact Business Results," while the International Federation of Training & Development Organizations (IFTDO) focused on "Business Development Through Human Resource Development" at their world convocation. Note the recent report for the American Society for Training and Development in its new series, *Human Capital: A High Yield Corporate Investment* (Carnevale, 1983). Its major points deserve our consideration:

- Educated, healthy, trained, and spirited people are the ultimate source of economic growth. They are not simply the passive consumers of an autonomous and inhuman economic yield.
- People—not machines—are the wellspring of productivity. Productivity is the human art of getting more with the same or fewer resources.
- Human resources, historically, have been replacing all other resources (such as natural or machine resources) as the basic building block of production, and the value of human time has been increasing.
- Human motivation and cultural differences are the key differential factors in the economic development and productivity of both organizations and nations.
- Although human resources are seemingly inexhaustible, in the near future there will be a shortage of workers, especially the technically qualified.
- Investments in the development of human assets by employers will improve the immediate bottom line and have long-term pay-offs for organizations.

Figure 5 provides an illustrative summary of Carnevale's study by contrasting human and other factors of economic growth from 1948 to 1990.

Thoughtful managers, especially in new industries and technologies, understand the importance of training and education for career development, employee productivity, and corporate profitability, both for themselves and for their colleagues. Therefore, they assume an HRD responsibility. They perceive the HRD professionals as a part of the management

Figure 5. Human Factors in Economic Growth.

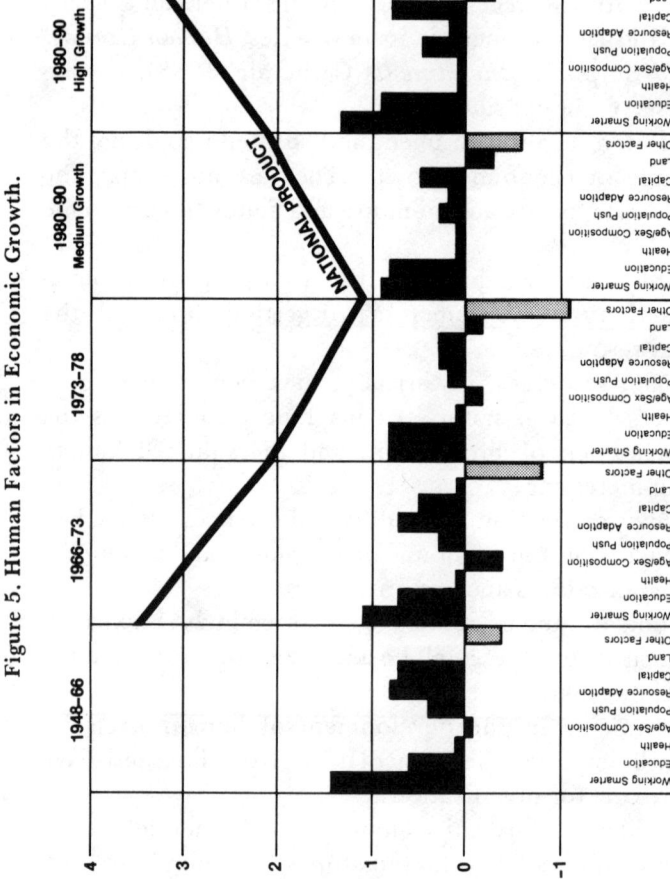

Growth in contribution from Human Factors (working smarter, education, health, age/sex composition, population push, resource adaption) + Land + Other Factors = Growth in Economic Output.

■ Human Resource Factors

Source: Human Capital: A High Yield Corporate Investment, Executive Summary, Washington, D.C., American Society for Training and Development, 1983. Reprinted with permission.

process and utilize their resources (Desatnick, 1983) when they are available internally, or seek the aid of external HRD consultants and learning materials. Occasionally, they read HRD journals and books or attend conferences and workshops so that they can be on the cutting edge of human resource development. They do not become so enamored with the new technology and robots as to neglect the human factors that contribute to the effectiveness of any enterprise.

In a national study of companies identified as productivity leaders, A. T. Kearney, Inc., of Los Angeles found that 71 percent have made the management of employee capabilities and contributions of critical importance in their strategic planning for the future, while 81 percent of their less successful competitors simply react to human resource needs as problems arise. What differentiated the leader companies from the others? In their examinations of these high-performing corporations, whose revenues ranged from $350 million to $500 billion, the investigators measured them in terms of higher net profit margins for 1981 as well as five-year returns on total capital and equity. As a result, Robert W. Miller, principal for the consulting firm, identified five managerial practices that contributed to their success: (1) The human resource role was defined as a major participant in business decisions and strategy implementation. (2) Current human resources focused on important problems before adding new programs and resources. (3) Human resource staffs initiated programs and communicated with line management. (4) Corporate staffs shared responsibility for human resource policy formation and program administration across organizational levels. (5) Line management shared in the responsibility for human resource programs.

To assist thinking managers in increasing their human resource management capabilities, the International Division of the American Society for Training and Development (ASTD) recently issued *Global Strategies in Human Resource Development* (Harris, 1984). The HRD megatrends analyzed in this report are of significance to metaindustrial managers and thus are summarized here:

1. Human resource development should be directed

toward the emerging work environment dominated by the new technologies related to communication and information processing, microelectronics, and genetic engineering.

2. HRD should utilize strategic planning methods for each stage of the business cycle, as well as for each stage of the employee's life cycle.

3. HRD should be systems oriented and employ the technology of systems analysis for a wholistic approach to personal development and performance management.

4. HRD should be future oriented and employ the technologies of future research, such as technological forecasting and environmental scanning.

5. HRD should focus on transformational management; that is, it should emphasize preparing institutional leaders to assist in the transition to the new work culture—leaders who will be skilled change agents for the creation of the information society.

6. HRD management should be decentralized in operations and accountability while providing a wide variety of internal and external consulting services.

7. HRD should be a high priority of corporate executives in terms of both the organization as a whole and themselves in particular.

8. HRD should be research oriented. Human factor data collection, analysis, and reporting are important in maintaining organizational health, in meeting training needs, and in program assessment.

9. HRD should be given a human capital emphasis and be performance oriented with goals that are specific, measurable, achievable, and compatible.

10. HRD should be multifaceted in the services rendered to personnel—from training in the new technologies and automation to management development that helps people redefine roles while coping more effectively—and fosters growth in organizational excellence.

11. HRD should facilitate organization development efforts to transform the corporate culture and humanize the new work culture.

12. HRD should be promoting *synergistic* training, edu-

cation, and networking; that is, it should be preparing people for collaboration, team management, and peer sharing through personal and electronic networks.

13. HRD should be international in content and global in the scope of its concerns, especially by providing cross-cultural skills training and comparative management development (Harris, 1984, pp. 12-31).

Perhaps Alfred North Whitehead offered the best insights into developing human potential when he observed that education is the process of teaching the application of knowledge. But then he wisely reminded us: "The old foundations of scientific thought are becoming unintelligible. Time, space, matter, structure, pattern, functions, etc., all require reinterpretation" (Moran and Harris, 1982, p. 341). The renewal of our human systems so that they are attuned to the new work culture will come through learning and the intelligent use of the new technologies.

To dramatize the importance of Whitehead's statement, we refer to a current special management strategy report. It was assembled by Opinion Research Corporation (ORC), an Arthur D. Little Company subsidiary, and is entitled "Managing Human Resources, 1983 and Beyond." Prepared by ORC's Center for Management Research, the results of this massive data survey of employee attitudes revealed that managers are becoming more like hourly workers in their attitudes toward key work place issues, that compensation plans are viewed as having major pitfalls and are in need of drastic alteration, that worker confidence in top management is at an all-time low, and that employee attitudes are in the midst of profound change. It is information like this that permits the creation of relevant and appropriate human resource management strategies. Such trend analysis can help set new directions in labor relations, compensation, and job satisfaction while counteracting high stress and burnout, symptoms of the society in transition. However, for real impact, such national studies should be supplemented by internal human factor data gathering on one's own personnel. Thinking managers seek feedback, formally and informally, from their employees.

The Conference Board in 1983 held a series of meetings

for corporate executives on "Strategic Human Resource Management." One of the presenters, Ray Amara, president of the Institute for the Future, predicted that human resources would be the driving force for corporate America throughout this decade. Human resources will occupy center stage in management concerns because (1) high growth rates in the United States labor force will change in the mid 1980s, and labor will become relatively scarce; (2) corporate activism will turn inward, and intergroup conflict in the work place likely will increase (for instance, mid-career people versus older workers, women versus men, and so on); and (3) human resource management will be viewed increasingly as the critical path toward achieving corporate objectives and may even constrain its growth in some industrial sectors.

The Conference Board sessions pinpointed as the principal shapers of the corporate work force the following:

- the changing profile of entry-level workers;
- the mismatch between demand and supply for particular job categories;
- the continuing revolution of women in the work place;
- the deepening of the generational conflict;
- the changing of the work ethic;
- the changing map of employee values;
- the growing degree of employee risk taking and number of entrepreneurs;
- the push of competition for new markets;
- the pull of information technology;
- the growing participation and activism of employees within corporations; and
- the uncertain role of trade unions.

The implications of such findings for the thoughtful manager are manifold, especially in enhancing people's competencies. And, if the authors of *Industrial Renaissance* (Abernathy, Clark, and Kantrow, 1983) were right in saying that most managers view their role through a haze of outdated assumptions and expectations, then the preceding insights may provide the basis for creating some new ones.

Educating the work force in new directions must take place at all levels, but in organizations it should begin with the so-called leaders—executives and managers. It is their responsibility to ready their colleagues, as well as their families, for the changes in the work culture. In a recent volume entitled *Developing Managers,* Manuel London (1985) emphasizes the career development of the beginning manager. At the other end are experienced managers who may find themselves displaced as organizations trim back on their management personnel. Such employees also need training, coaching, and counseling for new positions within a corporation, to start up their own businesses, or to obtain management employment elsewhere.

Workers need corporate support in coping with the transition to the technological work environment. Thinking managers also can make a major contribution to national and community renewal of formal systems of education. They can get involved in reducing the learning gap—in schools and colleges, in universities and professional schools—between what is being taught (often obsolete) and what is relevant for a postindustrial society. The same may be said for education and training within industry and government. But it is not just the content of the curriculum or course that may be archaic, but the means of teaching or instruction. Metaindustrial managers can take the initiative, both in their companies and in their communities, in reforming instructional methodology so that better use is made of new educational and communication technology, of self-learning packages and programmed learning. In the emerging work culture, this is necessary and vital; learning is now a dynamic and continuing process for a lifetime. Knowledge means both wealth and power.

Since human factors have such a great impact on the bottom line, thinking managers would do well to understand what is involved in HRD and then to effectively utilize available resources through either internal or external consulting services. Further, it behooves all managers to increase their own competencies in human resource management and development, especially in small or newly founded enterprises in which professional resources may be limited. The trends indicate that in the metaindustrial work culture, general management will be more directly involved in HRD. To help us understand what is encompassed in the people area of business activity, the ASTD competency study provided a "Human Resource Wheel," which is reproduced in Figure 6.

Figure 6. Human Resource Wheel.

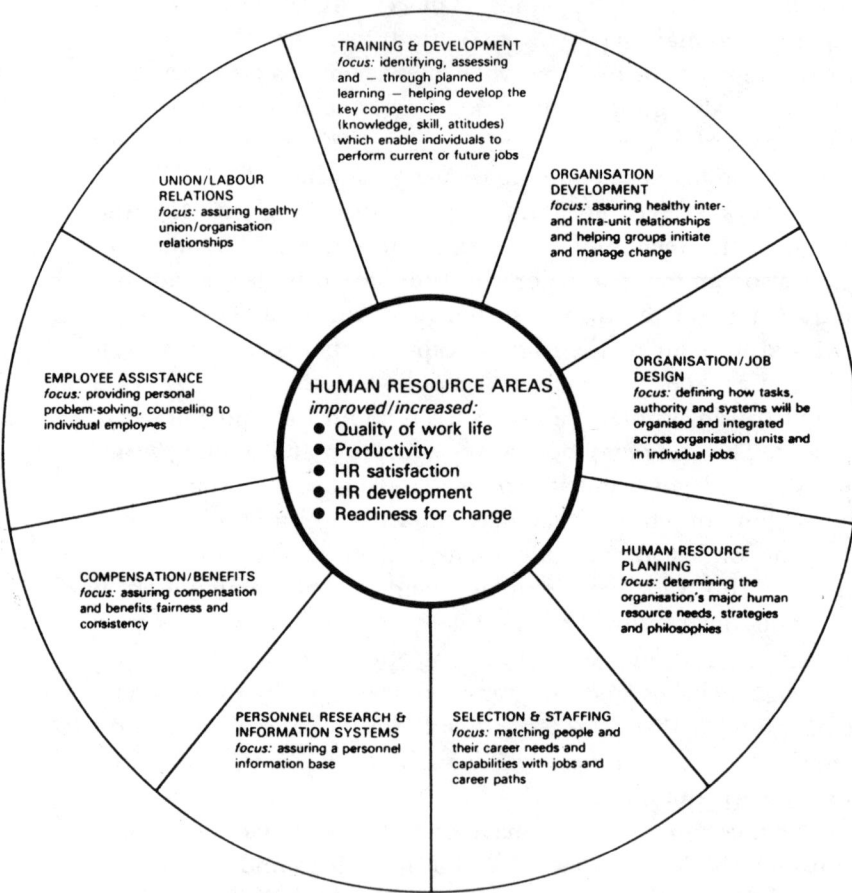

Source: Copyright 1982, American Society for Training and Development, Washington, D.C. Reprinted with permission.

To illustrate the shift in attitude and approach in meta-industrial organizations, take the issue of staffing and selection. In the new culture, managers become more directly involved than in the past in the process of recruitment, and if personnel specialists are available, they act as consultants. Sometimes an outside contractor, such as an executive search firm, may take care of recruiting talent, but with guidelines developed by management. The actual interviewing and decision making regarding who is hired is often the work of a management task force, because knowledge workers are difficult to obtain and retain; managers can ensure that there is a match between the person hired and the organizational culture. Furthermore, new technologies are being utilized to facilitate the procurement of competent personnel—televised or videotaped interviews, simulations and computer games, computerized credential checking, and like practices.

Just as there has been dissatisfaction on the part of management with the unrealistic approaches in schools of business, the same complaints have been directed toward some corporate HRD efforts. The new management seeks to promote learning that is: (1) performance related—knowledge that can be related to job needs or problems; (2) problem finding—having the skills to analyze and discover needs or problems and the ability to solve them; and (3) real world business—with the focus of instructional methods and efforts on realistic issues of managing resources that also demonstrate pay-off in organizational effectiveness, rather than teaching about paper management and figures manipulation.

Sterling Livingston (1983) founder of the Sterling Institute in Washington, D.C., confirmed this, urging more applied management development that features:

• Convenience and mobility: Decentralize education and training and bring it to where the trainees are at work or at home; make it portable and accessible at any time of day or night without instructors and suitable for either individual or group learning.

• Communication and educational technology: Utilize satellites for teleconferencing, instructional program transmission, or recording for later video playback; employ computer-based seminars and miniature flat-screen video players that can be carried and accessed at any time.

• Content relevance, application, and pay-off: Emphasize practical skills acquisition that is measurable for performance improvement.

Livingston demonstrated these principles in a training program in balance sheet management for GTE Corporation. Conducted for 6,300 employees, this learning investment in human resources cost $1.4 million for 345 classes, including all expenses. The return on investment (ROI) to the company that was measured was $94 million in approved investment reductions and $50 million in expense reductions. With a grand total of $144 million in improved working capital, Livingston said it is easy to justify investing in other performance-oriented training that can produce quantifiable results.

The education of people for the information society has broad social implications. In the Third World, for instance, 750 million persons will enter the work force by the year 2,000. Can we afford to waste such human assets through inadequate or obsolete educational endeavors? Since so many companies do business in developing countries and employ indigenous workers, it would seem advantageous to get involved in ensuring that appropriate education, training, and jobs are available to such people. In fact, many international contracts now require the contractor to further technology transfer with major training programs. In the more advanced technological countries, the issues center around (1) reorientation of displaced workers in "sunset industries" in which crafts are being eliminated or replaced by high technology and automation; and (2) educating people—especially the young, women, and minorities—for new technologies, careers, and the work environment.

Thinking managers have the capacity to provide innovative solutions to such problems. When we consider the hundreds of thousands of new jobs created each year in the United States alone, primarily in the electronics industries, there is a need for urgency. The irony is that there are vast numbers of unemployed people in every land who want and claim the right to work in the technological culture but who are not qualified until educated for the new careers. Others are unemployable because they resist new learning or will not relocate. Such critical issues require the synergistic collaboration of industry, government, and school systems.

One prototype solution may be being implemented in California as this book goes to press. There, an employment training panel has been formed (contact MIC 64, 800 Capitol Mall, Sacramento, California 95614). The panel resulted from 1983 legislation to provide funding to teach laid-off workers new technical skills required by employers and to ensure job placement. The money comes from employer taxes to put unemployment insurance recipients to work. The private sector receives contracts to provide the technicians with training in word processing, machine repairs, microwave servicing, space shuttle servicing, and other high- and low-tech positions. Also, the federal government is already providing funds for worker retraining (for example, $75 million in 1983). With over two million workers already displaced and millions more to follow, the new United States Job Training Partnership Act addressed the problem with expenditures of $3.6 billion (1984) for "retraining." It is commendable that the private sector is involved with government in this endeavor. Since manufacturing jobs eventually will make up only 5 to 10 percent of the work force, management leadership now is indispensible.

To confirm that this is a global issue, note that Britain in 1985 has 3.3 million people out of work but has trouble finding qualified persons for high-technology jobs, such as systems analysts, electrical engineers, and robotics technicians. Apart from efforts by the government to develop cooperative solutions with industry and academia, the United Kingdom Department of Trade and Industry has been fostering with grants the establishment of Information Technology Centres. To be operated by private industries, these centres are aimed at preparing idle youth for high-tech occupations.

Another key issue for the new management centers around the competencies of the current crop of managers and HRD practitioners. One recent survey of leading United States corporations revealed that 97 percent of their managers and 80 percent of their in-house trainers were not computer literate ("Finding A on the Keyboard," 1983). As one frustrated manager confessed, "I run a $300 million division on a daily basis, and now I am having trouble finding 'A' on the keyboard." Some corporations, such as United Technologies, are facing up to such a training and education challenge—they put 1,100 executives through a three-day personal computer course and, upon successful graduation, rewarded them with $4,500 in hardware and software. Managers must cultivate competencies in both technology and people management. The latter should also include the management of meetings and ways to facilitate adult learning. But for those in the new work culture that consider themselves human resource development professionals, both greater compensation and broader skill are to be expected. The HRD professional now must function as manager and learning specialist, strategist and change agent, group facilitator and counselor, instructional technologist and needs/task analyzer. No wonder the American Society of Training and Development's 1983 competency study for such internal or external consultants concluded that human resource responsibilities require:

- understanding about adult learning dynamics and career development;
- proficiency in cost-benefit analysis, counseling, facilitating, group process, negotiating, delegating, and organizational relations;
- ability in oral communication, presentation, and giving feedback, in model building and preparing written materials, as well as in performance observations and questioning;
- capacity to do research, including data gathering and analysis in human factors, organizational diagnosis, and future studies and to utilize information resources, such as libraries, computer data bases, and networks;
- knowledge in the nature and management of business, especially of the client organization and its industry, as well as of organizational behavior and culture; and
- adroitness in identifying the content and skills requirements of jobs, tasks, and roles, as well as in developing contemporary strategies, procedures, and techniques for actualizing human potential.

Thus, if the size of the organization warrants employment of HRD professionals, these are the qualities to be sought in such persons or in HRD contractors, as well as the competencies that all managers should cultivate to improve their human resource management capabilities. Furthermore, the meta-industrial organization involves HRD professionals in general management and offers such persons the same opportunities for advancement into the executive suite that are available to marketing or financial specialists.

Since 1958, according to Leonard Nadler (personal communication with the author) there has been increased concern for, and research into, the need for higher education institutions to provide learning experiences for HRD practitioners (then called trainers). George Washington University is the only university that has been offering degrees in HRD since 1948 rather than just offering occasional courses. Since the latter part of the 1970s, HRD has become one of the growth areas in universities. By 1983, over 100 universities claimed to offer HRD programs, though in many cases they merely relabeled whatever (communications, counseling, media technology) they had been offering previously. The significant trend in universities has been the inclusion of the private sector through the use of advisory committees and internships. Managers are serving as classroom resource people and graduate students are conducting research projects in the business and industry world, encouraged by thinking managers.

The thrust in people development is toward performance improvement and quantifying results. That is the kind of thinking prevalent among such innovators as professors Lee Brummett, University of North Carolina, and Eric Flamholtz, UCLA's Center for Human Resource Management. These accounting professionals have been integrating their own field with behavioral science research and promoting human resource accounting. To better capitalize on organizational human assets, they provide an analytical framework and quantitative techniques to assess human resource investment and returns. They advocate a revision of the traditional balance sheet to accommodate such data—or at least the addition of a supplement to report on value increases or losses on this human dimension.

Education of executives and managers for the new realities also needs to provide knowledge of strategic planning and management (Ansoff, 1984). The new learning should include analysis of social and business trends and forecasting, of culture change, especially as it affects the work place and worker values, and of managing for organizational effectiveness through such strategies as those described in Part Two of this volume.

Finally, there are a growing number of professionals, such as scientists, attorneys, and physicians, who need knowledge of business and management. This is necessary either to maintain their own professional practices or to enter an entrepreneurial enterprise. Numerous attorneys make it to executive suites, and we have many examples of medical practitioners starting health care or high-tech businesses. Such reeducation applies equally to engineers, nurses, architects, and those in other career specialties that have neglected fundamental business, financial, and people skills.

In the emerging work culture, the compartmentalization of knowledge and disciplines, segmentation of academia and industry, and distinctions between formal and informal learning are diminishing. The information society, with its new technologies, already is promoting convergence and facilitating more synergistic approaches to human resource development. The need for such synergy, even between labor and management, was confirmed in a recent study by ITT Educational Systems. Its 1984 report surveyed 300 senior human resource executives of *"Fortune* 1500" firms. While 74 percent of the respondents reported having personnel who were positively inclined toward retraining, collaboration between management and employees seemed to be the reason for this. That is, both must work together to devise solutions that provide the most suitable education and training for technological changes.

New Educational Technologies and Strategies

An electronic university has been established by a consortium of twenty-four engineering schools—among them M.I.T., Stanford, and the University of Southern California.

Advancing Human Resource Development

Called the National Technological University, it is issuing guidelines for the accreditation of "electronic" schools and will offer accredited master's degree programs across the nation. The seed money for this project came from the U.S. Department of Defense, IBM, General Motors, General Electric, Eastman Kodak, and many other major corporations. The experimental university will offer videotapes or simultaneous broadcasts of courses taught in the sponsoring institutions of higher education. Executives are responding enthusiastically to the educational innovation because of quality instruction, convenience, academic credit, and accessibility to remote work areas.

Federal Express is innovating with videoconferencing as a means for facilitating worldwide corporate meetings and HRD. On June 24, 1984, for example, a record was broken when 25,000 employees and their families "attended" conferences in 240 different sites from Brussels to Honolulu. Federal Express used Lunar Productions for presentations and Holiday Inns' HI-NET to provide a satellite communications network. The global audience examined issues of corporate and personal achievement, employee resistance to technological innovation, and competitive challenges. James Barksdale, chief operating officer, confirmed that there was very exciting response from the participants and that corporate family feeling was revived.

These two illustrations highlight how far technology has progressed in revolutionizing learning and communication. Experts in media, such as the presidents of Computer Based Education Systems (Franz Fauley) and International Technical and Commercial Services (David Matthews) have identified five relevant trends ("High-Tech Training . . . ," 1984, pp. 78–79):

1. machine-independent courseware—software learning programs that are compatible with any model of microcomputer;
2. downloading/uploading—use of mainframe computers and "downloading" them for microcomputers or "uploading" microsoftware into the mainframe systems for greater flexibility;
3. teletraining/teleconferencing—satellites or cable transmis-

sions that permit trainees to interact with a speaker or instructor at a central site;
4. miniaturization—highly portable learning aids, many with computer-assisted instruction (CAI) or computer-based training (CBT) capability;
5. interactive video—CAI that combines computer text and graphics with realistic images and sound of videotape or videodisk (the computer asks the learner "if... then" types of questions for multiple-choice answers and the user can talk back).

Such electronic innovations further individualized learning, expedite training, reduce related travel costs, provide expert input, and increase learner retention. They enable the creation of sophisticated learner simulations.

The growth in such human performance technology and the demand for computer literacy have prompted a profound observation from Jean Jacques Servan Schrieber, director of the Paris World Centre for Personal Computation and Human Resources: "Computer science is not just a field among others. It is a new language, a fresh way of learning. Only this new technology can help solve our vast unemployment and literacy problems, because only the personal computer can make learning an attractive proposition again. It does away with classrooms and lectures. You can immediately become active with your own computer, in effect teaching yourself. Most of all, the student with a computer is not a passive listener to television or blackboard knowledge. He is not judged by someone else, but by himself" (Newman, 1983).

We may not agree totally with this prophetic vision of how computers will change our working universe, but we all might concur that they are very powerful intellectual tools that metaindustrial managers must master. We also know that advances in telecommunications will force the courseware for human resource development to be problem oriented instead of content oriented, while education and training facilities will shrink in size as telecommunication centers begin to dominate learning environments.

Nancy Weingarten, publisher of *Data Training*, confirms that computer-based training is no longer used primarily for data processing training (*Data Training*, 1984, 3 (10)). Now it is being used for sales and product training, knowledge and technical training, management development, and personal growth. No wonder she is sponsoring publications, conferences, and expositions for the expanding CBT market.

For management concerned about how these new technologies can be used more effectively to capitalize on human assets, some unusual challenges wait to be confronted. For example, experts in information technology understand the hardware but often have difficulty creating software because they know less about how people learn than about the technology itself. Also, although the computer is only a tool, an artifact of the new culture, some data processing managers would make people an extension of it. Another challenge relates to the fact that more than half of our current jobs did not exist forty years ago; how can we design instruction and programs for occupations yet to be?

For those thinking managers that wish to make the most of the new technology, perhaps it would be helpful to answer a few pertinent questions:

1. How may we employ these new communication tools for our own personal and professional development, as well as for the improvement of our organizational communications?

2. How may we better utilize these new capabilities for the human resource development of our personnel on the job, at home, or in educational centers?

3. How may we personally promote greater collaboration in educating and training the work force by the joining together of business, universities, and government in joint technological endeavors?

4. How may we create more balance between learning and life needs, education and occupational needs, through the more intelligent use of information technology?

5. How may we develop human potential for greater organizational effectiveness by using communication technology to promote alternative forms of HRD, especially more self-learning?

As managers work together to answer such queries and to solve problems posed by the introduction of the new technologies into the work place, perhaps we will form a helpful balance between our human and machine resources.

A survey in 1983 of 1,000 subscribers to the *ASTD Training and Development Journal* revealed that 91 percent of the respondents were still using texts and workbooks in their HRD programs. The technology in use was mainly overhead projectors and films (70 percent each) and slides/tapes (68 percent). Only 40 percent utilized computer hardware or planned to buy such in the next year. Among these 1,000 HRD professionals, only 31 percent used or planned to use interactive video systems or other media equipment. A decade from now those percentages should rise dramatically as high-tech learning tools begin to dominate the instructional field. Computer-assisted instruction and interactive video will be the principal acquisitions for corporate HRD centers. Soon, it has been predicted, 15,000 or more installations employing microcomputers in training will be functioning nationally. CAI permits learning in a one-to-one situation while saving 30 percent of the time of more traditional methods. Learners benefiting from CBI can focus on individual problem areas while retaining more of the information. Ford Motor Company found that CAI reduces the time it takes to train sales personnel while increasing the trainee comprehension of the material offered.

Angus Reynolds of Control Data Education Technology Center, Rockville, Maryland, called computer-based learning a technological multiplier. He reported on projects all over the world that are successfully using computer-supported educational technology (Harris, 1984, pp. 50–57). Computer-based learning (CBL) becomes a technological multiplier when it multiplies the power of a person to serve many others that otherwise might not be served. Reynolds demonstrated how CBL also can be cost effective, as in the case of United Airlines. In that company's "new hire" pilot training, computer-based learning reduced the traditional training course by an average of zero to one half elapsed days, for a first-year savings of $72,000 and estimated continued savings annually of $175,000. The same

Advancing Human Resource Development

success stories are being demonstrated in other industries, such as petroleum, manufacturing, university medical education, and government, such as in the education of air controllers. To further CBL, computer manufacturers are donating equipment to schools and colleges, and some universities are requiring all new students to have their own microcomputers. Learning centers in corporations and government agencies are in the midst of transition to learning technology that is centered in the computer. It is a new tutor that becomes an interactive learning system when it is mixed with video, audio, and graphics. Such multimedia education enforces correct answers and procedures (Dean and Whitlock, 1983).

These mind tools may receive their ultimate applications to education and work in a decade or so. Research is underway in both Japan and the United States to produce a fifth-generation computer (Feigenbaum and McCorduck, 1983). The power of this artificial intelligence machine will not be just its speed of processing but also its capacity to reason with an enormous amount of information, which it can constantly select, interpret, update, and adapt. The new computers, which may reach the market in the 1990s or sooner, will not require specialized machine languages as now; we will be able to use conversational language, show pictures, or transmit messages by keyboard or through handwriting.

But for the thinking manager or the HRD professional to make the most of the new learning technology, the computer should be combined with the advantages of video, whether in tape, cassette, or disc format. This new capability can be used for training or work both in the home or office and in learning centers and resorts. Knowledge Industry Publications of White Plains, N.Y., referred to our times as the "Video Age" in its new review of video's potential to grow from video text to corporate television. Sterling Institute uses both computer simulations and interactive video case studies in its training strategies. Forum Corporation uses both audio- and videotapes for recording its customized management development programs for clients. Ford Motor Company combines CAI with videodisc and compatible television system, for the disc has the advantage of fast random access of selected information (each has 54,000 frames and each frame has a digital code). AT&T refers to "teletraining," which uses existing telephone lines to connect speakers with learners at remote sites while employing an array of audio-graphics services and equipment. The advantages of video use are timely instruction, reduced travel costs, and greater on-the-job productivity. This technique brings together the advantages of the small seminar group and ready access to experts, and it has been used in plants for university-credit courses.

The new technology has powerful educational and organizational communication implications. Aided now by satellite transmissions, videoconferencing utilizes electronic blackboards, videotapes, slides, and live lecturers. Such mixed media enables us to conduct case studies and role playing and practice exercises and tests, as well as experience a variety of instructional techniques from vu-graphs to interactive writing. The larger the audiences involved, the less the interaction or use of the Socratic method. But to use such electronic wonders for personnel development also requires careful planning, much practice, and a vivid imagination for media techniques. Multinational organizations will develop the in-house expertise to facilitate the manager's use of these new communication technologies. Smaller firms will learn where the best external resources are for taking advantage of these new learning techniques. In either case, thinking managers will learn about these opportunities and capitalize on them to facilitate both human resource development and organizational effectiveness.

Gordon Shea, president of Prime Systems Company in Beltsville, Maryland, sagely observes that lifelong learning and new-age opportunity go hand in hand. Tomorrow's winning organizations will be managed by those who are being well trained and educated today. Author of such management books as *The New Employee* (1981) and *Creative Negotiating* (1983), Shea appreciates that in these times of transition employees are constantly confronted with staggering technological advances, intense competition, and complex work place demands. Thus, managers need HRD strategies to create a growth environment for knowledge workers. Let us examine four innovative approaches that are attuned to the demands of the new work culture.

Electronic Middle Management. The Delphi Group, a Tucson-based management consulting partnership, became convinced that traditional educational systems involving short bursts of stand-up training were on the wane and that teleeducation was the way to go in management development. The principals, Raymond Payn and Irving Schlafman, undertook action research on learning applications models that incorporate the personal computer. They now assist in the installation of such learning, the monitoring of results, and the support systems. They use microcomputers in project management training (scheduling, cash flow management, change control), and in problem analysis. They are broadcasting their efforts over public service television in Arizona via videotapes in order to reach a wider audience for management education. They are linking up with the Western Behavioral Science Institute (WBSI) in La Jolla, California. What WBSI has done for executive development through its computer-based School of Management and Strategic Studies the Delphi Group hopes to accomplish for middle managers, especially in high-tech industries.

Performance-Based Engineer Development. All career fields are faced with rapid advancements; sometimes the knowledge base doubles every five years or less. This has been especially true in engineering. Thus, the American Society for Engineering Education funded a study of applications of performance-based instructional technology to meet this challenge. The project is headed by Janet Fiero of Motorola Training and Education Center in Schaumburg, Illinois. The expected outcomes are identification of companies already using such systems for engineering training, increased effectiveness of engineering technology, improved engineer performance, and reduced cost of current training. State-of-the-art methodology, new reference materials, quality control methods, evaluation procedures, and other such benefits will result from this undertaking. Since engineers are so critical to success in high-tech companies, this should be a welcome resource for managers.

Laser Disc Video In-Service Training. To boost employee

productivity and reduce turnover, Sizzler Restaurants produced ten laser training programs for its workers. The new training technology offers standardized learning through the use of record-like discs that contain high-resolution TV pictures and hi-fi sound tracks. The programs, along with laser disc players, have been distributed nationally to over 400 restaurants for a learning system that is both involving and interactive. Personnel work in teams while on the job and use break time to play each disc. Segments are repeated until the message is learned. Feedback on the method has been very positive.

New Meeting Technology Via Videoconferencing. The magazine *Successful Meetings* (March 1982) reminds us that video/teleconferencing can be used for regular meetings or for educational seminars. All types of allied gadgetry are coming on-line to enhance this method—"smart" registration systems, radio pagers, computer-generated signs and badges, and so forth. Leasing and resale of satellite time is now possible for business and educational conferences. Even professional and trade associations are offering assistance. Videoconferencing for continuing education is now available through the American Law Institute and the American Bar Association on a monthly basis. Merrill Lynch has its own in-house video network, studio, and staff, producing, for example, investment seminars. It has linked together staff and clients in thirty cities for educational purposes, annual meetings of stockholders, discussions on employee benefit packages and new tax laws. Whenever the firm cannot produce something in-house, it goes to external resources for supplementary assistance (such as VIDEONET in Woodland Hills, California).

Managers and meeting planners are learning the logistics of putting together videoconferences and where to obtain help in that regard. MEDIASENSE of Boulder, Colorado, suggests that planners know: (1) who needs to exchange what with whom—define the needs, desires, and budget of the group to be involved; (2) the meeting's purpose (decision making, sales, training, and so forth)—which determines a set of considerations affecting the tools to be used; and (3) the required physical design—the building for the meeting, the set, the transfer of slides or film to videotape, the broadcast time and point of origin (lower costs go with the use of daylight hours and larger cities). HRD or departments will have to maintain information on video service suppliers and terminology, as well as on the techniques required to make the most of this new media.

Alternative Higher Education Opportunities

Since lifetime learning is essential in the new work culture, thoughtful managers seek to obtain this for themselves or others in a way that not only is convenient but that possibly provides academic credit. Adults in business or government often find it difficult to go to university or college campuses for the traditional degree-offering or extension services. As a result, Carnegie Foundation studies into alternative forms of higher education have stimulated new possibilities in this regard (Eurich, 1984).

This report entitled *Corporate Classrooms: The Learning Business* indicates that United States companies are paying for twelve million courses, educating nearly eight million people, spending upward of $100 billion in the process. Continuing corporate education for workers today is big business in itself: getting mass numbers of people into this learning business is a matter of survival for corporations, according to Del Lippert, vice-president for educational services at Digital Equipment Corporation (*Time,* Feb. 11, 1985, p. 74). These corporate programs often are conducted on a contract basis with employees, are performance oriented to the job, are programmed for efficiency and accessibility, are technologically up to date, and often have academic legitimacy. In fact, the Carnegie study indicates that this type of corporate education often is superior to that offered by the universities.

Entrepreneurs have started legitimate fast-growth universities, such as National University in San Diego, California. To avoid becoming involved in "rip-off universities" that offer worthless degrees, it is wise to ascertain whether the educational institution has regional accreditation (such as by Middle States or Western Association of Schools and Colleges) or approval for its programs by a professional association in a specialized field (for example, the American Assembly of Collegiate Schools of Business accredits M.B.A. programs). So as not to waste financial resources in the pursuit of advanced learning, consult *Credentials: A Guide to Business Designations* (Milbrath, 1982).

Employed people today have many options for obtaining undergraduate, graduate, or professional degrees while working full-time. Some corporations have their own internal universities that offer accredited degrees. For example, General Motors Institute has a long history of educating engineers and technicians with a degree curriculum and is now independent of its corporate founder. Similarly, the Wang Institute of Tyngsboro, Massachusetts, offers graduate programs in computer science and software engineering, while Northrup University, an offshoot of the Los Angeles aeronautical corporation, has a full degree program. By 1988, eight more corporations plan to develop nineteen degree programs. Innovative consortium arrangements with universities and colleges enable organization courses to be recognized for academic credit. The American Council on Education's (ACE) Commission on Educational Credit and Credentials evaluates a company or agency's course objectives, content, teaching materials, methods, and procedures for performance assessment. Presently, ACE Publications has credit recommendations for 1,700 such courses in more than 140 organizations nationwide. The latter include *"Fortune 500"* companies, professional institutes and associations, and federal, state, and local government agencies.

Since America is a credential-minded culture, why not capitalize on the huge investment organizations are making in the management and technical HRD of their people? Why not let employees enjoy an additional benefit to the training and development they receive on the job—namely, a college or advanced degree or accredited credential? One illustration of this industrial/academic collaboration in human resource development is the business certificate program of Ebasco Services Incorporated and Pace University of New York. Since the company is in engineering, construction, and consulting, its HRD department designs and develops its own courses, curricula, and teaching methodology and conducts instructional activity. Using the ACE Noncollegiate Sponsored Instruction program in conjunction with the University of the State of New York, Pace University provides Ebasco with review services of its HRD programs, as well as a certificate for credit-worthy courses completed. Pace, with a successful track record of satellite and outreach programs, considers the certificate an interim step toward awarding an Associate in Applied Science Degree. Such institutional cooperation can be created by thinking managers with local universities for all types of credit and degrees.

Another type of professional development involving credits and degrees is independent study. This can range from correspondence courses to enrollment in the University of Mid-America (UMA). The latter is part of a national university consortium and is based on the British open university model. UMA uses videotapes and public television to offer a variety of credit courses. In conjunction with the American College Testing Program, many universities offer external degree programs. One such example is the University of the State of New York. It offers useful publications for managers and their employees, such as *How to Study Independently* (1982) and *Directory of External Graduate Programs* (1982) (contact Regents External Degrees, Cultural Education Center, Albany, N.Y. 12230). The latter lists fourteen innovative programs for college graduates in business or the professions who seek advanced degrees with a minimum of seminar attendance and a maximum of self-learning and research but who wish academic counsel.

Universities themselves are becoming more flexible and innovative in reaching out to local industry with more relevant programming that supports the development of knowledge workers. The University of California at San Diego, for instance, has just inaugurated in its extension division an executive program for scientists and engineers. To meet the needs of high-tech managers for continuing professional development, this nontraditional program features a small, select group of participants (twenty-five) nominated by their companies; the instruction is proficiency based, and the content emphasizes managing technological innovation and improved communication to enhance productivity. Those enrolled attend classes every Thursday from 3:30 to 9:30 P.M. for nine months and function together like a communication laboratory and peer network. As another example, Charlottesville Institute of Textile Technology offers a Master of Science program attuned to high-tech manufacturing and management skills.

The information age will spawn many unique ways of educating people by taking advantage of the new technologies. Under the leadership of James Grier Miller (1978) of La Jolla, California, a University of the World project is under development. It plans to use video, audio, computer, and other electronic instructional technologies for credit and noncredit education from existing schools and colleges at preliterate, primary, secondary, baccalaureate, and graduate levels. The first three levels are especially intended for developing nations, but the other levels could be equally useful for management and employee development. This plan is an expansion of a successful model of Miller and his associates called EDUCOM that created an educational network of interconnected and established institutions of higher education. Through this means, seventeen major American universities provide access to computerized data banks, electronic mail services, computer-aided instruction, and other educational resources.

The above are creative strategies for developing human resources that metaindustrial managers track and explore. Keeping the citizenry or employees informed during the ongoing knowledge explosion challenges management to utilize such imaginative HRD approaches. The scope of these efforts can be appreciated when one visits Xerox's 2,265-acre educational complex in Feesburg, Virginia, where 1,200 company students are in training; it is confirmed at the AT&T educational center near Princeton, New Jersey, and at the IBM supercampus in Thornwood, New York.

The growth of the "training industry" in the United States is an entrepreneurial movement responding to the need for a constantly changing work force. In 1982, the Hope Reports of Rochester, New York, indicated that the sales of instructional materials and services for the HRD industry amounted to $1.7 billion; 55 percent of this was for off-the-shelf materials and packaged programs, 27 percent for public seminars, and 18 percent for custom-designed learning programs. This figure does not include the dollar investment in training equipment, meeting facilities, travel costs, and related HRD expenses. But it is enough to underscore that adult learning, whatever it is called, is big and costly business. For bottom-line reasons alone, thinking managers factor human resource development into their strategic planning.

New Work Culture Management Development

As previously noted, the impact of new technologies on management is causing a shrinking of the middle level while enhancing first-line supervisory and top executive roles. The problem is worldwide, as one study by Durham University business school in the United Kingdom indicates. Their survey of 91 large British-based corporations found that two thirds had thinned their managerial ranks between 1979 and 1984 ("Innovative Unemployment," 1985). The question naturally arises about how companies plan for such redundancies, and how they prepare the management personnel involved. That same news report in *The Economist* cites IBM as everybody's favorite example of how to equip executives for such organizational changes. Through a career counseling program, IBM seeks to avoid managerial layoffs by readying such people for job changes. A system for scrutinizing management performance annually is supplemented by eight days of yearly management and technical training. Thus, on the average, 40 to 60 percent of Big Blue's managers change their positions within IBM every year. By sticking to their managers, such personnel are loyal to the corporation, and only 5 percent a year leave, including the retirees. In addition, there are "outplan" units for entrepreneurial types to become venture managers of new product lines and services. The next chapter will further discuss this issue of technology's impact on role changes.

The University of Southern California's Center for Futures

Research admits that business schools are becoming less relevant in light of new realities. Its faculty members envision dramatic changes in business that will vastly alter how students and trainees will be prepared for their managerial functions. They cited the rapidly changing nature of information resources, worker participation, business ethics, and government interaction as examples of vital elements transforming business strategies and management's activities.

In a recent volume on work, organization, and technological change, Mensch and Niehaus (1982) quote George Kozmetsky on the subject of technology in managerial education. As both a venture capitalist and a former business school dean, Kozmetsky should be taken seriously on the direction of management development. He believes these are the strategic research areas to consider in preparing managers for the technological work culture:

- managing productivity, efficiency, and competitiveness;
- managing innovation, research, and development;
- managing international business;
- managing human resources, including manpower, compensation, rewards, and quality of working life;
- managing strategic relationships and social responsibilities;
- managing entrepreneurship, venture capital, and business development;
- managing finances and marketing, including capital requirements and investment decisions;
- managing information and MIS;
- managing the environment, especially in the interests of enhancing the quality of life;
- managing and developing new growth industries;
- managing technology assessment and evaluation as a value, national, and world resource;
- managing public risk analysis and the influence of technology on the organization, education, and training.

Kozmetsky advocates that professional management development includes more linkage with the basic sciences, prepares leaders to deal with macroengineering problems (pollution, energy, and resource scarcity). He believes that it is important "to manage our human resources in a technologically based society in such a way that we actually anticipate change, and not just accept or react to it. We must develop the ability to organize work in such a way that for most individuals—regardless of race, color, creed, sex, or intelligence quotient—work becomes more complementary to human needs, and thus more fulfilling and self-satisfying" (Kozmetsky, 1981, p. 24).

It would be impossible to analyze here all these points as to their appropriateness in the metaindustrial work environment. However, one element was missing in much management and executive development in the past—learning on culture and its influences. It is implied in the previous listing, for such awareness and skill is essential for managers that hope to improve international business and productivity, technology transfer, and human resource development. A rationale was provided in Chapter Two for cross-cultural management education.

The Future of Management Education (Kakabadse and Mukhi, 1984) indicates that management development is of global concern and may involve breaking old ways and styles of management. Further, the scholars contributing to that volume think that managers need to be educated not only in present and emerging practice but in understanding the changes and complexities surrounding work life today.

If I were to select areas of priority in management development, my choices would be computer literacy and meeting dynamics as offering the greatest return on investment. Since it has been estimated that 65 percent of United States managers are expected to be using computers before the end of the decade, this would seem a logical point of focus for management training. Personal or microcomputers will be vital to managers for both operations and learning. The delivery of corporate training at all levels up to the executive increasingly will be accomplished through the use of computer discs and videocassettes. The human resource management function also requires computer knowledge and skill. Many organizations, such as Manufacturers Hanover Trust, have computerized their HRD systems from recruitment, training, and assignment to centralized documentation, testing, and performance evaluation.

Staff meetings offer unique opportunities for management development, especially when carefully planned as to content and methodology. The president of Xerox Learning Systems, S. S. Anderson, predicts that 70 percent of management time in the future will be spent on this prime activity. He estimates that key executives will devote five hours of every working day to attending or leading meetings, either in person or electronically. That amount of time and visibility offers career development opportunities for both executives and those exposed to them. Among the many self-learning courses offered by Xerox is one on leading meetings for better communication, leverage, productivity, and use of power.

In a 1983 *Meeting News* interview, "megatrend" author John Naisbitt commented on this matter with reference to the "high-tech/high-touch" phenomenon: "The more technology in this society, the more people want to get together. Meetings will be one of the great growth industries in this country because of technology; people will want to aggregate more, in a compensatory way." If human energies are to be more effectively used and human potential actualized, our meeting management competencies also will have to be increased. This imimplies learning more about group meeting dynamics, the use of technology for greater meeting effectiveness, and the cross-cultural factors to be considered in planning meetings, especially on the international level. Perhaps the following two illustrations will help underscore the last two guidelines:

Meeting Technology. One way to promote learning at meetings is to ensure that they are interactive; here is a way technology can accomplish this with large audiences: The Group Response System (GRS) consists of a set of calculator-sized keypads connected by flat ribbon cable to a microcomputer. The latter is connected to a video display that is visible to the audience. To use GRS, the speaker or instructor poses a multiple-choice question either verbally or through a projected slide. The meeting participants provide a response by pressing a button on their respective keypads. In seconds, the system can display the audience's total preference in a color bar chart on the monitor. The same approach can be used to administer a quiz, test, or employee survey inventory. This method can help a lecturer get a quick profile of the audience knowledge on the subject so that the presentation can be customized; their response thus can be used as the basis of small- or large-group discussions. GRS enhances the flow of information and facilitates more intimate learning.

International Meetings. When planning a meeting abroad that is a major activity involving many others, the following strategies will ensure that the objectives of such sessions are achieved: (1) Personally inspect meeting facilities in the host culture and negotiate directly with suppliers and vendors to minimize perceptual and cultural differences. (2) Observe the local business protocol, such as in the use of business cards, last names, respect for titles, following the chain of command, selection of competent interpreters and their equipment, translation of visual and written materials. (3) Carefully choose a cosmopolitan and professional travel agent who is knowledgeable about meeting sites, local resources overseas for banquets, tours, and conveniences, and customs regulations regarding transferring meeting equipment, currency, dietary differences, and AC/DC power requirements. Managers operating in a global environment make a point of knowing the dynamics that affect the productivity of business meetings in a local culture, and consciously seek to promote synergy in international staff development (Moran and Harris, 1982, Ap. C).

Conclusion

Better educated knowledge workers want to learn continuously and are always seeking opportunities to upgrade their jobs competencies. The thinking manager aims to provide a creative work environment that will energize people and satisfy such needs. The new work culture offers many options in developing human resources for improved performance and productivity. This may be through the creative use of new technologies in HRD. It may be in the provision for employees of varied opportunities for structured or unstructured learning and updating. Or it may be through lateral transfers or counseling about job change or second careers. In the new work cultures, better meeting management can also enhance the human assets of participants, especially by creative use of communication technologies.

FIVE

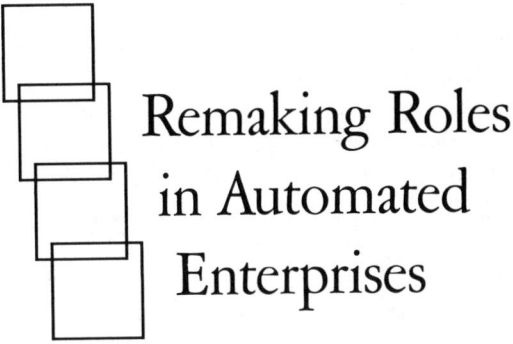

Remaking Roles in Automated Enterprises

Executive Summary. The linkage of new technologies in computers and communication represents an enormous leap for human interaction. Since this advances our capability to process and utilize information, managers are expected to master the new tools to some degree; and responsible management exercises leadership in the further introduction and integration of information technology into the work place. The scope of the challenge is evident, with electronic work stations expanding rapidly and predictions indicating that there are likely to be millions by the end of the decade. A case is presented in this chapter illustrating how to manage the various stages in the transition to office automation.

Whether in offices or factories, the spread of automation is changing not only how and where we work but also our roles and our relationships to one another at work. Nowhere is this more evident than in management, which is experiencing a realignment in levels and types—such as fewer middle managers and more information resource managers. But the information technologies are also altering how the manager operates. Managing for automation opens new dimensions for innovative leadership. We consider three such issues here: changing corporate culture, human factors, and supervising home workers.

The challenge for new learning by both supervisors and subordinates in this regard is both varied and continuing. Personnel need to learn about the benefits and challenges of automation and robotics, particularly in terms of emerging occupations and impact on the work place; the communication possibilities and patterns that develop through intelligent use of micro-mainframe computer interface, electronic mail exchange, and video/teleconferencing; the redefinition of roles, relationships, authority, and influence that comes with the sharing of information resources and power; the value and uses of relevant hardware and software, as well as the skill development necessary for their effective application; the emerging issues of privacy, security, and accountability that come with more ready access to organizational information; and the requirements for more innovative management techniques and organization structures to suit the new technologies. With the wider application of management strategies resulting from such learning, automation and robotics will cause a reconfiguring of work culture reality.

Occupational Transformations

We all are aware that the new communication technology has been changing our world, especially at work. (I, for one, have been struggling with a new electronic wizard, an IBM personal computer (PC), as a replacement for a more comfortable electric typewriter.) The introduction of new technologies is disrupting the traditional roles of workers, while creating new ones. Charles Delaney, system vice-president for New York's Chase Manhattan Bank, suggests that the introduction of the PC is only the most visible ripple of a tidal wave that is irreversibly engulfing organizations.

Popular business and professional literature has been documenting such changes, along with consequent alterations in work relationships. Following are ten published critical incidents that highlight the challenge:

1. The explosion in technology is transforming the communications field itself and its employment marketplace. Those with the right skills and personal savvy to market themselves may become part of an emerging group of elite technocrats.

2. The middle manager, badly battered by recessions, may become an endangered species, for the future of this function is in jeopardy. The computer is the principal force behind this trend as businesses seek to become more efficient while using fewer people. One study of major industries in 1983 resulted in a consultant's prediction that middle-management ranks in American companies would become permanently depleted by 30 percent within the following few years.

3. Michigan has a vigorous effort underway to replace lost jobs in the automobile industry by encouraging the manufacture of robots for export throughout the world. The most difficult problem to be faced in this regard is that of retraining workers for high-technology jobs that do not yet exist. However, even that state's president of the American Federation of Labor-Congress of Industrial Organizations (AFL-CIO) agreed that such diversification is essential to broaden the state's economic base, cultivate new industries, and create new work opportunities.

4. A recent conference of the Diebold Research Program featured a speaker who reminded the audience that change from a traditional clerical environment to an automated one involves negative factors, such as job insecurity, fears of incompetence, loss of job control, and career development ambiguity. But with proper planning, these negative factors can be counteracted. A 1981 Diebold study on the subject found that 60 percent of the respondents reported positive impacts on the quality of work life of the introduction of office automation.

5. According to a 1982 report of SRI International, one out of every four white-collar offices will have an automated work station by the end of this decade. Nearly half of these are expected to be multifunctional—that is, merging both office data and word processing capabilities. This study predicted that by 1990 professionals will use up to 25 percent less time on office-related chores than in 1982, while the clerical staff will use up to 36 percent less time.

6. Computer-mediated work is the subject of much research by Harvard Business School psychologist Shoshana Zuboff. Her studies of man-computer relationships in the work place indicate that many people forced to work with the new

technology feel uneasy and frustrated. Some are afraid that it demands skills they do not now have, and so they resist these innovations.

7. Another example of role change being brought on by new technology is in the pharmaceutical industry. Drug manufacturers are cutting down on expensive detail personnel by sending physicians videodisc players. Then, instead of having their technical sales representatives actually visit the doctors' offices to explain their new products, these companies send videodiscs to provide an attractive and comprehensive media presentation the M.D. can watch at his or her convenience.

8. Bethlehem Steel saw a drop in its employment from 115,000 in 1975 to 48,500 in 1983. Yet, it was the first major United States corporation to help displaced workers understand that the end of their steelmaking jobs does not signal the finish of their careers. The giant corporation offers a comprehensive program to deal with the emotional impact of permanent lay-offs. Through "career continuation centers," displaced employees are counseled on problems related to unemployment as well as on job-seeking techniques. Other services include psychological testing, a telephone hotline for help with personal crises, job listings, and searches. Bethlehem reports that those who stay with the program usually get a job within ninety days (some 55 to 65 percent), although they may receive a lower salary. Others go into business for themselves, many with the help and encouragement of their former employer.

9. A public broadcasting television series on *Connections: Technology and Change* noted that much of the alteration in worker relation to work is unconscious and unplanned. It cited a shift toward service and high-technology industries as examples, as well as the move from fabrication to processing industries (such as chemicals, plastics, and synthetics), in which automation flourishes. Yet such changes, including the growing use of industrial robots, may eliminate physical drudgery and anomie from the work place.

10. Stanford University completed a study for the National Institute of Education in 1983 on "The Educational Implications of High Technology." One conclusion of the study

was that since we cannot predict what kinds of jobs people will hold during the next forty years, it is best to seek a good general education while cultivating the ability to adapt to changing occupations and careers.

These ten media accounts have personal and social implications. They indicate somewhat the scope of the enormous transition underway in how we organize work and manage the people and resources related to it. The reality of the world in which we now live and work is that telephone, television, and computer increasingly are being linked together. With this linkage will come whole new ways of learning and working, as well as of relaxing and playing. For many, the fine line between work and leisure is eroding. This is especially true for telecommuters who are now able to stay at home and do their work electronically. Teleworkers save commuting and energy-related costs, as well as time.

When Sara Lee Bakeries created one of the country's first cybernated factories in the 1970s, it was a strategic decision of great import. It meant that, instead of opening many bakery plants around the nation, the company could concentrate its resources in one facility at Deerfield, Illinois. Rather than employing thousands of bakers at many locations, the new automated system enabled the firm to have fewer personnel at a central site. Now computers control the baking machines and a new generation of technicians regulates the equipment. The baking operation is totally cybernated, with minimal human intervention. However, there are occasions when people do enter into the manufacturing process. For example, when the CEO of this futuristic factory invited me to visit the plant, the banana machine broke down and workers were rushed in to take over the peeling procedure!

Union officials have complained that, in designing a production process that minimizes human participation, worker control and initiative is frozen out. They are concerned also about employees who are slotted between two centrally controlled robots, lest they again become mere cogs in a larger machine. In counterpoint, the new management argues that the old industrial assembly lines, many of which still function, are not very humane working environments. They maintain that the new systems both free people for more human activities and create new technical positions requiring greater knowledge and skill. Not only does productivity improve with automation, but robots often undertake work that is too dangerous or boring for people to do. Others fear that the robot revolution renders humans superfluous in many jobs, thus creating vast displacement in the work force. The counter argument again is that people will be leaving tiresome and hazardous positions for retraining in more satisfying work that offers more challenge and freedom.

There is concern that a two-tiered work force may be emerging: one level of elite executives, scientists, professionals, and technicians at the top, but a majority in an underclass of low-paid "labor surplus" at the bottom. It is possible for two work cultures to develop if sufficient education and retraining opportunities are not provided to displaced workers, the underemployed, and the unemployed. This is where enlightened management can exercise corporate social leadership to minimize the problem. But there is also a third kind of work opportunity in the metaindustrial society for those willing to provide a variety of services required by the changing circumstances. Many of those who have lost factory jobs are learning to become entrepreneurs and to provide such services—some companies are helping ex-employees in this process. One consequence of a dynamic, growing economy is job displacement, but this can also result in career enlargement.

The new information society is forcing formal school systems at all levels to reexamine their curricula and to bring their course offerings into line with the changing economy. John Opel, IBM president, advocates greater cooperation between industry and universities in training and educating people who can make the most of the new technology. For this reason, IBM has set up a $50 million program of money and equipment grants to help universities upgrade and expand courses in manufacturing and engineering, especially those related to the use of robotics, CAD/CAM, and resource planning. Such actions demonstrate how metaindustrial management can exercise creative leadership in the community to deal with the transitional challenges.

The impact of the technical change underway is dependent on the rate of its diffusion and adoption. Office automation, as a case in point, is slowed down by the enormous costs involved in both equipment purchase and the training of personnel, as well as by the necessity for redesigning the organizational structure and roles to accommodate it. Some functions or trades gradually will fade away; draftspersons, bookkeepers, and production welders are typical of occupations scheduled for eventual replacement by computers and robots. Despite the loss of over a million jobs in declining industries, the Federal Bureau of Labor Statistics (BLS) forecasted a net increase in manufacturing jobs by 1990, although these may be outside the traditional centers of heavy industry. But the bureau also predicted that the greatest number of job openings in the decade ahead will be neither in manufacturing nor in computers but in low-tech positions—occupations of service that are low in skill and salary, such as secretaries, cashiers, sales clerks, nurses' aides, and janitors; the creation of 3.7 million such jobs is anticipated by 1990.

Hank Koehn of the Trimtab Consulting Group warns managers, however, to be cautious in interpreting the predictions of government statisticians. The BLS regularly makes such projections based on past data on personnel needs. But with the economic shift to high technology, information processing, and services, there could be an increase in productivity, profitability, and economic growth without any increase in employment (Koehn, 1984). Government extrapolations on the present work force are unable to reflect the impact of change on the future. Thus, a growth in the "service" economy may mean fewer "servers" and more direct interface between producers of goods and consumers.

Opinion analysts Daniel Yankelovich and John Immerwahr confirm these observations. They foresee blue-collar and manufacturing jobs shrinking to make up as little as 7 percent of positions in the work place while white-collar and service jobs increase. These forecasters maintain that, with the spread of the new technology, robots and computers will take over routine work tasks, freeing people to do the thinking work that requires skill and discretion. The issue for management, according to Yankelovich and Immerwahr, is how to structure such work so that it appeals to job holders' increasing desires for autonomy, creativity, community, and entrepreneurship. The trend demands that workers exercise more judgment and discretionary competencies. Such developments also pressure both union leaders and managers to reevaluate their traditional adversarial relationships and to place more emphasis in their negotiations on nonmonetary rewards and people's need for self-fulfillment through their jobs. (See American Society of Personnel Administrators, *Work in the 21st Century,* 1983.)

The transformation of work is causing other trends that new management types should monitor and perhaps capitalize on. These include rising female labor participation, decreasing number of hours on the job, older people staying on the job longer, more frequent changes of occupations, long-term automation producing growth in new jobs, and out-placement services for displaced workers. In trying to cope with turbulent alterations in the work place, innovative management is experimenting with creative strategies.

Employee Assistance Programs. High technology is creating a need for human resource counselors who can help personnel sort out the problems and possibilities while trying to cope with the transition to the new work place. Employee Assistance Programs (EAP) range from rehabilitation efforts to deal with alcohol and other substance abuse and chronic absenteeism/tardiness to career development programs that can extend from retraining to assistance in new business start-ups.

Downsizing/Closing Operations Guidance. Enlightened management can take more humane steps in dealing with the effects on workers of declining market share, overcapacity, redundancy, or obsolescence in plants, work units, functions, or positions. To delimit employee shock, anger, and lawsuits, the new management involves workers and union leaders, where applicable, in the planning process for such necessary economic changes. Assuming that the decision is sound from a financial and long-term perspective, employees need to be adequately prepared for the eventuality. Rather than calling workers off the line and simply telling them they are no longer needed, as Atari did in 1983, with security guards escorting them out of the plant, or simply putting a notice of a plant or division closure on the bulletin board, the announcements can be staged and can emphasize the positive side. Thus, the employer communicates to workers why the decision was necessary and what the company is going to do to help displaced personnel get back on their feet. This involves more than just informing these employees of severance pay and extension of employee benefits. For example, Ford Motor Company cushioned the blow by taking funds from a closed plant sale to help laid-off workers in this manner: (a) continuing health insurance for 80 percent of them for an additional twenty-five months; (b) providing a $6.7 million training, education, and placement program (partially funded by state and federal programs); and (c) providing data for the new job opportunities in a high-technology industrial park to be created by developers on the site of the demolished auto plant.

Bethlehem Steel is another example of a corporation learning to survive and adjust to new realities through downsizing. As part of its remodernization, the company is planning to be smaller and make greater use of automation and robots. Along with plant closings and reduced work force, the company is learning more effective ways of employing existing facilities by using high technology to produce products with a future. In seeking products and markets that offer very competitive earning potentials, it is learning to withdraw from unprofitable geographic areas while using income from property sales and other savings to gain upside leverage. Trimming down and making better use of internal renewal are enabling many industries to reverse decline while gearing up to the postindustrial challenge.

Preparing People for the New Jobs. In addition to corporations, universities and communities can innovate in creating programs that inform people of the emerging occupations and then helping them prepare for these new roles. Management leaders can contribute much to this process by providing trend indicators of the new vocational opportunities and activity descriptions and then assisting in the design of suitable education or training for such positions. For example, there is evidence of growing need for computer farmers, robot technicians, CAT-scan readers, computerized paramedics, new technology services providers, hazardous waste managers. In fact, technicians will be required for lasers, energy, housing rehabilitation, materials utilization, genetic engineering, bionic medicine, holographic inspection, computer graphics and design, and a host of new fields, such as space (Cornish, 1984; Sheffield and Rosen, 1984).

Instead of contributing to the surplus in many professions, such as lawyers and physicians, the dramatic shift in the job market calls for more geriatric social workers, engineering professors, dietitians and nutritionists, accountants and auditors, and even competent elementary school teachers. Identification of the vocational fields with a future should be a critical concern not only for school administrators, parents, and graduates, but also for thinking managers who will be seeking the work force with these new capabilities. With the spread of the computer and telecommunications, it is fairly obvious, for instance, that we will be seeking more software designers, specialists in teleshopping, editors and writers for telenewspapers and telemagazines, professionals in teleconferencing, as well as experts in video publishing, interactive video, narrowcast table, and other new communication technologies. In Exhibit 1, S. N. Feingold provides a summary of occupational titles of the future for which people should be preparing now (Feingold, 1984).

The information society is creating knowledge industries and a demand for "knowledge engineers"—people who can create, manipulate, and send information or data. Capitalizing on emerging employment markets for ourselves or for those who depend on us means developing effective strategies for acquiring new skills and insights. Here are a few tips in that regard for thinking managers to consider:

• Search for instructed experiences—opportunities and events that permit us to learn more about ourselves, our professions and occupations, and the future of work and technology. These chances to gain new input, skills, and even contacts may be formal or informal, in person or electronic.

- Seek cross-cultural fertilization. Integrate information and insights from distinct data bases, knowledge areas, or disciplines. Encourage interdisciplinary activities, synergistic relationships, and interchanges with people who either think differently or are culturally different. Graft their mental differences or perceptions onto one's own when appropriate, and look for unchartered career dovetails.
- Monitor trends and look for linkages. Anticipate trends in one's own field, business, or technology by scanning the environment and analyzing developments. To be on the leading edge of occupational developments during transitional times, we must have our eyes on trends and be able to project their meaning beyond the present horizon. By not restricting our reading, contacts, and communications, we become generalists, able to string together bits of data, envision connections, and draw inferences. The bane of technologists is to succumb to tunnel vision and to be too narrow in perspective. Thinking managers cultivate intuition, watch trends and forecasts, trust personal instincts, develop action plans and then implement them.

Case Study of the Automated Office

To appreciate how electronic technology affects the work environment, consider the process of transforming an office into electronic work stations. For organizational managers, this means facing a variety of important issues regarding planning, designing, testing, implementing, and evaluating the new automated systems that are being introduced (Ruprecht and Wagoner, 1984). Since the tools in question not only cause significant organizational change but can be radically changed themselves in a relatively short period, dynamic planning is advisable. The Sterling Institute in Washington, D.C., accomplished this by: (a) a simplified form of operational analysis, which focused on the work to be done in terms of objectives, structures, and methods of operations; and (b) systems analysis of performance functions and results to be sought in the new design.

For the purposes of the following case, call the company

Exhibit 1. Occupational Titles of the Future.

Aquaculturist
Armed courier
Artificial intelligence technician
Arts manager
Asteroid/lunar miner
Astronaut
Battery technician
Benefits analyst
Biomedical technician
Bionic medical technician
Cable television auditor
Cable television salesperson
CAD/CAM technician
Career consultant
CAT scan technician
Certified alcoholism counselor
Certified financial planner
Child advocate
Color consultant
Communications engineer
Community ecologist
Community psychologist
Computer:
  analyst
  camp counselor/owner
  designer
  graphics specialist
  lawyer
  microprocessor technologist
  programmer (software writer)
  sales trainee
  security specialist
  service technician

Fiber-optics technician
Financial analyst
Financial consultant
Forecaster
Forensic scientist
Fusion engineer
Genetic biochemist
Genetic counselor
Genetic engineer technician
Geriatric nurse
Graphoanalyst
Hazardous waste technician
Health physicist
Hearing physiologist
Hibernation specialist
Home health aide
Horticulture therapy assistant
Hotline counselor
House- and pet-sitter
Housing rehabilitation technician
Image consultant
Indoor air quality specialist
Information broker
Information research scientist
Issues manager
Job developer
Laser medicine practitioner
Laser technician
Leisure counselor
Licensed psychiatric technician
Market development specialist
Massage therapist
Materials utilization technician

Orthotist
Paraprofessional
Peripheral equipment operator
PET scan technician
Physician's assistant
Planetary engineer
Plant therapist
Plastics engineer
Pollution botanist
Power plant inspector
Protein geometrician
Radiation ecologist
Recombinant DNA technologist
Relocation counselor
Retirement counselor
Robot:
  engineer
  salesperson
  scientist
  technician (industrial)
  trainer
Security engineer
Selenologist (lunar astronomer)
Shrimp-trout fish farmer
Shyness consultant
Software club director
Software talent agent
Soil conservationist
Solar energy consultant
Solar energy research scientist
Solar engineer
Space botanist
Space mechanic

Contract administrator	Medical diagnostic imaging technician	Sports law specialist
Cosmetic surgeon	Medical sonographer technician	Sports psychologist
Cryologist technician	Microbial geneticist	Strategic planner
Cultural historian	Microbiological mining technician	Systems analyst
Cyborg technician	Mineral economist	Tape librarian
Dance therapist	Myotherapist	Telecommunications systems designer
Dialysis technologist	Naprapath	Thanatologist
Divorce mediator	Neutrino astronomer	Transplant coordinator
EDP auditor	Nuclear fuel specialist	Treasure hunter
Electronic mail technician	Nuclear fuel technician	Underwater archaeologist
Energy auditor	Nuclear medicine technologist	Underwater culture technician
Ethicist	Nuclear reactor technician	Volcanologist
Executive rehabilitative counselor	Nurse-midwife	Waste manager
Exercise technician	Ocean hotel manager	Water quality specialist
Exotic welder	Ombudsman	Wellness consultant
Family mediator/therapist	Oncology nutritionist	

Source: Feingold, 1984, p. 13. Reprinted with permission.

The Fortune Corporation (TFC), since the problems and solutions outlined are not unlike those found in *"Fortune 500/ 1000"* firms. The transition to a computer-mediated office often goes through the five stages described. It is both a painful and a joyful process, for it reorganizes the way we typically do business. The transition is a realignment that alters organizational structure, as well as roles and relationships. It means a reconfiguration of reality, abandoning traditional procedures, and learning new ones. The electronic office redesigns both information systems and jobs. It transforms not only clerical functions but also the nature of management, even turning professionals into some new hybrids. For technology improvements to enhance operations, the organization's people must be involved. Since this transition is a prime management concern in the 1980s and 1990s, this idealized case summarizes many dimensions of the challenge facing us. As a consultant to The Diebold Group, international information systems experts, I am grateful for the many insights I am able to include here as a result of my participation in their plenary conferences. The five-stage model in the case is based upon an adaptation of the hypothesis promulgated first by Richard L. Nolan of Nolan, Norton & Company (refer to *The Consultant,* Jan./Feb., 1985, pp. 1-5). Nolan believes that the fifth stage calls for readaptive strategies as automation transforms organizations from a pyramid structure to a diamond format.

Stage One: Conception. This initial stage has been described in The Diebold Research Program as recognition of the need to improve office worker productivity. It begins with piecemeal cost displacement solutions to specific problems:

Tom Brown, CEO of TFC, was proud of his company's innovation in the introduction and use of mainframe computers. Now that the electronic data processing (EDP) division was firmly in place and management information systems (MISs) were functioning smoothly, he felt it was time to do something about the proliferation of desktop computers. Shrewd managers in control of their own budgets were bringing in their own microcomputers to supplement EDP services. The trouble was that this equipment often was incompatible with other equipment and was not tied into the whole MIS operation. Brown felt that the time had come for some corporate policy on the matter and for a systems approach to replace a fragmented approach to office automation.

Brown asked Ted Stone, TFC's vice-president for information systems, to hire an external consultant of some repute to look into the situation. The professional resource, Jay Ferr, reported that the data processing people were going one way while those in headquarters administration and telecommunications were going another. Ferr had demonstrated to Stone that some TFC personnel were already using word processing, other departments were using voice telecoms, and still others were using time-sharing plans to get their information services. The consultant indicated to Brown and Stone that, if coordination were to take place, it would mean a restructuring of principal support and staff relationships while trying to gain user support for an office automation (OA) corporate plan. Ferr's comprehensive report had already included a process analysis of the company's document creation and modification system, as well as its communication, reproduction, storage retrieval, and destruction.

Since Brown realized that productivity in the offices was likely to go down as TFC evolved to more fully automated systems, he and Stone decided to accept the consultant's recommendation to facilitate the changeover. If in the long run the new technology would raise productivity, their people would have to be involved in planning at all levels of TFC. Thus, Brown established an OA task force that was to concentrate on both the people and technology aspects of automation. It was to distinguish between data and information, examine both software and hardware issues, and plan for everything from personal computing to telecommunications. This representative group was to deal with issues such as data base administration and integrity, technical support and security, policies and procedures, and external services.

Stage Two: Initiation. This is the process of developing OA tactical and strategic plans while testing alternative approaches in isolated or limited work environments:

The task force began by studying some of the existing corporate competition for control of the new technology, analyzing how systems already in existence could be integrated, listening to vendor briefings, and considering cost displacement. The group decided to inaugurate, test, and evaluate several pilot projects. One project was a clerical situation, another focused on work stations for professionals, and a third was just for managers. In each, "ergonomics" was a key consideration—that is, the study of the relationship between humans and machinery. Work place ergonomics seeks to defuse employee and union opposition to the new technology by designing products and work stations that are more compatible with human needs. The task force sought input from users on furniture and equipment, getting their reactions to its ease of use as well as seeking feedback on various approaches to "dumb" and "intelligent" terminals and on various software packages. They presented a report on their findings entitled, "First Steps Toward an Integrated Information System." Then an executive planning group on automation and telecommunications, including Brown and Stone, worked seriously on the recommendations for their larger and long-term implications for the company's future.

Interesting human factors were being revealed from the pilot efforts. For instance, some managers were resisting personal computers, since they thought that the use of the keyboard was menial—something for a typist to do. The human resource department at TFC then organized helpful workshops for managers and their secretaries to examine their changing roles with the introduction of office automation. Managers were trained to maintain their own electronic calendars, address directories, and mail and message exchanges, as well as taught how to network by wire with other managers. Now that secretaries were being relieved of many clerical duties, they were free to take on greater administrative and creative responsibilities. It was also discovered in the preliminary studies that people had difficulty distinguishing between data and word processing. An analysis of those doing word processing tasks revealed that they still had a "linear work approach." They had been conditioned in linear, time sequence patterns—input, process (typewrite a letter, duplicate it, mail original, store copies), wait for answers, and if they come, then respond. But the ball game had changed —electronic mail and files provided immediate feedback. So the OA training now had to emphasize a "cyclic" approach to word processing-type work—input directly on-line to a group of recipients, for the technology now makes it possible to get immediate results. The pilot efforts revealed that personnel in word processing centers were not yet taking full advantage of the new technology to increase productivity. Thus, supervisors were assisted in coaching their personnel to change the ways the tasks in the office traditionally had been done. This is but one example of the kinds of white-collar productivity issues that began to surface in the early stages of OA.

Stage Three: Contagion. Valued-added OA systems are implemented in a variety of user environments to improve managerial, professional, and executive performance:

Gradually, there was more widespread use at TFC of automation, especially with common managerial processes. The results of the user pilots were integrated into mainstream operations, and OA even began to cause change in business plans. As Brown struggled with his colleagues to obtain an integrated information system, they confronted such issues as strengthening central control and local autonomy. They were very surprised at how some of the EDP people were threatened by the spread of OA; the latter often viewed it as an erosion of their power over information and failed to grasp the big picture. Brown then set up an executive conference on information flow and services. He explained to top management the message he wished conveyed throughout the entire corporation: that an office exists for every business area in the organization—manufacturing, distribution, marketing, sales, and accounting. An integrated information system means that each of these subsystems is directly connected electronically. In the new architecture of information, even the different physical locations within the corporation, whether domestic or international, were to be integrated through automation. The new policy is that information as a resource is to be shared and utilized to achieve company goals, and it is not to be the preserve of a few specialists, or one division, or one location.

Acting on another recommendation from Ferr, TFC also

began to plan for the establishment of a headquarters' information resource center that would feature professionals from previous staff functions, such as corporate communications, data processing, and word processing. Its mission in a distributed environment was defined as: (a) keeping management informed as to what data and information are available; (b) ensuring that interpretations of that data and information are consistent and correct throughout the enterprise; and (c) acting as a resource to users for techniques for accessing, processing, and managing such information and data.

The prototype OA studies also resulted in new challenges for executive problem solving, such as the creation of systems for integrating electronic mail, text editing, and textual data base access; redesigning and modifying rewards and measurements (for example, high-performing managers were given the privilege of having a company personal computer in their homes, which were electronically connected to their offices); and the need to improve business intelligence systems and to integrate information systems of subsidiaries and acquisitions into the main TFC/IS.

From an initial concern with office automation, management began to think and plan in larger terms of information as a corporate resource. And this led to reexamination of some traditional work roles and the creation of new ones, more appropriate for knowledge workers. For instance, it became obvious that the function of a secretary had to be restructured within an automated administrative support team. After study, the position of office information systems specialist was designated; this person inputs, formats, and edits on terminals, maintains data files, and operates the electronic mail system. Another, called an administrative secretary, handles mail and telephones, types and files correspondence, coordinates travel arrangements, and conducts other general secretarial activities. Such changes also altered career paths and opened up new professional opportunities for incumbents.

It leads to the elimination of some middle managers, while creating the post of information resource manager. This highlighted the growing importance of information processing to a successful business, for such professionals are architects who design information systems to meet user needs based on their input; consultants who counsel managers on the effective use of information technology, both hardware and software; synergizers who bring together many parts of the information system so as to create a whole; and educators who assist in training management to use information tools. In this latter role, the information resource manager assists general management in planning for the changes in technology, roles, and relationships.

Stage Four: Consolidation. This stage involves the development of integrated information systems based on the experience in the previous stages, with special emphasis on gaining operation efficiency and capitalizing on common learnings:

Brown was pleased at the progress TFC was making in the advancement of office automation. While encouraging stronger central information controls, he also allowed for local autonomy. Automation of common managerial processes was on-line, and even business planning was improving as a result. Ferr was enabling the corporation to improve intergroup systems exchanges and tying various management groups together in electronic networks. This, in turn, was augmenting marketing effectiveness.

Indeed, TFC personnel were beginning to understand that data are bits of information. But that information has to be pared and shared, interpreted and shaped, selected and transformed into knowledge. In order for information to be used effectively as a resource, TFC employees had to appreciate their own vital involvement in seeing that it was adequately gathered, analyzed, and distributed. But Brown also knew that such concepts were changing the very nature of their business, as well as the corporate culture.

Brown thought that Stone had developed a winning strategy when he promoted intergroup team building with the word and data processing people. Until OA, the latter had had exclusive control of data, and now DP personnel had to be reoriented to share information power and to work cooperatively not only with all management but with their OA counterparts. Sophisticated computer professionals had much to contribute to the organizational changes and new information designs if they could broaden their technical perspectives.

Stage Five: Creative Evolution. This stage involves the furtherance of integrated information systems and designs that create opportunities for business expansion and new competitive advantages—a continuing and dynamic process to improve organizational communications through an innovative information environment:

With more centralization of information controls, TFC was now in a position to allow more decentralized management control. To capitalize on new business opportunities, entrepreneurial groupings were fostered, often with only electronic connection to the parent corporation. Personal and electronic networking became a catalyst to enterprises stimulated by the shared perceptions and information. Teleconferencing was beginning to decrease costly and time-consuming meeting travel. For the first time, TFC showed the potential to become a global corporation in the fullest sense of that term. As employees became more comfortable and experienced with the new technology, they became more creative and productive in its use.

With technological maturity, Brown could measure how the wise use of information resources was giving his organization a distinct edge over the competition, so he increased the amount of money invested into information R&D to maximize that advantage. Some of this research is taking place in a consortium of companies doing research in artificial intelligence. And some of these funds are underwriting new interactive authoring systems to improve training and HRD efforts in the corporation. Since TFC was rapidly becoming an organization of knowledge workers, Brown wanted to use electronic "books" to facilitate their learning.

Case Conclusions. Analysis of the TFC case raises some questions to stimulate our thinking:

1. What were some of the new skills employees had to acquire with the introduction of office automation?
2. What were some of the new attitudes and working patterns they had to develop with OA?

Remaking Roles in Automated Enterprises 155

3. How were communication practices and time sense altered by OA?
4. Why did points of influence, authority, and control have to be redefined with the evolution of these new information systems?
5. Why were roles, relationships, and reporting responsibilities modified?
6. What is the value of introducing a staged approach beginning with a pilot project when planning for OA and computer technology?
7. What new corporate strategies and sequences are to be recommended?
8. How critical was the involvement of the chief executive officer in this major organizational transition?

The clues to the answers are all in the case study, at least by implication.

Tremendous growth in the adoption and application of information technology may also mean a growth in associated people problems. In the early stages, anticipate and delimit, where possible, user confusion, frustration, and resistance. In the beginning, expect some people to be threatened by learning difficulties and seeming loss of control of their work space; in time, most do gain the necessary skills and find that the new tools provide them with more control over their work.

Although one would expect computer specialists to provide leadership in the changeover to OA, they are sometimes the most resistant. After all, it is "their" computer that is in the forefront of the communications revolution. Yet, many MIS/DP managers find themselves in an identity crisis—as the case study indicated, they are now having to share their position and power. When they are called upon to assist in office transformation, they too often concentrate only on technical aspects, overlooking the human dimensions.

Management's responsibility is to help personnel comprehend how information technology is altering the nature of their work. Through orientation and training sessions, employees can be assisted in learning how OA can contribute to work simplification and standardization. They can be involved in planning and task forces on task elaboration and variation, on health and safety concerns, on electronic mailing or computer graphics, and on achieving their potential through creative applications of the new tools.

Management development should focus particularly on how OA requires alteration of traditional managerial roles, more delegation and synergy, and skill acquisition in calendar management, electronic files, and the like. Office automation also affects the distribution of authority, work flow, and issues of centralization and decentralization. At the bottom line, it affects productivity and profits: Studies confirm that white-collar productivity has steadily increased in the past five years with increased use of information technology. Where the middle manager's role survives, it will be restructured around information. That person will be more an interpreter and communicator, an interpersonal facilitator and influencer, a decision maker on information, its use, and technology. Richard Nolan, of Nolan, Norton & Company, notes that a computer functional executive (CFE) is emerging in some large organizations. Such a role requires someone who is not only competent with complex technologies, but can act as a critical source of information for the executive group (*The Consultant*, Jan./Feb., 1985, p. 4). The transition to the new information environment or "thinking businesses," Nolan believes will take ten years and means a thorough recharting of the organization, so information and its technology is perceived as an asset and not an expense.

Automated offices will necessitate a new way of thinking, a new logic of management. The case study in this chapter was based on experiences of major corporations in introducing automation (such as Honeywell, Aetna Life & Casualty, and Citibank). It involves technology such as is illustrated in Figure 7 on the automated office of the future.

The lesson for managers is that it is best to go step by step into this automated office and that careful planning is called for in stages of development. In summary, here are some successful tips for positive technological transformation of the enterprise.

- Start small, with a pilot project approach—one department or division at a time until the whole corporation is involved.

Figure 7. Integrated Office Automation.

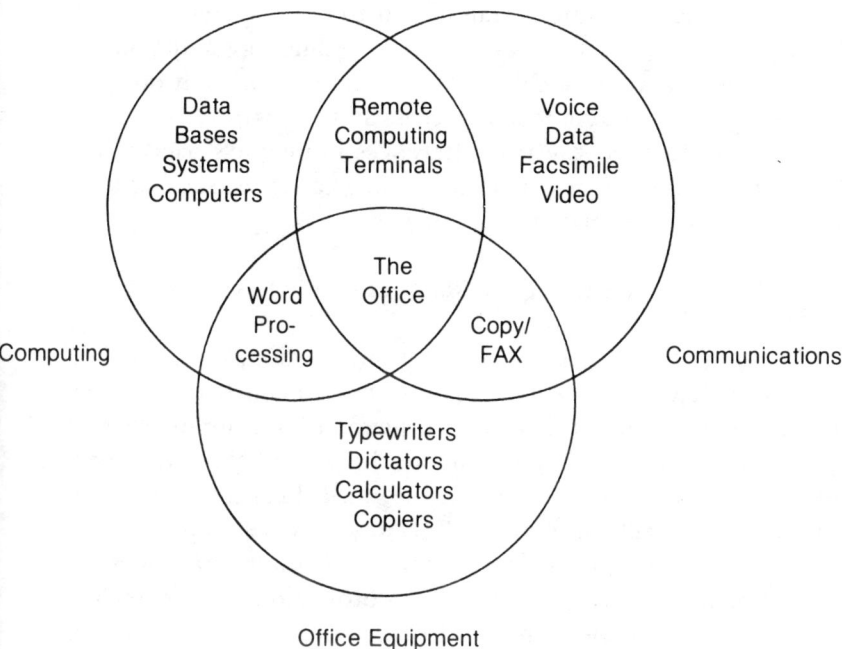

Note: Reprinted with permission of The Diebold Automated Office Program, 1983.

- Focus on the greatest need. Begin where the organization is hurting and OA benefits are immediately needed, and results will be more evident.
- Consult with users before starting and get their input and involvement in a dynamic planning process.
- Proceed gradually; phase in new automated systems and services as supplements and productivity aids for secretaries and support staffs (rather than replacements).
- Strive for integration—first with existing office structures and capabilities, then between and among various entities within the emerging information system.
- Select for compatibility. Equipment and software

should not only fit the needs and preferences of the users, but they should fit with information systems now in place, when feasible.

- Offer continuous training on the new systems at each stage of development. Relate the new technology and skills to alterations in corporate culture (for example, work stations provide access and are symbols of success and status).
- Be flexible toward differences in people's pace of adjustment to the changes, in their learning capacities, and in their creative use of automated equipment.

Altering the Manager's Role

John Diebold, the prophet of automation, stated in a recent interview: "Very early on, we put out a construct in which we said that the first thing that happens with a computer is that you change the way a job is done; the second thing that happens is that you change the job; the third thing that happens is that technology changes society" (Narayanan, 1984, p. 11).

Among the jobs being changed as a result of automation is the manager's, along with other professionals' and technicians' jobs. As implied, the electronic office is one of the major catalysts altering the traditional approach to management. One international consultant, however, bewailed that in a way office automation presently is a joke—it requires transformation of the work environment, and managers give it lip service as the way to go, but they do not want to change themselves. It is okay to let the new technology change the secretary or draftsperson's job, but too many managers want to play in the old ball park and not make the transition to a new way of carrying out their function. Automated communications provide multiple opportunities to improve the management of time, meetings, and information exchanges, but this vast new array of communication alternatives is already causing "options shock" among managers.

The possibilities for data and voice communications for network analysis often overwhelm both management and their organizations. The very thought of having to learn computer languages becomes a deterrent, and managers fail to realize that there is now software to minimize that problem until such time as direct voice communication to computers becomes standard operating procedure. Then there is the matter of learning the new, ever-changing terminology of the automated enterprise. For example, Harry Katzan's *Office Automation—A Manager's Guide* has a glossary of over 1,400 office automation terms (Katzan, 1983). No wonder "uninitiated" managers and other professionals unfamiliar with computers are intimidated by the new work stations.

For this reason, information expert Joseph Ferreira, former vice-president of The Diebold Group and now a principal of Business Research Institute, (Narayanan, 1984, p. 13) advises that personal computers should be a discretionary tool: "The PC gets very much into personal work styles. It's part of a person's work space. Most of what people do in that work space is largely discretionary. They have options on the way they do things—like in the use of the telephone. The same thing applies to personal computers. The PC is a tool that supports people in the way they work; it influences their personal style; it changes the way they think." Ferreira thinks that the new technology should not be forced on managers but that they should be enticed into its use gradually. Rather than putting a computer on every white-collar worker's desk, he would provide the tool to those who are ready to use it intelligently. His strategy has been to give the technology to those executives who are comfortable with it and let them create their own constituencies. This distinguished consultant believes that we are in a shift from a work culture that is very control oriented to one that creates a context in which people work for a common good. Ferreira maintains that we are in evolution to the office of the future and that the personal computer is but the initial stage in that transition (Narayanan, 1984).

The key to winning managers and professionals over to regular use of the new technology in their work is training. Xerox Office Systems realized this in terms of such personnel at its Palo Alto Research Center. Xerox researchers (Kingston, 1981) discovered that the higher a person's level was in the organization, the shorter was his or her attention span. Office automation training for them had to be intuitive, easy to use and to remember. "Keep it simple" became the motto when preparing learning programs and materials on document preparation (text entry, editing, formatting, graphics illustration, and page makeup) and management (electronic filing and mail, printing, communications, magnetic media interfaces). This approach was extended to instruction on information processing (forms and records processing, user programming and calculating). And the pay-off in improving managerial and professional productivity is impressive. It began when such highly paid personnel started giving up their handwritten and typed drafts of material in order to produce more attractive documents, gradually realizing the power and control the new tools were giving them over their own work. They stopped sending things to administrative support staffs and started keyboarding for themselves. Using the new Xerox "Alto" systems, impressive savings in workdays and costs began to amass.

Essentially, the Xerox researchers proved that (1) steps in work processes could be eliminated, (2) reduction in turnaround times could be effected, (3) time needed to complete tasks could be reduced, and (4) many intangible, unmeasurable benefits occurred. The latter included reduced dependency on other departments (such as word processing and graphics), better remote communications electronically in real time, and improved writer efficiency, flexibility, and availability. Participants in the new electronic networks reported feeling less isolated because they were "plugged into what was going on in the organization." Users of the information systems felt that they had more status and access.

The strategic impact of information technologies on managerial work has not escaped the attention of researchers at the University of Southern California. There, at the Center for Futures Research, a two-year study began in 1984 on how developing capabilities in computers and communications affect the manager's role. With financing from major corporate sponsors, the research will develop and validate diagnostic tools for evaluating the effectiveness of information management infrastructure and its capacities for aiding managers and professionals in carrying out their tasks. The study will also engage in impact assessment of different types of organizations in various stages of transition and utilization of information technology. The USC futurists will construct scenarios of future roles for managers and professionals as a result of the information technology changes. They will, furthermore, focus on the policy variables that can be manipulated in addressing the what, when, how, and where of implementing technologies. (For further details, request document F-52, CFR, Graduate School of Business Administration, University of Southern California, Los Angeles, Calif. 90089-1421.)

Information technology is beginning to remake the manager's job in many ways. Currently, only about 3 percent of the 25 million managers and white-collar professionals in the United States are using computer work stations; but their exploration and experimentation may well set the pattern for what is likely to become standard operating procedure for their successors in the future. The results will transform not only their roles but the organizational structures in which they work. One such result, for instance, is a flattening of the management pyramid that affects the middle management role because information availability becomes more instantaneous and there is less need for the layers between top and first-line management.

Since increased managerial and professional productivity also results from the installation and use of the new information technology, organizations would be wise to spend more on equipment, training, and support services for these knowledge workers. In using the 3.2 million computers now active in United States business, management has had perceptual blinders up to now. We are gradually moving from mainly accounting applications to wider and more creative employment of the technology.

Here are some of the contemporary innovations by managers and professionals with microcomputers:

- Analysis of pricing, competitive product lines, and promotional allocations. By utilizing the computer's memory, Pfizer Pharmaceuticals, as a case in point, was able to cut 50 percent of its cost in promotion of a product and save time compared to a comparable search of market research books.
- Improvement of decision making at all levels of man-

agement. Managers are now able to combine company data with outside information to get broader perspectives on industry-wide statistics or national and global economics. Hours, instead of months, can now produce data that can become meaningful studies of one's businesses, markets, competition, and forecasts.

- Increase in organizational communication effectiveness through voice-store-and-forward telephone systems that avoid time-wasting repeat calls or through electronic mail exchange which simultaneously transmits memos, reports, drafts to colleagues. Teleconferencing can link remote managers to one another while also cutting down travel costs.
- Facilitated scheduling, planning, and calendar management, as well as inventory control. James Collins, a Litton Industries materials manager, reported that the computerized inventory and scheduling system installed at his Kentucky plant changed his job drastically by eliminating 95 percent of the emergencies, thus enabling him to spend more time planning instead of reacting.
- Tracking of trends in one's company, industry, or field or in the economy. Such uses can range from environmental scanning to monitoring new patents in a specific market. For instance, in Bedford, Massachusetts, the air force has a computerized system to keep track of $3 billion worth of electronic bids made to the government.

The results of such activities contribute to the remaking of the manager's position in the organization. Some of the results being reported are:

- A 25 percent reduction in unproductive time formerly devoted to waiting for telephone calls to be returned, meetings to be held, and information to be sent. The desktop computers are also proving their worth in expediting routine tasks from making copies to arranging reservations.
- Gradual replacement of the old middle managers by new information resource managers who study, analyze, and report on the newly available data, as well as coordinate the information support system. The value of these new information professionals is in servicing other managers, especially by winnowing the information they provide for its more salient meanings and applications.

- Coordinating more effectively office and factory activities while promoting a new synthesis among manufacturing, marketing, and finance for better corporate team management. As Richard Starr, director of management systems for TRW's Reda Pump Division, indicated that now there is so much more information, teamwork is tighter and more attuned than it ever was before.
- Decision making is being pushed downward and first-line supervisors are better informed.

These effects of information technology are most dramatic in terms of supervisors. The new automation and communication systems are reshaping the role of first-level management. With access to data formerly denied them, supervisors now know more about the business. They not only are permitted to participate more in making decisions, but they have more time to engage in planning and forecasting. Perhaps the best pay-off in terms of morale is that such supervisors have more time for their people. Career development opportunities then improve for such persons, who gain wider experience and skills. At Ford Motor Company in Edison, New Jersey, the automated systems have stimulated the "enabling functions" among factory supervisors. On the assembly lines, supervisors now have time to listen to workers, to use their ideas, and to focus on problem solving instead of being overly concerned with discipline. The computer-based technology often takes over the control and monitoring of production flow and quality, freeing supervisors for more coaching and training of personnel. But first-line supervisors need to be trained for their new role and power, especially as facilitators of self-management work teams, whether in office or plant. Supervisory development now has to concentrate on cultivating participatory style and on synergistic skills in worker counseling, negotiating, and maintenance.

New Dimensions in Managing for Automation

In the analysis so far of the impact of automation on the management function, many indications have been cited as to how the role will be altered. This discussion concludes with two issues that require innovative leadership: (1) human factors, including personnel development, and (2) supervising workers at home.

Human Factors. The introduction of computers and robots into offices and factories involves more than technical change—it also means organizational and human change. For over thirty years, behavioral scientists have been doing research and developing methods for planning change. Now managers in automated enterprises need to benefit from this by learning about the management of driving and resisting forces related to such changes. Books and workshops on the management of change are more readily available to managers either through international or external resources.

Among the psychological factors managers must learn to cope with as computers and robots are introduced into the work environment are cyberphobia and cyberphrenia. Since cyberphobia is excessive fear of the new technology, it may be accompanied by feelings of severe anxiety, hostility, and resistance in various forms. For some workers, having to learn to use a computer may prove disturbing, even dysfunctional—the machine may prove too intimidating. Computer-generated decisions, for instance, are perceived as being unchallengeable, stifling personal judgment and creativity. For others, the new machine threatens the ego or sense of self—seemingly, for some, creating a feeling of loss of control over their work space.

Cyberphrenia, on the other hand, is addiction to the new technology to the extent that it totally dominates one's life. We witness it in elementary and college students who become absorbed in computer games or processes, as well as in managers or brokers who become so obsessed with their electronic work stations that they forget other people in their offices, work too late, and even neglect eating and exercise. Such people sometimes become mechanical in their responses, narrowing their life-style and focus and substituting machine for human relationships. They are often prone to deviant behavior and become amoral, such as the computer whiz who ends up using the computer to steal millions of dollars from a bank employer.

Although managers should become familiar with the symptoms of both types of extreme reactions to automation, they are not expected to provide therapy. The manager's job is to try to prevent such aberrations from developing when possible and, if and when they become apparent, to make referrals to qualified professionals within or outside the organization who are capable of counseling employees with such problems.

The average individual is uncomfortable with change and tends to resist it while holding onto the status quo. However, through the application of planned change strategies, education, and training, the normal person will adapt and accept the challenge. After all, learning and career development depend on openness to change in our attitudes and perceptions, as well as in acquisition of new information and skills. Managers can do much to prepare people for the new technology. Gradual introduction is the most desirable; this may include using staff meetings to orient personnel to the fundamentals of computers or robots, to familiarize them with terminology and buzz words, and to show films that take the mystery out of these new tools. To reduce embarrassment and strangeness, executives and professionals might relate their initial experiences in mastering the personal computer; word processing operators might act as tutors; training specialists might schedule workshops for beginners or more advanced classes in the special software that advances work proficiency. With these and similar procedures, managers should exercise initiative and leadership in helping their staff grow in computer literacy and power.

The greatest resource available to most companies is the human resource of information professionals already in the organization's MIS or EDP departments. These are potentially the new "knowledge brokers" who already possess competence in computer and communication technology; line managers must learn to build organizational relations with them. In this manner, the in-house resources can be more fully used in the furtherance of office automation and managerial work stations.

The information technology environment is also transforming the human resource function within organizations. This will require many changes on the part of management and is more completely treated in Chapter Four, along with other development and management concerns.

Supervision of Workers at Home. When the factory age came into being a few centuries back, cottage industries were in vogue. Like the parents of William Shakespeare in Stratford-upon-Avon, many people worked in their homes. With the dawn of the information age, a similar prospect confronts us through the medium of the electronic cottage. A pop prophet of *The Third Wave* called it a breathtaking social change that ties into trends toward smaller work units, decentralization, de-urbanization, and the shift from the manufacturing of things to the processing of information (Toffler, 1980).

Employers are admitting that up to three quarters of their personnel might work at home if the company provided them with the right communication technology. Think what such a transition in the work force could do to urban overcrowding, traffic jams, and auto pollution, to say nothing about improving the quality of work life! The National Academy of Sciences sponsored a 1983 forum on "Office Work Stations in the Home," estimating then that the known number of 15,000 could swell to 10 million by 1990.

Since microcomputer technology is well on its way to revolutionizing how America works, this is another manifestation of its capabilities, especially when the corporate data bank is linked to the home office. Since a relatively small number of companies currently are experimenting with the new possibility, research is underway to understand better the technical, economic, psychological, legal, and management, as well as social, implications of the phenomenon. Among the leaders in such investigations is Margrethe H. Olson, a business professor at New York University (NYU). Her studies at NYU's Center for Research on Information Systems are examining work-at-home programs relative to impact on performance, work attitudes, work patterns, and supervision, especially through the use of computers and communications technology. It is the issue of supervision and administration of home workers that most interests us here. How is management changed when the manager is mainly connected electronically with a worker and only occasionally meets that person face-to-face?

In preliminary studies, Olson reported that management did not find such distancing to be an insurmountable difficulty ("The Practicalities...," 1981, pp. 21-24). Instead, they reported these benefits from having their information workers at home stations:

- ability to utilize otherwise unavailable talent;
- reduction in travel and commuting costs and stress;
- elimination of tardiness, absenteeism, and break-time issues;
- cutting down on turnover problems;
- improved worker satisfaction because of flexible work schedules, easier family management, personal savings in time, money, energy, and clothing costs by not having to commute daily, decrease in direct supervision, and improved relations in the community.

However, these same investigations by Olson also indicated some of the management challenges that occur when supervisors are physically separated from the people for whom they are responsible in the corporate sense:

- need to develop new trust levels with employees who are allowed to work where and when it suits them without the usual controls;
- tendency of home workers to underestimate their working hours, as well as requiring a system for monitoring and compensating overtime beyond normal weekly hours of work time;
- difficulty dealing with poor performance and disciplining some employees when operating from a distance;
- coping with matters of family interference with worker productivity, lack of clerical and peer support for the at-home employee, decline in company loyalty with increase in independence, temporary feelings of inequity among peer groups that continue to work in the corporate office;
- social isolation created by work at home, more so for women than men, and concern for loss of image and status in the organization and for career development.

Obviously, effective managers can discover ways to prevent or resolve such problems experienced by at-home workers. For example, the social isolation can be reduced by electronic networking, periodic group meetings of such employees with their supervisors, invitation to corporate special events, and various other means to keep at-home workers plugged into the corporate dynamics and culture.

The initial studies seem to indicate that, for both the individual and the organization, the benefits outweigh the disadvantages. For example, the remote workers reported increased concentration and reduced stress, while the supervisors indicated reduced costs and improved worker morale, especially when individuals are allowed to control their own work space and pace. Management experience to date with this new alternative is very limited but generally satisfactory. However, labor specialists and union officials are expressing a strong distaste for the development. Not everyone is suited for telecommuting, so care must be taken in selection, as well as in choice for those who wish to become teleworkers or who wish to come back into company offices after trying to work at home. But for those who find it a viable option, organizations will increasingly be expected to provide it. Apparently, the technology of teleworking is relatively easy, but the management of it requires new expertise and higher levels of cooperation.

In a global economy, America's choices are "Automate, Emigrate, or Evaporate"; so said Charles McMillon in both title and conclusion of his article (McMillon, 1985). As director of an industrial policy project for the U.S. House of Representatives' Small Business Committee, he believes that automation is the only way the country can regain a lead in productivity. He advocates the establishment of a central facility for broad dissemination on information and education modeled on the Agricultural Extension Service.

Conclusion

Managing technological changes effectively implies more than ensuring that hardware and software are user friendly and do not endanger people's health. It means applying positive strategies for helping workers adapt when their world is in flux and they feel discomfort with uncertainties. Effective managers assist their colleagues in developing new frames of reference and reality, in maintaining some sense of control over the automated work space, in gaining office automation skills. As the enterprise goes through the various stages toward the full integration of these new technologies, managers are concerned with more than cost avoidance and reduction. Thinking managers counteract potential word processing/data processing infighting by promoting synergistic efforts between data processing and office automation specialists, particularly by encouraging both to become information professionals. If decision making is to be improved by use of these electronic wizards, then decision support systems have to be created. Above all, wise managers appreciate that continuing technical training and consultation should be provided if all are to transcend into the office of tomorrow with grace and wit. For it is this transition that is the principal force forming the new work culture.

SIX

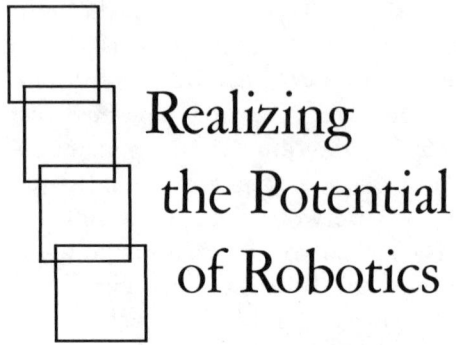

Realizing the Potential of Robotics

Executive Summary. Before the year 2000, most managers will interface with some form of robots or computer-controlled machines. These are among the new technologies that are reconfiguring management and changing the way we plan, schedule, control, and manage, especially in manufacturing. Since such automated tools are transforming our work culture, this chapter provides a guide to increasing management understanding of robotic capabilities.

Even while we ponder potential applications in the work place, robot powers of perception, decision making, and mobility are continually being improved by their creators. Eventually, robot sensors will enable them to see, touch, and move, as well as respond to the unexpected. After all, robots are machines that perform in a manner ordinarily ascribed to a human being, so the possibilities for refinement beyond the primitive models now in use are tremendous. Management is challenged to do more than comprehend robotic technology; it should work cooperatively with engineers and technicians in creating desirable work uses that improve both productivity and society.

There is a direct correlation between robots and jobs. Just as the industrial stage of development substituted mechanical for human energy, the metaindustrial revolution utilizes

Realizing the Potential of Robotics

computer power in place of brain power to control machines and industrial processes. The shift is so significant that even the United States Census Bureau will now count the number of robots engaged in industrial use. Robot labor is adopted, at first, to replace humans on dangerous or unpleasant jobs and later to supplement or enhance human vocational activity. Managers must weigh the advantages or disadvantages of the tin-collar worker over human personnel in specific situations. Whether the judgment is to use a robot replacement or a combination of robot and human workers, managers must be ready to cope with alterations in work roles and environments caused by such decisions.

The work force also must be prepared by management to deal with the new reality. When robots take over undesirable, tedious, and automatic jobs, human effort can be conserved for more enjoyable, changeable, unstructured, and creative activity. Some researchers think the threat to unemployment is overrated, for robot use in industry is growing at less than 35 percent a year, and that obsolescence is the real culprit. On the other hand, just like computers, robots create many new occupational opportunities to manufacture, sell, install, and service the new technology. Obviously, the transformation is toward a computer/robot-based economy that creates more wealth for more people—one that will affect all careers and professions, industries and organizations. The reeducation process for this transition offers management rare opportunities to seek synergistic solutions with the help of robot manufacturers, as well as government and universities.

Management leadership is needed to counteract "robo-shock"—excessive fear of robots and the job loss they supposedly cause. Management strategies are discussed here for anticipating or alleviating the problems related to robotic implementation that may range from medicine to the military, as well as home and personal use. However, it is in manufacturing that the most exciting applications are underway. There, robots, along with computers, are opening new dimensions of integrated and flexible production systems. As we experiment now with the factory of the future, management must confront many vagaries of the new technologies. On the one end of a continuum are safety issues because the stupidity of unsupervised robots may lead to injury or death of their human coworkers. At the other extreme is the potential for artificial intelligence with their expert systems that will liberate professionals in many fields because of their data and knowledge base. Research into both the human brain and automation may lead to the new architecture of tomorrow's computers, robots, and automated machines.

Occupational Transformations

Cybernetics was the term coined by the late M.I.T. mathematician, Norbert Wiener, to describe the emerging science concerned with control and communications between man and machines. Today, we might refer to this as advanced automation, the mechanical management of machines by programmed computers. "Automata," the name originally used to describe mechanical devices in human or animal form, may have first appeared in historical writings between 400 and 350 B.C. Technically, automation now refers to techniques, methods, or systems for operating mechanical or production processes by highly automatic or electronic means. In the previous chapter, we examined the impact of automation on our work roles and environment, especially with reference to the office. Now, let us focus on this phenomenon in terms of robots, particularly as they will affect manufacturing. Thinking managers realize that there is a robot in their future, whether in the factory, office, or home. What we need to appreciate is the significance of this development—robotization of manufacturing, for instance, is comparable to the mechanization of agriculture. Again, a sampling of random media reports may help increase awareness on this vital subject:

• Japan manufactured 28,000 robots in 1983, a 13 percent increase in volume over the previous year, estimated at $766 million in value. Japan now produces 60 percent of the free world's robots, and the Japanese expect to quadruple their own robot use by 1990. By that date, one Japanese company alone—Matsushita Electric Industrial Company—expects to install 100,000 robots.

Realizing the Potential of Robotics

- Britain is introducing the devices into its businesses faster than either Japan or the United States. Taylor Hitech, one of the United Kingdom's materials-handling equipment makers, has been commissioned to build a remote-controlled "robot arm" to pick up hazardous material, such as radioactive components.
- In 1984, American companies spent $343 billion on new plants and equipment. Aging factories are being refitted with high-technology equipment—computers, robots, automatic welders, laser, and ultrasonic probes.
- In the next decade, robot sales are likely to increase 35 percent, and the United States market alone may rise to $2 billion. The global stock of 31,000 robots in 1982 may climb to 330,000 by 1990.
- Within ten years, General Motors will probably purchase 20,000 robots that could displace upward of 50,000 assembly line workers.

"Robo-shock" is here—both for those who actually design the things and for those in whose imaginations sleek mechanoids already serve every conceivable human need. Some writers see robotics as the symbol of American technology, a bellwether indicating the direction of industry, employment, electronic intelligence, and the human use of human beings. Certainly, microelectronics and robots have captured the imagination of business. Managers especially need to be concerned about the growing human-machine interface.

What Is a Robot?

Robots got their name in a 1921 play by Karel Capek from a Czech word for forced labor. A form of automation, these machines can be programmed for a variety of manipulative, routine tasks. Stand-alone, independent devices, they are sometimes called steel- or tin-collar workers. The Robot Institute of America defines them as reprogrammable, multifunction manipulators designed to move material, parts, tools, or special devices through variable programmed motions for the performance of tasks.

The basic parts of a robot's anatomy are the manipulator or mechanical arm, the controller or computer, and the power supply. The two major types of robots in use are: (1) *nonservo-controlled:* sometimes called pick-and-place or point-to-point robots, they usually are pneumatically operated and electronically controlled (cost range is $5,000 to $30,000); and (2) *servo robots:* a more sophisticated kind with servomechanisms for quick change of arm/gripper, they can move in a continuous path or in irregular, nonlinear routes (cost range is $25,000 to $125,000). The latter can be guided physically by a human operator or by push-button instructions that can be stored in the robot's computer memory for replication or reprogramming. Sensors tell the robot where to go and how to respond, while its internal memory contained in a programmed computer enables encoders, for instance, to measure distance. A sensory servo robot is a computerized model with one or more artificial senses, such as sight or touch.

Roboticists remind us that only 1 percent of today's robots are mobile and that the other 99 percent are stationary or placed on a fixed-rail system. Distinctions are made between true robots, which have intelligence on board, and functionoids. ODEX 1, made by Odetics, Inc., has been described as the latter —a drone—because it is remotely controlled by radio waves from a human operator within twenty feet.

Perhaps we can clarify further by distinguishing robots from other automated devices, thus describing what robots are not:

- Teleoperators—remote operators that control and direct a machine. Sometimes called telepersons, these are mobile, operating proxies that go where humans cannot, should not, or do not want to go. For example, there is the remotely controlled underwater vehicle, and other wonders are soon to come out of our university laboratories for artificial intelligence. Soon one will be able to wear a jacket with sensors and tiny motors, and his or her body motion will be reproduced at another place by a mobile device, such as a mechanical hand.

- Mechanical or moving dolls—not robots, despite their popularity at Disneyworld. Robots are independent, stand-alone devices, not like the Ideal Toy Company's mechanical imitation.

- Cyborgs—hybrid combinations of human and machine. These are created when mechanical parts, such as a prosthetic arm or leg, replace those of nature. Thus, the devices or mechanical organs operate on electromyographic signals and are extensions of human senses or physical powers.

Androids, conceived of as being human-like in every way but functioning only because of electrical mechanical systems, currently exist only in science fiction.

Although robots often are designed in a human image, looking human is not a prime attribute. We are only in the early stages of robot research and development; their costs must come down and their sensing abilities increase before they will be widely put to use. Eventually, robots will be able to respond to a variety of sensory cues—visual, auditory, and tactile; they will learn by experience, analyze tasks on their own, and be capable of self-diagnosis and repair. In the near future, we can expect rapid improvements in assembly robots that are extremely fast, accurate, and dexterous. Designs are already being developed for these to use graphics databases that describe the shapes of parts to be made and how the assemblies should be constructed. But, for the moment, we mainly have a primitive use of robots to transfer materials and engage in certain processes, such as welding.

Hank Koehn, former vice-president of futures research at Security Pacific National Bank, suggests that our most sophisticated and complete robots to date are unmanned spacecraft, such as Viking, which explored Mars, and Voyager, which visited Jupiter and Saturn (Koehn, 1981). These were designed to do their own navigating, maneuvering, repairing, and landing on other planets with a minimum of human interaction. How can we characterize the Canadian-built mechanical arm operated by the astronauts on the Challenger shuttle for the first time in September 1983? While the shuttle circled the globe at 17,500 m.p.h., this fifty-foot robot arm snatched the wayward satellite, Solar Max, from space and placed it successfully on a platform in the cargo bay so that repairs could be made on the ailing robot. The California Space Institute has just completed a study on the use of automation for space exploration and exploitation

(Criswell, 1985). The Soviets too are making extensive use of robots in their space program.

Tools, even machines, are human artifacts—extensions of ourselves. This often is very evident in the design of robots with human-like appearances, characteristics, and names. However, since experiencing errors and failures is part of the human condition and creative process, we have a problem with boredom with inorganic zombies that do not make mistakes. Although our robotic creations plod along relentlessly, logically, and tirelessly, they never act on intuition or impulse or fantasize. Yet despite the threat that many perceive with the growth of robotic technology, it has immense potential to enhance our life quality and work environment. Our quest to perfect and expand this new capability will lead to more self-knowledge.

In the metaindustrial work culture, robots with microprocessors or computers will move from hot, heavy, dangerous, and repetitive assembly line work to more difficult and delicate tasks requiring great visual and tactile skills. Business leaders see them as a viable alternative to win the productivity battle while counteracting poor-quality workmanship and rising labor costs, especially relative to safety and other benefits. Here are the arguments, pro and con, relative to robots:

Robot Advantages:

- work twenty-four hours a day 95 percent of the time—no breaks or holidays;
- immune to safety hazards and regulations;
- nonunionized and unprotected by government regulations;
- cost-effective over the long term—no entitlements;
- easily adjusted to new tasks—do not get bored or careless;
- increased productivity and profitability—quality with no mistakes.

Robot Disadvantages:

- high front-end investment and uncertain, long-term ROI;
- high costs of both installation and maintenance;
- threaten some human workers who fear impact for unemployment;

Realizing the Potential of Robotics

- alter work environment/relationships—workers need training;
- limited current use—no sophisticated, creative work yet.

Since the pace of adopting robot technology has not been as fast as with computer technology, enlightened managers still can exercise creative leadership to delimit the social and economic dislocations that might be caused (Ayres and Miller, 1983). In the early 1980s, for example, there were only about 7,000 robots in the United States. With an expansion rate of 30 percent annually, which may result in 200,000 robots in the United States by 1990, management must plan and act now for the intelligent introduction of this new technology. That way, human hardships in this transition can be minimized. Thinking managers may wish to consult a manual on the subject—*Robotics in Practice: Management and Applications of Industrial Robots* (Engelberger, 1980). Another recommended resource for those seriously interested is *Robotics and Automated Manufacturing* (Dorf, 1983). Managers also will find it helpful to attend seminars on the topic, such as the Data Processing Association's (P.O. Box 3608, Torrance, Calif. 90510) sessions on "Man-Machine Interface" (MMI). MMI is an emerging field of study in successful systems performance. Wayne Zachary of Drexel University examines in such seminars the design, best operation, and evaluation of this interface, especially as it relates to emerging capabilities with artificial intelligence.

Robots and Jobs

The tonic of high technology being administered to rejuvenate American industry has been called a bittersweet brew. Yes, the army of robots, optical scanners, microchips, and other forms of automation is revolutionizing the way companies produce and people work so that costs can be reduced and foreign competition met; but the trend of these technological changes is away from labor-intensive activities. It means more output from fewer people, more sales, and less pay. The move to modernization also is taking a heavy toll on traditional jobs in basic industries, such as auto, steel, and textiles. However, according to some executives, automation is the salvation of our economic system—industry must automate, emigrate, or evaporate. Not only are new types of jobs being created in the process, but a whole industry, called "high tech," is coming into being. Already it employs from 3 to 6 million workers, depending on how the term is defined, out of a total United States work force of almost 103 million.

Management guru Peter Drucker predicted that robotization alone over the next twenty years will eliminate ten to fifteen million jobs, causing the Americans involved in manufacturing employment to drop to less than 10 percent of the total work force (Koehn, 1983). On one end of the spectrum there is the view of Isaac Asimov (Koehn, 1981, p. 1), who quipped, "Robots don't kill people, they kill jobs." The other view was aptly expressed in a headline of the columnist James Flanigan: "Robots won't take jobs, only reshape them" (Flanigan, 1984). Economist Anthony Carnevale (1984) recently prepared a report for the American Society for Training and Development titled *Jobs for the Nation*. In it he maintains that worries over worker displacement by robots are unfounded and that the dislocation is relatively limited in the whole economy. Although he admits that workers in traditional heavy industries are trapped in transition, displaced workers of the new technologies suffer only temporary loss of income and the major changes will affect where they work and what they do. For the last twenty years, his report concludes, high technology has created new manufacturing jobs. In counterbalance, the United States robot industry is expanding rapidly and may grow by 1990 to a $4 billion market in both devices and peripherals. In this country alone, sixty corporations make and distribute industrial robots, principally Westinghouse's Unimation and Cincinnati Milacron. The human reality is that from the mid-1980s on in this nation, one robot will likely displace four to six assembly workers; at present, there is only a net redundancy of about 1.5 workers per robot. For intelligent management, the implication is an immense challenge to prepare and retrain workers who most probably will be dislocated.

Manufacturers, as a case in point, have no choice but to opt for robotization, or they risk losing their competitiveness

Realizing the Potential of Robotics

and more jobs in whole sectors of their industries. Besides, industrial robots are valued for high and consistent standards of quality, low rejection rates, rapid production, and reduced unit costs. Two corporate "mini" cases illustrate this transition:

1. General Electric, Erie, Pennsylvania. General Electric management transformed a drab, seventy-year-old building into a factory of the future through high-technology applications. Thus, they saved the company's locomotive and land transportation business, along with many jobs and the area's economy. Instead of going offshore with their manufacturing, they invested $316 million in the changeover. The principal instrument of this rejuvenation was the robot that operates like a giant praying mantis with long metal fingers. Snatching tools from a shelf and delicately placing them into machines that mill motor frames, it demonstrates uncanny ability to make the right selections. Initially, the decision to automate here cost 2,300 jobs; but, in the process, it not only has saved the city economically, but it has sparked a $100 million development plan called Erie Tomorrow. The renovated plant increased its production capacity by one third; with the help of robots, its 3,200 employees can now machine a 2,500-pound locomotive frame in sixteen hours instead of the previous sixteen days. Furthermore, General Electric invested $6.5 million in a modern training center to help workers cope with the new technology. The union also supports the effort, contending that such older factories created the profits to pay for such automation.

2. Fanuc, Ltd., near Mount Fuji. In this Japanese complex, two plants with cavernous, bumblebee-yellow buildings operate with automatic machining centers and robots. During the day, there are only 100 workers per plant for 10 robots, but production is almost $8 million monthly. A 54,000-square-foot machining center is supervised at night by only 1 human controller, who watches the machines on closed-circuit television. If something goes wrong, that single worker can shut down a particular part of the operation and reroute work around it. With only subdued blue warning lights, unmanned delivery carts move like ghostly messengers through the eerie semidarkness. The automated plants make robot parts and machine tools,

which are presently assembled manually. These Fanuc factories are five times as productive as conventional counterparts would be.

These two illustrations point up the potential for automation, whether revitalizing an existing manufacturing facility or creating a new model. In both instances, there are fewer human beings involved than would have been true in the past. Veteran roboticist and writer Isaac Asimov admits such human displacement but argues that any job a robot can do is beneath the dignity of a human being (Koehn, 1983, p. 7). Instead of mindless drudgery, he proposes that more human jobs be created and that we focus on the tasks that are intrinsically human, such as sports, entertainment, and scientific research.

Before we reach that ideal state, there is going to be a painful transition for many a blue-collar worker. It is a time that cries out for transformational leadership. Back in 1981, the chairman of General Motors, Roger B. Smith, blissfully observed that "every time the cost of labor goes up $1 an hour, 1,000 more robots become economical." Perhaps such reasoning explains why General Motors will spend more than $200 million in 1983 to convert to high-tech automation. Eight hundred robots will weld the bodies of virtually all their cars. By 1985, that number jumped to 5,000, and is likely to be 14,000 by 1990. Richard Beecher, head of General Motors' machine perception and robotics department, estimates this to be a $1 billion investment for robots of varying size and sophistication. Some will assemble components; others will paint or load and unload machines. The conversion of older General Motors plants to automated and robotic systems is credited partially for the dramatic turnaround in the corporation's financial performance; analysts noted record earnings of $5 billion in 1984. General Motors is so committed to this new management strategy that it acquired Electronic Data Systems as a subsidiary division to create the "paperless" corporation and established the Saturn division to produce cars in a modular and more automated fashion. In the process, the United Auto Workers union predicted that humans on the assembly line would be cut by 50 percent. Yet, because of the surge in imported cars and components, these American labor leaders admit the robots offer vastly improved quality control and are cooperating with management in transforming the auto factories.

Such robotic strategy and labor-management synergy are vital in view of developments in other nations. Consider the Japanese challenge. Nomura Research Institute reported that the Japanese robot industry in 1985 recorded $1.2 billion in sales and forecasts double that by 1990, when they predict their industries will be using a million robots. Toyota Motor Company has a new plant that employs total use of robots in all production stages. Honda Motors reports its Sayama Works will have no human workers in the paint factory. Nissan Motor Manufacturing Corporation has built its most automated plant in Smyrna, Tennessee, with 219 robots, plus other automated and computerized systems. But that Japanese-American plant also will employ 1,000 workers, who will benefit from participative management and quality control circles.

Anywhere mechanical devices can be programmed to perform useful acts of manipulation or location under automatic control, a robot can be made to do the job. James S. Albus, chief of the Industrial Systems Division of the National Bureau of Standards, reminds us that robot capabilities are constantly improving. Within a decade, he expects that robots will be used in construction to carry, lift, and position building materials; in the mining of seabeds; in erecting large structures in space, as well as for planetary observations and space defense; in futuristic factories for automatic management of inventory and tools; for machining assembly/finishing; and for inspection and component production (Albus, 1981). This expert predicts that a robotic-based economy will not necessarily foster widespread unemployment but will create new jobs and industries while raising the level of affluence. So anticipate that robots will be picking our fruit, disposing of our garbage, cooking in fast-food restaurants, and even babysitting. In the near term, the shift to a new economy will require:

- robot manufacturers—people who will make, market, and distribute robots and related parts or services;
- robot operators—trained people to operate or supervise robots;
- robot technicians—people to maintain and service robots—to take charge of "care and feeding" functions;
- robot consultants—people to analyze occupational functions and work needs that lend themselves to replacement by automated, mechanical means and to counsel on the robotic systems that can best address these possibilities;
- robot designers—creative engineers and computer specialists to do the research and development on the next generation of robots that will demonstrate greater artificial intelligence; and
- robot programmers—computer professionals to develop robotic information systems, as well as program individual machines.

These are but a few of the jobs emerging as a result of the development of robotic technology. Thinking managers will have to consult specialists or literature on job forecasting and analysis to determine types of occupations, skills, experiences, and training required for this purpose. This requires more than simply identifying what work the robots can perform; it means examining what human activity should be done in tandem and then preparing personnel for these new roles. Some of the existing work force can be recycled, but other new technicians may have to be trained or recruited. The robot operator, for instance, needs a different set of skills than does a blue-collar worker doing tasks comparable to what the robot now undertakes.
Honeywell Systems and Research Center in Minneapolis has been doing research on what is necessary in a monitor and controller, such as dictating the robot's processes and effective communication with robot programmers, maintenance staff, and other such human specialists. Furthermore, maintenance personnel for robots have to acquire new electrical and mechanical skills. Thus, a principal management challenge is massive re-

education of employees. This can only be accomplished through collaboration with universities, government, and robot manufacturers.

The application of robots will take place in both the private and public sectors. For example, robots will be very important in the United States Postal and Weather Services. And, in the military there will be a growing demand for the speed, precision, and cost effectiveness of robots, and new defense contractors are likely to rise to the challenge of this expanding market. Research at the Strategies Studies Institute of the Army War College indicates that many of the routine and dangerous jobs of soldiers can be taken over by robots. The army's Future/Long Range Planning Group at the Strategies Studies Institute has prepared a report on the military use of robotics and artificial intelligence (Crumley, 1982). Some of the future battlefield activities envisioned for this technology include identifying aircraft, controlling air traffic, and transmitting deceptive noises to confuse the enemy; identifying and tracking targets and selecting from among them the high priority ones; handling materials contaminated by accident or by war circumstances; loading weapons, setting fuses, and transfering ammunition from storage areas to weapons; digging ditches, making craters, or building obstacles; and detecting or laying mines on land or under the sea.

One's imagination could conceive other prospects for saving human lives while defending the country—perhaps even having robots do the fighting instead of people. The army report also indicates that the near-term application of robots with artificial intelligence might include conducting physical examinations and aptitude testing, issuing uniforms and equipment, and numerous administrative duties. Undoubtedly, these forecasters are correct when they envision something like the "Manhattan Project," which developed the atom bomb in World War II. Something comparable involving all branches of the military in cooperation with the scientific and engineering communities will be necessary to make AI applications feasible.

Management, in any event, should introduce robotic technology in stages: (1) undertaking unpleasant, unsafe, or uninteresting tasks avoided by humans; (2) supplementing or enhancing tasks that humans are still required to do or oversee; and (3) expanding to totally new applications giving the robot tasks other than those for which it originally was designed. Let us examine three work situations that illustrate these in terms of developmental stages.

Stage One: Arc Welding. Hot, dirty, and unpleasant for humans, this task requires heavy, protective clothing to cope with flying sparks and choking smoke. Human welders cannot keep a torch on the work for more than 30 percent of the time they are working. Robots can focus the torch on the work 90 percent of the time and turn out three times as much work. The productivity gain is realized through repeating the same welding tasks many times without reprogramming. Although today's robots need human assistance to help in work set-up, they probably will become intelligent enough to assemble and set their own work. Eventually, they will be able to analyze a job, know where the welds should go, and work from plans stored in their memories without supervision.

Stage Two: Commercial Jet Flying. Boeing's 757 and 767 airliners are so automated that pilots need not intervene from brake release through landing rollout. The new jets are able to accelerate to speed, rotate, take off, climb, cruise to predetermined locations, approach, land, and stop—all without human intervention. However, the Federal Aviation Administration (FAA) limits their automatic use currently to fifteen feet above the runway on landing, at which point the pilots must intervene. This is the closest thing we know to a truly automated system working in an unpredictable, uncontrolled environment, but even then the human pilot is retained.

Stage Three: Self-Regulating Robots. By the turn of this century, we are likely to have robots that can take care of themselves; that is, they will be able to design, manufacture, market, install, program, and repair themselves and other robots. With artificial intelligence enhanced, it is difficult to predict how these super robots will change the world of work and their relations with us.

Managers concerned with planning for the transition to

Realizing the Potential of Robotics 185

the robotic economy should be cognizant of the difficulties that may be encountered and the problems that will have to be solved. In the next section, we will deal with some of the sociological issues. But there are also larger economic and technical matters that will require innovative management. Converting industrial-age plants to automated and robotic systems may take a quarter century or more, will be quite costly, and will involve a transitional human work force engaged in ad hoc roles that eventually will disappear. The real problems will be in industries that delay or postpone adoption of the new technology, for as they fall behind in productivity, they are likely to have the biggest lay-offs. Those that gradually introduce the new systems into their operations are more likely to seek intelligent ways to retrain their employees for the changed circumstances.

Currently, economic considerations sometimes delimit the shift from human to robot. General purpose robots today often are too slow and expensive for adoption in mass-production assembly tasks. But they can compete in small or batch assembly. Software costs are another inhibitor until techniques for more structured programming and high-level language are refined.

Technically, robots have many limitations, especially when the tasks are complex, unstructured, and subject to unexpected happenings—things that humans can cope with more effectively. Until we have sufficient experience with robot applications and research progress, we can look forward only to the next generation of robots, which may be more dexterous, graceful, mobile, and intelligent. For example, TRW is working on such prototypes with its new R202 model. Their intrapreneurial engineers face many hurdles as they try to develop an adaptive, autonomous robot. There is a variety of challenges that will temper the changeover to the new technology.

As Albus reminded us, people have to be convinced that robots are going to bring more benefits than problems; for instance, they need to be shown the alternative income-producing occupations that will emerge with the conversion to robotics and other automated systems. But will we have the workers ready for the new positions in computer-integrated manufacturing, machine maintenance systems, and robotic manufacturing—the high-growth industries of the future?

Robots and People

Probably the effects of "robo-shock" will be greatest on the 3.8 million United States workers that may be displaced or dislocated by sophisticated robots. Thus, the fear of robots and their impact on us may be the biggest deterrent to their adoption. Public perception or misperception about the social implications of robots also may facilitate or retard the advance of robot technology. Here is an arena in which thinking managers can again exercise real leadership. Labor groups, threatened by the implications of new technology, are already mobilizing their spokespersons. Harley Shaiken, a manufacturing consultant with the United Auto Workers, articulated their position: "By designing a production process that minimizes human participation, you freeze out the worker's control, and we often overlook the impact of robots on the jobs that remain.... When the worker is slotted between two centrally controlled robots that dictate the pace, he becomes a mere cog in a machine. These things matter" (Condon, 1983, p. 17).

Psychological Implications. Integrating robots smoothly into the work force without unduly upsetting the human employees is not always possible in the real world. We already are hearing a new term—*technostress*—to describe a condition resulting from an individual's inability to adapt to the introduction of new technology. The possibilities for managing the ailment seem to be dependent on the age of the worker, his or her past experience with technology, his or her perceived control over new tasks, and the organizational climate (Brod, 1983). The last two factors are items managers can deal with to some degree. As with the previously mentioned cyberphobia or computerphobia, the resistance to the technology can be lessened, the anxiety and hostility reduced. However, business planners have not given sufficient attention to (a) behavioral science strategies for planning change, especially with technology; and (b) the psychological factors relating to transitional experiences,

Realizing the Potential of Robotics 187

such as altering the work culture with computers and robots. Work behavior is directly related to the processes of perception and judgment, and managers need to be more cognizant of how to influence such positively.

Let us examine two more "mini" cases relative to the worker's psychological reaction to robots—the first is a white-collar situation, the second in a blue-collar context.

1. *The Office.* Citicorp has thirty-six robot mail carriers on its work force. These devices look like filing cabinets on wheels. They page elevators to move from floor to floor, follow a track underneath each floor, and announce their arrival at each department they service. However, the robot-human connection went awry at this major New York banking institution: The mail machines unwittingly undermined one of the major organizational values of the human mailpersons who formerly had covered the pickup circuits in one and a half hours. There was no longer the cheery interface among the humans or the gossip and corporate communications provided firsthand when the mailperson made the rounds. Then the schedule had been a bit more casual and it had been possible to make private arrangements for favors and the transfer of special messages. Now the electronic carts conditioned people to set up a new internal clock. The change in routine has been described by one worker: "After nine and a half minutes, you began to steel yourself for it—the incessant warning beeps and the heavy rattling. We frequently considered getting a can of spray paint to lay down an enticing new trail for the robo-cart to follow that would lead directly down the stairwell" (Stein, 1983, pp. 51, 90).

Much has been written about designing computer systems that are user friendly, and the same may be said about robotic systems. The field of human engineering, especially ergonomics, is trying to design such machines so that they are not only more friendly and satisfying to people but also more safe and compatible.

One other costly element was overlooked in the management decision by Citicorp in favor of mail machines—clerical help assigned to the mail deliveries had used this as a learning experience in understanding how the organization functioned.

Now, the bank is finding it quite expensive to give new clerks the knowledge they previously had picked up on the mail routes.

2. *The Plant.* Our next case was obtained from the studies of three Carnegie-Mellon University professors (Argote, Goodman, and Schkade, 1983). It is one of the few investigations that have been completed on how robots affect both the worker and the organization. The research took place at a manufacturing plant engaged in the forging and machining of metal alloys. A nonunion work force of 1,000 was fairly stable, and labor-management relations appeared good. The company used various strategies to gain employee acceptance of the introduction of robots in one department, and it took a year to ready workers for the change. The target group of 40 employees worked in three shifts using grinding and milling machines on tasks that were primarily sequential.

The robot was placed at the beginning of the work flow, loading and unloading milling machines. The investigators interviewed workers about their attitudes regarding the robot before it actually was introduced and then again two and a half months after the change. Initially, the subjects reported that the robot would increase productivity and quality, reduce costs, make jobs easier and less boring, and increase skill requirements. However, after some experience with the robot, worker attitudes became more complex and somewhat more pessimistic: 87 percent of them felt that while robotics will make the United States more competitive, it also will require more job retraining; half of the interviewees realized that it would displace workers. Although these workers still had positive attitudes toward the robots, they had become more realistic. They were more concerned about having to compete with the robots, about the possibility of accidents, lowered quality of work, and alterations in their jobs as now performed (more activities, more watching, more programming). It was also evident that, at least in this beginning stage, personnel were experiencing more stress and pressure from the new tasks and responsibilities, more isolation, and less communication with fellow workers. But there were advantages as well—the robot operators were gaining new recognition, heavy and fatiguing work was being eliminated, more interactions were taking place with support personnel from engineering and maintenance. The study also confirmed that some jobs would be eliminated and others would have to be upgraded in classification, but there was no evidence of planned change in the pay system.

What insights do these previous cases offer to managers faced with the prospect of introducing robots into their work environment in the new future? Here is a summary:

• Weigh carefully the management decision regarding robots—will this particular robot plan have more advantages than disadvantages?

• Seek to develop a user friendly attitude toward the robot: Involve workers in the planning process, let them have contests to name the mechanical device, conduct initiation parties for the new robot, emphasize its positive applications, inform employees' families about the development.

• Communicate openly and effectively about the anticipated changes well before actual introduction. Resolve beforehand concerns about job security and pay. Provide demonstrations of the machine and its potential. Establish feedback mechanisms for worker reactions to information received. Focus first on informing supervisors about the program and winning their support, then encourage supervisors to hold regular discussions with workers on the subject. Prepare personnel for changed patterns in social interaction as a result of robots.

• Anticipate problems that might arise and prepare coping strategies. Plan for new job activities and rotation. Attempt to maximize the fit between new job characteristics and personal characteristics of current workers. Involve the support specialists early in the planning and implementation phases.

• Train personnel in advance and thoroughly, not only in the technical aspect of robot operations but also for the new work culture that will evolve—this also implies having back-up operators and maintenance people prepared for any eventualities that might occur. Have a continuing HRD program in robotics for all stages of its implementation.

• Stagger the implementation of robotic technology—begin with a pilot project, evaluate the results, and apply the learnings to the next phase. Include workers from departments adjacent to the target group in the training process. Lastly, institutionalize the whole procedure for robot introduction so that it becomes a regular part of the new organizational culture.

The Human Factor. Robots affect people, and seemingly people affect robots. Isaac Asimov (Koehn, 1983, p. 7) proposed three laws of robotics: (1) A robot may not injure a human being, or through inaction, allow a human being to come to harm. (2) A robot must obey the order given it by human beings except where it would conflict with the first law. (3) A robot must protect its own existence as long as such protection does not conflict with the first and second laws. Although Asimov wrote these laws for a futuristic handbook of robotics for 2058 A.D., we must start thinking about such guidelines before our present primitive robots get artificial intelligence.

There have been strange reports, as well, about the impact of humans on robot performance. Robotics expert Joseph Engelberger (1980) tells one such story about a sick robot named Clyde that worked in an auto plant. It seems that poor Clyde had something akin to a nervous breakdown, pulled in its arm, and refused to move, despite efforts by mechanical specialists to diagnose the problem. Clyde's fellow workers decided that their mechanical friend needed cheering, so they organized a party, heaping flowers and get well cards on the dormant frame, and before long Clyde recovered.

IBM's David Grossman thinks robots can appear egocentric, even hypochondriacal, in monitoring the state of their own health. He has noted the similarities between diagnosis of robot problems and medical diagnosis. IBM's robot model 7565 monitors its own entire robotic system every 20 milliseconds, shuts off if this self-examination uncovers anything abnormal, and logs the problems. Grossman remembers a test robot that kept turning itself off for no discernible reason until the engineers discovered that it was responding to a trivial problem—a clogged hydraulic filter that someone had forgotten to replace but that caused static electricity to build up a charge, which shut off the machine's computer (Stein, 1983, p. 90).

Barry Brownstein of Battelle Memorial Institute confirms that some robot problems are like human ills. Thus, Battelle is designing robot-to-human communication systems so that remote robots can report back from far places—such as space, undersea, or a nuclear plant. The humans back home then can compensate for problems met by the robots. Battelle also is designing robots that can repair themselves or that have compensation components for breakdowns. Instead of creating a superclass of robot doctors, the designers hope to produce robots that relatively unskilled people can care for and maintain (Stein, 1983, p. 90).

Education and Training. Obviously, a mythology about robots has built up in popular literature over the centuries: Either we endow robots with human-like qualities or we view them as a threat, taking over in our place. It is the job of management to counteract the fantasy through education and training and to emphasize the possibilities that robots offer to liberate humans and develop our potential. The learning programs should focus on attitude and technology.

At our present state of robotics, training is most often available through vendor companies. These training opportunities range from fully equipped learning centers to which employees are sent to consultation and learning packages at the work site. As an example, IBM has a Robotics Assembly Institute that provides customers with three weeks of hands-on training in basic and advanced robotic concepts and applications. Sometimes, the vendor will send a consultant or project team on-site to assist a client's programmers, technicians, and maintenance personnel, as well as to provide management training upon request. Although vendor training can be customized, it is not always of high quality, since suppliers tend to be more sales oriented than concerned about an existing client's needs. Sometimes a company's internal HRD staff can be instructed to conduct the robotic training. Unimation's director of technical training, Pat Rosato, advises viewing each installation individually and tailors the training to suit. Westinghouse is reputed to have the most elaborate and extensive program in employee robotic education. It used videotapes to win over union officials to robotic conversion, and it even flew some of them with senior management to Japan to view robots at work there.

Some corporations, such as General Electric, are so committed to automated technology that they have established their own education centers to provide instruction to their employees. General Electric's Learning and Communication Center is a $6 million facility with fully equipped classrooms and high-technology laboratories for training in machine tool control and system applications, diesel engine maintenance, rotating electrical machinery, and locomotive maintenance. Other firms are beginning to take advantage of new educational technologies that offer media packages for skill development of personnel in various new technologies. A multinational company, for instance, will be able to instruct paratechnicians in robotics via satellite anywhere in the world in which their operations are located. Through such means, the best experts in any new field can be brought in person to learners or by film, videotape, or computer-assisted instruction.

The Society of Manufacturing Engineers publishes an annual *Directory of Robotic Education and Training Institutions.* It lists 8 universities with four-year degree programs in robotics and 173 schools that offer courses on the subject. Of these, Carnegie-Mellon, Duke, and Lehigh Universities are the only ones with both undergraduate and graduate programs. M.I.T. and Rensselaer Polytechnic are also among the leading institutions of higher education in robotics, but there are also technical schools that may offer assistance to management, such as Worcester Polytechnic Institute and Piedmont Technical College. Industry support for robotic learning is also available through some community colleges, such as Macomb Community College, so it is wise to check with local educators.

The collaboration between business and educational systems needs to be two-way in educating for new technologies. For example, Baxter Technologies Corporation of Canada, a major machine tool manufacturer, is assisting schools with computer-aided manufacturing (CAM) equipment. In order for schools to provide the next generation of technicians or to assist industry in retraining the current work force, schools and colleges need the latest in equipment. Baxter has come out with a low-cost CAM system for training today's students in new technology. Personal computers also will be used to control lathes; one is called "Future Builder" and was designed specifically for vocational schools.

University extensions and professional associations are beginning to offer courses in all facets of the emerging technologies. For example, San Diego State University's Center for Continuing Education has a two-day course in "How to Use Robots in Manufacturing," while the Technology Transfer Society of Torrance, California, offers an intensive, two-day seminar on "Robotics and Artificial Intelligence." Some engineering societies are offering to members teleconferencing courses for updating in the merging technologies. IEEE Educational Activities Board (345 E. 47th Street, New York, N.Y. 10017) provides, among its programs, a self-learning one in "Hero 1," which teaches the principles of robot technology. But more than just private sector support is needed; government at all levels, as well as trade and professional associations, must join in synergistic efforts with business and academia to prepare qualified people for the new work reality.

In examining the robot-people connection, it might be wise to consider the developing market in household or personal robots. Although the mass market for manufacturing is five to ten years away, seven companies are now building personal robots or parts, and these devices are priced between $1,200 and $8,000. With exotic names like Hero, Jenus, or Comros, they usually are mobile, have sensor systems, can lift objects, sometimes can speak or respond to verbal commands, and contain a built-in microcomputer. Nolan Bushnell, founder of Atari and now chairman of Androbot, Inc., is producing for retail stores two creations, B.O.B. and Typo. The cost of these personal robots ranges from a few hundred to thousands of dollars. If the growth of the personal computer market is any indicator, personal robots also may have a bright future with consumers.

Just as computer networks have been formed by people as a positive coping mechanism to deal with the intricacies of the new technology, the same can be done among those at home or work who are involved with robots. The human exchange of information, insight, and intuition about robots and other such technology can be both helpful and fun, counteracting some of the trauma of the transition to the high-tech way of life.

The word that best expresses the ideal interface between humans and the new machines is *symbiosis*. For many years, for example, there has been an ongoing debate within NASA and the aerospace community on the issue of manned versus unmanned missions in space. Addressing this argument of man or machine during a presentation at the California Space Institute, William Haynes, Manager of Crew Systems for the Aerojet Corporation, ended his lecture with this pithy observation: "Not man or machine, but man *and* machine. We see this happening all around us. Until recently, our human/machine interactions have been at arm's length. What we are beginning to see are true symbiotic relationships, where man and machine operate as a closely coupled system augmenting each other's strengths, correcting each other's weaknesses. In perfecting our machines, we are learning more about the machines and a great deal more about man. It's exciting, it's fun, and there is more than enough for all of us. . . ."

Future of Robotics and Manufacturing

Joseph Engelberger (1980), president of Unimation, Inc., argued eloquently in his writings for pressing ahead with robotic developments for both financial and humanitarian reasons. He maintained that every job that is debilitating to human beings should be turned over to these nonhuman slaves. Further, Engelberger projected ahead fifty years and predicted that the pain of the present dislocation will be compensated for in the future, when robots and other automated devices enable us to have a three-day work week, clean air and water, and a desirable metaindustrial life.

Virginia Coates, vice-president of J. F. Coates, Inc., a Washington futures research group, suggested that we consider the transition to the robotic economy in terms of the Technology Diffusion Model developed by her husband, Joseph (Coates, 1983, p. 28). In the first wave of technology diffusion, the Coateses believe, the impacts come from substitution—the user substitutes a new technology for older systems because it can fulfill functions more efficiently or effectively. The second wave is described as accommodation—industries make internal changes to make better use of the technology. The third wave is *innovation*—new uses for the technology are discovered. In the future, when we reach the third stage of robotic technology in the twenty-first century, robots will be doing activities that are now only faintly perceived—on the earth and under it, under the oceans, lakes, and rivers, and especially in space, exploring the far corners of our universe. These future robots will have sophisticated artificial intelligence and be designed in unfamiliar shapes and sizes. They will protect the environment, engage in hazardous missions, serve the global market of human needs, and help limit the consequences of human fallibility and error.

Arthur Hawkins, director of futures research at the University of Minnesota, alerts us to the prospect that when we create perfect artificial intelligence toward the turn of the century, it will become increasingly difficult to distinguish robots from humans, either physically or in terms of capabilities. Hawkins muses that robots as surrogate human beings could have their metal, fiber, or carbon filament covered by artificial skin with the warmth and texture of the real stuff ("Factories: Flexibility Is the Future," 1983).

The factory of the future could have robots operating around the clock, seven days a week, year in and year out. Whether on this planet or in the high frontier, such a system would require minimal supervision and have tremendous implications for both the economy and defense, as well as for developing countries. Raj Reddy, director of Carnegie-Mellon's Robotics Institute, believes that within ten years there will be factories using thinking robots that will sense changes in a production process when they occur and automatically make adjustments. Within twenty years, he estimates that people will own robots in their homes; they will be able to simply tell a machine to do a chore, and the robot will figure out a way to do it, no questions asked ("Factories: Flexibility Is the Future, 1983). Research is already underway to turn these visions of the future into near-term realities:

- In Boca Raton, Florida, at its GSD plant, IBM has "Project White Cloud" underway to do this for industrial robots.
- In Japan at Waseda University, Professor Ichiro Kato is now developing medical robots capable of tactile detection, such as of breast cancer; each has twenty-five "fingers" that relay its findings to a computer system that detects the cancerous growth and other abnormalities.
- In Sweden, ASEA has a new partner in Electrolux and expects to become the dominant industrial robot supplier of Europe. The merger matches ASEA robots with Electrolux's pneumatically powered machines for high-tolerance inspections and improved arc welding. Now ASEA has opened a robot center in Detroit, Michigan, that brings together sales, service, and research staff close to the American auto industry, its biggest market—this after ASEA captured an $8 million order for 105 robots from West German automakers BMW and Daimler-Benz.
- In Fremont, California, Apple Computers has a new $20 million automated factory that can produce one MacIntosh computer with 450 parts every 27 seconds, or 500,000 a year—all this with only 300 workers, automatic conveyor belts, and robots attached to circuit boards.
- In Richmond, Virginia, AT&T Technologies has a frontier-breaching printed-circuit board plant from which computers receive complex instructions from a dozen Bell Laboratories design centers around the country.
- In Japan, Pioneer Electronics Corporation now uses about 100 robots, which have cut the cost of installing electronic parts in circuit boards by 75 percent.
- In Houston, Texas, NASA's Planetary Materials Laboratory examines solid samples from other worlds. The robot landers and rovers, such as Surveyor, Viking, and Lunokhods, carry out experiments and transmit their findings; the next step will be the return of solid samples to Earth for analysis. In the case of the moon, Americans brought back lunar materials, but the Russians accomplished this feat with three robot spacecraft.

In the near future, the United States also will have spacecraft that go to the target planet and dig up and secure samples while another robot spacecraft automatically brings the materials back here.

Thinking managers are aware that new technologies are reshaping society and its institutions. Nowhere is this more evident than in the manufacturing process. The technical revolution going on in factories has profound implications for all management, for it is restructuring the role of the manager. Figure 8 illustrates integrative manufacturing systems, with their automated and computer-based technology, including robotics. The focus of the factory of the future seems to be on flexible systems of production. The tasks to be accomplished are both complex and changeable, not simple or routine as in the industrial stage of development. Frequently, they are undertaken to meet customer need for customized goods and parts, and the tasks are very interdependent. Products and processes are often altered and adapted; ultrastability is the norm. The work requires high-level skills, because problems and opportunities often cannot be anticipated. The quality of the work is often more important than the quantity, and meeting exacting standards requires cooperation among all the people involved—designers, producers, and marketing and sales personnel together seek to serve the customer. Flexible manufacturing systems (FMS) are transforming the economics of production. But for FMS to function effectively and be well coordinated, it must be computer based. The key to its increasing productivity is research and development in CAD/CAM. This involves advancing our metaindustrial capabilities in both artificial intelligence (AI) and robotics.

AI requires the fifth generation of computers that will come into being before the end of this century (Feigenbaum and McCorduck, 1983). Previous generations of computer technology were centered around vacuum tubes, transistors, computer chips, and very large scale integrated circuits (VLSIC). Japanese and American researchers are struggling with the next generation of VLSI chips that will enable users to process many operations simultaneously with vastly increased speed and pow-

Figure 8. Integrated Manufacturing Systems.

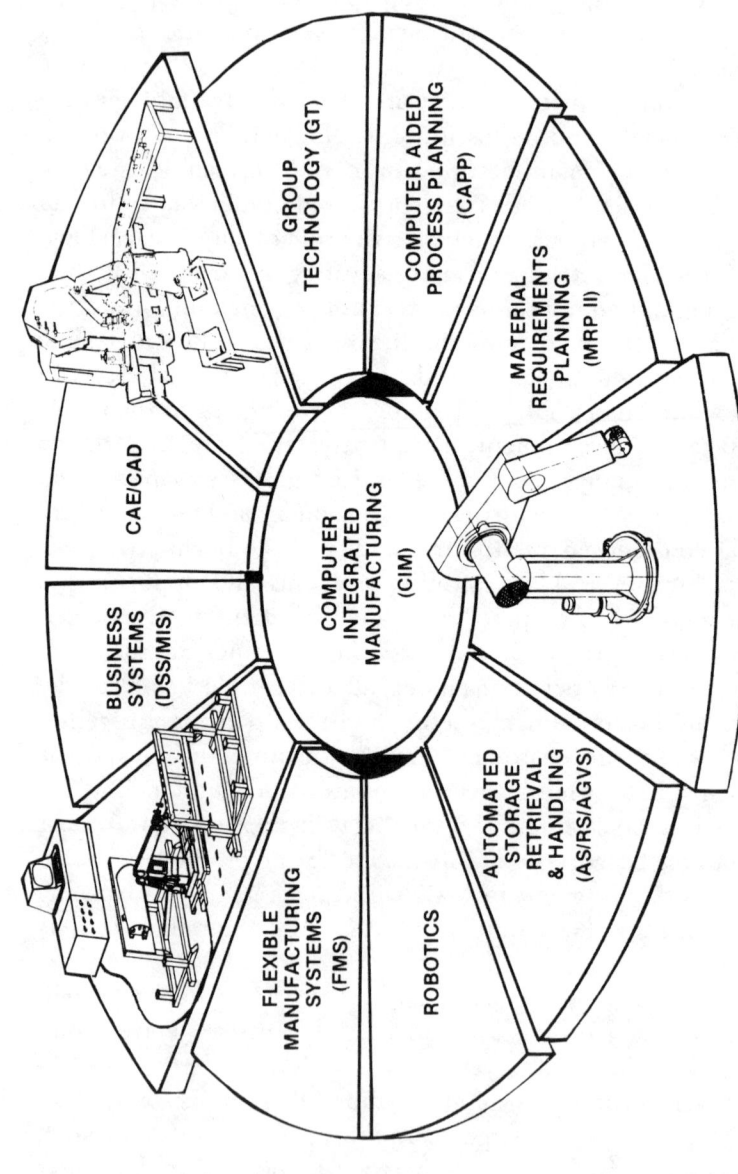

Note: CAE = Computer-Assisted Engineering; CAD = Computer-Aided or -Assisted Design.

Source: Technological Marketing Society, 3420 Kashiwa Street, Torrance, California 90510. Reprinted with permission.

er. The Defense Advanced Systems Research Projects Agency planned to spend $50 million in 1984 and $95 million in 1985 on this advanced computer technology. Industrial giants such as IBM, Hewlett-Packard, Texas Instruments, Control Data, MCC, Schlumbergers, Ltd., and Xerox, as well as smaller research corporations, have ongoing major AI research efforts. Academic researchers at M.I.T., Carnegie-Mellon, Yale, Stanford, the University of Texas, and the University of California at Los Angeles (UCLA) are in the mainstream of this research on artificial intelligence.

Over the years, AI research has progressed to the point of mimicking human intelligence and expertise in complex ways, such as assembly line scheduling, guidance of advanced missile systems, and computer designing. The aim is to devise machines that do more than compute and store information—they can see, touch, smell, recognize spoken commands, and even speak languages. These are thinking machines that use intelligent tools to duplicate the human brain's capacities; they can analyze problems, make judgments, and even acquire emotions. But the 1,000 or so scientists engaged in this research are running into many problems, such as trying to teach computers our common sense, perceptual abilities, language nuances, and even our capacity to forget nonessential information so as to avoid overload.

The applied side of AI is called expert systems—the development of computer programs that result from combining textbook knowledge with the experience of top-performing practitioners and then applying this body of knowledge to solve problems. This experience includes the "tricks of the trade," the "rules of thumb," and other insights professionals gain in the long course of doing something well. Using a knowledge engineering procedure, researchers interview reputable authorities in a field and gradually build an expert data system that reflects both the formal and the informal learning on the subject. Such systems already have been developed for patient diagnosis and treatment, decision support applications, diagnosis of oil drill bit problems, naval task force threat analysis, and geological explorations. Others are underway for "missionized robotics";

software specification, production, and verification; tactical air targeting; analyzing structural defects in buildings and bridges; and tracking movements of toxic waste. Essentially, these experts are computer advisers that provide high-level information at low cost. Expert systems preserve civilization's critical know-how.

But it is in the flexible manufacturing system that a convergence takes place between automation and computer-directed materials handling. With the enhancement of robotics and artificial intelligence, the factories of the future are beginning to emerge. The Boston Consulting Group uses a football analogy to try and help management appreciate the significance of the change. They liken it to the introduction of the forward pass in football, which changed both offensive and defensive strategy. As a result, selection, preparation, and training of coaches and teams had to be radically altered. Similarly, flexible manufacturing systems by means of new technologies is a whole new ball game that will fundamentally transform production and the work environment. In fact, once these new thinking machines move beyond the laboratory into the work place, civilization will be as changed as when the printing press was invented five hundred years ago!

To get a better sense of tomorrow, enter UCLA and head for the School of Engineering and Applied Science. There, the staff in the Department of Manufacturing Engineering is doing research to advance smart CAD systems that will lay the groundwork for improved future automated factories. The UCLA laboratories in robotics and AI will seek to integrate these two fields to enhance dynamic production scheduling and tool management. As their director, Michael Melkanoff, noted: "The idea behind the FMS approach is to develop a system that can adjust itself with as few as possible manual steps in the production of various-sized lots of different types of parts. . . . Our goal is to develop a dynamic system that can change from minute to minute as manufacturing requirements change" (Melkanoff, 1984, p. 80). Through these computer-assisted techniques, designers of automated manufacturing will be able to standardize parts and operations while minimizing the number and size of tools. Such computer programs monitor the manufacturing process.

Algorithms, some expert systems, and computer graphic simulations are used to increase robotic capabilities. The result will be advanced robots with high-level language that integrate mechanical and electrical subsystems. The eventual pay-off will be to the consumer, who will be able to order and afford a product that is customized and stylized to that person or company's unique needs or personality.

Universities, such as Carnegie-Mellon, have begun to introduce courses in manufacturing management and the new technologies into their curricula. Thus, it is no wonder that IBM's president, John Opel, observed: "There can be no factories of the future unless there are universities of the future educating those people now" ("Manufacturing is in Flower," 1984, p. 51). Despite the transition to an information and service economy, we would be wise to heed the counsel of Hewlett-Packard's president, John Young, that manufacturing is the base that creates many of those services.

If today's managers are to transcend their industrial age conditioning and adapt to the relevant use of computers and robots in administration, production, and the professions, they will have to make monumental adjustments. The scope of the transformation can be readily seen in flexible manufacturing systems: Not only do they eliminate scores of craft specialists, but the traditional foreman is replaced by a systems operator. Furthermore, FMS demands more intimate communication and cooperation among corporate units, blurring traditional functional distinctions and lines of authority. It also is dependent on "teamwork" among computers—they must be able to "talk" to one another. Management at General Motors, for instance, had to solve the problem of such incompatibility among computer manufacturers' equipment by setting standards in this regard for the 40,000 intelligent devices it already has on its production lines. General Motors' manufacturing automation protocol (MAP) may set the norm both for its own automobile industry and for the computer industry. The issue demonstrates the uncharted management waters that transitional executives must sail and why management must familiarize itself with the intricacies of automation and robotics.

But the automated factory that is emerging with more

sophisticated robots that benefit from artificial intelligence may not be the ultimate invention. At IBM, David Grossman further boggles a manager's mind because he thinks that molecular biologists can find ways of manipulating genes and thus make biological machines that can do the same thing as computers that control robots!

These times of transition allow for no complacency. *The Economist* ("Japan Invents Robots...," 1984) reported that Japan's 250 or so robot makers are already struggling to give birth to a new generation of robots. These "third-generation" robots will be aware of their environment and able to react to it instead of merely repeating a series of predictable motions. That country's Ministry of International Trade is spending $100 million over the remainder of this decade on this research for robots that will be able to learn or adapt programs while operating. The aim is to have the third-generation robots ready by 1990 for linkage to the fifth-generation computers, which are expected to be available around the same time. Meanwhile, we will have to be content with researchers' efforts to perfect the seeing, touching, and walking abilities of the 40,000 second-generation robots the world is currently using.

Thinking managers realize that the use of automation, whether in terms of computers or robots, can no longer be ignored in government or business. Rather, these new technologies must become an integral part of strategic management, and managers need to learn now about their present and potential applications.

SEVEN

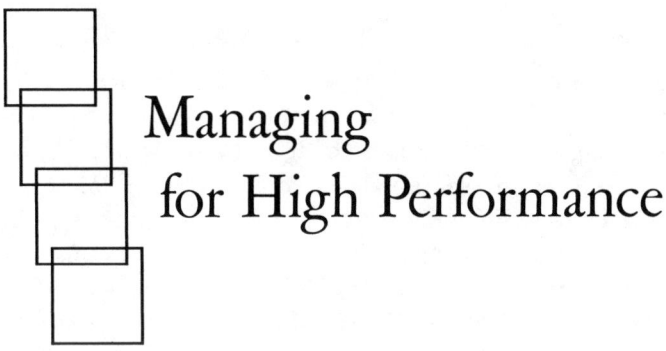

Managing for High Performance

Executive Summary. To maximize worker performance, meta-industrial management not only seeks to obtain and retain very competent personnel, but it also establishes a link between on-the-job activity and compensation. Furthermore, mutual goal setting with employees relates such to specific performance targets. Managing for greater productivity in the fast lane requires positive reinforcement and constructive feedback, as well as innovative experimentation with job schedules, roles, and functions. A creative corporate environment stimulates people to energize themselves, especially if their work is meaningful, allows for self-development and career advancement, and offers recognition and rewards.

When the corporate culture supports metaperformance, the focus is on actions and the results personnel achieve. To obtain and sustain peak performance, companies provide for learning in the new information technologies, project/team management, and meeting/time management. Human performance can be further enhanced by high-performance interviews, making work fun, stimulating innovative activities, seeking cultural match, fostering participative management, encouraging the competence norm, enriching compensation, and improving organizational communications. In addition, performance and productivity can be improved and costs contained through the development of a flexible and diversified work force.

Strategies for Performance Improvement

- Some Blue Shield offices are offering productivity incentives to video display terminal workers and are using computer monitoring for work measurement and assessment.
- Workers at International Harvester's plant in Melrose, Illinois, voted overwhelmingly to approve a plan that links wages with productivity. The incentive plan gives bonuses if workers increase productivity above a plant performance index. The United Auto Workers unionists also agreed to pay cuts if productivity drops.
- Pitney Bowes Corporation of Stamford, Connecticut, has been using the classic "suggestion box" successfully since 1943 to save money and improve performance. Employee suggestions implemented during the past five years alone saved more than $2 million while enriching personnel with an added $400,000—awards can reach a maximum of $30,000 per person.
- Diamond International in Palmer, Massachusetts, improved management and labor relations through a performance incentive plan called the 100 Club. Productivity went up 16.5 percent and error rate down 40 percent while decreasing grievances 72 percent and accident lost-time to 43.7 percent. The formula is simple—employees are allocated points in recognition of above-average performance, perfect attendance, or working a year without industrial accidents and the like. The earned points can be converted into modest prizes. The real value is in recognition of excellent effort and a visible sign of company appreciation.
- Honeywell, Inc., took a national survey of secretaries and managers: 40 percent of the bosses responded that they felt their secretaries were too busy. But the secretaries indicated that they wanted more responsibility—75 percent said that they were not too busy to take on extra chores, while 40 percent said their supervisors saw no need to delegate more work to them.

- Drake Beam Morin of New York City surveyed 1,300 top manufacturing and service companies. They discovered that 88 percent of lay-offs were based on seniority, not on performance, and that only 44 percent of them took into consideration federal legislation regarding formally documented and legally sound measurements of work behavior.

Management does not in itself connote leadership. In the four opening critical incidents, management was demonstrating innovative leadership in order to encourage high performance, while in the latter two cases management seemed to be operating on obsolete principles. Numerous research studies are confirming that under more traditional management approaches there seems to be a commitment gap—workers admitting that they are not doing their best but becoming willing to achieve more when performance is tied to pay, bonus, and other incentives, either financial or psychological. A recent best seller, *The One Minute Manager* (Blanchard and Johnson, 1983), also proposed three other pragmatic ways of turning "payroll sitters" into job doers: (1) goal setting in which workers and managers together set job goals that are short enough to be read in one minute; (2) reinforcing workers as they seek to achieve such goals with management support, particularly through short verbal praisings when tasks are accomplished; (3) redirecting workers who do things incorrectly through such means as timely and brief reprimands or constructive feedback.

The work culture now emerging has two characteristics that affect productivity and profitability: emphasis on worker competence and high performance as organizational norms. In the disappearing industrial work culture, government regulations, union interference, and management sloppiness often contributed to declining work standards. In contrast, entrepreneurial enterprises, particularly in the high-tech fields, are seeking enthusiastic, top-performing knowledge workers. Increasingly, setting high standards encourages many employees to stretch beyond their current efforts and achieve greater potential. This often can be accomplished by giving personnel more responsibility and flexibility.

Established organizations also have been searching for

ways to revitalize their businesses and services, such as through improved job designs and practices. Research by the Work in America Institute confirms that, both in the public and the private sectors, workers are being offered more options that enable them to concentrate their job time more intensively and productively. Toward such ends, innovative managers are experimenting with flex-time and part-time alternatives, job and work sharing, even by spouses, and lateral transfers and sabbatical leaves in both corporations and government.

Real leaders have always sought ways to motivate their people and to increase productivity. Therefore, contemporary thinking managers attempt to provide a creative corporate environment that stimulates employees to energize themselves. Among metaindustrial workers, a new pattern of motivators seems to be emerging, particularly among those in start-up, fast-growth, high-tech situations. For example, when I surveyed colleagues at EAN-TECH, Inc., in Mountain View, California, the top principal motivators were spread down the hierarchy of human needs:*

1. the chance for self-development and improvement;
2. the opportunity to do challenging and meaningful work (1 and 2 might be classified as self-actualizing needs);
3. the means for promotion and advancement;
4. the feeling that my job is important (3 and 4 might be considered ego needs for recognition/reward);
5. the receiving of appreciation feedback when work is well performed;
6. the means for knowing what is going on in the organization (5 and 6 might be characterized as inclusion or belonging needs);
7. the existence of clear organizational objectives, so that "I know where I stand"; and
8. the compensation of good pay (7 and 8 are considered security needs).

*Based on the research and paradigm of the late humanistic psychologist, Abraham Maslow.

Incidentally, the last-mentioned motivators received the highest rankings; none chose needs at the physiological or survival level. Readers are challenged to do motivational data gathering with their own personnel, especially with those considered to be high achievers. (In addition to the data-gathering instruments in the appendixes at the end of this volume, the leadership motivation inventory is available through Management Research Systems, P.O. Box 1585, Ponte Vedra Beach, Fla. 32082.)

In the new work culture, the role and performance of first line management—from supervisors to project managers—becomes more critical. Jack Phillips (1985) suggests that those who directly oversee the work of other employees can make the difference in the success or failure of an organization. To ensure high performance for persons in such roles, he proposes a systematic HRD approach that extends from selection of the most qualified candidates to a program for their professional improvement.

High-performing companies are learning ways to maintain productive behavior in their work force: (1) Adopt a consensus and reinforce a few key objectives and policies—keep it simple. (2) Reduce the levels of management and size of the business activity—keep it lean. (3) Focus on employee actions, rather than attitudes, that improve or impair performance, such as care for details versus careless work habits—be specific. (4) Reinforce the positive job behavior on a continuing basis and help subordinates become winners—give immediate feedback and encourage the setting of achievable goals or quotas. (5) Recognize and reward directly those who perform well—provide specific incentives. (6) Capitalize on employee differences instead of seeking conformity—use a team approach to optimize individual contributions. (7) Create a corporate culture that sustains high performance, innovation, and flexibility while avoiding an overconcern for authority, deference, status, and moving up. Such a creative environment avoids adverse behavior controls—fear, threats, and intimidation—while downplaying undue attention to problem employees. It is a constructive approach to discipline (Hess, 1983).

By computerizing the employee evaluation system, it is

possible to identify high and low performers in terms of their positions within a group making up a particular job classification ("Developing a Computer-Assisted Evaluation System," 1983). The CAPE system has been developed and tested successfully for this purpose, and used to determine who gets bonuses, salary increases, promotions, or terminations. Its creators claim that it is fair and legally defensible, and based on a consistent, data-oriented methodology for staff improvement and increasing overall productivity.

Since metaperformance is directly linked to a strong self-concept, it is noteworthy that a California legislator is seeking to establish a state commission on self-esteem. Assemblyman John Vasconcellos introduced a bill in 1984 asserting that most individual behavior is motivated by self-perception and self-image and furthermore that increased self-esteem tends to make people become more achievement oriented, confident, creative, productive, and successful ("How Do You Feel About Yourself?", 1984). These are certainly words of wisdom worthy of management consideration!

A five-year study of top performers has just been completed by a University of Chicago education professor. After interviewing 120 of the nation's leading artists, athletes, and scholars, Benjamin Bloom concluded that drive and determination, not great natural talent, led to their outstanding success. Although they began to express their interest in a field of eventual high achievement early in childhood, it was the continued encouragement of parents and other adults that was a key factor. Bloom's findings indicate that individuals can achieve extraordinary levels of performance given the right moral support and training ("The Key to Success? . . . ," 1985). Thus a work culture and its leadership can influence the exercise of human potential.

High-performing professional or research personnel are not always able to transfer that same capacity into administrative positions. Before promoting an excellent engineer or technician into management, careful assessment might determine whether such a person would be effective in the management of people. Often, experience as project or task force managers, when supported with training, can develop specialists into skillful supervisors. High-performing companies also offer counseling to inadequate managers as to whether they would be more productive and happier back in research or their own specialties. Conversely, interpersonal skill development may possibly turn such persons around.

Harris International (Box 2321, La Jolla, Calif. 92038) found that high-performing personnel also can be effective problem solvers when brought together in small groups for that purpose. Surprisingly, when assembled in a High Performance Management Workshop, some top performers admitted that this was the first time the organization had ever given recognition to their outstanding efforts. Apparently, many managers fail to confirm the high-achieving employees. Via videotapes of their participation in these problem-solving sessions, participants can be used as behavior models for "ordinary" employees. The video feedback to management is most powerful (Harris, 1980, pp. 85-90).

In *Managing for a High Performance,* three professors of management maintained that attainment of individual, group, or corporate performance is dependent on effective planning, organizing, leading, and controlling (Ivancevich, Donnelly, and Gibson, 1983). But it takes more than that. Andrew Grove, president of Intel, a premier high-technology company, thinks in terms of leveraging peak performance through teamwork. In *High Output Management,* Grove (1983) explains that the manager's highest leverage activities are those that affect the work of the greatest number of people or the work of one person over a long period of time. To maximize such leverage, he advocates the following:

• No more than six to eight subordinates should report to a manager.

• Put on well-run meetings where information is exchanged concisely, objectives are set, priorities are determined, and decisions are made.

• Before making decisions, settle what decisions have to be made, when each has to be made, who decides each, who needs to be consulted first, who ratifies or vetos each, and who needs to be informed about each decision.

• When planning, managers should establish projected

needs, determine the current status of production, and project what must be done to produce what the environment will demand.

- Decentralize large operations with mission-oriented hybrid and functional groups for maximum resource utilization.
- Coordinate mission-oriented units with functional groups so resources of the latter are allocated and delivered to the former by means of dual reporting.
- Utilize a management style suitable to the situation, such as Task-Relevant Maturity (TRM), so that the amount of monitoring is relative.
- Communicate task-relevant feedback to subordinates, for performance appraisal is a high-leverage activity—such reviews focus on what skills employees need and how to obtain them as a means of intensifying subordinate motivation.

Grove believes managers should spend most of their time developing the company "stars" because such top performers account for a disproportionately large share of the work accomplished in any organization. After several years of being noted for its innovative work environment, Intel is experiencing defections and high turnover among its most talented personnel. As often happens in high-tech businesses, outstanding managers, engineers, and computer specialists on the fast career track are beginning to leave this leader of the semiconductor industry. But why? Despite Grove's wise counsel cited above, *Business Week* ("Why They're Jumping Ship at Intel," 1983) reports reasons for the defections: (1) strain of the recent recession and business downturn; (2) inappropriate steps to improve performance that undermine "esprit de corps" (management shuffles, longer working hours, pay cuts, and other such disincentives); (3) inadequate people management as the corporation experiences fast growth and hard times in a volatile industry. There has been some question as to whether the matrix management approach can work when such an organization as Intel grows rapidly into a more complex entity.

In any event, even if such problems challenge a leader in the microprocessor field, there are lessons to be learned from its efforts to maintain a high-performing position. Job-hopping among top performers is currently endemic to Silicon Valley, but the phenomenon is spreading. Thus, we should listen again to Andrew Grove when he admits to shifting corporate emphasis to cautious growth, product quality, and more careful management of people, especially by training managers how to better manage their own staffs ("Management: Large-Scale Integration," 1983). When successful start-up enterprises experience rapid growth, the real challenge is to keep the spirit and values of young high-performing companies while quickly bringing in additional competent personnel and management systems.

One such new venture, People Express, has done this by being totally people oriented in its management practice. Its founder and chairman, Donald Burr, keeps costs down and performance up by hiring only customer service managers; regardless of the tasks undertaken, that is the title of 4,000 employees who perform multiple jobs. All personnel are owners with a minimum of 100 shares of corporate stock. Burr's life-style improvement philosophy is: "We want to maximize profits, and we want to do very well at that. But we can find a better way to do it, a way that is more friendly and more conducive to people getting out of life what the hell they're trying to get out of it. You don't just want to make a buck. You want people to become better people.... We've proved that if you give people space, room and freedom, you get trustworthy behavior" ("Donald Burr: The Perfection Imperative," 1985, p. 70).

Maintaining High Performance

How can managers help employees move beyond average, acceptable levels of performance? One can pursue a number of other strategies in addition to those already mentioned. In this section, we will review eight such strategies.

1. *Conduct high-performance interviews.* Jerry Fletcher (1983) advises this approach with subordinates, especially if one wishes to obtain good results without causing undue stress and burnout. As CEO of High Performance Dynamics, Inc., in Richmond, California, Fletcher has found that such encounters, whether with individuals or in groups, can ascertain: when work-

ers perform at their best, and what happens to cause or sustain that peak performance; and how to identify that behavior pattern from a series of critical incidents that can be repeated so that a job is routinely done exceptionally well in the future. Managers need to realize that this performance pattern differs with individuals and adjust their management styles accordingly to increase the performance. Furthermore, managers would do well to reinforce those qualities or procedures that contribute to that person's successful endeavors. The very analysis of this pattern can prove motivational, even with average workers—all of whom have had some periods at work during which they did things surprisingly well. This strategy is also useful in a hiring or regular performance appraisal interview.

2. *Make work fun.* People like to have fun. Charles Dwyer (1984, p. 71) of the University of Pennsylvania's Wharton School suggests that fun can be deliberately built into an organization. Any number of strategies can convey the basic message, "We can have fun here as long as we reach production goals." These can range from joke boards and candid photographs to Apple's skull-and-crossbones flag, which flies from the building in which a new computer is being developed, to "beer busts" for socializing purposes. The point is to ensure that work is a joyful experience, as is evident often in entrepreneurial activities in which informality, teamwork, and fellowship reign. Dwyer has seen the concept of fun on the job cause remarkable attitude changes—in people who have wonderful days on dull-as-dust assembly lines or who even come to work when they are sick because the experience there is intrinsically satisfying—it is fun to be there!

3. *Stimulate innovative activity.* Encourage personnel to be more creative, to go beyond the boundaries of current logic, especially with reference to R&D and new technology. This can be done by fostering a spirit of risk taking, by brainstorming regularly, by rewarding creative breakthroughs, by challenging employees to remove their perceptual and psychological constraints. Naturally, this is best accomplished when the manager is a behavior model of innovative leadership.

If innovation potential for an organization is to be actualized, Barry Minkin, president of Minkin Associates in Mountain View, California, recommends that executives take a long-term perspective and provide continuing management support to innovators (personal communication to the author). Minkin cited as examples former colleagues at Stanford Research Institute, such as Doug Englebart. For over twenty years, Englebart was an unsung hero at SRI, doing augmentation research that laid the groundwork for the office of the future. Although rarely understood or appreciated by his peers, he had the active support of management. Later, Englebart became a success at Tymshare, where he now innovates for better use of computer systems.

Many are understandably alarmed that Yankee ingenuity is slipping, because more than half of the applicants for United States patents during the past few years have been foreign born. But R&D directors in major United States companies assure us that we have not lost our inventiveness and advise:

• Avoid the M.B.A. syndrome of trying to minimize risk by betting on only that which seems a sure thing and economically feasible.

• Lengthen the innovation cycle through long-range thinking and planning—the time lapse from investment to market impact is usually seven years.

• Cultivate intuition, whether in research or in decision making, by encouraging personnel to believe in their abilities and by training them to more fully use their capacities, especially intuitive insights.

There appears to be a direct relationship between high performance and creativity in its various manifestations. Therefore, it would seem a wise strategy for management to target innovation as a desirable work norm. In problem solving, such as on the issue of productivity, examine alternative modes, generate a large number of ideas from personnel, and then urge them to build on each other's input. This often can be best accomplished through the group process of brainstorming, according to the tested guidelines of Walt Disney (1920s) and Alex Osborne (1950s): (1) Create time frames and pressures. (2) Rule out criticism and defer judgments while ideas are being generated and recorded. (3) Encourage quantity input in a freewheeling manner. (4) Use teams to synthesize and refine the raw data. (5) Present these subgroup reports to the larger cluster for synergistic solutions.

Creative top performers seem to be whole brained—that is, they use both the right-brain capability of perception and intuition and left-brain logic. The process of management manifests creativity when managers orchestrate and integrate the multiple talents of their human resources. To be a high-performing manager is a creative art requiring the practice of many skills. This is evident in James F. Beré, president and CEO of Borg-Warner, who transformed a collection of ill-fitting operations into a successful conglomerate with $3.2 billion in sales. As Beré sums up his secret: "When you are in manufacturing, the whole essence of the business is to serve. . . . If you communicate with people, you can release their creativity. Then they can go to work and be part of the decision tree" ("Healthy Smokestakes, 1983, p. 59).

4. *Seek cultural match.* To ensure high performance, carefully recruit individuals who fit the corporate culture. If the culture rewards outstanding performance through teams, select people who will work well in such groups. Or, if top performance is a cultural norm, employ only those capable of meeting that standard. However, it is possible to create an organizational culture that fosters creativity and productivity while using an assessment system to integrate and promote those who will match the work environment.

Ellen Wallach (1983), a career development consultant from Lexington, Massachusetts, has developed an index for this purpose. Table 3 illustrates the person-system match in terms of three types of organizational cultures—bureaucratic, innovative, and supportive. (For a more comprehensive inventory on this subject, see the organizational culture survey instrument in *New Worlds, New Ways, New Management* [Harris, 1983]. It is also available from Management Research Systems, Ponte Vedra Beach, Fla. 32082.)

5. *Foster participative management.* This concept has been applied increasingly over the past thirty years to improve

Table 3. Organizational Culture Index.

Please select the number on the following scale which most closely corresponds with how you see your organization's culture. Then insert that evaluation in the parentheses after each word. 0 = does not describe my organization; 1 = describes it a little; 2 = does describe my organization a fair amount; and 4 = describes my organization most of the time.

a) risk taking ( )	m) stimulating ( )	
b) collaborative ( )	n) regulated ( )	
c) hierarchical ( )	o) personal freedom ( )	
d) procedural ( )	p) equitable ( )	
e) relationship oriented ( )	q) safe ( )	
f) results oriented ( )	r) challenging ( )	
g) creative ( )	s) enterprising ( )	
h) encouraging ( )	t) established/solid ( )	
i) sociable ( )	u) cautious ( )	
j) structured ( )	v) trusting ( )	
k) pressurized ( )	w) driving ( )	
l) ordered ( )	x) power oriented ( )	

Scoring Profiles
BUREAUCRATIC CULTURE: c, d, j, l, n, t, u, x
INNOVATIVE CULTURE: a, f, g, k, m, r, s, w
SUPPORTIVE CULTURE: b, e, h, i, o, p, q, v

Source: Ellen J. Wallach, 1983. Reprinted with permission of *Training and Development Journal.*

both productivity and performance. Involving employees in the business, whether in planning or in decision making, usually has profitable results. General Electric, Cummins, and Signetics are just a few of the many corporations learning to enlist workers in the task of enhancing quality and productivity. In addition, the 1982 annual report of the Ford Motor Company states that Ford's participative management program played a significant role in improving Ford car quality—by an average of 59 percent over previous levels.

This same strategy seems to be the secret of Warner Communications, the entertainment conglomerate. Its CEO, Steven J. Ross, promotes a family atmosphere, especially through a pilot executive group—an intimate, free-form coterie of long-time associates. Although one of the nation's 100 largest industrial enterprises, Warner's headquarters is described as the nucleus of an extended family of creative artists, and its management sees its role as providing a supportive environment for its many autonomous and creative business units. Like other excellent companies, the hallmarks of this corporate culture are not only family spirit, small central staff, and divisional autonomy, but also decentralized authority with participative management and organizational informality and creative intrapreneurialism. By encouraging its people to get involved in everything at Warner, management strengthens loyalty and prompts personnel to stretch beyond average performance.

The transition going on within the cultures of hierarchical structures is most evident at Westinghouse. The executive vice-president of its Power Generation Group, Gene Cattabiani, explains how the company is using ad hoc groups to solve specific problems ("Westinghouse's Cultural Revolution," 1981). Performance is enhanced by small clusters of these excited entrepreneurial types of employees who take on tasks close to their abilities and interests. He cites personal experiences within this large electric giant, where the introduction of participative management caused people to work harder—not from fear but because their work was no longer muffled by layers of middle management and supervision.

Because of its effectiveness, there are many advocates of WAM (Walk- or Wander-Around Management)—in which key executives get down into the organization by visiting assembly lines, taking a refreshment break with workers in a cafeteria, or otherwise evidencing visible management at the lower operational levels. Best selling author, Thomas J. Peters (1983b), is the prime advocate of this strategy and found in revisiting excellent companies that he had actually underestimated its importance. Such visiting can become an opportunity to let members of the "crew" get involved in and with management. The approach can be extended to all those associated with the enterprise's success—from suppliers to customers. Peters (1983b) quoted Lord Sieff, the seventy-six-year-old chairman of Marks & Spencer, the most successful mass retailer in Great Britain, relative to the exceptional quality standards of his store merchandise: "Of course, each of my vice-presidents and I visit at least fifty suppliers a year."

Collegial partnerships can involve a wide range of people whose high performance contributes to the achievements of the enterprise. Perhaps the philosophy of the quality circle movement sums up this strategy best: people are the experts in the work they do; everyone has ideas and wants to contribute; people care about the success of their organization; and everyone can help solve problems if given the opportunity.

General Motors executives admit that their involvement with Toyota in their joint venture, New United Motor Manufacturing (NUMM), is a learning experience in participation. At the NUMM plant in Fremont, California, personnel practices are not the kind traditionally seen in United States assembly factories. Instead, hourly workers experience shop floor involvement in decisions, multiple job skills as a norm, and frequent morale builders. Japanese partners at NUMM even got the unions to agree to flexible work rules, including choosing workers on the basis of ability, not seniority ("Meet America's No. 4 Automaker . . . ," 1984).

6. *Encourage competence.* Metaperformances are possible only with competent people. Competence implies possession of the knowledge, skill, experience, and/or qualifications required to do a task or job well. Without sufficient ability, exceptional performance is impossible. Competence would seem to be at the heart of true professionalism. Competence can be given the highest priority in an organization's policies of recruiting and selecting only the best. Competence as a norm is then reinforced by providing learning and support services that keep such high performers on the cutting edge of their fields. Further, rewards and promotions are offered as a result of outstanding performance. High achievement can be built into the system so that the company or agency becomes known as "high performing." With knowledge workers, proficiency breeds respect. Competency becomes a part of corporate culture, whether in terms of slogans, myths, or heroes (Pascarella, 1984).

When Ford Motor Company inaugurated a policy on employee involvement (EI), president Philip Caldwell indicated that it would be company policy to encourage and enable all employees to become involved in and contribute to the success of the company. Since then, that strategy has permeated every activity of Ford's North American Automative Operation. But this policy was also backed up by participative management and a competence process. With the assistance of Teleometrics International of Woodlands, Texas, a competence analysis was undertaken to establish benchmarks and to survey employee opinion. To foster high management achievement and organizational performance, Ford's HRD professionals used Teleometrics's "Models for Management" seminar. Such training for managers and work teams reinforced changes in participation, quality, and performance. The process began with 1,280 managers and cascaded down to include 15,000 subordinates. Ford considers this only the beginning of its renewal. No wonder it outdistanced its competitors in 1983 with a robust increase of 76.8 percent in sales!

Jay Hall, president of Teleometrics and author of *The Competence Process,* demonstrated through his research that there are quantifiable and measurable dimensions of organizational competence. He maintains that managers are directly responsible for creating a work life in which individual competence is encouraged through participation, commitment, and creativity. Ron Zemke, research editor for *Training,* adds that rapid technological change demands not only real expertise but also definition and certification of basic competence in the new technologies.

Although the spirit of entrepreneurialism is one of the characteristics of the new work culture, it does not eliminate the need for professional management in high-flying start-up enterprises. Entrepreneurs who can inspire early enthusiasm for their products or services might either transform themselves into competent managers or acquire this capability through the recruitment of others so that the fast-growth business can move on to a more complex stage of development. Once the size of the work force moves beyond fifty, founders are wise to heed this counsel.

7. *Enrich compensations.* Peak performance also can result when employees are given a piece of the action or when increased benefits are linked to improved productivity. Stock

Managing for High Performance

incentives, once the prerogative of top management, are being shared with personnel on a broader basis, and now the government offers a tax break when company stock is given to employees. Thus, employees today own 70 percent of Dan River, 33 percent of People Express, 20 percent of Sherwin Williams, and 7 percent of Dow Chemical. The trend toward turning American workers into share-holding capitalists was evident at AT&T before its break-up, when one out of seven shareholder accounts belonged to an employee. In the current negotiations to "privatize" Conrail, a push is underway to have the U.S. Department of Transportation allow the workers to buy it, and a bid has been made to the government on their behalf.

Before he became famous with the United States Olympic Committee and as Baseball Commissioner, Peter Ueberroth built First Travel Corporation into a spectacular success, offering stock incentives to high-performing workers and rewarding talent without prejudice. As the airline industry began attempting to rebound from recession and deregulation, Western Airlines offered 27 percent of company stock to employees, Continental proffered 35 percent, and Eastern also proposed extensive stock ownership to its personnel. The trend is evident in both low- and high-tech industries. As previously mentioned, a plant closure caused the 6,000 employees of National Steel's facility in Weirton, West Virginia, to purchase the whole operation through an employee stock ownership plan. High turnover in personnel, at the other extreme, causes genetic engineering firms to counter with generous stock option plans.

To emphasize the message of this strategy and its impact on performance, consider the case of Peter Kiewit Sons, Inc., the Omaha-based builder. In a *Forbes* feature ("The Ultimate Meritocracy," 1983), the company was highlighted because of its $1.5 billion in revenues and $660 million in cash and securities. Among its sidelines, the corporation is one of the top ten coal producers in the United States. When founder Peter Kiewit died recently, he directed his sons and estate to sell the company back to the employees—now eight hundred of them are shareholders! No wonder the firm's outstanding characteristics are employee loyalty and high performance, which have produced, in turn, one of the country's most successful business records. The founder wanted the company to be remembered as "only the best," and he ensured this in both life and death by rewarding productivity with shares in the enterprise.

Other innovative employers have created a variety of financial incentives to stimulate employee performance and productivity. For example, Hewlett-Packard, the Palo Alto-based manufacturer of electronic instruments and computers, has had a tradition of setting aside a portion of pretax profits to reward employee effort. Currently, this is generally 7 to 9 percent of a worker's base pay. Thus, it was only natural when its president, John F. Young, was appointed to the White House Commission on Industrial Competitiveness, that his leadership would force the group to examine profit sharing as a successful method for improving both motivation and productivity in the work force. Marginal rewards then rise and fall with business conditions. As another example, take the case of General Motors. To restore its preeminence in the global auto market, in 1983 it announced the resumption of executive bonuses and employee profit sharing, both tied to increased revenues.

Travel incentive awards have become more popular as a means to bestir salespersons to exceptional endeavors. To prove that employees are a company's most valuable asset, 1,000 United States corporations are currently sponsoring travel programs. As a motivator, these firms make available through the company discount group packages and lowered prices to their personnel for vacation or weekend trips.

Another approach offers a varied menu of employee benefits that workers can customize to their family needs. At Flour Corporation in Los Angeles, for instance, personnel may choose more money or more time off when vacation time is due; they can literally sell that paid time off back to the company if they so wish and stay on the job. Over a hundred major corporations have adopted flexible benefits systems that allow choices of options relative to various insurance and investment plans, child care services, and even prepaid legal aid. The tax advantages of receiving such benefits over being pushed into a higher tax bracket by salary increases are one stimulus. But the flexible fringe benefits can also save the employer money at a time when the United States Chamber of Commerce reports that traditional benefit payments are equal to 37 percent of a typical worker's salary and rising. In the new work culture, benefits need to take into account dual-income households and give employees more responsibility for making their own decisions in this regard.

Today's metaindustrial workers often would prefer more leisure as an incentive or compensation. The Conference Board survey of 3,000 companies confirmed the trend toward "paid time off" as part of the new benefit packages. They found that in the 1980s, a five-week maximum vacation is typical, the number of paid holidays has risen to ten a year, and more company health plans are allowing compensated time for all types of illness, including mental illness or rehabilitation from drug/alcohol dependency. People are attracted to progressive firms that offer paid or unpaid time off for retraining or higher education, such as a "sabbatical" leave. Although recessions can cause temporary cutbacks in such varied allowances, the postindustrial work scene is likely to feature more, not less, of this phenomenon.

Retirement alternatives also are changing in the emerging work environment. Some workers are enticed to retire earlier, such as at AT&T, by offers of one or two years' salaries paid for early leave taking. Others are attracted to improved pension plans complementary to Social Security benefits plus features that adjust the plan to inflation or that permit workers to take the benefits when they leave the organization.

Enlightened management periodically reviews all aspects of the compensation and benefit programs, seeks employee input, and then creatively tries to link any improvements to performance.

8. *Improve organizational communications.* Problems with labor-management communications are a perennial source of undermined productivity. In high-performing companies and agencies, effective communication systems usually are operating. Let us examine proven innovative strategies for performance improvement at three different levels within enterprises:

Institutional level. Productivity and profitability can be enhanced when an organization has a common culture and speaks a common language, according to Harold S. Hook, chairman and CEO of American General Corporation, the fourth-largest shareholder-owned insurance group in the United States. When Hook introduced his change strategy, called "Main Event Management" (MEM), into that company in 1975, annual revenues were $1,289.1 million. Eight years later, after employees had benefited from training and application of MEM's "Model-Netics" systems, the 1983 financial report listed revenues of $3,953.4 million. This implementation of ten integrated systems of communication, according to Curtis Reed, president of E. F. Hutton's La Jolla Associates, contributed to the revenue doubling and such bottom-line results as operating earnings up to $289.8 million! It was Hook's diagrammatic and symbolic models that produced change in management activity, as well as in organizational memory and performance. That is why Reed's consulting efforts are focused on taking these 151 conceptual models to other industries and even to the public sector. The success of La Jolla Associates in doing this seems to stem from Model-Netics facilitating the standardization of organizational culture and communication, especially relative to performance improvement.

Individual level. Managers who engage in on-the-job coaching of their subordinates or team members also achieve higher productivity with such personnel. Thomas Jaap, managing director of Human Resource Associates in London, says the strategy can be successful if we understand that: learning is a continuous process and must be related to specific job tasks; learning improvements at work must be reinforced; and learning is the responsibility of the learner, not the coach. The coaching process not only improves interpersonal communication between managers and subordinates but also requires: new skill acquisition by the manager in listening and counseling or mentoring; linkage to measurable performance standards and integration into everyday work routines; dynamic development of opportunities for coaching as an employee learns and changes for greater performance improvement; and creation of a growing relationship between the coach and the performer that is trusting and task oriented while increasing delegation and interdependence. Jaap, also publisher of *HRD International,* has demonstrated that managers can be trained to develop a coaching climate, use a coaching language, and apply coaching strategies. In an era of knowledge workers, this type of management development would seem preferable to the classic boss style.

Consulting level. Whether by internal or external consultants, process consultation can be used to facilitate organizational communication and problem solving. The client can be either an executive or manager or a team or business unit. The effective consulting relationship involves this client in both diagnosis and solution, especially if ownership and commitment are to result from the endeavor. If high performance is the immediate concern, the consultant helps the client formulate the problems, identify, evaluate, and select strategies for solutions, and implement for results. Process consultation involves such phases as initial diagnosis, data collection, team skills training, data confrontation, intergroup building, team building, and action planning. If a company's own human resource department does not possess such consulting skills, management should turn to external professionals for this purpose. It is an organization development strategy that can be used for performance improvement.

Capitalizing on a Diversified Work Force

Human resource management that employs any of the above strategies is likely to improve performance and productivity. However, there is another reality to be considered. In the dying industrial work culture, "manpower"—as it was called—was stable. People tended to devote a lifetime to one employer if they could and to find a niche in some department or division where they would stay many years, often until retirement. But in the metaindustrial environment, workers are more mobile, not just within one organization but within an industry or professional field. For quality-of-life reasons, workers also are becoming more selective in the amount of time they wish to devote to a job; their loyalty often shifts from an organization that employs them to personal and professional development wherever it can be found. The new work culture tends to mean a more diversified work force, even in terms of a single organization; that is, workers are seeking more options and alternatives relative to employment for income. Figure 9 illustrates this trend.

Figure 9. The Diversified Workforce.

[Diagram showing concentric groupings: outer labels SELF-EMPLOYMENT, AGENCY TEMPORARIES, SUBCONTRACTING, INCREASED OUTSOURCING; FIRST PERIPHERAL GROUP — SECONDARY LABOUR MARKET — NUMERICAL FLEXIBILITY; FULL-TIME CORE GROUP — PRIMARY LABOUR MARKET — FUNCTIONAL FLEXIBILITY; SECOND PERIPHERAL GROUP with SHORT-TERM CONTRACTS, PUBLIC SUBSIDY TRAINEES, DELAYED RECRUITMENT, JOB SHARING, PART-TIME.]

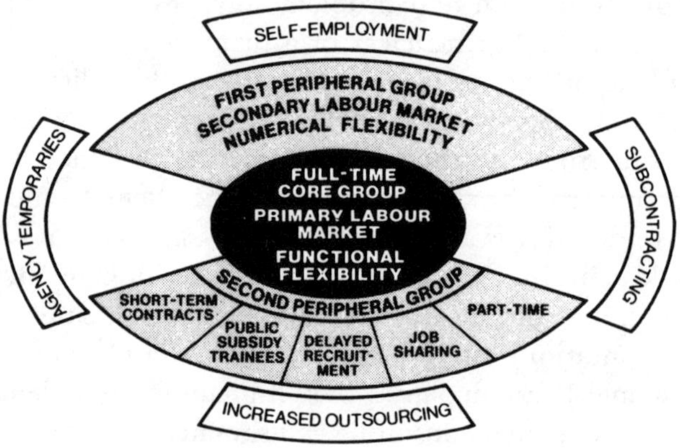

Source: The Economist, September 29, 1984, p. 63. Reprinted with permission.

Those who seek a more stable relationship with a corporation or agency are depicted as the "core professionals." These are key employees, carefully selected and few in number. Such full-time persons are known for the quality performance described in this chapter, and it behooves an organization to focus its human resource strategies on this group for long-term development purposes. These individuals are also known for functional flexibility—they are able to switch from one job to another within a work unit or from one plant to another because of their critical core skills. These are the people the organization seeks to retain, perhaps using approaches such as those identified in *The 100 Best Companies to Work for in America* (Levering, Moskowitz, and Katz, 1984). The common characteristics of these successful corporations so attractive to personnel are promotion from within, reluctance to lay off employees in hard times, and development of a strong family spirit.

It is conceivable that high performance is cultivated even in peripheral groups. For example, if contract and part-time workers are proficient former employees of the organization, they would carry the competency norm into other and newer relationships with the employer. By having the flexibility to set their own work schedules with reduced hours on the job, such associates may be more energized when they work for the company or agency. In fact, if they are in an entrepreneurial relationship with the organization, they may even exceed performance levels of regular core employees.

By permitting more variety and diversity in affiliation, the metaindustrial organization in this schemata also has a second peripheral group of human resources from which it draws. These are qualified personnel who are permitted to share a single job, may work only part-time, and are contract workers or are supplied by agencies as temporaries. This set-up benefits the organization by keeping its work force lean and containing labor costs; it permits expansion of personnel when the market demands it and contraction when income slows down. But such approaches are also of benefit to persons who have family or other responsibilities that do not permit them to work full-time or who prefer to work out of their homes. It provides more flexibility for both the employer and the employee. Consider some corporate illustrations of this trend:

- F. International, a British-based company, has 850 freelance computer experts worldwide, 80 percent of whom work out of their homes. This computer services company supplies contract workers to multinational corporations and government agencies for inexpensive part-time service.
- Manpower is an American temporary help firm that offers 600,000 temporary workers to do everything from cleaning offices to processing data. No wonder the Organization for Economic Cooperative Development reports an increase in part-time employment in all twenty-four countries that have membership in that organization!
- Rank-Xerox in the United Kingdom facilitates execu-

tives who wish to leave their companies and sell their services back to their companies and others. It has a network of former top management people working out of their homes, available when needed.

• Federal Express has a core of high-performing professionals but can expand its work week and number of personnel through a variety of part-time arrangements. Like Federal Express, the smart companies are treating such part-timers as fairly and creatively as they do their full-time people.

Top-performing executives, managers, and consultants in the new work culture also are learning to negotiate varied work relationships with employers. At the vice-president level, particularly, high performers may decide that they do not wish to work for a company full-time. There may be a variety of reasons for this—entrepreneurial desires to own one's business or to have more free time for personal and family growth or to go back to school for further education. Whatever the rationale, such creative executives are vital to their organizations and are in a position to work out a mutually beneficial contract that is different from the traditional arrangement. The new relationship may be as a part-time employee, retaining benefits and perhaps three quarters salary in return for agreeing to certain annual deliverables to the company. Or the relationship may be that of a contract worker and consultant that receives a retainer fee plus expenses. Or the employer may agree to the executive's establishment of a subsidiary in which that individual is totally in charge; another variation is that the former employer company invests in the executive's new enterprise and agrees to purchase its products or services.

To conclude, the new work culture offers both flexibility and variety of affiliation to retain the "brainpower" of the highly competent. In addition to the performance strategies discussed here, consider those analyzed in greater depth in the next three chapters—teamwork, networking, and wellness.

EIGHT

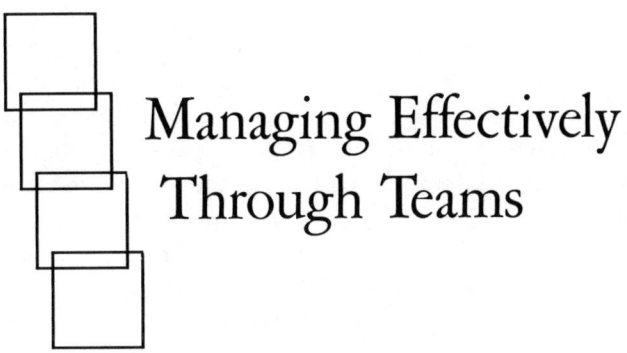
Managing Effectively Through Teams

Executive Summary. If high performance is to be sustained in metaindustrial organizations, cooperative action among personnel becomes essential. The explosion of information today and the complexity of our times demand it. Team management, then, is vital to achieving and maintaining high output amidst rapid growth. Thus, thinking managers are committed to learning the skills of group dynamics, including how to influence team processes and activities, norms and values, task and maintenance functions. Increasingly, they practice group leadership, which implies clarifying roles and relationships and sharing unique talents and decision-making responsibilities. Furthermore, they acquire new tools, such as the computer, to control the diverse elements involved in matrix, project, or product management.

In such ways, an effective team culture can be created that improves performance beyond the sum of individual member efforts. To help in this process, behavioral scientists can provide team-building activities to ensure group productiveness and synergy. Successful management not only actively promotes a team spirit but installs team mechanisms and the means to develop team skills.

Team Management

Consider the following description: "a paternalistic organization where mediocrity is condoned, where personnel policy is very similar to civil service (with a rigid hierarchy and people of similar rank paid about equal regardless of results), where there is no incentive to be innovative, where there is a big emphasis on short-term profits at the expense of longer-term investment, where there is limited understanding of the difference between sales and marketing, and where the emphasis is on the tactical rather than strategic thinking" (Weisler, 1984, p. 28). Does it sound familiar? Most readers are likely to have experienced that disappearing industrial-age work environment. What is remarkable is that this quotation by James Weisler, vice-chairman of the Bank of America, describes the situation at his institution, which cries out for organizational change. Having been exposed as a consultant to that creaking financial elephant, I can confirm the accuracy of the analysis. The bank's culture, as reported above, is counter to almost every one of the eight strategies discussed in Chapter Seven as a means for ensuring high performance!

In contrast, consider First National Bank of Chicago, which was featured in the same article on the transformation of international banking. First Chicago did not limit its renewal to new technology—such as automated tellers, new financial systems, asset/liability management, or such new marketing strategies as capitalizing on the consumer-oriented nature of its business; First Chicago executives committed themselves to altering the culture of their rather staid institution through team management. A task force group of senior managers was formed in 1982 and spent eight months studying how the existing organization functioned and how to build on its strengths. Middle management was involved in the group's mission, and the strategy that emerged was directed toward first-line supervision and account officers. The approach centered around development of teamwork, because that was the staff's preferred style, along with increased risk taking and innovation. In Chapter Two, we reviewed team management as a central feature of the metaindustrial work culture. Now we will consider ways to apply it in matrix, project, or product management to increase performance and profitability, as well as service.

For our purposes, a team is a work group or unit with a common purpose through which members develop mutual relationships for the achievement of goals/tasks. Teamwork, then, implies cooperative and coordinated effort by individuals working together in the interests of their common cause. It requires the sharing of talent and leadership, the playing of multiple roles. The ideal number of persons engaged in such joint action is usually no more than eight, although that figure can be expanded to include a natural grouping. Team performance is highest when the dynamics of group process can occur; this is more likely to happen when the number of participants is limited for maximum interchange. Teams are developed through training and experience; the skills to be acquired for improving their management are a combination of technical, organizational, and interpersonal. For the team leader, the new learnings include allocation of expert time and talent, as well as the dynamics of small groups and their meetings. Mike Woodcock (1985) has created a systems approach to team development that includes forty-five activities that trainers or managers can undertake to enhance team effectiveness.

The fundamental reality that demands a team approach today is the increased complexities and uncertainties with which organizational leaders must cope, both now and in the future. People teams at work enable us to focus more brainpower while performing a variety of functions together. In the high-tech, fast-growth environment, "ad hocracy" through teams or task forces is standard operating procedure, while "ultrastability" is becoming the norm for dealing with rapid organizational change. However, this means creating a meta-industrial environment in which specialists and separate business units are interdependent and practice collaboration with one another and those in functional activities on a daily basis.

UCLA professor William Ouchi wrote a book called *The M-Form Society* (1984), which is an analysis of how American teamwork can recapture the competitive edge in business. His thesis is that not only United States business but also American industry, government, and academia could learn something from Japanese-style cooperation in work groups. But the flip side is that Japanese tradition dictates that the individual should be very cautious in a group and never speak his or her mind openly. It is for that reason that Link Consulting Associates in Kyoto introduced the American team approach of The Executive Committee (TEC). In this peer executive network, Japanese CEOs are encouraged to be more candid, sharing, and helpful in the small-group experience. When altering work culture, we have to create both the mind set and the institutions for facilitating collaboration in planning and problem-solving activities. The postindustrial scene and the global economy make this necessary, because our problems and challenges are becoming increasingly complex.

In North America, there is ample evidence of this trend toward synergistic management actions. For example, consider the endeavor in which major corporations, including IBM, are joining in a task force effort with the U.S. Department of Defense in cooperative research on very high speed integrated circuits (VHSIC) for computers. At the manager's level, the team is where the action is, so new learning is required in cooperative relationships.

Competition is strongly embedded in the American culture, as is evident in the adversarial posture between labor and management. The new team training involves a reanalysis of how we view and interact with others, of how we can learn from each other and gain more by working together rather than engaging in vicious struggles and put-downs of one another. The new work environment requires more cooperative support of peers, mutual growth activities, and attitudes that enhance high team performance.

Team training is even possible within an organization for both union and management leaders together. Digital Equipment Corporation provides cross-skills training and learning; thus, at its electronics plant in Enfield, Connecticut, Digital uses the team approach to replace the standard production assembly line. Each team member is trained to perform twenty different job functions involved in producing circuit board modules. In this high-tech factory, there are three autonomous manufacturing groups, each consisting of four teams with eighteen members. To be fully certified to work on the total product, members undergo three months of team training for acquisition of both technical and group interaction skills. The pay system reinforces learning by tying increases to acquired knowledge and competency. The plant manager, Bruce Dillingham, emphasizes that it takes a certain type of new manager to make the team strategy work—one who assumes a teaching or facilitating role and who knows when to step back and let people grow and develop.

Ralph Kilmann, a professor at the University of Pittsburgh, offers sage advice related to the issues of performance and teams. He maintains that no one new management approach will work toward creating and sustaining an organization's high performance and morale. Instead, one must use an integrated combination of strategies. In his book, *Beyond the Quick Fix* (1984), he suggests five tracks to organizational success: (1) the culture track, which shapes an adaptive work culture that encourages trust, commitment, and information sharing; (2) the management skills track, which helps managers acquire skills to solve complex problems and analyze decision assumptions; (3) the strategy-structure track, which presents ways to set and align an organization's direction and structures with strategy and goals; (4) the reward system track, which provides a process for creating compensation and incentive systems that attract, motivate, and retain able individuals for the organization; and (5) the team-building track, which infuses into work group cultures the norms and management skills that ensure high performance and high-quality decision making. It is a message in harmony with the thrust of this book, and the last track is the focus of this chapter.

Team Process

There is a new form of playing golf in groups, which is called "scramble." It can be an excellent means of team building. Individual scores are replaced by team scores obtained by combining the best performance of each member for each shot on every hole. The total score represents the top performance of every participant in the foursome. I found the game to be a profound learning experience and a most enjoyable one (especially because although a mediocre golfer, I won a prize through the team approach). The peer pressure was on for everyone to do his or her best for the good of the team. Would that such an approach could be converted to the game of business!

Teams are effective when they produce outstanding results, succeeding in achieving despite all the difficulties. For this to happen, members must feel some responsibility for one another and for their personal contribution toward the desired outcome. Two British consultants, David Francis and Donald Young, collaborated on a useful volume, *Improving Work Groups* (1979), which contains an examination of the process for making this happen. They cited characteristics of high-performing teams:

- Output. Together the group can deliver more than the individuals who comprise it could do in isolation—the right combination produces results.
- Objectives. Participants understand their purpose and share their goals—the combination achieves mission.
- Energy. Members take strength from one another and build on the capabilities of their fellows—the combination is energized through synergy.
- Structure. Mature members create mechanisms for dealing with issues of procedures, organization, roles, control, and leadership—the combination becomes orderly, directed, flexible, and responsive.
- Atmosphere. Members create a spirit and culture that is open and supportive, permitting risks to be taken and confidences to be shared—the participants become comfortable with one another and cohesive.

Because of this group identity and morale, the team is effective. Synergy results because individuals have created a real team culture (group attitudes, climate, customs, norms, and practices) that fosters the accomplishment of the team's mission.

Work teams can be formed for a variety of purposes—to accomplish a specific task, train together, problem solve, and/or plan a product life cycle. Successful quality circles are one example of effective team management. Increasingly, pressures resulting from transitions and complicated undertakings are forcing organizations to adopt a matrix management design. This style usually involves establishing project teams with members reporting to both project and functional managers. Such matrix organizations may produce pitfalls because there may be a tendency toward anarchy, power struggle, excessive overhead, decision strangulation, and other group problems. However, with proper team development, there can be many benefits—such as more flexibility and adaptability, more timely and balanced decisions, and more rapid management response to market and technology. The team can become a learning community, training members to deal with greater complexity, educating them for higher management, focusing energy and improving motivation, and retaining in-depth specialists because the team approach makes greater use of their capabilities. The project team then becomes interdisciplinary and couples different technical specialities and perceptions.

Jack Baugh (1981), a Hughes Aircraft executive, wrote his doctoral dissertation on decision making in matrix organizations. He suggests that the matrix should be considered when simultaneous dual decisions are needed, when a company is faced with uncertainties generated by very high information processing requirements, when strong financial or human resource constraints are a factor, when decisions must be sped up because of rapid technological advances, and when the sheer quantity of data, products, and services makes it necessary. Baugh believes that matrix provides a transitional bridge between old and new management situations.

To use matrix, or any form of project or product, management requires an understanding and practice of group process. The process is the action or way of operating by which a team achieves its purposes. High performance in groups can be aided or undermined by this.

When leadership is shared on a team, these multiple functions are performed by different members at various times; team capability and energy are enhanced. Thus, the individual who can develop a computer simulation provides task leadership. The one who tells a joke in a moment of crisis and releases tension offers maintenance leadership. The person who helps the group deal effectively with minority opinions or people contributes norm leadership. Detailed definitions of tasks, maintenance, and norms/values follow:

Task Behavioral Orientation. This is the behavior of team members that affects the "doing" of work. A central issue is how the group makes decisions—is it by consensus, majority rule, leader fiat? Then there is the matter of leadership—is it shared, is it by subgroup or clique, or is it the realm of some authority figure? How does the group solve problems—is there a method, and if so, is it systematic? Finally, how does the group communicate—who initiates, proposes tasks, defines problems, and suggests procedures to solve problems? Who seeks information by requesting facts, asking for suggestions, searching for data? Who gives information or opinion by providing relevant facts, data, or ideas? Who clarifies, elaborates, interprets, or reflects on ideas or suggestions, clears up confusion, gives examples, offers alternatives? Who provides syntheses and summarizes by pulling together ideas, restating, or articulating conclusions? Team effectiveness can be increased when a facilitator or observer sits in on team meetings to evaluate the process underway, using some form of data-gathering instrument to record individual behavior and performance. (Resources B and C, at the back of this book, provide means for analyzing team synergy or group maturity.)

Maintenance Behavioral Orientation. This is the behavior of members that maintains the group's cohesiveness as a working unit and affects its morale. A central issue in this regard is conflict resolution and utilization. This implies questioning how members handle conflicts with one another: Do they envision such differences as energy that can be constructively channeled? How open are members to giving and receiving feedback, and how sensitively is it handled? How well do teammates deal with feelings and emotions? High team maintenance is evidenced by demonstrations of individuals caring for one another and by the amount of encouragement that is offered.

Maintenance is also manifested in supportive ways through warm feelings and friendliness, as well as a certain amount of acceptance, sharing, and recognition offered to one another. Some group participants contribute to this maintenance process by being sensitive to others' moods, by harmonizing or reconciling differences, by reducing tensions, or by getting the members to explore positions and feelings on an issue. Others do it through negotiation and compromise, admitting errors, or practicing self-discipline in the interest of group cohesion. Again, it is useful to have an observer assess such matters by means of a data-gathering instrument and then give feedback to the team on both the task and maintenance aspects of such behavior. (I have developed instruments I503 for this purpose, which are available from Management Research Systems, P.O. Box 1585, Ponte Vedra Beach, Fla. 32082.)

The new approach to managing the people dimension at work, and especially in teams, is called behavior technology (Wellin, 1985). It involves activities that range from defining performance requirements and appraising performance to managing conflict and working in groups.

Norms/Values. Among team activities, there are behaviors and functions centered around norms or standards, as well as around values or priorities. This may be seen in the customs and traditions the team develops and in the protocols that influence how the group works. These are key factors in team culture.

Team Task Activities

Having distinguished the team's maintenance activities that sustain its internal workings from its task activities, let us examine in some depth what the latter are. Essentially, task activities are achievement activities that enable the group to attain its goals and targets within a specific time frame. For example, project managers must be concerned not only about interpersonal dynamics but also about technical aspects of managing a specific project. The latter include such tasks as defining the project and analyzing work to be performed; planning for the use of project resources to achieve the mission; setting project objectives, priorities, and performance standards; developing a project scheduling system and milestone reviews; developing a project budget and getting it funded; building a project organization by recruiting, orienting, and developing team members; installing project controls and meaningful supervision; and establishing project communication, reporting, and evaluation systems.

The more team members can be involved in these major tasks, the more likely it is that the project will succeed. Each of these tasks requires the application of specific competencies. For example, project planning and scheduling means selecting appropriate techniques for network analysis, critical path analysis, or cost analysis. Staffing a project may include preparing job descriptions, qualifications statements, and forecasts for "manpower" requirements; choosing selection methods and procedures; and possibly developing performance appraisal criteria. Readers who wish to advance their team management capabilities in this regard may wish to review *Project Planning and Management: An Integrated Approach* (Goodman and Love, 1980) or *The Principles of Productivity Management in the Development of Computer Applications* (Keane, Keane, and Teagan, 1984).

A most powerful management tool for controlling the diverse elements involved in project or matrix management is the personal or microcomputer. The lead feature in *PC World* for September 1984 discussed how to use a personal computer in project management. The authors, William Dauphinais and Leonard Darnell, indicate that new software is available to help project leaders increase the quantity, quality, and timeliness of information. To make a complex project more manageable, a computer can assist with planning, monitoring, and tracking. It can help project teams identify tasks and sequences to be performed, establish and follow a schedule with its milestones and deadlines, and estimate resources as to what will be needed and when and how much it will cost. The personal computer can even be used to manage accountability, analyzing, clarifying, and evaluating roles and relationships. Dauphinais and Darnell make an interesting distinction between project tracking and monitoring—the former involves more record keeping and is historical, while the latter is more subtle, forward-looking in nature, and takes into account unexpected changes. Project monitoring is real-time planning that alters the project in progress and observes changes in plans. The information collected via the computer is a compilation of team history and can be used from project to project to improve team performance.

Now software packages are available to assist team leaders with a variety of project functions, from maintaining the calendar to task definition and sequence, resource and cost definition, and compilation of charts and reports. Software companies, such as Digital Marketing, Earth Data, Harvard, North America Mica, Omicron, Primavera Systems, Scitor, VisiCorp, and Westminster, all have such programs and can offer descriptive catalogues on their distinctive features. Whether small or large projects, software packages are becoming more sophisticated and helpful to team leaders.

Ideally, members should work as a unit to create the team charter, which deals with some of the needs described above. Essentially, it describes what the group agrees to focus on in order to function together effectively. Figure 10 provides a visual overview of what is involved in project management and the systematic development of people to engage in such team activity. It is a profile of a three-day workshop on this subject offered by the Delphi Group of Tucson, Arizona.

We are beginning to appreciate the fact that the management of macroprojects requires special understanding and competencies. A consortium of universities thus has devised an Institute on Large Scale Programs, which is now headquartered adjoining the University of Texas and can provide helpful information for those so concerned (2815 San Gabriel, Austin, Tex. 78705).

Team Skills

As indicated in the previous section, an effective team member needs a combination of both technical skills, such as those outlined for project management, and interpersonal skills.

Figure 10. Project Management Team Development.

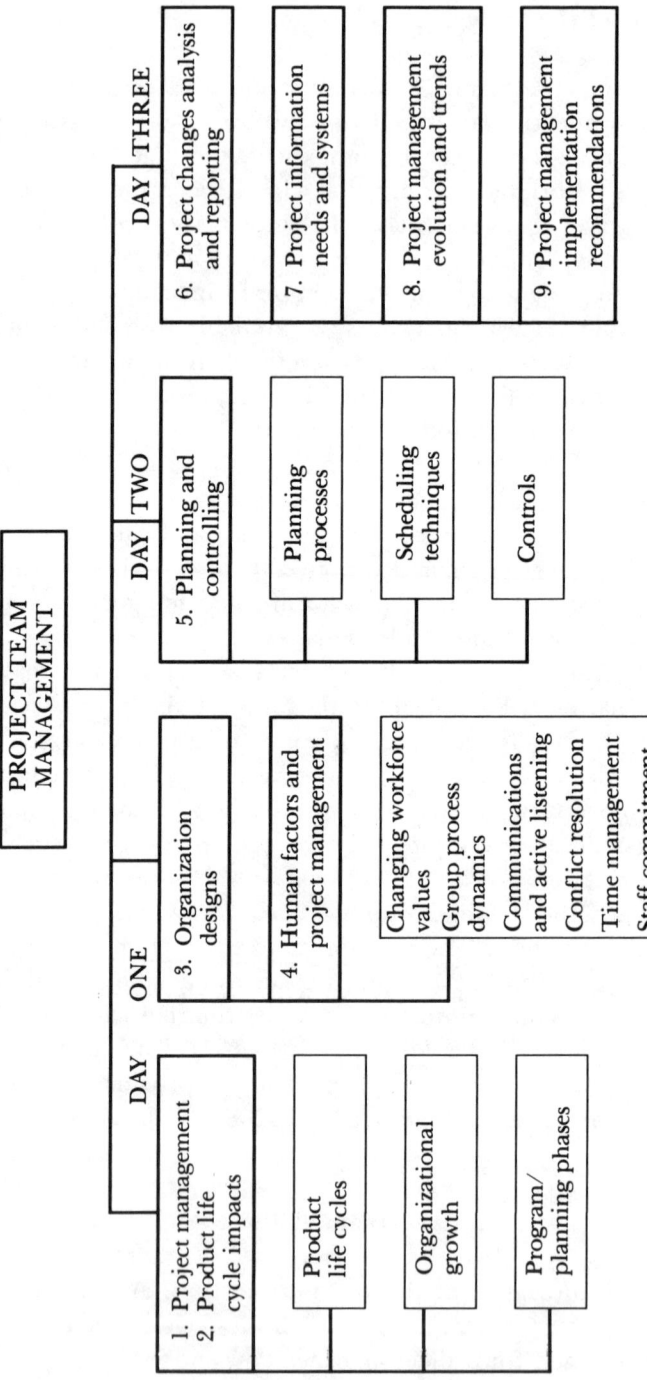

Source: The Delphi Group, 4625 E. Broadway, Tucson, Arizona 85711. Reprinted with permission.

Managing Effectively Through Teams

Let us concentrate here on some of the human relations competencies required for high-performing teams. The most obvious of these is the most important—an ability to communicate both in writing and orally and at both the interpersonal and organizational levels. This ranges from being able to compose a concise project plan with supporting documentation to promoting its acceptance and funding and compiling periodic and final reports. However, communication at both the cognitive and feeling levels is what determines the success or failure of the team. Team communication training will address not only such interchanges and how to improve them but also the group's interface with other business units. Resource B offers a team synergy analysis inventory to facilitate member assessment of team skills, while Resource C provides an instrument for assessing the maturity of a group in terms of team relations.

The team leader needs to develop, particularly, skills as a synergist—first, bring together both technical and human resources to ensure team accomplishment; then, bring together both team and organizational relationships (Corning, 1983). Plugging the team activities into functional structures requires sensitive negotiations. Managing inevitable differences and conflicts within the team and with other groups also requires additional proficiency. When such skill development cannot be obtained internally from the organization's own human resource division, there are ample external consultants available to bring such training in-house. The Sterling Institute in Washington, D.C., for instance, has a videotape learning package on team building, and many educational film producers offer a variety of audiovisual aids on the subject. Among many books now available on such issues, I recommend *Working in Teams,* by James H. Shonk (1983).

Although we cannot cover the subject extensively here, it is possible to offer some tips to readers to help them improve their participation in groups. The team is a microcosm of the larger organizational world and the way people act. Although the group experience may be temporary, it provides an opportunity to learn with and from colleagues and to practice new skills. Team meetings challenge us to share insights based on unique professional backgrounds and organizational experiences. Both task achievement and group learning can be maximized when members follow these guidelines:

- Be experimental. Test new styles of leadership and communication, different kinds of behavior and attitudes, new patterns of personal participation and relationships.
- Be authentic. Be honest in team communications and avoid game playing with each other; care about team members— enough to confront them when necessary and tell it like it is.
- Be sensitive. Express your own feelings, and be conscious of the other person's feelings. Respond empathetically and reflect on the sender's real meaning in message exchanges. Be aware of a whole range of nonverbal communications and cues.
- Be spontaneous. Respond creatively to here-and-now data produced in the group, especially to personal revelations of self; not only confirm others in their sharings, but avoid being manipulative.
- Be helpful. Accept others' perceptions of themselves, others, and of situations as being valid whether you agree or not, and avoid imposing your opinions, values, and systems on others; unless others perceive your intervention as helpful, it is not; others must be aided to discover new dimensions through you.
- Be open and flexible. Consider other viewpoints, alternatives, and possibilities, rather than being closed minded or locked into previous positions; be adaptable, not rigid, in responding to innovative ideas or perceptions of differences.
- Be time conscious. The group has limited time together and schedules to keep, so limit personal inputs and avoid dominating team communications or diverting the group from its mission; cultivate conciseness, preciseness, and listening skills while bringing the wayward back on target.
- Be a group leader. Share distinctive competencies and permit others to make their unique contributions to team task and maintenance functions; team participation is an opportunity to practice a range of leadership skills, whether as initiator or follower.

As the field of project management and computers converged, researchers at Keane, Inc., a data processing and software services consulting firm, speculated on the skills that project leaders should possess. They contracted with behavioral scientists at McBer and Company to undertake a job competency analysis based on their methodology of interviewing outstanding performers as to their critical tasks for successful accomplishment of their role. The subjects were superior DP project managers, and the findings, according to Bander and Giber (1985), resulted in this model of the type of competencies project managers should possess:

- Problem-solving cluster: diagnostic, systematic, conceptual thinking, plus monitoring and information-gathering competencies.
- Managerial identity cluster: strong project manager identity, self-confidence, and flexibility competencies.
- Achievement cluster: results and business orientation.
- Influence cluster: interpersonal astuteness, influence skill, team building, developing others, client orientation, and self-control competencies.

Bander and Giber then created a development program for project team leaders to replicate this model and foster these competencies.

A. Samuel Cook, a senior partner in the law firm of Venable, Baetjer, and Howard, provides a short course in human relations with a circular that in essence encompasses great implications for those who would improve team performance:

> The six most important words: "I admit I made a mistake."
> The five most important words: "You did a good job."
> The four most important words: "What is your opinion?"
> The three most important words: "If you please."
> The two most important words: "Thank you."
> The least important word: "I."

Research at the East-West Center in Honolulu (Moran and

Harris, 1982) indicates that some behaviors and attitudes manifested by members contribute to high performance in teams, particularly those operating cross-culturally in international marketplaces. A summary of these data may be transformed into applications by those concerned about team development. These are the characteristics found to facilitate team success:

1. tolerance of ambiguity, uncertainty, and seeming lack of structure;
2. interest in both the group and each individual's achievement;
3. ability to give and accept feedback in a nondefensive manner;
4. openness to change, innovation, and creative joint problem solving;
5. ability to create a team atmosphere that is informal, relaxed, comfortable, and nonjudgmental;
6. capacity to establish intense, short-term member relations and then to disconnect these for the next project;
7. desire to encourage group participation, consensus, and decisions;
8. appreciation of effective listening and communication that serve group needs and that stay on target and on schedule;
9. capacity to cultivate a team spirit of constructive criticism and authentic nonevaluative feedback;
10. group attitude that invites members to express feelings and to be concerned about team morale and maintenance factors;
11. clarification of member roles, relationships, assignments, and responsibilities;
12. shared leadership so as to fully utilize all member resources;
13. periodic reexamination of maintenance functions that affect team progress and communication;
14. fostering of trust, confidence, and commitment within the group;
15. sensitivity to the team's linking functions with other working units;

16. promotion of group norms so that members are respectful and supportive of one another and realistic in mutual expectations;
17. use of approaches that are goal directed, that divide labor fairly among members, and that synchronize efforts; and
18. providing for team-building opportunities in the midst of task concerns and pursuits.

Team Building

Team building is a behavioral science technology for achieving many of the preceding characteristics in work groups. It is best accomplished with the help of a third-party facilitator, preferably a trained consultant, either an internal or external resource. Persons who are known as organization development (OD) specialists are usually capable of conducting team-building skill training. Preferably, this training begins with one off-site intensive experience of two or three days duration, such as on a weekend. Then, it may involve periodic on-site team meetings—perhaps a half day every other week or monthly. Team development can be accomplished with regular functional work units or ad hoc teams or on an intergroup basis. Although the investment may require considerable time, energy, and funds, the pay-off is usually worth it.

When TRW Systems used matrix management to participate successfully in NASA's Apollo Program, it used such a strategy to improve work team performance. Sheldon Davis (1970), then TRW's vice-president, concludes that over the years TRW Systems has undertaken team building hundreds of times and that it has had positive impact almost every time. As a result, the technique appears terribly relevant in terms of some of the issues technical people face when they must work together to reach a common goal. The issues considered in such team building are:

1. What are we here to do and how do we do it?
2. How do we work through problems and make decisions?
3. What is our relationship to other groups?
4. Who cares about our success?

5. What is it like to work here or on this team?
6. What is my job, and what makes it hard for me to accomplish it?
7. What are my perceptions and expectations of my role and responsibilities?
8. What changes would I like to see in my role, and what changes would be necessary for me to be able to assume broader responsibilities?
9. How could my work unit work more cooperatively, and what must I do toward that end?
10. What does each member need to do differently in order for the group to be more effective and productive?
11. What changes are needed in relationships with other groups, supervisors, or subordinates?

The strategy examines the dynamics of the group and enables members to practice skills in data gathering and analysis, feedback, negotiations, conflict utilization, and problem solving. The main effort is working through blockages toward group progress so that team energy is focused and not dissipated. The outcome is improved team collaboration and accomplishment.

The greatest return on investment in team building is with new groups and start-up enterprises. For example, when General Dynamics brought together project groups to develop the Shuttle-Centaur rocket, it was able to call on experienced technical teams from its prior Atlas-Centaur project. Because of the company's previous investment, the team building in this case could focus on creating even higher performance through better management of complexity, better quality of decisions, more rapid response. The emphasis in experienced teams whose members are comfortable with one another is on honing the proven relationships, skills, and systems so as to capitalize on their collective strength.

Team building can be used to improve either intra- or intergroup relations. Functional work teams can be brought together, in the latter instance, to analyze each group's perception of the other units and how communication and cooperation between them can be promoted for the good of all.

In the new work culture, we often establish task force

teams that cross conventional lines in organizations. Furthermore, the makeup of such problem-solving groups usually cuts across ranks and organizational levels. The concern is to gather personnel with the expertise and diversity to provide a variety of perspectives, such as from marketing, manufacturing, and management backgrounds or disciplines. In this way, team building is essential for maximum contribution of each member's potential toward group tasks and goals.

Team Roles

In many ways, the team represents a miniature version of the organization that sponsors it. It involves a set of interacting roles that often must be negotiated and that always result in the forming of relationships. The more the group understands these roles and relationships, the better accountability can be managed. Team development often involves reassessing and clarifying roles and relationships. (Resource D provides an organizational roles and relationships inventory that can be used to help team members with this clarification process.) The more roles can be integrated and made synergistic, the more effectively jobs and tasks can be performed.

Research has been conducted abroad on management team roles by Roger Mottram (1982), personnel director for Woolworth in Australia. The ten-year study of managers attending workshops at the Administrative Staff College in Henley found them to take on eight fairly distinct styles or team roles. Mottram discovered that managers consistently adopted one or more of these roles in teams, not necessarily associated with their functional role in the organization.

The Chairperson. This person displays powers of control and coordination of group resources; he or she operates on a democratic, participative basis but can assume control when necessary. The personality profile is that of a dominant but relaxed character who can be aggressively nonassertive—a steady, cool type who is both creative and enthusiastic and people oriented. (This person may not necessarily be appointed the designated team leader.)

The Shaper. This team member prefers to shape decisions

directly and personally, likes action and quick results, is a willing follower, and seeks a course that best sums up the situation and can cut through difficulties. This person is so results oriented that he or she pushes for ideas believed best so as to get the job done and thus be in charge. The personality profile is assertive and extroverted with somewhat nervous and restless tension. The shaper avoids constraints, seeks expedient routes, and is unduly sensitive to criticism, although quick to criticize others. Although at times compulsive, intolerant, and very competitive, when operating well, this person can command respect, inspire enthusiasm, and make things happen. A shaper operates best in an informal team of peers and needs to practice self-discipline in a mixed, structured group.

The Innovator. This person's strength lies in his or her capacity for advancing new ideas and strategies independent of his or her professional expertise. The innovator has a fertile, fluent mind capable of original thought. If properly plugged into a team, this person can transform his or her thinking and contribute to its success. The personality profile indicates someone who has high intelligence but who is not naturally geared to survival in organizational structures. The innovator emphasizes ideas, not people, while underemphasizing pragmatic feasibility. Yet, he or she can transform team efforts through new insights that focus issues and cause thinking breakthroughs. This person needs team support to stay with the group and to alter this style.

The Company Worker. This team member accepts situational limitations and conventions while buckling down to getting the job done. He or she translates concepts and plans into working realities through care and thoroughness, determination and common sense. The company worker needs objectives and procedures to be clearly spelled out so that he or she can follow them exactly. The personality profile indicates that this person rates high on sincerity, integrity, self-discipline, and character. Reluctant to change and experiment, this manager's strengths often mean promotion to senior levels. Because of lack of vision and inability to deal with unstable situations, plus innate conservatism, this member is less effective as a team head than as its backbone.

The Monitor Evaluator. This manager is able to think critically, analyze ideas, and evaluate feasibility. A strategist and judge, this member provides overall perspective but needs the input of ideas and knowledge of what is going on around the group. The personality profile indicates weakness in persuasive powers and a tendency toward the negative or overcritical; but when used properly, these traits may prevent the team from taking on ill-advised projects and help members deal with complex information and optimal decisions when data are ambiguous. Intellectually competitive and often right, this person may overpower colleagues and stifle their contributions. When feeding ideas to others to use, this person is at his or her best.

The Team Worker. This team member puts people at the top of the list of priorities and is concerned about the feelings, needs, and concerns of members. He or she observes the strengths and weaknesses of each participant and capitalizes on individual assets while delimiting liabilities. Low key and pervasive, the team worker plays a facilitator role and minimizes frictions and antipathies. The personality profile reveals a stable extrovert with a strong competitive streak and a need for power. Beginning as a behind-the-scenes helper, this person develops into an adept delegator and staff developer.

The Resource Investigator. This is a person with a drive to explore resources and ideas outside the team and to develop a wide range of useful contacts. When actually present in the group, he or she maintains good relations, encouraging colleagues to use talents and to experiment with new ideas. The personality is cheerful, resourceful. Although capable of stimulating ideas in others, if the impetus is lost, this type may become bored or demoralized or may overextend him- or herself. At best, the resource investigator helps the team avoid introversion, defensiveness, and becoming out of touch with the wider world.

The Completer. This person keeps the team on its toes, helping it avoid errors of commission or omission. He or she is concerned about the project staying on schedule and about the completion of details and demonstrates a sense of urgency. The personality profile indicates a worrier with great self-control, strength of character, and purpose, but someone who is highly anxious, compulsive, and introverted. This nervous energy can be used to get a project completed, despite the irritations it may cause.

The great contribution of Mottram's research is its confirmation of roles that have both strengths and weaknesses. It is the balancing of these positive and negative factors that makes a great team. Each role can contribute to team success, as well as failure. While all the roles are needed to some degree, the right combination makes for effective team management; for participants, this may mean role sharing or sacrifice. Mottram's research provides helpful clues as to what to seek in people if a balanced team is to be composed. Implications for high performance are that we should gather together a team of people who can play these various roles. The challenge is to recognize and capitalize on each member's strengths while minimizing natural or acquired weaknesses. In the synergistic combination lies the key to increased team effectiveness.

Conclusion

Teamwork and its development can be utilized at all levels of the organization—literally a way of managing. The team strategy can be employed from industrial job training to complex matrix management. It can be used with volunteers, part-time or hourly workers, and right up the organization to executive development. Teams can be formed with people from a horizontal or vertical distribution of the work force. Teams in the forms of task forces or ad hoc groups can cut across organizational barriers and boundaries to create a talented mix of human assets that enhance problem-solving capabilities. A team strategy is standard operating procedure in the new work culture for more effective energizing of people and for improving their interfacing.

NINE

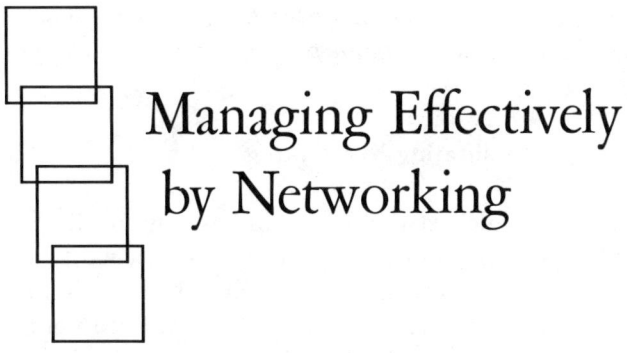

Managing Effectively
by Networking

Executive Summary. Networking is another strategy for performance improvement that is prominent in the emerging work culture. It involves a system of interrelated people or groups, offices or work stations linked together for information exchange and mutual support. This can be accomplished personally or electronically, informally or formally, locally or globally. Advances in telecommunications have opened up undreamed-of opportunities for networking, either within a multinational organization or among like-minded individuals, institutions, and systems. Creative managers employ computers and other communication technology for networking by electronic mail and bulletin boards, teleconferencing, or video text exchanges. Increasingly, management is subscribing to specialized, commercial networks offering particular information and services that advance their businesses. As more information and knowledge are shared by this means at a faster pace, the nation, indeed the world, is moving toward a network marketplace.

Personal networks of executives, professionals, scientists, and technicians help participants cope with high-growth challenges and the turbulence of transition to the new work environment. Consultants, whether internal or external to the organization, also benefit from networking and make it easier for management to utilize their resources. Groups with special needs, such as women and displaced workers, find networking a helpful coping mechanism. When person-to-person networks add electronic capabilities to their interchange, they enhance their potential for increasing human performance through synergistic action.

Facilitating Networking

The idea of people networks is as old as time itself. Yet the concept of networking is very relevant to the new work culture and complementary to team management. The two in tandem connect resources in such a way as to contribute significantly to the improvement of both technology and productivity. The effective use of networking strategy can stimulate high performance in people and their organizations by advancing information exchanges and sharing problem-solving skills.

Networking is in harmony with the American culture. As a people we like to organize, so we form associations for varied purposes, but especially around occupations—from manure spreaders to information professionals. Benjamin Franklin probably began the tradition in this country in 1727, when he organized the Junto professional and civic association. This was a group of young tradesmen seeking personal and professional development who held weekly meetings and exchanges. The Junto network operated on the basis of twenty-four standing queries that facilitated the sharing of member interests in both getting ahead and doing good. These questions related to everything from sharing new books read and technological advances heard about to giving positive recognition and support to a fellow citizen for outstanding performance or encouragement for the pursuit of "honourable designs." As Franklin, whose genius was later to be demonstrated in many ways, declared: "Individuals associated can do more for society and themselves than they can do in isolation" (Zemke, 1982, p. 106). Out of this synergistic experience, many good things flowed, such as the founding of the first American library, municipal fire department, life insurance company, and philosophical society.

Social critic Philip Slater maintains that as American society becomes more complex, it is transforming itself from a community to a network. This has profound significance for management at a time when the business environment is volatile, unpredictable, and marked by rapid growth of new technologies and enterprises. Instead of small, tightly knit communities in which "constituencies" know and help one another, business leaders must cope with networks of "stakeholders" among suppliers, unions, consumers, environmentalists, and public interest groups. These often form homogeneous networks mobilized around a central theme or cause, often connected by computer. For society and business, this offers both opportunities and dangers. A network society is more permissive, according to Mitroff and Kilmann (1984), allows for a greater range of behaviors (including deviancy), and is more susceptible to psychopaths and sociopaths, which the community seeks to exclude.

Networks, however, can be used for positive contributions that improve both society and the work environment. Executive and architect Charles Luckman proposes a network that would counteract the adversarial relations existing among companies and unions by promoting more synergistic relations for the benefit of the economy and the workers. He advocates and will financially support a Round Table Foundation that would bring together representatives of labor and management for joint learning by labor and management leaders in the most enlightened methods for making our economy produce a higher standard of living for all. The resulting network would facilitate understanding of each other's perspectives and roles and might aid some common understandings for mutual benefits to employees and employers.

Networking has long been used to increase sales performance. The Million Dollar Roundtable (MDRT), headquartered in Des Plaines, Illinois, is a network of 23,000 insurance salespersons who qualify for this association through their record of $1.9 million in new sales of life insurance in a year. The MDRT study groups of five to ten individuals meet three or four times a year for long weekends of concentrated study, sharing management and marketing information and true peer support. One outcome is that these high performers frequently meet with and contact one another informally throughout the year. Although we have long been aware of the informal "old boys' network" and what it does for career development, only recently have women in management and the professions begun to use the network concept seriously. Today, there is not only a formal organization, "All the Good Old Girls," but in many cities women concerned about moving up in their fields and companies or agencies have formed local networks for mutual assistance.

Presently, the most exciting developments are in information networks and services that make electronic linkages among people possible because of the integration of computer and communication technologies. Advances in satellites, teleconferencing, and personal computers have opened up limitless opportunities for networking. Networking, furthermore, is the key technology fueling the spread of office automation—the linking of multiple information processing systems to shared resources. Multipurpose networks become the freeways for the flow of business information because of the interconnections provided. The full potential of office automation cannot be achieved without the right network technology.

The J. C. Penney Company (Norris, 1983) devoted a whole issue of its corporate publication, *Forum,* to the topic of networks, calling them a matrix of exchange. In that issue, John D. Adams, an independent consultant, astutely observed that people use networks to help them either avoid problems or solve problems. Networks provide a new kinship that offers both social and emotional support, as well as advice and intimacy. When one seeks to initiate planned change, networks become a useful mechanism for identifying and energizing those who support the alteration in the status quo or the innovation. Furthermore, coalitions of networks with a common cause can become a powerful social, political, or economic force. We have seen this recently in both the consumer and nuclear freeze movements, as well as in the "Greens" in West Germany and the advocates of equal rights for women in the United States. Within large bureaucracies, networks can be effective change strategies—witness the Delta Task Force within the United States Army that bypassed rank as reason for inclusion and substituted competence, courage, and commitment to renewal as their criteria for membership. Aimed at improving the army, this network of 400 has small group sessions, produces instant books, edits and distributes concept papers, and generates problem solutions—it is a catalyst for change in the military, especially with reference to leadership.

Networking is a growing phenomenon that provides linkages and exchanges among those with common concerns. In an information society, it is an essential communication tool for knowledge workers. Advances in both telecommunications and transportation make the network mechanism even more attractive as a medium for the interchange of both information and insight. Networking can be accomplished formally or informally, personally or electronically, locally or globally, externally or internally. The authors of *The Network Nation* (Hiltz and Turoff, 1978) believe that because of the new technologies, networks will cause more information to be shared by more people at a faster pace than at any other time in history. The futurists at the University of Southern California are more specific in their helpful volume, *The Emerging Network Marketplace* (Dordick, Bradley, and Nanus, 1981); they discuss not only the network information services but also the structure, components, trends, markets, and issues involved. They believe that there are significant socioeconomic, technological, and other factors moving the United States toward a network marketplace. These include economic growth demands, flexible and fast response requirements, rapidly changing demographics, and business communication needs—all factors in the progress of high-performing enterprises.

Personal Networking

The authors of *Networking: The First Report and Directory* (Lipnack and Stamps, 1982) define a network as a web of free-standing participants linked by one or more shared values. They envision a network composed of self-reliant people and independent groups, a new/old organizational tool. Megatrend forecaster John Naisbitt (1982) sees information networks as one of the forces shaping our future, replacing hierarchy and organization charts. Personal networks, according to the late sociologist Virginia Hine, are often multileadered, segmented or composed of autonomous segments, and ideological. The latter gives the grouping the power of a unifying idea.

Personal networks are free-forming and adaptive; often, the process is characterized by: (1) relationships that are both abstract and qualitative—the person is more important than the paper he or she creates; (2) unstructuredness: its boundaries are fuzzy and its autonomous participants function independently both as wholes and parts, or "wholeparts" as Stamps and Lipnack designated them; (3) distribution of power, responsibility, and decision making duties; (4) multiple roles, because networkers play varied and existential roles as "nodes" (entry points or end recipients) or "links" (connectors or conveyors of information); (5) balance in terms of the integrity and importance of personal worth and collective purpose (I/we); and (6) shared values and concerns that cause temporary coalescence and cohesion—the ideological glue that holds together the participants.

Thus individuals or groups have formed a wide variety of networks that serve human needs, including the following:

- Transnational Network for Appropriate/Alternative Technologies (TRANET) in Rangeley, Maine, operates on five continents from this tiny village.
- The 24-Carat Club in New York City and New England, which is a network for independent jewelry saleswomen.
- The Office for Open Network Resources in Denver, Colorado, offers network services to those seeking to find others of similar interests from inventors to investors.
- Communications Era Task Force of Spokane, Washington, and Winlaw, Canada, is an international network for those aware of a new reality emerging and who wish to examine new directions, ideas, values, and models.

Networks also have been formed to promote wellness or to help people cope with substance abuse—alcohol or other drugs or smoking. The essence of their success is that they are person-to-person exchanges of information and support, often self-help in nature.

Since collegial networks are helpful, informative, and perceptually enlarging, it would be most helpful to cultivate certain behaviors that support networking. Carol J. Pierce (Norris, 1983, pp. 20-21), a New Hampshire process consultant, suggests the following:

1. Assertiveness: willingness to stand up and be counted in expressing ideas and acting on behalf of our beliefs;
2. Willingness to take risks: willingness to extend and commit oneself by signing up, making unpopular decisions, supporting minority causes or even nonviolent actions, such as picketing;
3. Initiative: willingness to form or support networks that integrate both personal and group goals;
4. Autonomousness: ability to work independently and interdependently in relation to individuals and the whole network;
5. Communicativeness: ability to interact effectively by listening and contributing, by facilitating and maintaining group morale.

For people networks to function effectively, participants must be open to differences in each other and promote sharing of unique opinions, attitudes, insights, and perceptions. Personal networking requires members to be understanding and accepting, to be encouraging and creative, to share leadership and be democratic in the best sense. Networks work best when they are synergistic.

In managing personal networks, consideration should be given to the four C's, according to sociology professor Charles Kadushin of the City University of New York (Norris, 1983, p. 18):

> CONTROL is difficult within informal networks, and is often dependent upon leadership of organizations and communities from whence members come. . . .

CONTEXT is the social atmosphere and reality in which the network operates and is somewhat dependent upon; informal networks are rarely independent centers of power. . . .

CLIQUISHNESS is the tendency for networks to view themselves as unique and elite, and to practice exclusiveness; social status is achieved through membership in a network or its inner circle. . . .

COST is the reality that all networks, even informal ones, incur expenses which must be borne; since most have no budgets coming from public support, they devise means like barter, member investment, delayed payments, or low-cost operations based on volunteers, contributed services, and the like.

When the network operates within a larger and more formal organization, support may come directly or indirectly from that entity. When an informal network grows in terms of number of members, services offered, and influence exerted, it usually is formalized with contracts and payments and the introduction of management systems. In a high-tech company, for instance, an informal network might exist to accomplish certain tasks. When operating in a project management mode, the network concept may be formalized, such as through the creation of a third-party support system. This is an ancillary but disciplined group of software professionals who become a supplementary resource for project managers to call on, in addition to the regular in-house technical staff of the corporation. Sometimes technical specialists within fast-growth enterprises form networks with colleagues in other companies or industries in order to keep up with the state of the art in their field. Network participation contributes to their performance improvement and assists in problem solving, especially with emerging technology.

The need for such networking was underscored by Andrew Grove, president of Intel (1983a), when he indicated that rapid change makes it imperative to mix position power with knowledge power. Networking strengthens the latter by keeping

Managing Effectively by Networking 257

the executive on the cutting edge of business knowhow. Sometimes these network relationships may be formalized, as with CEOs in San Diego County's "Valley of the Chips." There, key management in high-tech, fast-growth companies are forming a San Diego Technology Executives Network (SDTEN, Box 2321, La Jolla, Calif. 92038), which is being connected in turn to university knowledge and data bases, as well as various government research centers and programs. But the most valuable service of such local networks comes from peer relations, support, and problem solving.

Networks are often formed as a result of membership in some trade, technical, or professional association. This may begin with attendance at an interest group meeting of an existing organization or within an industry and with an exchange of business cards. Often, this ends with an expression of thought, such as "keep in touch" or "we must get together again"; if someone becomes a catalyst and takes on the "weaver" role to bring such people of common concern together physically or electronically, then a new network may be born.

Figure 11 offers an overview of the process of networking with reference to innovators. In it, Parker and Hedin of the Center on Technology and Society in Cambridge, Massachusetts, describe how isolated innovators may—intentionally or not—create a network that then can be institutionalized or dissolved or spun off into another network. In any event, people networks can be a powerful resource to high-performing managers, for tapping into brainpower ensures success in a knowledge society.

Electronic Networking

The formation of electronic information networks is facilitated by rapid developments in telecommunications. Some people have networked frequently in the past via telephone and conference calls, but the computer now extends this possibility to a new level. The magic of electronic mail is its capability for message exchange through computer interface, allowing retrieval at a time convenient to the receiver. The electronic interchange may be made among employees of the same company within a

258   Management in Transition

Figure 11. Process of Creation and Change in Personal Networks.

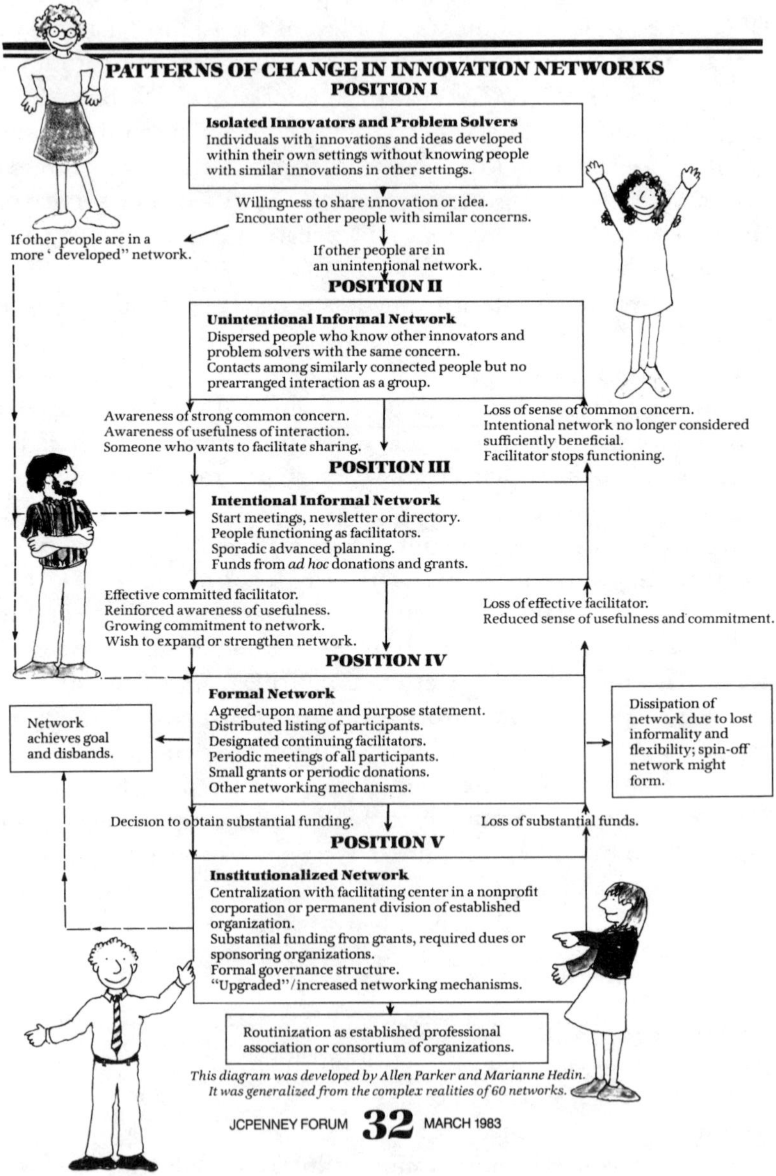

PATTERNS OF CHANGE IN INNOVATION NETWORKS
POSITION I

Isolated Innovators and Problem Solvers
Individuals with innovations and ideas developed within their own settings without knowing people with similar innovations in other settings.

Willingness to share innovation or idea.
Encounter other people with similar concerns.

If other people are in a more "developed" network.   If other people are in an unintentional network.

POSITION II

Unintentional Informal Network
Dispersed people who know other innovators and problem solvers with the same concern.
Contacts among similarly connected people but no prearranged interaction as a group.

Awareness of strong common concern.   Loss of sense of common concern.
Awareness of usefulness of interaction.   Intentional network no longer considered
Someone who wants to facilitate sharing.   sufficiently beneficial.
                                             Facilitator stops functioning.

POSITION III

Intentional Informal Network
Start meetings, newsletter or directory.
People functioning as facilitators.
Sporadic advanced planning.
Funds from *ad hoc* donations and grants.

Effective committed facilitator.
Reinforced awareness of usefulness.   Loss of effective facilitator.
Growing commitment to network.   Reduced sense of usefulness and commitment.
Wish to expand or strengthen network.

POSITION IV

Formal Network
Agreed-upon name and purpose statement.
Distributed listing of participants.   Dissipation of
Network   Designated continuing facilitators.   network due to lost
achieves goal   Periodic meetings of all participants.   informality and
and disbands.   Small grants or periodic donations.   flexibility; spin-off
                   Other networking mechanisms.   network might
                                                              form.

Decision to obtain substantial funding.   Loss of substantial funds.

POSITION V

Institutionalized Network
Centralization with facilitating center in a nonprofit corporation or permanent division of established organization.
Substantial funding from grants, required dues or sponsoring organizations.
Formal governance structure.
"Upgraded"/increased networking mechanisms.

Routinization as established professional association or consortium of organizations.

This diagram was developed by Allen Parker and Marianne Hedin.
It was generalized from the complex realities of 60 networks.

JCPENNEY FORUM **32** MARCH 1983

Source: *JCPenney Forum,* March 1983, p. 32. Reprinted with permission.

single plant or among many facilities of that organization. Or it may be made with friends and acquaintances in other firms and locales with whom we are familiar. The interchange may even take place with professionals we have never met but have only written to or talked with by telephone. What may begin as a message exchange dictated by the need to communicate rapidly and economically with a geographically dispersed group of people may in time become an electronic network. In other words, the electronic "mailbox" and "bulletin board" can be transformed into an informal or formal network exchange.

The World Future Society devoted a whole issue of its journal (*The Futurist,* June 1984) to the theme of networking as a global communication tool. In that unusual edition an article appeared by C. Jackson Grayson, Jr., chairman of the American Productivity Center, on networking by computer (pp. 14–17), in which he indicated how such networks could be of assistance to business firms for electronically linking corporate officers to divisional managers; for linking plant managers and supervisors to share common problems and information; for linking technical personnel across divisions and projects; for developing organizational relations among those who share the same functions in large corporations, but across work unit affiliations; for linking together members of quality circles, productivity teams, and various involvement groups. Obviously, the network can be extended outside the company to connect corporations to legislative services, varied data bases, and associations.

Grayson suggests that the computer network can facilitate participation in industry associations and professional societies. The possibilities range from connecting information among members, to planning meetings or actually conducting special theme conferences electronically.

A group of scientists, for example, began with an information interchange that evolved into Science Net; now it is managed by a Boston company, Omnet, Inc., and is the world's largest R&D communications network apart from the United States government's ARPANET. Intergroup or intercompany networks have been formed to cater to particular interests within and among systems of people. Network training and management seem to be the key to effective electronic intercommunication. Some companies, for instance, prefer to purchase a commercial service for this purpose rather than get into their own hardware and software costs plus the cost of training managers and technical personnel in the proper use of networks. For some participants, there may also be the added issue of security, so passwords have to be devised and codes developed.

For those with access to a micro- or personal computer, communication becomes possible with mainframes and local and public networks. Many personal computer owners form their own networks to facilitate their use of particular hardware, such as IBM, Apple, or Kaypro, and to exchange data on software possibilities. These networks enable users to improve long-distance communications, to emulate the functions of large terminals, to use protocols for file transfers, to ensure computer security, to solve performance problems, and to assess resources or vendor offerings. In this age of information networks, voice, data, and image can be integrated electronically, tying together dissimilar, intelligent devices, terminals, computers, and data bases. Figure 12 illustrates the components and communication possibilities for a local area network, which can also be expanded regionally, nationally, and internationally.

It is the modem, the box-like connector of computer and telephone, that makes it possible for people to form electronic networks. Furthermore, those in search of information, colleagues with similar interests, or just friends may access networks to serve particular purposes. The most popular of the pay-for-connect-time utilities is The Source, with 40,000 subscribers, and Compuserve, with 70,000 members. Plugging into an existing data base can give one a variety of specialized information, as well as news, games, travel tips, and so on. Networks have been brought into being to serve the needs of professionals wishing to interface with colleagues, aviators in a particular area, those who are handicapped with special disabilities, or persons seeking legal or personal counsel. For many, it is exciting when an audience is created that is interested in their ideas and responds to personal input.

Figure 12. An Electronic Local Area Network.

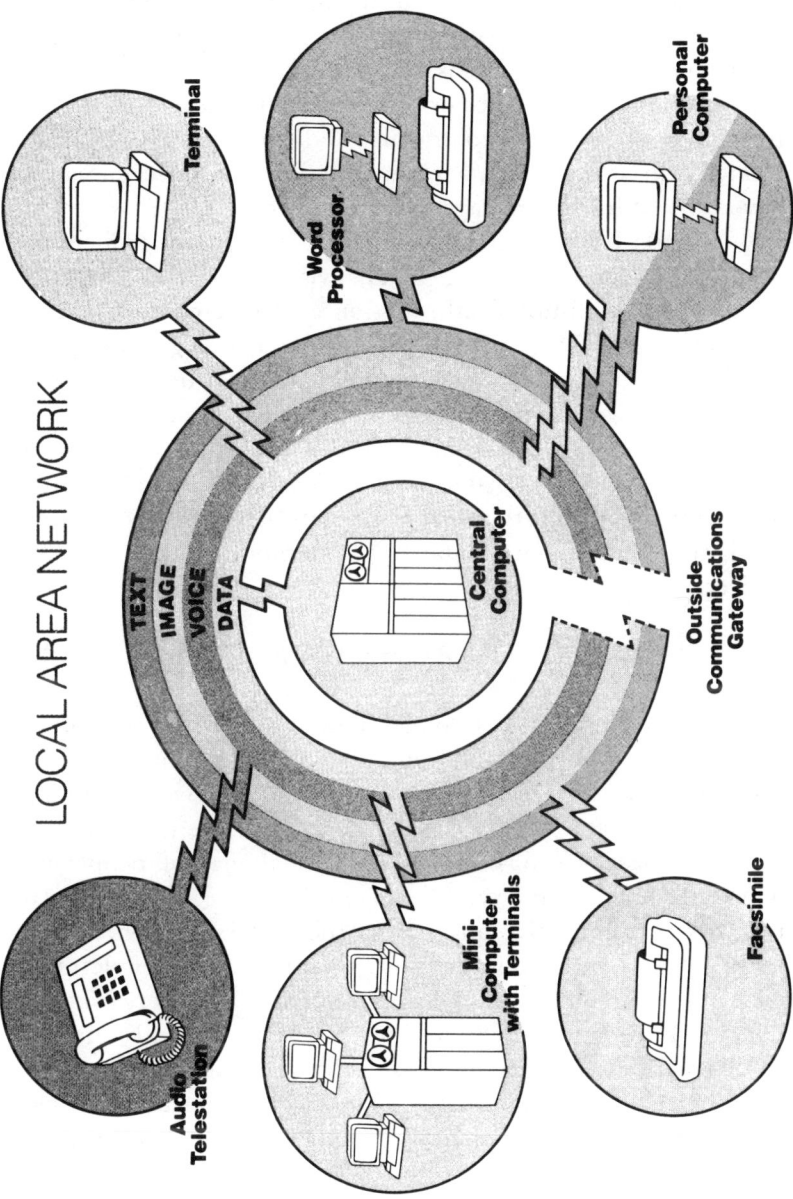

Source: The Diebold Group, 475 Park Avenue South, New York, New York 10016. Reprinted with permission.

Managers concerned about high-output management in an enterprise or an industry might, as a case in point, create an electronic network for this purpose. Those interested in the topic of high performance or human resource development may form a conference tree to organize and store messages being exchanged on this subject, such as practices and procedures that have worked for the managers in the network.

Similarly, managers coping with the growing phenomenon of "telecommunicating" might wish to set up an electronic network for continuing information exchange on this trend in the work force. They might exchange data on legal and regulatory news, supervisory and technology issues. In fact, at least one such network now exists and has spawned a newsletter entitled *Telecommuting Review* (Telespan Publishing Corporation, 50 West Palm Street, Altadena, Calif. 91001). Members share information on everything from security issues related to home work terminals to long-distance telecommuting from offshore offices.

Management and Consultant Networking

Networking makes connections between and among human resources. In fact, the four and a half billion inhabitants of Earth make up a collective nervous system, a network of human consciousness and energy. The Network Institute (Box 66, West Newton, Mass. 02165) acts as a clearinghouse of people networks throughout the world, ranging from the Tarrytown 100 network for innovative business to the Professional Writers network. The institute publishes not only a book and newsletter on this phenomenon but also a directory of these networks. We will end our analysis of the subject of networks with reference to several that will be of interest to thinking managers.

One of the oldest and most successful successful networks of CEOs is The Executive Committee (TEC), a subsidiary of Vedax Sciences Corporation (3737 Camino del Rio South, San Jose, Calif. 92018). In California alone, TEC enrolls more than 350 presidents of small, usually low-tech corporations. The group meets formally on a monthly basis, devoting its morning session to input and discussion with a guest expert of its choos-

Managing Effectively by Networking

ing. The afternoon is then spent with a TEC facilitator for peer problem solving. That same TEC consultant meets at least monthly with each member for counsel. Each executive team consists of no more than twelve persons, and members occasionally meet with other groups through workshops, regional meetings, or telephone conferences. Members value highly the executive development and peer support values of such experiences. Reports indicate that participants receive help with such practical matters as establishing a successful telemarketing program, decisions on a single-interest venture versus a partnership, turning a company around from insolvency, forming highly satisfying friendships with counterparts, using network resources to locate qualified specialists, using colleagues as a sounding board for wrenching decisions, and learning to restructure a company for more delegation. This sampling of results points up some of the positive outcomes from a network catering to top management needs.

Ronald Richards, a fellow TEC consultant, offers some guidance to those who wish to be effective in such networks:

1. Be candid, open, and helpful in participation.
2. Support the group by regular and active attendance, but extend friendships beyond the monthly meeting.
3. Use hosting a meeting as an opportunity to acquaint fellow members with one's company, just as if the group were a board of directors.
4. Exchange annual reviews or reports with a view toward improving your own.
5. Share written discussion issues with members prior to problem-solving sessions; think out and prepare issues before the session in which you might be helpful because of personal competence.
6. Challenge ideas and concepts in the peer sessions.
7. Invite the network facilitator to visit your plant or headquarters, and seek feedback on that professional's observations.
8. Use network tapes for additional learning and develop a library for use with your own management.
9. When contemplating major corporate moves, such as di-

vestiture, contact for advice other network members with similar business experience.
10. Consult colleagues for recommendations when searching for management personnel suitable for your firm.

Steven Panzer, founder of Southern California Technology Executives Network (12011 San Vicente Boulevard, Los Angeles, Calif. 90049), ascribes much of the success of high-tech executives in his geographic area to their connections and information exchanges with counterparts in other companies. They learn through network sharing that they are not the only chief executives with such problems. Panzer believes that the power of the organized network is in the member, as well as the consulting, resources that can be brought to play on particular executive needs. In this safe forum they can confront the question of why so many high-technology companies fail to go beyond their first product. The principal benefit from such networks is peer dialogue and mentor relationships.

Consultants also create networks for their own development, and these can be very valuable for independent practitioners suffering from isolation and lack of colleagueship. One such group is the International Consultants Foundation (ICF) (11612 Georgetowne Court, Potomac, Md. 20854), which publishes a newsletter, proceedings of its annual meetings, and referrals for services. For managers interested in its services, ICF has an annual registry of its members and will sell proceedings volumes to externals. (For example, in 1980 this text was *Innovations in Global Consultation,* edited by Harris and Malin, and in 1981, *Systems Thinking* by Lippitt and Lippitt.) A 1983 ICF workshop on "Networking" examined the advantages of interdisciplinary, interorganizational, and cross-cultural cooperation. It pointed out how this mechanism can enable consultants to share their personal stresses and concerns, their professional services and resources, their knowledge of future trends and projections.

The Consultants' Networks (57 West 89th Street, New York, N.Y. 10024) offers both a personal and electronic network. Its DATAFILE system—consisting of a computer file on each consultant and his or her individual expertise—should be of special interest to executives. A matrix summary of resources is available on request without charge; a user subscription gains access to printouts on members' backgrounds. Consultants' Networks' founder, Stan Berliner, believes that this resource-finding system facilitates the linkage of executives and external consultants.

Another example of how networking can aid high-performing management is the video distribution network concept. Through such a system, organizational communications and training are dramatically improved. Within a national or international enterprise, timely information is obtained on marketing, policies, strategies, and other business matters to be distributed simultaneously in various locations. RCA Services Company (909 N. Orange Avenue, Hollywood, Calif. 90038) is at the forefront of this video network technology.

Managers and consultants with mutual concerns formulate networks to satisfy specific needs. For example, there has been a growing awareness among managers and human resource development specialists of the value of human factor data gathering—that is, the use of some instrumentation to collect, analyze, and disseminate information from members in an organization or industry; this may be accomplished through inventories, questionnaires, checklists, or other such diagnostic survey techniques for seeking opinion and feedback. This awareness first led to a sharing of information about the subject in training publications as to what existed and where to obtain it; next, a seminar was held for information exchange and evaluation on existing instruments of this type. Finally, an Instrumentation Network (Suite 334, 15612 Highway 7, Minnetonka, Minn. 55345) emerged. Its director, Mari Lou Goodacre, is maintaining a file of samples of existing commercial instruments and data profiles on each filled out by the suppliers and publishes a *Directory for Training and Development Instrumentation*.

To further cooperation and trust by multiplying connections, Network Builders International of Atlanta, Georgia, a consulting firm, offers computerized networking directories relative to learning and resource opportunities for people willing to share skills, knowledge, and experience. Many professional groups are also publishing network services to specialists in various fields. The University of Michigan's ERIC Clearinghouse on Counseling and Personnel Services in Ann Arbor hosts CAPS: HITECH, an electronic network for professional counselors, that involves message exchanges, consultation, and computer conferencing.

Computer networks are spreading rapidly for the purposes of management and professional development or problem solving. The National Society for Performance Instruction (NSPI) reported in *The Performance and Instruction Journal* (1983) that in the fields of science and technology alone there now exist over 1,000 data bases used at least two million times a year by searchers. In addition, NSPI notes that there are 530 bibliographic data bases with seventy million citations. To cope with the information explosion, thinking managers and other professionals create their own prototype knowledge data bases and networks. Colleagues join together to input, synthesize, and update this information; often updating is done monthly by a panel of experts. Thus, if management has a particular concern about developments in corporate health services or advances in biotechnology, a task force of volunteers can be formed to establish its own select computer network.

Table 4 provides a sampling of such network resources.

Another example of commercial electronic networks serving new management and consultant needs is PLATO. Founded originally to service schools through computer-assisted instruction, it now provides a note file on various academic subjects which can be entered into by users who wish to leave and receive messages in a certain category of information. Metaindustrial management already utilizes many international and national information exchanges, such as The Source and Compuserve, for communication with special interest groups, for market research, and for other purposes. However, many managers and consultants in transition need orientation not only to the potential for networking but also to the possibilities opened up by electronic networking. To understand sophisticated wideband transmissions for video, data, voice, graphics, facsimile,

Table 4. Managerial Network Resource Sampler.

In addition to the networks already mentioned, this listing may be of interest to thinking managers seeking network resources.

- Network Institute, P.O. Box 66, West Newton, Mass. 02165; a metanetwork that links members to other networks by means of a directory of 2,000.
- Metasystems Design Group, 1401 Wilson Blvd., #601, Arlington, Va. 22209; computer linkage to transformationally oriented futurists for electronic mail exchange and computer conferencing.
- Office for Open Network Resources, P.O. Box 18666, Denver, Colo. 80218; subscribers' service for information and idea exchange.
- Transnational Network for Appropriate/Alternative Technologies (TRANET), P.O. Box 567, Rangeley, Maine 04970; a global clearinghouse and resource matchmaker for local self-help technology.
- Institute for the Information Society, 2-15-29 Shinjuku, Shinjuku-ku, Tokyo, Japan; to implement networking in Japan, in cooperation with the government's economic planning agency.

Special Network Resources

- Microcomputer Information Support Tools (MIST), 695 Fifth Street, Lake Oswego, Oreg. 97034; software system for converting personal computers into network stations.
- *Computer-Mediated Communication Systems,* by E. Kerr and S. R. Hiltz, published by Academic Press, 52227 Stevens Creek Blvd., Santa Clara, Calif., 1982; tells how to do electronic networking through computers.
- *Manager's Guide to Local Networks,* by F. Derfler and W. Stallings, available from the American Management Associations Book Club, 135 West 50th Street, New York, N.Y. 10020, 1983; shows how to use local area networks to increase productivity and knowledge about the latest in communications and computer technology.
- *Complete Handbook of Personal Computer Communications* by A. Glossbrenner, published by St. Martin's Press, New York, N.Y., 1983; provides everything needed to know to go on-line with the world.

Source: Noel McInnis, editor of *The Futurist* (June 1984) special section on networking, kindly provided the above information.

and the like, computer network capabilities (such as Ethernet and Wangnet) require special briefings either within organizations or by going outside to public seminars.

Organizations invest considerable funds in sending personnel to special meetings, workshops, seminars, and other information-gathering conferences. As I have observed with my own clients, too many sponsors fail to get sufficient pay-back or ROI on such expenditures. That is, there is not enough follow-up with individual employees or members to allow the data obtained to become internalized into organizational knowledge. One way of doing this is through some form of debriefing—that is, providing an opportunity for the participant to share his or her experience and information with colleagues either orally or in a report, particularly as to how they can benefit the company or agency that paid for participation. The other possibility is for personal or electronic networking to occur among the attendees in such programs in order to continue their exchange.

Ellen Nan Velsor, a research associate at North Carolina's Center for Creative Leadership in Greensboro, has conducted a study that points out the networking possibilities for members of a management staff who attend a training group together. In the center's *Issues & Observations,* Velsor proposes forming issues groups during the sessions; these groups would communicate across divisions and deal with working relationships. After the training ends, program alumni groups can continue to exchange dialogue on the issues and might even be allotted organization time for this purpose.

Conclusion

Networking is a powerful synergistic tool that wise meta-industrial management employs in order to remain well informed. It is a means for improving professional and organizational relations and for furthering career development. Networking systematically builds on a set of relationships and contacts that can both facilitate and provide support to thinking managers. When used properly, it leads to knowledge and growth; when abused as a gimmick for self-aggrandisement at the expense of others, it debases human relationships.

TEN

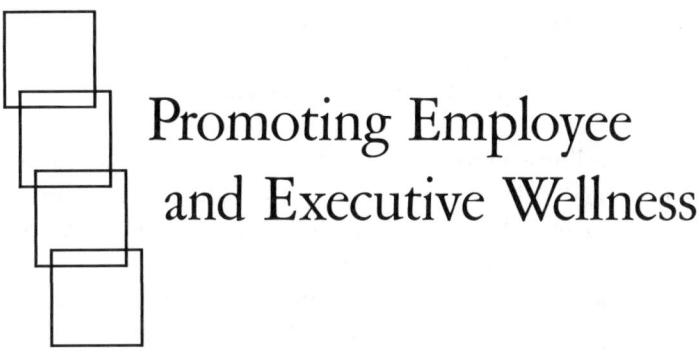

Promoting Employee and Executive Wellness

Executive Summary. As society shifts to a different work culture centered around information processing and new technologies, many people are exhibiting symptoms of future shock—increased substance abuse, personal and systems breakdowns, burnout and technostress, and self-violence and suicide. Such destructive trends point up the need for corporate strategies to counter these negative adjustments while improving employee coping skills during the profound social transition. New age management efforts in this regard go beyond traditional medical benefits and safety training, advocating instead wellness in both life and the work place. Such strategies contain rising health care costs for business, as well as for individuals, and contribute directly to enhancing performance and productivity on the job.

Thinking managers lead in developing healthier life-styles for themselves and their corporate colleagues. They foster innovative efforts to delimit medical and hospital expenses while promoting a behavioral health approach—taking self-responsibility for a wellness quality of life. Metaindustrial managers are concerned about stress management, the fit between the individual personality and the work environment, being a wellness behavior model, making use of wellness resources, and creating people support systems. They realize that corporate health, literally and financially, requires active involvement in programs to protect and enhance the health and well-being of both personnel and the public affected by corporate activity.

Corporate Behavioral Health

- A "wellness epidemic" is breaking out in factories and offices, helping workers modify life-style factors that may set them up for strokes, heart attacks, cancer, and other health disasters.
- A scientific revolution is underway. Among its manifestations is the growing popularity of "taking responsibility" for one's health through running and other forms of exercise, through diet and life-style modifications, and through intense preoccupation with wellness and prevention.
- A connection has been made between personality type, stress, and occupational environment. Researchers at SRI International have confirmed that person-fit factors may cause job stress. That is, the combined fit or lack of it between a manager or worker's life-style and the demands of the work environment can be a cause of job satisfaction on the one hand or stress on the other.
- A radical alteration of the work environment through various new technologies is disrupting the lives of millions of workers. In addition to the severe stress and depression frequently caused by lay-offs from traditional jobs and industries, those who manage to hold onto their positions often are filled with fear of operating in a deregulated industry, of having to learn new skills, or of being replaced by some automated machine.

This is a sampling of current news reports. The message indicates both positive and negative aspects of work life, when society and organizations are in turbulent transition. In the old work culture, companies and agencies primarily were concerned about physical safety during work hours or basic medical benefits as part of a total compensation package for employees. Larger corporations might even have had a medical department with a physician and/or nurse and occasionally a dietitian—the primary concern was for medical record keeping, annual physicals, some first aid or simple treatment, and limited health information.

In the new work culture, there is a major change of attitude regarding employee health and well-being and the employer's responsibilities in that regard. Corporate wellness strategies and facilities attempt to obtain higher performance and productivity as well as to contain the exploding costs of health care. Human resource development efforts within organizations now include a bewildering variety of both mental and physical fitness offerings for personnel. Furthermore, individual and group therapy is paid for in whole or in part by employers assisting employees to overcome abuse of alcohol and other substances. However, little is being done to help executives and other workers improve their ability to cope with the changes underway. Thinking managers concerned about their own health, as well as about the health of their colleagues and the corporation, should address such issues as part of their strategic planning for the future.

As Joseph D. Matarazzo and his associates (1984) summarized, three major categories for healthiness deserve management's support: (1) preventive health services—related to high blood pressure control, family planning, pregnancy and infant health, immunization, and curbing of sexually transmitted diseases; (2) health protection—occupational safety and health through toxic agent control, accident prevention and injury control, fluoridation and dental hygiene, and surveillance and control of infectious diseases; and (3) health promotion or wellness—through reduction or elimination of tobacco smoking, curtailment of misuse of alcohol and other drugs, control of undue stress and violent behavior, promotion of balanced nutrition, physical fitness, and exercise, use of seat belts, child daycare provisions, and other such practices contributing to a healthier life-style.

Encouragement of wellness among employees is more than an exercise in corporate social responsibility—healthy workers are more happy and productive; unhealthy ones are a financial drain on employers. Millions of dollars are lost each year in corporate profits and productivity because of employee illness and accidents. Peak performance levels may be undermined by employees whose functioning is impaired by various physiological or psychological ailments. Increasingly, such loss in worker efficiency is related to abuses of alcohol and other substances. Whether this destructive behavior is an inherited tendency or due to an inability to cope with future shock, repairing the damage or compensating victims of impaired employees can be disastrous to the company's bottom line. (Consider the position of railroad executives facing lawsuits against their companies because inebriated locomotive engineers caused serious train wrecks.) Then there is the matter of skyrocketing medical costs and how these affect the organization's contribution to employee health insurance.

Surely such negative factors should be reason enough to stimulate management interest in employee health and well-being. But thinking managers have more positive motivations for improving their own health and that of their associates at work. They realize that wellness can enhance both quality of life and human performance while preventing or delimiting health hazards and catastrophes. Such matters are integral to management concerns in the new work culture—successfully dealing with these issues contributes significantly to the maintenance of a healthy organization.

Historical Perspective

During humankind's initial stage of development as primitive hunters, health concerns largely were related to survival. Often, such needs were handled by medicine men or faith healers. It was in the agricultural stage that communal living led to a new level of health need and treatment. With the emergence of food shortages and infectious diseases, more formal medical care and institutions came into existence. In the previous 300 years of industrial work culture, the human condition witnessed both improved health service and extended life span while experiencing increased hazards from nuclear accidents or destruction and occupational risks. During that period, there were major advances in modern science, such as the revolutions in biomedicine and pharmacological research. Such developments have not only eliminated many diseases that plagued our ancestors, but they also have spawned huge health and hospital industries, as well as rising health care costs. The industrial age has produced a strange mix of progress and regression. Advances in public health, microbiology, and food production and processing have reduced morbidity and mortality, while factory workers are being exposed to unprecedented chemical and other substance contaminations. In fact, the factory itself often has contributed to environmental pollution and threatened community well-being. The disaster at the Union Carbide plant in 1984 at Bhopal, India, should convince skeptics of the need for greater industrial safety and greater environmental protection.

Industrial-age medicine, now called traditional, operates on models of cure and rehabilitation only. It often produces marvelous applications, but principally in First and Second World countries. In the twentieth century, business and industry used such health resources not only to promote safety and hygiene but also to experiment with preventive health models for their workers. In the last decade, far-sighted management has promoted the clean-up of pollution caused by its corporate operations and sought to preserve ecological balance. In other cases, irate citizens and government intervention have forced companies to exercise social responsibility.

As we create a postindustrial society, our health consciousness is being raised further. We have more knowledge and information on illness and wellness, on overcoming disabilities and handicaps, and on increasing longevity and dignifying death. At the beginning of the 1980s, the United States Surgeon General, Julius Richmond, stated that the health of Americans had never been better. But at what price and for whom? Midway through the decade, we are now aware of fellow citizens suffering in increasing numbers from lack of food, shelter, and health services. In 1982, over $321 billion was expended to provide health care for our United States population of 230 million people. Yet, although that figure was 10 percent of the national gross product, whole segments of the society did not share in these benefits. As we move toward a new work culture, the trend is toward health enhancement and taking responsibility for preserving one's own well-being.

According to Matarazzo, a professor at Oregon Health Sciences University, and his associates (1984), a consensus is emerging among professional, business, and government leaders. They agree that: (1) the financial and human costs associated with currently preventable dysfunctions (such as lung cancer, cardiovascular disease, alcohol and other drug abuse, and vehicular accidents) are a waste of this country's human and fiscal resources; and (2) the behavior of the individual (use or abuse of tobacco, alcohol and other drugs, and salt; poor practice relative to dental hygiene or automobile seat belts, and so on) is the unexplored frontier in the study and understanding of good health. Today there is more willingness in the metaindustrial society to go beyond traditional medicine as commonly practiced by established physicians and to consider alternative forms of health care. As Norman Cousins, author of *Anatomy of Illness,* so eloquently explained in a television production on his book, the art of healing is still a frontier profession.

Medical sociologist Aaron Antonovsky (1979) suggests that one of the remarkable accomplishments of our times is the majority of living persons remaining healthy in the presence of so many pathogens; he recommends that more attention and research be directed toward discovering the reason for that phenomenon. He surmises that persons who have a strong "sense of coherence" in their lives are less apt to succumb to microbiological and psychological pathogens (stressors). For Antonovsky, *coherence* means maintaining control over one's own health; developing a basic personality structure that has a global orientation; cultivating a dynamic feeling of confidence that one's internal and external environment are somewhat predictable and that there is a high probability that things will work out as well as can be expected. Perhaps there is a clue here for wellness in times of turbulent transition—namely, build into our lives more self-regulation, more openness and flexibility, and more positive mental attitudes. Yet, Antonovsky issued a warning—radical changes in one's structural situation (in marital status, occupation, place of residence) can lead to significant modification of one's sense of coherence. I agree strongly with Antonovsky, for my experience indicates that any form of major culture shock or life crisis also triggers a major reevaluation of our psychological constructs—that is, the way we read meaning into our lives. This is what is happening to workers generally as the new technologies bring about profound shifts in work itself, in the way it is done, and in the roles we play. This issue will be discussed further in the next chapter.

Health Care in the New Work Culture

There are many forces shaping the future of health care, such as sweeping redistribution in health delivery systems and the revolution in medical technology. Let us focus here on one trend in this new work culture—the involvement of the corporation in health care—and conclude by connecting it to another previously identified trend—the movement toward behavioral health. Perhaps a brief sampling of what some companies are currently doing regarding employee health will underscore the transitional strategies:

- The healthier life-style program at 130 General Motors plants has produced a 60 percent drop in sickness and accident payments, a 50 percent decline in the number of reported accidents and grievances, and a 40 percent reduction in lost work time.

- Kennecott Copper Company inaugurated an exercise program that has resulted in a 55 percent reduction in medical costs, while New York Telephone Company reports that its smoking cessation program produces savings of $2,045,000 a year because of reductions in absenteeism and medical costs.

- Speedball Corporation of California gives a $7 weekly bonus for not smoking on the job. Colonial Bank & Trust Company of Chicago gives personnel who complete required fitness activities a certificate from the Illinois Governor's Council on Health and Fitness. Bonnie Bell Corporation of Ohio offers financial incentives to those who regularly exercise, as well as providing facilities for this purpose.

- Scherer Brothers Lumber of Minneapolis has snack machines that dispense fruit instead of candy. Faultless Starch Bon Ami Company of Kansas City advocates meditation for stress reduction among its personnel. Cannon Mills of North and South Carolina has a voluntary health maintenance screening program for 23,000 employees.

In *Health Promotion at the Workplace* (Ainsworth and O'Donnell, 1984), the authors documented this corporate push toward healthier life-styles as a means for improving productivity, reducing absenteeism, and deflating medical benefit costs. Endeavors range from company gyms, pools, and jogging trails to corporate programs in nutrition education, hypertension screening, and yoga classes. Many employers are now spending an average of $1,200 to $2,200 per year on medical benefits—sums that outstrip pension costs. Experts project a savings of major proportions for every preventive health program inaugurated (for example, $600 a year for every worker who stops smoking). This explains why in Nebraska, for instance, the Omaha Wellness Council represents a coalition of seventy companies with 60,000 workers engaged in good health programs at their work site. That council is proving the validity of its claim that most people need corporate assistance to help themselves to better health.

According to *The Social Transformation of American Medicine* (Starr, 1982), more than thirty-four million Americans have no health insurance, and a national plan is not likely in the near future. In the book's final chapter, "The Coming of the Corporation," Starr reminds us of a 68 percent jump in profit-making hospital chains and the failure of the fee-for-service medical approach. The corporation also is getting into the health business indirectly through its large expenditures on research and development—this is above and beyond the pharmaceutical, food, and cosmetics industries. Further, there is a convergence going on between the information sciences and bioengineering technologies on the one hand and the field of medicine and hospitals on the other: Business is providing computers for thermal imaging, computer-aided design for genetic engineering and screening, closed-loop control of blood pressure and drug monitoring, and many other innovative medical

Promoting Employee and Executive Wellness

applications. The merger between science and industry is an exciting aspect of the new work culture; it can be witnessed in wide-ranging entrepreneurial, technological endeavors ranging from optical waveguides to nuclear magnetic resonance.

However, for our purposes here, it is the private sector management of health care costs for which managers have the most concern and from which managers have the most to learn. The following six case studies best convey the trends:

Johnson & Johnson. Its Live for Life program helps employees make positive choices in life-style behaviors that not only permit them to control their own health destinies but that moderate health care costs. It combines the advantages of work site participation, concrete goals, company incentives, and peer influence. The initial health screening includes a questionnaire plus biometric and aerobic fitness tests. The company-paid action programs that follow offer choices that focus on weight control, exercise, nutrition, smoking cessation, stress management, and health knowledge. On the average, 40 to 60 percent of the 18,000 employees in thirty locations participate.

Owens-Illinois. Its health care cost containment campaign encompasses 47,000 employees and retirees. Benefit coverage has been reshaped to encourage use of less expensive health care alternatives. Videotapes, newsletters, and handouts are an ongoing part of the plan. Cost-effective alternatives can range from home care service in place of hospital treatment to second opinions on the desirability of surgery to consultation on outpatient services. Health centers also have been established to provide wellness counseling.

John Deere & Company. To counteract a tripling in employee health care costs, this company has required a physicians' peer review system. That is, if a doctor requires hospitalization of an employee, that decision becomes subject to review by medical advisers. Length of stay also is subject to review. Whether Deere will cover all or part of the hospital costs is dependent on this self-administered, self-policing process of the local medical community. The utilization review program has cut the average hospital stay of Deere employees from 1,500 days annually before the plan was inaugurated to 20 days annually. For its 130,000 employees, Deere uses external monitors, such as the Iowa Foundation for Medical Care, to conduct reviews, cutting the annual growth rate for hospital care costs by 20 percent.

Quaker Oats. Its health incentive plan seeks to manage health benefits more effectively through an annual dividend to employees if health care costs are actually lower than forecast. Also included is a $300 yearly health care expense account, which can be used for tax-free reimbursement or taken in cash. Although Quaker does provide comprehensive medical benefits, these are available on a cost-sharing basis, which protects the company against catastrophic losses. Annual adjustments keep the plan's value current with economic changes.

DuPont. DuPont's Medical Care Assistance Program (MEDCAP) offers choice and flexibility to meet personal health needs. One MEDCAP option is to have the company pay for basic medical expenses while supplementary coverage is paid monthly by employees; if employees choose not to pay the latter, incentives are provided to use more convenient, cost-effective outpatient or home care services. A continuing organizational communication program informs employees about MEDCAP and offers feedback on employee health care use data for each plant site and for the entire company. Prior to the plan, DuPont was spending four times as much on health as on other benefits; but with the new approach it was able to hold expenditures on medical benefits to $156 million!

Polaroid. This firm uses the Health Maintenance Organization (HMO) with its employees to manage health costs. The HMO provides comprehensive health care for a fixed prepaid fee. Doctors are paid on a salary basis; the physicians' group must deliver quality care at a cost within the monthly figure of its corporate agreement. Fifteen percent of Polaroid's workers have signed up for the HMO plan. Employee family memberships are free; routine health insurance coverage is also available. In all, the new approach has reduced health insurance costs by 5 percent.

Others. Some corporations are directing their health care efforts toward the executive suite. Since top management is costly to recruit, develop, and compensate, investment in those with problems can have pay-off. Consulting groups such as Beam Pines Human Resources and Goodrich & Sherwood specialize in executive renewal. They deal with work-related problems of executives that result from behavior, medical, and alcoholism problems, as well as situational issues brought on by organizational change. Costs for confrontation and counseling, as well as therapy, often in the executive's own office, may range from a flat fee of $5,000 for forty hours with HRD consultants to $150-250 an hour, plus consultant travel expenses. Clients include PepsiCo, Time, Warner-Lambert, Cahners Publishing, and others.

Many of the corporate endeavors described are in harmony with an innovative concept called behavioral health. As explained by Matarazzo and others (1984), behavioral health is an interdisciplinary field dedicated to promoting a philosophy of health that stresses individual responsibility in the application of behavioral and biomedical science knowledge and techniques to the maintenance of health and the prevention of illness and dysfunction by a variety of self-initiated individual or shared activities. Despite the academic verbiage, the idea is a refreshing health model that is attuned to the new work culture. It is based on the premise that the origins of good health are found in life-style behaviors that can be altered in more positive ways.

When issuing the Surgeon General's report on healthy people in 1979, Department of Health, Education and Welfare Secretary Joseph Califano summed up its essence in this observation about Americans: "We are killing ourselves by our own careless habits. We are killing ourselves by carelessly polluting the environment. We are killing ourselves by permitting harmful social conditions to persist—like poverty, hunger and ignorance—which destroy health, especially for infants and children." Business can be the principal social institution in the emerging information society to provide leadership in a behavioral health movement that would counteract such self-destruction. Managers not only can take responsibility in this regard but must encourage their companies' HRD departments to include health educators on their staffs and wellness programs in their activities.

Stress Management and Ambivalence Skills

Stress, according to Joan Borysenko of Harvard Medical School, is an interaction between a life situation requiring readjustment and a person's ability to cope ("Ways to Control Stress and Make it Work for You," 1984). Stress is one of the byproducts of significant shifts in life patterns—such as is happening with the microelectronics and information revolutions. In the past thirty years, stress has been cited as taking a heavy toll on the national well-being—70 percent of today's physical problems in advanced technological societies are associated with stress and life-style. Let us deal with the former in this section and the latter in the next part of our analysis.

We know that stress is a major management problem when "*Fortune* 500" corporations increasingly invest in elaborate stress management programs for their personnel. In *Technostress: The Human Cost of the Computer Revolution* (Brod, 1983), the author examined the cost of the transition to the electronic work place and found that, if not managed intelligently, technostress can contribute to reduced productivity, burnout, low morale, absenteeism, and high turnover of employees, especially among technical types. Uncontrolled stress, regardless of the cause, can be a debilitating medical and social problem, leading to lost or inadequate work days and diminished capacity and creativity. Mismanaged stress can lead to loss of large sums of corporate monies, as well as to death itself. Yet reasonable stress can be a catalyst to high performance when properly converted and channeled by workers (Hockey, 1983). People can be trained to manage stress in their lives, but this requires fostering in them a sense of self-esteem and self-responsibility. Controlling stress does not mean passivity and underachievement.

The Stress Mechanism. So what exactly is stress and how do we cope with it? Among health professionals, multiple meanings are given to this term and its causes. Hans Selye, a pioneer

Promoting Employee and Executive Wellness   281

in stress research, considered it the "spice of life," as well as the rate of wear and tear on the body. Others think of stress as the source of productivity in the human species. For the average person, it is the psychological or physiological response of the body to aversive or positive events. Stress also affects behavioral or mood systems, stimulating us to be more creative and productive or more anxious and irritable. Stress triggers chemical change in the brain and alters the body's chemical balance. The result is elevated levels of hormones, including adrenaline or epinephrine, norepinephrine, and beta-endorphin. This can happen with major life crises, such as the death of a spouse, a divorce, or even the loss of one's job. Scientists at the Salk Institute in La Jolla, California, have synthesized a substance that duplicates corticotropin, a chemical produced in the brain that triggers stress reactions; they hope through their modified substitute to be able to block the body's reponse to stressors. Other researchers at the University of California at San Diego School of Medicine have been studying acetylcholine, a potent brain chemical that acts as a messenger among nerve cells and "turns on" the body's reactors to stress. When your heart is pounding and you feel scared, it is because of this hormone; the new theory is that acetylcholine may be the master gear that drives relevant systems in the brain.

There seems to be an interconnection between our behavioral activities and our biochemistry at any moment. Stress symptoms can warn of potential health problems. The signals include prolonged dizziness or gastrointestinal pain, persistent heart abnormalities or visual disturbances, exceptional fatigue and bodily dysfunction. The physical warnings of overstress are evident when the stomach churns, the muscles tighten or knot, the blood pressure rises alarmingly, and sometimes we perspire. Diminished immune responses resulting from stress, as may occur during a bereavement, may cause a person to become more susceptible to disease. Psychologically, those suffering from too much stress may have deep feelings of guilt, fear, anxiety, strain, and panic. At worst, this can result in an erosion of self-control and competence, as well as increasing isolation.

Such symptoms, according to psychoanalyst Douglas Bier

(1985, pp. 73-74), are especially manifest with hi-tech and fast-track careers. In his research for the Project on Technology, Work, and Character, Bier has found that these symptoms are often translated into physical complaints, such as headaches, backaches, stomach problems, insomnia, and eating difficulties. Bier believes this sometimes results from inappropriate trade-offs and compromises in pursuit of career; for example, some professionals feel guilty for betraying themselves for organizational career development, so suppress rage. Young, urban professionals seem to get caught up in the materialism of a successful career, yet experience conflict in the process. For ambitious women, it may take the form of trying to balance at a price the demands of career and motherhood. For members of minorities who stifle anger because of real or imagined racism in a white-dominated business culture, the adaptation may involve suppression of their own cultural conditioning and heritage. Bier thinks that new employees of the eighties want a better trade-off in the struggle between career demands and personal needs or goals. Compromising in the race to get ahead may cause suffering in terms of distorted values, shallow relationships, and even substance abuse. To maintain balance and to grow may often require serious reassessment of one's lifestyle and pursuits.

Stress Management. The key to stress management is how we deal with stress (Beech, Burns, and Sheffield, 1984). Stress is neither weakness nor wellness, but it is very relative. That is, what is stressful to one may not be stressful to another. Further, the amount of stress one can handle differs for each person. Stress is situational and depends on how we perceive it. The Chinese word for *crisis* has a double meaning—one character means danger, the other refers to opportunity. Stressful situations can either stimulate or overwhelm us. The following true case of Jin Miaolin is an illustration: Jin is a make-up artist who works at the state crematorium in Shanghai. His main occupation is to prepare the faces of the dead for their funerals. Singing to himself cheers him up and takes his mind off his work. His avocation thus became writing songs, and today he is the most popular composer in China. Eighty of his songs have been recorded, and the two biggest song hits in the country are his. In a recent interview with United Press International, he said: "The pressures of my work gave me the inspiration to write songs. I've seen so much sadness in my job that it has given me the feeling I should write happy songs" ("Shanghai Composer Works with the Dead," 1984, p. 18).

Even time pressure can encourage productivity, efficiency, and well-being. Perhaps that is why we build time frames into creative brainstorming sessions or project management. Deadlines can cause adrenaline to be secreted and energy to be increased so that we rise to the challenge of the occasion. However, when there appears no way of meeting those deadlines, anxiety, panic, and mistakes may result. In orienting new employees to their organizational culture, many of the best-managed companies build stress into the indoctrination period, just as the military does in the "boot camp" experience. Procter & Gamble, IBM, and Morgan Guaranty Trust are a few among many with sophisticated socialization programs for their recruits that train the newcomers, especially for management positions, how to deal with high-volume, intense work situations. They learn how to cope with long hours, rigorous deadlines, exhausting travel schedules, and related stress while remaining high performers.

All of this has great significance for thinking managers. If those in supervision can maintain balance in themselves and in a work group regarding stress, then productivity may be furthered. If they can recognize when stress is getting out of control, they can initiate mechanisms to counteract damaging effects. We can learn to control habitual reaction patterns and break conditioned cycles of response. The choices with stress and tension are flight or fight, or, better still, managing them. For example, we know that there are Type A personalities—many of whom are found in leadership or executive positions. These are hyperreactors—hard-driving, time-pressured, super organizers who always keep their motors set on "high" and never "idle." They are prone to cardiovascular disease and other traumas, and they find it very difficult to relax. Being of this type and having had to have open heart surgery because of it, I can assure readers that it is possible to change one's life-style and to improve one's quality of life. The trick is to do it on one's own *before* tragedy strikes!

One might consider stress as a matter of degrees on a continuum. On the left-hand side are those positive or "pro" forces that result when stress motivates us, while on the right-hand side are the contrary or "con" factors resulting when there is not enough tension. Obviously, to manage stress more effectively, we need to be challenged in our life and work, as well as committed to what we do as true professionals. We need to take control over our life space or private world and assume self-responsibility. In this effort, we must communicate with others and seek peer support. Without any stress or tension, life can become dull and we become lethargic and nonparticipative, increasingly drawing inward and becoming isolated from others. It is a choice between becoming a world maker or world squatter, unless one is content to be in between and maintain perfect equilibrium between the positive and negative factors.

Managers concerned about the work environment examine the "fit" between an individual's personality and the job situation. For example, Margaret Chesney, a psychologist at SRI International, suggests that Type A managers need job autonomy and independence, while Type B people require more structure—and, if it is lacking, they will leave their positions. Behavior is the function of both the person and the environment: We change our environment, and it changes us. Stress becomes unhealthy when there is a serious imbalance between the two. Thus, if we have a personal preference for high visibility and we are in a role that denies us that visibility, our work environment may be unsuitable for us. If we like a work situation that is regular, predictable, and dependable, we seek a position with high structure. If we enjoy wide latitude where risks are high and things are hectic and somewhat disorganized or changeable, we should apply for careers or industries that provide such—for instance, becoming an entrepreneur or going into the high-tech companies. If one has a high need for affection, perhaps one should enter a people-oriented or service profession. In other words, unless we are prepared to change our personalities and preferences, undue stress can be avoided by seeking harmony between our job and work climate. That is why some managers, long conditioned by the work culture in a basic industry, may not be able to make the transition to a high-tech situation.

Managing with Ambivalence. In educating and training people, it is well to bear in mind that in a high-technology firm it is often necessary to manage ambivalently (Maidique and Hays, 1984). Unlike the industrial work culture's commitment (in the manner of the assembly line) to order and organization, a high-tech company is built on norms of change, innovation, and entrepreneurial activity. That corporate environment may involve alternating periods of control and relaxation; of tension, action, and excitement interspersed with times of reflection, evaluation, and revitalization. Rather than becoming tense, frustrated, or discontented, people who are suited to this seem to thrive on the irregular rhythm or work pace, as any computer manufacturer will confirm. The shifting of one's internal gears frequently becomes par for the course in an organizational culture in which change is built into the system—people cope with such instability and operate on a norm of ultrastability.

The following actual case illustrates this point. Peter Shaw, founder of Syte Information Technology of San Diego, California, works six days a week and up to twelve hours a day. In running this start-up computer company in a fiercely competitive field, he is under constant pressure. It is a life that would be stressful for most people. Yet the thirty-seven-year-old executive looks quite relaxed. He attributes this to a philosophy that most pressures are self-induced. He operates on three rules—don't sweat small things, because they aren't that important; most things are small things; and go with the flow. By the latter, he means do not fight it—figure out the best way to navigate the course. He also practices not bottling up his feelings, leaving office cares at work, and sharing responsibilities with fellow workers, as well as with family. Even business travel can be relaxing for him (Bry, 1983).

Help with Controlling Stress. Whether one's difficulties with stress are psychological, physiological, or situational, excessive stress can be controlled. For those with overactive sympathetic nervous systems due to their genetic programming, physicians can assist with prescribed drugs or therapy, such as biofeedback. Others may benefit from training offered on managing occupational and personal stress by psychologists, such as Henry Singer of Westport, Connecticut's Human Resources Institute. For example, in preparation for the 1984 Olympic games, the staff of the Los Angeles summer events went through a "Stress-Reduction and Customer Service Program." To cope with the thousands of visitors from around the globe, personnel were given training in multicultural communication, defusing hostile people, and stress relief.

Within organizations, HRD professionals may use packaged programs, such as John Adams's *Understanding and Managing Stress* by University Associates (8517 Production Ave., San Diego, Calif. 92121) or Nancy and Donald Tubesing's *Structured Exercises in Stress Management* (Whole Person Associates, P.O. Box 3151, Duluth, Minn. 55803). The latter offers assessment instruments, relaxation exercises, and skill-building mechanisms for coping with stress. Among the stress management strategies proposed by the Tubesings (1983, pp. 49-52) is this interesting ABC model:

A. Alter it. Remove the source of stress by problem solving, planning and time management, organizing, or direct communication.

Avoid it. Remove oneself from the stressful situation by withdrawal or delegation, thus conserving one's energies.

Accept it. Come to terms with the reality of the situation, and equip oneself physically and psychologically to cope with it.

B. Build resistance and increase one's stress toleration—physically, through proper diet, exercise, systematic relaxation; mentally, through positive affirmation and mental health habits, such as clarification of goals/values/priorities; socially, through building and maintaining a people support system; spiritually, through esthetic activities, meditation, religion, or service.

C. Change through planned alterations in one's perceptions, expectations, and situations.

In addition to self-help learning activities on stress management obtained from "how to" books and audiocassettes, health professionals are teaming up for comprehensive neighborhood services. For example, the La Jolla Clinic of Family and Preventive Medicine offers medical and alternative therapies that deal with anything that will ensure fitness, from diet to relaxation exercises. The same approach can be found nationwide as part of a holistic health movement, which has established centers in many cities.

Wellness Life-Style for Executives and Employees

In this century, we have moved from medical models that are strictly corrective and rehabilitative to those that are preventive and wellness oriented. The Health Insurance Association of America describes wellness as a freely chosen life-style aimed at achieving and maintaining individual good health. Fundamentally, this means that a person takes responsibility for creating a healthy life-style while avoiding attitudes and actions that lead to illness. Thus, each must map out his or her own plan for positive undertakings that would accomplish this goal while eliminating mind sets and habits that undermine well-being.

In the metaindustrial work culture, business policy at all levels is beginning to support this wellness trend. The reasons are not altruistic, but economic. As was mentioned earlier in this chapter, healthy workers have a very favorable impact on the profit margin, while those who are not are a drain on cash flow. The American Association of Fitness Directors in Business and Industry has amassed statistics that make the case for managerial involvement in wellness—over $5 billion is lost to American industry each year by the premature death of employees; over $700 million annually is lost by United States businesses because of illnesses that keep personnel from their work; and up to $2,200 per employee is spent each year on medical benefits. Thus, it is to the organization's, as well as to the person's, advantage for workers to achieve and maintain these goals: (1) control over their own life space, (2) effective management of self-health, and (3) peak levels of mind and body performance.

The scope of corporate involvement in the wellness movement was indicated at the opening of this chapter. Let us cite more data to underscore the new reality:

- Over 500 United States companies are investing in employee wellness programs that emphasize fitness as well as management of stress and life crises.
- In 1984, 350 companies joined in the Corporate Cup Association's annual running relays. This not only is fun and builds camaraderie but it also supports company fitness programs.
- The National Fitness Foundation sponsors in May of each year a National Fitness Testing Week at 1,500 centers around the country. Many of the 500,000 who take the push-up, curl-up, arm hang, sit-and-reach, and running exams do so at company expense and with management encouragement.

The in-company wellness programs are wide-ranging, from behavior modification programs to curb substance abuse to courses in parenting, dental health, and weight control. If we focus in on one dimension, the possibilities for managerial innovation in other areas may become more evident. For example, there are more than 34,000 deaths and a half million injuries annually from vehicular crashes in the United States, many of these in company cars and trucks. Approximately 45 percent of those involved in police-reported accidents are employed persons who lose a total of eleven million work days annually because of injuries received. The routine use of seat belts could reduce such injuries and death by 50 percent; only 14 percent of drivers—and fewer passengers—in automobiles currently bother to wear seat belts. Yet, as David Sleet (1981), a professor at San Diego State University, reminds us, few corporate wellness efforts are directed toward a "buckle-up" campaign. Having served as a consultant with the National Highway Safety Administration, Sleet assures us that the United States Department of Transportation has done research and has information on cost-effective and efficient means for motivating employees and their dependents to wear safety belts while driving or riding in a motor vehicle on or off the job. He recommends that incentive programs, such as "Seat Belt Sweepstakes," which give prizes and rewards to continued seat-belt users, be adopted by companies and by entire industries. Such efforts, Sleet acknowledges, must be coupled with a safety belt education effort that offers employees options for improving their transportation safety.

Executives and managers need to become behavior models for their colleagues at work by beginning with their own personal wellness programs. Here are some strategies that might be initiated with key management and extended to the whole work force as appropriate:

1. A policy of requiring annual physical examinations in which the employer shares all or part of the cost with employees. This should include some form of stress test, such as a treadmill, and action plans.

2. A weight control regimen that not only includes information gathering on proper diet and nutrition but also prescribes practices to ensure such. For example, maintaining one's prescribed height-adjusted weight goal and not eating between meals are desirable practices.

3. An exercise program that is reasonable, regular, and customized to one's own needs and realities. This program should also utilize whatever corporate benefits are available relative to facilities, fees, and time allowances for this while at work.

4. A personal health management system that includes cultivation of habits for adequate sleep, recreation, and substance control (moderate or no use of alcohol or other drugs and tobacco).

5. A periodic assessment (for example, monthly or quarterly) of one's progress in wellness and in developing positive mental attitudes, possibly through a quality-of-life assessment.

With health costs doubling every five years, wellness needs to be built into the organizational culture, becoming a company or agency norm. Employees need management encouragement and support in the adoption of a healthier lifestyle that values wellness. Since researchers have indicated that persons who have a strong sense of coherence in their lives are less likely to succumb to illness, creating such congruence might very well be the goal of both personal and corporate wellness efforts. The reader might begin by utilizing the "Manager's Quality of Life Index" in the resource section.

Wellness Resources for Managers

Within organizations, the human resource development department or its professionals should take the lead in promoting healthiness on a corporationwide basis. Some of this assistance can be provided for individual self-help. It can begin with simple referrals to self-instructional audiotapes, such as "Managing Your Own Health" (ISHK Book Service, P.O. Box 176, Los Altos, Calif. 94022). It can extend to recommending computer software on wellness. For example, PLATO provides programmed learning in health education. Developed by Control Data Corporation for 23,000 of its own employees enrolled in its "StayWell" program, each software course has eight lessons; examples of these might include how to relax, how to maintain healthy blood pressure, how to lose weight, how to eat right, how to quit smoking, and how to be fit. The computer-based interactive training includes simulations, video- and audiotapes, and printed text. These, as well as other programs on nutrition, alcoholism, pediatrics, and the like, are available to others through Control Data's Life Extension Institute (8100 34th Ave. So., Bloomington, Minn. 55420-2028).

However, employees generally benefit most from a group approach to wellness, which might begin with classes in health education and extend to team activities. Such sessions can be enlivened by audiovisual aids, group simulations and games, and joint wellness tasks. The Center for Health Games & Simulations (College of Human Service, San Diego State University, San Diego, Calif. 92181) can provide further details.

As an illustration of what can be done with employee groups, the Tubesings (1983) advocate:

1. shared analysis of the qualities of the superwell;
2. identification of factors that will diminish the quality of one's life in one to five years;

Promoting Employee and Executive Wellness 291

3. consensus exercise on self-care strategies in six dimensions—physical, mental, emotional, relational, spiritual, life-style;
4. imagineering on previous illness and peak health periods, and learnings gained for future styles of coping with sickness or well-being;
5. sentence completion exercises on feelings and mental health;
6. planning together a corporate wellness fair or congress.

We are well aware of the importance of peer groups in rehabilitation, as Alcoholics Anonymous has amply demonstrated. That same group power for problem solving and mutual support can be utilized in wellness promotion.

Health networking with other companies can produce interesting ideas for incorporation into one's own organization. The *Executive Fitness Newsletter* (33 East Milnor St., Emmaus, Penn. 18049) provides biweekly reports in that regard. For instance, the Tyler Corporation in Dallas, Texas, sponsors an annual Invitational Cup—a two-mile foot race for top company officers who are at least forty years old and athletically inclined. In the 1984 event of this industrial and electronic manufacturer, the eleventh running included 180 executives, the oldest of whom was eighty-two years old (Al Gordon, chairman of Kidder, Peabody & Co., who was part of a three-member team).

Thinking managers will have recourse in their local universities and colleges for assistance with their company wellness programs. To illustrate, the University of Wisconsin at Stevens Point conducts an annual wellness promotion strategies workshop; and the University of California at San Diego offers extension courses and professional certification in fitness instruction and health management.

Local hospitals, health systems, and centers can be of assistance to managers seeking to formalize wellness efforts. As an illustration, the Scripps Memorial Hospital Foundation (9888 Genesee Ave., La Jolla, Calif. 92037) administers The Well Being, a health education center located in a shopping mall. Its varied programs extend from classes in physical fitness (jazz exercise, aerobics, yoga, computer risk assessment, and so on) to courses in CPR for heartsavers and in freedom from chemical dependency to workshops on nutrition, stopping smoking, and living with "parkinsonism." Furthermore, the hospital prints a monthly newsletter on fitness called *Prime Time*.

Various trade and professional associations, as well as unions, have resources to help further a corporate health and safety movement. For example, the California Board of Registered Nursing has a provider offering a series of workshops and seminars on "Well Within" (P.O. Box 8467, La Jolla, Calif. 92038). This is intended for wellness trainers and practitioners and is related to a nursing network. The programs are for continuing education credit, ranging from weekend wellness celebrations in the mountains, to emotional first aid, to Tai Chi Chuan or meditative relaxation, to counseling persons with grief.

The National Training Laboratories (NTL) Institute and Organizational Development Network conducts an annual conference on "Wellness in the Workplace" (P.O. Box 9155, Rosslyn Station, Arlington, Va. 22209). This three-day session reports on corporate wellness strategies, dealing with such diverse themes as high performance, reducing stress through work redesign or biochemistry, health enhancement for executives, work place emergency medical services, and the whole manager.

The emerging field of sports psychology also may offer managers valuable wellness insights. Through their Coto Research Center and the Institute for Advanced Learning (10800 Lyndale Ave. So., Minneapolis, Minn. 55420), a "Summit Conference on High Level Wellness" examines mind/body relationships and peak performance, plus research breakthroughs in wellness. The highlights include computerized life-style and nutrition analyses, computerized biomechanics, physiological versus chronological age comparisons, and even music as a relaxant. All this learning goes on at the Coto de Caza Resort in Trabuco Canyon, California.

Finally, for those who wish to pursue graduate studies in this subject, MIT's Alfred P. Sloan School of Management offers a master's degree in health management as part of its Fellows Executive Program. It is for senior-level health care practitioners, educators, researchers, and administrators who wish to specialize in executive health development.

This sampling should be enough to convince innovative managers that much aid is available for companies that see the connection between and among top performance, productivity, cost cutting, and wellness strategies. For those who prefer a cognitive approach through reading, we recommend: *The Unblocked Manager* and *50 Activities for Self-Development,* by M. Woodcock and D. Francis (Epping, England: Gower, 1982); *The Mechanism of Job Stress and Strain,* by J. R. French, R. D. Caplan, and R. Van Harrison (New York: Wiley, 1982); and *The Wellness Workbook,* by R. S. Ryan and J. W. Travis (Berkeley, Calif.: Ten Speed Press, 1983).

Including Family and Friends

Alvin Toffler reminds us that in the emerging Third Wave civilization, human relationships are more temporary, so we need new skills for developing intense, meaningful, global ad hoc relationships and then disconnecting. The phenomenon has been readily observed in terms of social, organizational, and marital relations. The traditional, more permanent nuclear family of the agricultural and industrial ages is breaking down and disappearing, as worldwide statistics on the growth rate of divorce confirm. In this transition period, new family alternatives and patterns are developing—such as the aggregate family made up of divorced parents with "his," "her," and "their" children in the same household; the single-parent or no-children family; the "mingles" family, who are unmarried heterosexuals or homosexuals living together. Society is becoming more open and diverse and offering more choice, but it also requires more cooperation and mutual support among people. That is why I emphasized in Chapter Nine the importance of networking in the new work culture.

To be healthy and to cope effectively in transitional times like ours, we not only need a sense of control in our lives and certain personality qualities, such as optimism and flexibility, but most individuals also require a network of family or friends to provide social support. Caroline Thomas of Johns Hopkins University studied over a thousand medical students who graduated between 1948 and 1964 (Matarazzo, 1983). She found that two of the strongest predictors among them of cancer, mental illness, and suicide were lack of closeness to parents and a negative attitude toward one's family. Another study of 7,000 people in Alameda County, California, in 1978 confirmed the importance of social support. Researcher Leonard Syme found that, generally speaking, people with few close contacts were dying two to three times earlier than those who regularly turned to their friends. The old saying "no man is an island" is still true.

Since we are social beings, wellness is dependent on some form of social support, whether it comes from family, peers, or networks. With serious illness and incapacitation, we become well aware of our dependence on others and of how valuable family and friends can be in rehabilitation. Furthermore, when one succumbs to the abuse of alcohol or other drugs or loses sexual control, we all realize the havoc this can wreak on family and friends, even when such people want to be helpful.

Only recently have we begun to appreciate how self-abuse can negatively affect others, such as in the relationship of pregnant mothers and their unborn children. Let us examine one seemingly "harmless" personal practice—cigarette smoking—and its effect on others close to the habitual smoker. In the 1984 report of the United States Surgeon General, Americans were again warned of the consequences of smoking. In 1983 alone, 362,000 deaths were directly linked to smoking, which contributed to lung and heart disease, as well as cancer. Surgeon General C. Everett Koops, after analyzing the evidence, commented that cigarettes are the most important individual health risk in this country, responsible for more premature deaths and disabilities than any other known agent—all this despite impressive gains through wellness campaigns that resulted in significant numbers giving up smoking.

What was most interesting to managers in that 1984 report was that smoking costs the nation $40 billion annually in health-related expenses and lost productivity! Further, there are troublesome findings of its impact on fellow workers, families, and friends of the smokers. *Passive smoking* is the term for nonsmokers involuntarily exposed to pollution in indoor environments by cigarette smoke; the problem is acute for children of smoking parents. The risk of death for heavy smokers is thirty times higher than for nonsmokers; but, at the same time, the smoker also increases the risk for those closest to him or her. No wonder the debate continues about banning smoking from the work place; in some places, such legislation has already been enacted. We are only beginning to become aware of health risks associated with nonsmoking tobacco use, such as "snuff" and "chewing."

Regardless of the cause, unhealthy practices have negative effects on those who live, play, and work with us. That should be a concern of management. On the reverse side, our wellness practices can be a source of positive influence as others emulate our efforts in this regard. But to maintain a healthy life-style, we still need to develop a social support system. That means not only developing skills in networking and friendship acquisition but also acquiring human relations skills for application both at work and at home. These revolve around communication, trust, positive influencing, cooperation, conflict management, and projecting self-confidence. Numerous books, courses, and learning aids are available for such self-development purposes. Thus, many companies are offering behavioral science programs centered around increasing one's effectiveness with people, something very much needed by those educated for technical and engineering careers.

There have been many horror stories about how the career demands on executives, entrepreneurs, and other professionals can demolish family and personal lives. We are familiar with the problems of entrepreneurs, hard-driving employers, workaholics, and those who suffer from burnout on the job. That is why the research at the Center for Creative Leadership in Greensboro, North Carolina, is so significant. Under the supervision of their research associate, Joan Kofodimos, a study was made of eighty-three highly successful managers on the interdependence between personal and professional lives. One aspect of the investigation focused on emotional well-being—that delicate balance between our lives at work and away from it. They found that many of these managers tried to set time and relationship boundaries, to separate personal and professional lives. These efforts were not always successful, for the problems in one arena would drift into the other. Since all the subjects were male, the corporate wife played a crucial role in contributing to her husband's career success when she was supportive, tolerant, and accommodating. Although divorce is now more common and acceptable, stability in marriage was found to be a factor in both management selection and promotion.

The issue today is that we have more dual-career couples and conflict can erupt unless there is a balance in the career orientations of both parties. Whether the manager, professional, or worker of any type is male or female, imbalance can occur between home and personal life. The danger seems to increase as one moves up in the organization. While success in career may prove rewarding, it may happen at the expense of personal life, causing failures with family and friends. Such persons may opt for the "veneer" of a happy family, or for pseudo-intimacy on the job, or for office affairs. In *More Than a Friend,* McGinnis (1981) points out that as more women move into the work force as well as into management, they are becoming more available to male management as peers and friends because they spend so many hours in one another's company and grow in mutual respect of one another's competencies. Furthermore, in our more open society, marriage partners are becoming more tolerant of office friendships with those of the opposite sex.

The organizational culture may also aid or undermine this balance. Some traditional bosses and companies demand the total absorption of their people at high costs to personal lives and families. The trend in the new work culture is not only to foster an integrated life-style and a more wholistic approach but to encourage family involvement. Tandem Corporation, for instance, goes out of its way to inform workers' families and involve them in company progress and goals and to provide social support to the families of its personnel. Metaindustrial work environments encourage qualities of both head and heart in their people. Many firms provide counseling to help employees cope with the devastation of marital break-up or to prevent it from happening. Other corporations are including spouses in executive development programs, thereby attempting to reduce the communication and intellectual gap that can occur when one partner grows and the other is neglected. When the company wants to reassign a manager or technician, whether in or out of the country, its relocation services usually offer job placement assistance if the employee's spouse has a separate career. Still other corporations include seminars on the challenges of two-career couples or "superwomen" as part of ongoing HRD offerings.

In her recent book on the "superwoman syndrome," Marjorie Shaevitz (1984) describes the physical and psychological problems of the all-knowing, high-powered female executive who may also combine the roles of all-loving wife, mother, and homemaker. To counteract unreal expectations of herself by herself and others, Shaevitz offers solutions and systems so as to avoid becoming victims of stress, overwork, and unachievable ambitions.

Organizational health is at its best when personnel, especially among the leadership, lead integrated lives. The organization can provide major support toward facilitating balance in the lives of its people. Having inculcated the manager, for instance, in the corporate culture's norms, values, and priorities, the company then rewards the individual for adherence to them. It is to the organization's advantage, therefore, to promote synergy between work and the family life of its personnel. Research evidence also indicates that corporate investment in fostering relations pays off, whereas imbalance in this aspect of managerial personality can prove costly to both the manager and the company. Organizational health is fostered when management demonstrates maturity, integration, and wholeness in business and personal life.

The welfare of executive families should be an organizational priority. In *Making It Together,* George and Ronya Kozmetsky suggest ways the leadership couple can create an "us" relationship that is a true partnership and that merges egos (Kozmetsky and Kozmetsky, 1981). They offer these practical tips for wellness in the relationship: (1) In addition to one's spouse, each needs at least another intimate friend of the same sex who provides accepting comradeship and reinforces individual security. (2) Such couples need to engage in constant value assessment and adjustment. (3) Taking a systems approach to family and personal management is helpful, especially when it comes to managing both time and information more effectively. (4) A balanced family has inner strength and mutual devotion, characterized by commitment to an active role in other institutions—that is, balance in both internal and external relationships. (5) The leadership family should be prepared to make the transition from the role of executive in one corporation to other opportunities or careers. George Kozmetsky, former cofounder of Teledyne and retired dean of the business school at the University of Texas, and his wife, Ronya, president of Austin's RGK Foundation, not only offer this guidance but are behavior models illustrating that it works. They more than amply demonstrate that the executive couple should be dedicated to promoting the general family welfare.

Conclusion

Since the wellness life-style is freely chosen, it aims to achieve and maintain good health, both physically and psychologically. Corporate-sponsored efforts toward that end represent a capitalization on the organization's human assets. Wellness can be built into the organizational culture and then extended into employee families. However, the maintenance of a social network for support is vital to the wellness process, and the corporation can assist in this development. Government reports in this decade confirm that Americans are getting the message regarding their health—in ever larger numbers they are eliminating, reducing, or otherwise changing their life-style behaviors that constitute risk factors.

ELEVEN

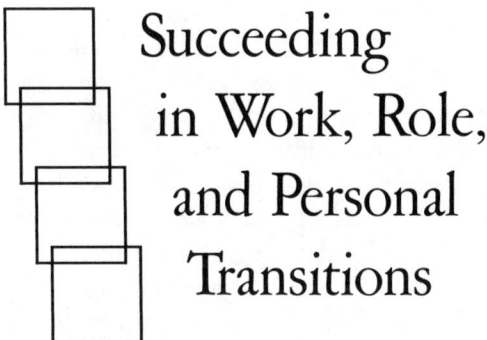

Succeeding
in Work, Role,
and Personal
Transitions

Executive Summary. Major shifts in life patterns bring on transitional experiences as we make significant adjustments to cope with a new reality. Such turning points in our lives trigger opportunities for personal and professional growth. They are related to both our physical and psychological well-being and can be brought on by everything from foreign assignment or career change to divorce or the death of a loved one. Personal upheavals alter our perceptions and behavior, and may produce various forms of culture shock. Currently, a great transition to a new work culture is being experienced simultaneously by masses of people.

This chapter analyzes the phenomenon of the transitional experience, especially as it relates to personal and role changes. In particular, special attention is directed to the transformation in the roles of women and managers. If we understand life transition as a dynamic process, we can increase our self-actualization while helping our families and colleagues cope more effectively with life's challenges, whether at work or in society.

Coping with Culture Shock

Back in 1965, Alvin Toffler began to popularize the notion of future shock, which had largely been the concern of social scientists. That year, I was overcoming the effects of "culture shock" and described it in detail to Toffler at lunch. Commenting on the larger meaning of that transitional experience overseas, Toffler noted that future shock is to the masses what culture shock is to an individual or family. Later he would describe the phenomenon in his classic volume on the subject this way: "Shattering stress and disorientation that we induce in individuals by subjecting them to too much change in too short a time.... Future shock is dizzying disorientation brought on by the premature arrival of the future. It may well be the most important disease of tomorrow.... Future shock is a time phenomenon of the greatly accelerated rate of change in society. It arises from the superimposition of a new culture on an old one. It is culture shock in one's own society" (Toffler, 1970, p. 290). Perhaps remembering my prior descriptions of myself as a bewildered American Fulbright professor in India, Toffler reminded his readers that culture shock is the effect of immersion in a strange culture on the unprepared visitor.

Travelers abroad, from missionaries and Peace Corps volunteers to multinational managers and those engaged in technology transfer, have experienced culture shock in various degrees and tried to describe it. In a previous work, I attempted to offer counsel on how to manage culture shock (Harris and Moran, 1979). Because of the importance of this concept to the new work culture transitions, it is worthwhile to review here some of the characteristics and effects of culture shock:

- Our reference points or cultural cues are "off" or even reversed. The meaning we read into communication symbols, such as gestures, are different—what is "yes" at home may be "no" in the host culture; what we consider good, worthwhile, or healthy may have the opposite designation abroad.
- Our environment is alien—that is, unfamiliar, uncomfortable, or even incomprehensible. All the absolutes and certainties of our own society and value system are now relative and tentative.
- Our psyche is jolted and we are bewildered. By misinterpreting or not understanding accepted behavior in the new culture, we experience frustration and even alienation, as well as more bizarre behavior.

- Our confusion in the strange culture may become more distressing. Over a period of time, the problem can become severe for some, with a breakdown in communications, misreading of reality, and inability to cope. This may lead to increased tension, nervousness, anxiety, and depression. The negative behavior may range from suspicion, apathy, and withdrawal to prejudgment, hostility, and possibly rebellion.
- Our emotional disturbances may produce physical symptoms, such as inability to eat or sleep, upset stomach, excessive concern for cleanliness, or some fixation such as hypochondria.

Severe culture shock may cause psychosomatic illness, alcoholism or other substance abuse, or nervous breakdown. The social impact of such culture shock may upset or undermine family, marital, and work relations. The results may extend from simple premature return to the home culture or firing to divorce or even suicide.

Culture shock has been designated by one anthropologist as a malady, an occupational disease of people suddenly transported out of their familiar context. Actually, it is neither good nor bad, necessary or unnecessary. It is a reality we face when in strange and unexpected situations; some even experience mild forms of it when relocating within their own country. It can be delimited when one is prepared for the new circumstances, minimizing the dysfunctional aspects of the unfamiliar environment while maximizing the opportunities there. As I have learned, it can also be a challenge to reevaluate one's psychological construct or way of reading meaning into daily activities. When the degree of culture shock is manageable, the experience can stimulate creativity and renewal, as well as extraordinary productivity.

The preceding descriptions have direct application to our transition into a metaindustrial culture, in which the notion of culture shock has been applied in various ways. Robo-shock is one form of it for individuals who acquire steel-collar workers, or robots, as colleagues. Organization shock is another extension of the idea, but this applies to institutions or human systems. A corporation, for example, may face this when it moves from domestic to international markets or when it must cope with a merger or acquisition. Since organizations are composed of groups of people, they can become disturbed and disoriented when corporate cultures clash because they are too different and not in harmony. Leveraged buy-out or a joint venture, then, might become the catalyst for activating this crisis in organizational cultures. Large bureaucracies, whether in the private or public sector, are subject to severe organization shock when there is a major change in leadership, market, or technology, such as is happening now on a large scale. Traditional manufacturing facilities, operating on the basis of obsolete management assumptions, practices, and processes, are victims of the phenomenon.

Equal employment opportunity legislation, for instance, caused mild culture rumbles in staid institutions that were not prepared to have minorities in the work force or women in management and the executive suite. Another illustration is the military work culture, which may conflict with that of civilian contractors, such as on a U.S. Department of Defense or NASA project. Again, a military officer conditioned by twenty or thirty years of that unique microculture—life in the armed services —may have difficult problems trying to adjust to civilian business.

Perhaps one of the biggest challenges lies ahead as we try to create a new space culture. Imagine the problems of humans trying to adapt to living in zero gravity or weightlessness for months and years at a time. Those pioneer technicians who will construct and then live on our first space station in the 1990s may experience unusual culture shock, but what about the families involved in the establishment of the initial space colonies? NASA began to confront such prospects in a 1984 summer study at the University of California at San Diego on space-based resources and operations in the next century. A cross section of distinguished scientists gathered to consider the extension into space of human presence on a more permanent basis, as will happen with the development of a lunar base. By 2010, those who work at moon factories may experience "space culture shock," particularly on their reentry to life on Earth (Harris, 1985b).

Succeeding in Work, Role, and Personal Transitions

The human transition at different stages in the development of the species has a counterpart in the life cycle of each individual. Our very sense of identity is involved as we pass through cultural and personal changes. This has direct implications for people trying to cope with the new work culture now being created. As we learned in Chapter Two, culture conditions our self-perceptions—our sexuality and nationality, our understanding of roles and relationships, our very personhood at different growth stages. When we go outside our home culture into an alien environment, our sense of self comes into question. Women, for instance, are not viewed the same way in Middle Eastern, Oriental, and North American cultures. Businesswomen from Western nations may be disoriented and distressed by the roles they are expected to play in Saudi Arabia or Japan.

When we interact with people or situations that are different from what we are used to, we have to learn coping skills that may involve changes in attitudes, ways of thinking, and vocabulary. We get new insights and inputs and develop a new data base for interpretation and decision making. Such transitional experience requires adjustment to the altered circumstances. For most of us, the first major experience of this type was the transition from adolescence into adulthood—which is sometimes an awkward and painful experience. For a time, we may have been confused and uncertain about who we were. Most people successfully manage this first identity crisis and learn to cope with a variety of minor transitions—from home to college life, from school to work, from minority to majority culture.

However, life is a series of passages with turning points. The passages are not always smooth—it can be rough when one is transported from the First World to live for a time in a Third World or developing country, or vice versa. But these are also challenges for growth, so that those who successfully cope with the transitional crisis usually become more mature and better persons for the experience. For example, expatriate managers who make it through "reentry shock" into their own home and organizational culture often are better people for this broadening experience. Those who have met and mastered megatransitional experiences, such as divorce, death of a spouse or offspring, or recovery from major surgery or severe illness, know the feeling—how one's sense of self-worth at first can be threatened by the crisis and then enhanced by the achievement of successful passage through it.

The survival of our species has always depended on extraordinary human adaptability—to all kinds of weather and climates, natural and human disasters, and changing circumstances; to diverse creatures, peoples, institutions, and cultures; and to different economic, education, and communication systems. Our transitional experiences are decision stages—from encounters that are debilitating to those that are exciting; from those that may be disintegrating to reintegrating; and from those that begin with dependency and end with independence. The transition is a learning process toward becoming more autonomous but synergistic persons. In this process, we pass through phases of identity struggles—from awareness, to rage, to introspection, to integration. With changing circumstances, growth occurs when we learn to incorporate the new information and insights into our previous perceptual field, and then to enlarge it.

The problem this developmental process poses for our species today is *time*. (Refer back to Figure 1.) In the distant past, change was slow and gradual. After the industrial revolution occurred, we, as a species, had only a few hundred years to adapt to that factory way of life before the cybercultural, or information, revolution began to take place. Now people have only decades for acculturating to this new information society. This compression of time is known as the acceleration of change —and it is causing increasing future and organization shock! Culture shock is being experienced by workers transitioning to the postindustrial culture during the 1980s and 1990s.

Compare our culture with that of the aborigines in the jungles of the Amazon, the Philippines, or New Guinea. The advances of both mass transportation and communication are forcing these stone-age people to leapfrog from the hunting to the technological stage of development. Consider those nations of people classified as preindustrial: The needs of the global marketplace are pushing such farmers from the agricultural into

Succeeding in Work, Role, and Personal Transitions

the metaindustrial way of life—as when multinational corporations or high-tech enterprises are formed within a Third World country. Less economically developed peoples in Asia, Africa, and Latin America—whether hunters or farmers—are having to jump into modern civilization within just decades, without the benefit of centuries in which to adjust. Their culture shock is enormous!

Similarly, factory and office workers—products of the industrial work culture—are being thrust into the technological and information work culture of automated or cybernated enterprises. If employees are to contain the impact of this future shock and become knowledge workers, it will be because thinking managers prepared and oriented their people for the momentous changes. If the majority of personnel are to be so transformed without excessive dependence on alcohol and other drugs, it will be because astute management insisted that company HRD programs train employees in change and coping skills. If we are able to delimit nervous breakdowns, mental illness, and suicides among the work force, it will be because metaindustrial managers insisted that enlightened corporate health programs be inaugurated that promote wellness and improve the quality of life. Only then can we begin to cope more effectively with some of the symptoms of inappropriate transition to the new work culture—burnout, technostress, cyberphobia, and other negative signs of our changing times.

Coping with Personal Change

When we relocate abroad or to an unfamiliar part of our own country, there are bound to be adjustment problems and a period of acculturation to the new scene. We go from places and people with whom we are familiar to strange locales and persons. We leave behind our points of reference, as well as customs, traditions, and life-styles with which we have become comfortable. We feel somewhat alien and uninitiated in the new environment. To limit the foreign or domestic culture shock, the individual must change, and that can be painful. We have to learn the local norms, preferences, practices—perhaps even a new language or way of speaking—in order to fit in. Such a transitional experience involves the acquisition of new cultural insights and skills.

Similarly, we who are products of the industrial work culture must go through comparable alterations in our life-styles and ways of thinking in order to adjust to the new work culture. Our laws, social institutions, careers, and work habits are manifestations of an industrial manner of living that is disappearing. Contemporary workers—regardless of occupation or profession—have been culturally conditioned by that industrial age. Often, the perceptions, the behavior, the data or knowledge base, and the solutions of that developmental stage are inappropriate. All of us, regardless of rank or position, must cross over to the unfamiliar postindustrial or metaindustrial way of life. Most educated individuals realize this and have begun the journey, making the necessary personal adjustments. For those who refuse to change, to face up to the emerging information society and its new technologies, there are likely to be hard times and slippage from the main thrusts of human development. The unprepared and unaware will experience the turbulence of the passage more profoundly than will those who have tried to ready themselves. Open communication regarding the transition into the new age helps people become more aware of the shared phenomenon so that we learn coping skills instead of blaming ourselves. We urge review of Chapter Ten, "Promoting Employee and Executive Wellness," and use of the Transformational Management Skills Inventory and the Manager's Quality of Life Index in the resources section.

Working people, from managers to laborers, are struggling with the stress and tension of the changeover. AT&T executives and technicians, for example, felt this when deregulation and divestiture caused upheavals and uncertainties in what had been a staid, comfortable public utility. Those in the airline and banking industries are in the midst of this experience. Further, employees of companies that have gone through mergers, takeovers, and joint ventures also faced increased stress and frustration when their work worlds were shaken; some may even have lost their jobs. Consider how the growing disregard for seniority, emphasis on meritocracy, and the cutting back on labor costs in order to be internationally competitive have shattered the complacency of unionists; those in the airline and steel industries especially are feeling the pains of the transition.

Under a government grant, the Oakland-based Institute for Labor and Mental Health has begun research on stress among workers. Lack of control over what is happening to them has been found to be a principal cause of the problem. Lower-echelon workers seem least prepared to cope with the massive changes around them and the personal adjustments required. So the institute has begun group counseling with several hundred union members in order to reduce stress in life, work, and family through changes in attitudes and behavior. For some, the new life-style may involve changes in their manner or hours of work, while for others it may require a different kind of occupation or more training; for still others, it may mean better utilization of support services and networks. Such services may include, for instance, biofeedback training—that is, gaining mental relaxation through recognition of body signals and practicing relaxation with the help of electronic instruments to measure muscle tension, brain wave patterns, heart rate, perspiration level, and body temperature.

"Everything nailed down is coming loose" may be a very apt description of our transitional times. When faced with the unfamiliar, the unexpected, and the unpredictable, these are the traits and qualities we should cultivate in ourselves (Harris and Moran, 1979):

- patience and tolerance, especially with ambiguity and discontinuity;
- listening skills and sensitivity, so that we not only hear what others are trying to communicate, both verbally and nonverbally, but can empathize with them;
- trust in our own intuition and feelings, so that we respond in a more balanced and less cognitive manner;
- respect for our own and others' inherent dignity and insights while transmitting positive regard for others, regardless of who they are;

- improved human relationships, especially at work, so that we are capable of more personalizing and reciprocal concern;
- openness to new ideas, inputs, and people while being less judgmental and evaluative of others;
- self-assessment of our values, opinions, and knowledge base to periodically update our perceptual field on the basis of new experience;
- ability to be more flexible, relative, and tentative instead of rigid and absolute;
- willingness to learn and develop continually, both formally and informally, regardless of the source of that learning.

As we grow older and perhaps more fixed in our ways, behavior patterns become more difficult to change. But if we strive to practice these qualities in our personal lives we will be better able to deal with profound alterations in our circumstances. Applying these strategies will facilitate the move to a new work opportunity, to a new career, to further education, or even to a different life-style. We should be as concerned about our own personal and professional development as we are about those for whom we are responsible (as was indicated in Chapter Four).

Life today gives us more choice to actualize potential, to utilize our talents more fully. In fact, that is the theme of the newsletter *New Options* (P.O. Box 19324, Washington, D.C. 20036). This newsletter reports what people are doing to expand their consciousness and to take advantage of current opportunities. Similarly, a group of managers and consultants has formed the Global Action Team of The Business Initiative (315 E. 65th St., New York, N.Y. 10021). This network of business and professional people examines how business enterprises worldwide create richer lives for everyone, be it by sharing authority, power, profits, or resources. Another illustration of new growth possibilities is the Citizen Planners (737 Sunset Ave., Venice, Calif. 90291). These are working people who take on responsibility for making neighborhoods more safe and friendly, for fostering full employment in the community, for promoting easy and reasonable transit, for cultivating the beauty

Succeeding in Work, Role, and Personal Transitions

of their area. They are a citizen task force formed to work with the public sector toward community transformation.

A typology of how we in the United States live and where we are going was provided in *Nine American Lifestyles* (Mitchell, 1984). Arnold Mitchell, of the Stanford Research Institute, did a psychocultural analysis and identified these primary life-styles:

1. Survivors, estimated at 4 percent of the population, are need driven, lacking in self-confidence, and often depressed and despairing.
2. Sustainers, who make up 7 percent of the population, are also need driven and do not trust people; they are often angry and resentful and feel left out.
3. Belongers (35 percent) are outer-directed, aging, traditional and conventional, content, patriotic, and sentimental.
4. Emulators (10 percent) also are outer-directed, but they are ambitious, competitive, ostentatious, and unsubtle—always striving to be like the rich and successful.
5. Achievers (22 percent) are outer-directed, driving and driven people who build the system and now are at the helm.
6. I-Am-Me's (5 percent) are transitioning from outer- to inner-directed and marked by spectacular ups and downs.
7. Experientials (7 percent) are inner-directed, seeking direct, vivid, and varied experiences.
8. Socially conscious (8 percent) are inner-directed people who focus concern on social issues, trends, and events.
9. Integrateds (2 percent) are equally outer- and inner-directed people who adapt easily to most conventions but are powerfully mission-oriented on matters about which they feel strongly.

Mitchell views these ways of life as steps up a ladder from the survivor level to full psychological maturity at the integrated level. These interesting categories may provide the basis for some self-analysis and planned personal change. However, by this reckoning, three fourths of the American people are need-driven and outer-directed. Although we may question the sample of those surveyed in the SRI study, it does provide some indications of where our transformation goals should be directed for a better life in the new society.

Our jobs or careers are the watershed down which our lives flow. For most people, more time is spent at work than at any other activity. One recent survey reported that the most important issues for Americans today are love and work, in that order. In this metaindustrial culture, people are seeking more meaningful work in which they can fulfill themselves as well as meet their financial needs.

In this postindustrial age, traditional employment in manufacturing, production, and distribution will wane. High-tech positions will provide only limited growth opportunities for work. During the past decade, two thirds of all new jobs were in businesses with fewer than twenty employees. According to the Futures Research Division of Security Pacific Bank, job growth will come in small entrepreneurial firms that provide flexible services to consumers, professionals, and other businesses or government. Increasingly, personal growth opportunities may be outside the context of work for income.

The really big personal changes related to work will be where, how, when, at what, and with whom we work. People will be more mobile regarding their work—they will have less expectation of staying with a single company, industry, occupation, or location. As part of the new life style, more people will have multiple careers. Their work will take them out of their home culture, perhaps even into space. The work will not only be with new technologies, processes, and information, but it will be more often performed with the help of automation and robotics (Criswell, 1985). Also, as telecommuting permits the use of alternative work sites, more frequently, work will be performed in one's own residence, often in conjunction with one's spouse or live-in partner. Many couples are learning to combine their work and love lives, while for others the fine line between work and leisure is eroding. What is work for some is play for others, and vice versa. For all of us, personal transitions are in order regarding our attitudes and perceptions toward work and the opportunities it offers in our future economy.

Since so much of our lives is involved with occupational activities, work relationships are of the utmost importance. They can give zest, joy, and enrichment to our lives, or they can bring us sorrow, frustration, and narrowness. They affect performance, productivity, and promotion. Since almost 50 percent of the American work force is made up of women, many of these relationships are bisexual, and the "boss" or owner is increasingly likely to be female. With equal opportunity legislation and more foreign partnerships or ownership of American firms, these relationships are often multicultural. Whether we are CEOs, middle managers, first-line supervisors, or students, our success depends largely on how we deal with others (Bolton and Bolton, 1984). In focusing on areas for personal change, social or leadership style would be a fruitful arena for improvement.

Even when we end our formal careers and retire, that does not mean we have to stop working. Second-career or retirement planning can lead us to the development of unrealized skills and talents, from art and music to crafts and technical activities. Senior citizens find that many service and voluntary work endeavors provide incredible satisfaction. For example, the International Executive Service Corps (P.O. Box 10005, Stamford, Conn. 06904) is a global network of retired executives and technical advisers working to upgrade management skills, basic technologies, and business productivity in the developing world. As the government Peace Corps and local SCORE (Service Corps of Retired Executives) programs learned, retired persons often make the best volunteers. In any event, one of the helpful changes in the metaindustrial work culture is that age is no longer an automatic barrier to significant work contributions.

Before we can ask family members, colleagues, or subordinates to change, we must first be willing to change ourselves. Over the years, all of us have constructed a system for reading meaning into the events and experiences of our lives. From time to time, mature persons revise and expand that psychological construct on the basis of fresh insights and circumstances. Before we can manage others effectively, we must manage ourselves in terms of self-knowledge, decision making and personal effectiveness, diagnosing and solving problems, analyzing and correcting errors, dealing with differences and conflicts, and understanding and improving communications. This implies continuing change or growth in the way we behave and relate. Some ask, "Why change?"—others reply, "Why not?"

Coping with Role Change

Some stability is brought into our lives by the roles society and its institutions create for us. At a point in time, our culture determines what these roles and relationships are and what is considered acceptable behavior as we fulfill such functions. Multiple roles contribute to our sense of identity as to who and what we are and how we are to act. In the past, social roles (such as parent or politician) and occupational roles (such as teacher or policeman) were well defined. People knew what was expected of them if they assumed a particular responsibility. However, with the acceleration of social and technological change, most roles are in transition, and many people are experiencing role crises. We are redefining the meaning and purposes of these life tasks. Parenting, for instance, is now considered a shared responsibility of both sexes and implies the practice of new skills and competences. Police persons can now be of either gender and act as both peacemakers and facilitators, as well as enforcers of the law. The new work culture not only eliminates some roles and creates new ones, but it forces a realignment of traditional work functions. (Chapters Five and Six discuss the contributions automation and robotics make to this process.)

The challenge for all of us is to reexamine periodically the multiple roles we assume in life. The contemporary situation may require us to alter our perceptions of some characters and change how we perform these roles. It would be impossible to review here all of the role changes, so let us focus on only two that have direct and profound implications for readers of this volume—the role of women, especially at work, and the role of managers or leaders in the work place.

Transforming Women's Role. On a global basis, at least in

more advanced economies, there has been a movement toward liberating women from the narrow interpretation of their function as wife and mother. The growth of feminist forces has resulted in significant social, political, and economic gains for women worldwide (Davidson and Cooper, 1985). Gender stereotyping, even in language, is receding. Both male and female consciousness is being raised in the struggle for equal opportunity, and men stand to gain as much as women from the role redefinition. The focus now is on the human person, regardless of sex, and the norm of competency is a benefit to all, since it is blind to gender, race, or rank.

Perhaps the scope of this role change in the United States can best be viewed in economic terms. Sociologist Linda Waite (1984) of the Rand Corporation reminds us that if women did not work, the economy would come to a grinding halt. Waite maintains that women are such a fundamental part of the labor force that, without them, the economy would not exist as we know it. Working women in America now total 50.1 million, outnumbering women who stay at home in the housewife role. The income produced by these working women not only is an incredible engine for economic growth but contributes much to family survival and progress. Career women are reshaping the economy and the work culture. A new periodical, *Working Woman* (342 Madison Avenue, New York, N.Y.), challenges women to picture themselves in jobs that enable them to fulfill their potential while giving them satisfaction, earning power, and prestige. Women are choosing to see themselves in the new roles. If these women are married, then that decision also affects their roles as wives, for their relationships with their husbands are profoundly affected and must become more of a partnership. If these women are also mothers, the role is further changed from the traditional function. Family responsibilities need to be shared, and added expenses may be incurred in using various kinds of childcare services. Multiple roles as worker, wife, and/or mother, especially in a single-parent situation, require improved home management and organization to cope with new stress and strain. Employers, too, have responsibilities to provide support services to facilitate this transition.

Yet, in these enlarged roles, most women not only are

succeeding but are gaining satisfaction. In the United States, for instance, women own more than 631,000 firms with gross receipts of $40.5 billion or more. However, of the 3.5 million businesses owned in this country by women, most are in the service arena and amount to only 3 percent of the economy. Women do not usually take jobs held by men; unfortunately, half of them concentrate in "female job ghettos," and only a small percentage gets into the male-dominated occupations. But equal employment opportunity legislation has opened the door for the next generation of women. For example, in 1983 the number of female practitioners of engineering rose 5.8 percent; of law, 15.3 percent; of medicine, 15.8 percent; and, most significantly, the number of female managers and administrators rose 32.4 percent.

Women may be moving up in management, but their acceptance into the executive suite has been slow. Although women now hold 30.5 percent of executive, administrative, and managerial jobs, they are largely in entry and middle ranks; unfortunately, fewer than 500 women are in senior management positions in corporate America, and these usually are not positioned to become CEOs. Only 36 percent of the *"Fortune 1,000"* companies have women on their boards of directors. Big business and its top management have been largely a male cultural phenomenon. If women do not become like their male managerial colleagues, they are often uncomfortable in the situation, and men are often uncomfortable with female peers. The major change in management will have to be cultural so that, as a start, the climate becomes more asexual and talented women are not excluded or underutilized. Too often now, key management treats female executives with benign tolerance or like wives or secretaries, not as equals. The transformation of organizational life is gradually making knowledge and competence the criteria of entry and promotion, not one's gender, race, or place of origin or the prestigiousness of one's alma mater.

Most career women reach executive positions as entrepreneurs, as did Dianne Sullivan, an aerospace contract negotiator, who founded Miraflores Designs with a partner and earned $3

Succeeding in Work, Role, and Personal Transitions

million in sales last year. Some satisfy a personal need, as well as other women's needs. For example, Tricia Fox started a daycare school franchise organization that generated a $12 million business in five years. Since the new economy will be service and information oriented, women may be in a better position to capitalize on the situation, as discussed in Chapter Three.

Rather than trying to overcome the obstacles of climbing up the corporate ladder, many women succeed by working for themselves. Thus, these women are learning to make use of venture capitalists to launch successful enterprises. Consider these female success stories: Discovery Toys, Inc., which has sold $11 million in educational toys; Netword, an electronic mail carrier that went public and netted $2.7 million in capitalization; BioSearch, a sanitation checking and testing outfit that merged after $.5 million in sales with Professional Services Industries, a company that does $25 million in sales. As *Forbes* humorously commented, "The Best Man for the Job May Be a Woman!" (1983).

As more women enter or move up in the work force, the role of husband and father, who must now share the management of home and family, is altered. Changes are required in corporate policies, as well. NBC, for instance, provides women employees with six months maternity leave with job and seniority guaranteed; CBS and ABC also offer paternity leaves. Six thousand United States corporations, including half of the "*Fortune* 500" companies, have employee assistance programs to protect their human assets, as well as to help personnel live and work more productively. Some of these new benefits are direct spinoffs of the women's liberation movement.

Working women have also affected business in other ways; for instance, new service industries have been developed to meet their special needs. Home and childcare businesses, convenience and restaurant industries, clothing and accessories firms—all have been positively influenced by the phenomenon of the career woman. But it is in the family, especially when the woman is the only parent in the home, that this role change is having its greatest effects.

Thinking women managers and professionals are overcoming sexism and chauvinism educating their male colleagues in the process. Many of us have to reassess our images of others' roles. For example, male misperception about the modern woman's role has led to job bias toward females and the locking of women into stereotyped positions. Male misperception also has contributed to unfair "gender gaps" in pay and benefits despite equal or better performance by women. It is not very productive for a country to have almost half of its working population thus underemployed, nor is it fair for such persons not to enjoy equal pay for comparable work simply because of gender. Even when technology creates new jobs, it may not be a great equalizer for females if women are restricted to lower-paying data entry jobs, for instance, and discouraged from positions as computer programmers or systems analysts. Changing the attitudes of male managers toward career women is both an educational and cultural challenge, especially relative to sex segregation and harassment at work.

But women are realizing that the major obstacles to female emancipation and equality may be the limitations they place on the development of their own potential. They now appreciate the fact that women must transform their own images of themselves and their roles before they can capitalize on their capacities. The United States Bureau of Labor Statistics estimates that by 1995 60 percent of the labor force will be female, and by the year 2000 women will likely find themselves performing quite different jobs than they now hold. If the quality of life and work is to improve dramatically in the information society, we will need more female leadership, whether in government or politics, industry or professions, religion or social services. This will mean changing the attitudes and behavior of both women and men toward the world of work and resolving ambivalences related to family responsibilities.

Transforming the Manager's Role. A bright administrative aide likes to stay on the cutting edge of management literature. After reading *New Worlds, News Ways, New Management* (Harris, 1983), one articulate woman penned a note to me about her experience with management in a copier service company: "Our manager, Fred, is the nemesis of all progressive management philosophy. I am constantly in trouble for unwelcome input as a result of my reading and continuing interest in people-oriented management practices. The issues are always basic—that there be integrity from the top down; that quality standards are never compromised; and that the dignity of the worker, particularly in this blue-collar field, is addressed. None of that is subversive or radical, but it sure threatens my manager. He recently fired a fine field service engineer who dared to read and think about such things and then to ask questions for improving our own work environment. Seems Gail quoted Drucker once too often, when our company 'leaders' prefer to manage by threat, intimidation, and quantitative measurements. Regrettably, they care nothing about people development!" These are remarkable insights demonstrating that managers can no longer control workers by withholding information. Knowledge about excellent management even makes the best seller lists today, so the rank and file have greater expectations of their own leaders.

Yes, antediluvian managers are still around who have ignored the consistent message of behavioral scientists for the past forty years. Though many of these types are rapidly being replaced, some may persist and be kicked screaming into the twenty-first century by frustrated subordinates and irate customers. Fortunately, most managers are changing their views about the manager's role. They listen and apply the research about productivity improvement through people. They turn to semiautonomous quality circles, flexible work hours, and self-development seminars for employees. They provide behavior models and give positive reinforcement or stroking to employees. Why? Because such intelligent business practice leads to less job turnover, higher employee morale and performance, and increased profits. Thinking managers have learned to stimulate workers through job satisfaction rather than just through promotions. The strategies and concepts that lead to high performance were reviewed in previous chapters. These approaches not only are the right way to go in the new management; they are correct practices in themselves.

The industrial age's traditional management hierarchy and its leadership style have outlived their usefulness for coordinating and controlling global enterprises. The alteration in managerial role comes out of this flattened organization, often at the expense of middle management, and the whole line/staff relationship changes as staff functions are taken over and simplified through telecommunications. With his or her own computerized work station and even an "electronic briefcase" to take on business trips, the new manager is connected to sources of instant and relevant information. Thus, hourly workers, organized in teams, can be given more responsibility—such as job redesign and participation—which was formerly exercised solely by supervisors. Clearly, for both managers and workers to be comfortable in these new situations, learning new knowledge, skills, and competencies is essential. If employees are to be involved but not taken over, they must be given the opportunity to learn about planning, problem solving, decision making, and self-supervision—once the exclusive prerogative of management. Those with leadership responsibility need to be educated, in turn, about new technology, team management, linking functions, information systems, influencing organizational culture, and so on.

Admittedly, the changed role of managers will include some classical practices that have been tested over time and found to work. CEOs, such as Erwin Zaban, know that "service" and close attention to detail are still ingredients of business success. His Atlanta-based National Service Industries (NSI), capitalized at $550 million, became a conglomerate by practicing these time-honored ideas, although in a new way. Consider, for example, its lighting division, which accounts for 29 percent of the profits. This division does not just sell hardware; it gives special attention to architects so as to provide a package of equipment that will fit into the overall design and structure of a new building. They sell a commodity product embellished with service that competitors cannot match. Not surprisingly, Zaban has only two vice-presidents between himself and division heads, encouraging the disparate divisions to be managed autonomously. Even in acquisitions, this top executive looks for excellent managers who will stay and shuns turnarounds. NSI's attention to detail also is obvious in the way it minds its money and controls spending, so that now it can keep earnings flowing by buying back its own stock.

Another example of timeless management practices is John McGillicuddy's adherence to his corporate slogan, "Quality, Loyalty, Consistency: Some Things Shouldn't Change." As chairman of Manufacturers Hanover Trust (MHT), he leads the nation's largest financial services company and its fourth largest bank. The three key words of the slogan describe this CEO, who loves his challenging work, especially the team spirit. MHT has posted eleven straight years of record earnings. McGillicuddy is said to be an extension of its whole, and he is known for the way he relates to people, whether inside or outside the enterprise. He believes MHT personnel are happy and successful because they really do work together as a team, regardless of level or position.

The current work environment, in addition to the tried and true, really does require new management approaches—unique leadership not prevalent among managers in the past. Among the new skills described throughout this volume, for instance, it was suggested that a metaindustrial manager should be an entrepreneur and a risk taker, a facilitator and an associative person, a futurist and a strategic planner. In the superindustrial arena, the transformational manager also needs to acquire these additional competencies:

1. Authentic communication management: the capacity to level with people and tell it like it is rather than play games. Intel's president, Andrew Grove, calls this constructive confrontation. Thus, in performance appraisal, the manager focuses on strengths and problems needing correction or solution and not on personality factors or avoidance behavior. Managing today means giving helpful feedback, communicating guidelines, negotiating, and seeking information through an established network.

2. Political/power management: the capacity to exercise interpersonal influence and implement planned change, as well as to take advantage of opportunities for organization development. Andrew Kakabadse, a British professor from Cranfield School of Management, has written two books on the subject.

In *The Politics of Management* (1983), Kakabadse refers to this skill as the people elements of the manager's work—the interactions, relationships, and complications that must be handled deftly. In a follow-up volume, *Power, Politics, and Organizations* (Kakabadse and Parker, 1984), power management is viewed as the constructive use of physical or human energy to achieve goals and influence people decisions and behavior in a particular direction. Leadership is the use of power for these purposes, while control is the end result or objective of influence. Power comes from expertise, access, accomplishment, timing, or presence. Rather than having an aversion for politics and power, managers must learn their positive use in order to perform effectively, to accomplish worthy objectives, and to facilitate the transition into the new work culture.

3. Energy management: the capacity to mobilize resources (human, material, natural) and guide them toward a desired end, such as an organizational objective. Whether psychic or physical energy is involved, the manager views every aspect of role responsibility in this context. Thus, when it comes to human energy, the concern with personnel is to stimulate their cooperation, confidence, competence, and commitment. This requires, for instance, creating a team atmosphere so that people become truly involved. Another aspect is performance management so that productivity remains high and rewards are given for increases in this regard. Performance appraisal and pay reviews, then, are concerned with assessment of how people conserve and channel their energies, or those of the organization, to achieve corporate missions.

4. Innovation management: the capacity to deal creatively with both changes and differences, to cope with unusual demands through unique solutions. For managers, this innovation can be applied to marketing or technology management, R&D in new products or services, human resource supervision or development—any area of the management and problem-solving process. C. Joshua Abend, president of the Syracuse-based Innovation America, Inc., thinks that this process needs to be focused especially on quality engineering, productivity, and performance. The Center for Creative Leadership in Greensboro,

Succeeding in Work, Role, and Personal Transitions

North Carolina, conducts an annual Creativity Week for managers and publishes the proceedings—the 1984 volume, "Blueprint for Innovation," is very much worth reading. The Center also has a research study underway on self-directed learning by executives. *High Hurdles: The Challenge of Executive Self-Development* is a report on this investigation by Kaplan, Drath, and Kofodimos (1985) which examines the effect of high position and power on getting developmental feedback; the nature of the executive job and the prospects for introspection; the need for competence and the ability to accept and learn from criticism; and the effect of career success on the prospects of behavior change.

For an inkling of what the manager's role is to become, examine the issues confronting those in high-technology management, regardless of the product or industry. Martin Apple, now president of Adytum, Inc., in Oakland, California, founded three start-up companies and raised a series of questions that highlight these concerns. There are no pat answers but in the search for creative solutions, new management will alter the traditional role of executive or manager. Following are some of the questions:

1. How can we best deploy information technology as a competitive instrument that gives a company more leverage?
2. How can we best use information technology to change what our company does, not just how it does it?
3. How can we best evaluate the value of new information, our emerging principal product?
4. How can we best cope with the stresses of fast-growth situations on corporate communications?
5. How can we best cope with and capitalize on rapidly occurring current events that threaten the life and future course of our company (such as formation of something like an OPEC for organizations engaged in worldwide food exportation; shift in historic weather patterns; women choosing the sex of their babies; availability of fusion energy; or utilizing space facilities and resources?

To these, Joshua Abend would add five other queries:

6. How can we best sense trends, opportunities, and potential disasters?
7. How can we best develop strategies, options, and alternatives to meet tomorrow's challenges?
8. How can we best do things better and maximize product wins?
9. How can we best turn around quickly when need dictates, and where should we do it?
10. How can we best cope with the unpredictable, the uncertain, and the unexpected?

The replies to these inquiries may help underscore why I earlier suggested that change today must be built into our lifestyles and that ultrastability must become an organizational norm. Metaindustrial management continuously responds to the challenge of change as a way of life! To live is to change, but to grow is to change often. The essence of life is transition—a pilgrimage, if you prefer. As Buckminster Fuller reminded us, we are all passengers on Spaceship Earth. Enjoy the voyage, and anticipate the future with pleasant optimism.

TWELVE

Succeeding Through Transformational Management

Executive Summary. Societies and their institutions, having life cycles, must either adapt or disappear. This book has been about the end of the industrial cycle and the transition to a metaindustrial civilization and work culture. Our thesis is that those in management positions are challenged to exercise leadership in this organizational transformation or renewal process. However, as Thomas J. Peters, coauthor of In Search of Excellence *(Peters and Waterman, 1982), commented in a recent television interview, such reassessment thinking has only barely begun among the vast majority of managers. Peters feels that ideally the transformation process must start on the plant floor; he estimates that it might take management upwards of thirty-five years to complete this process.*

For managers in the midst of this transition, vision plus candor, commitment, courage, and competence will be necessary if we are to reshape ourselves and our organizations, as well as work itself and the worker. In turn, this reshaping will contribute to the restructuring of the economy and of society. At the current crossroad, transformational management means exercising multidimensional leverage to create a more positive future. That implies learning and practicing new coping skills for personal, role, and organizational change. Managing between centuries calls for a combination of tried and true administrative practice and innovative practice. In order to transform human systems, vanguard managers must effectively employ human energy through authentic communications, including the intelligent use of politics and power. Furthermore, transformational management has the capacity to create surprise and even manifests a willingness to make mistakes.

The shape of tomorrow's organizations can be dimly perceived through the progressive practices of the more innovative and excellent companies or agencies. These twenty-first century prototypes are more technical and humanized, more creative and entrepreneurial than most of today's companies. They capitalize on opportunities to serve or to create new markets. They seek new institutional arrangements and relationships that are more synergistic. Increasingly, the new business frontiers they explore are regional, global, even interplanetary, in scope. But to actualize the future's potential, today's organizations require leadership and strategies dedicated to planned change, not business as usual.

Coping with the Big Transition

Products have life cycles—those who have studied or worked in marketing know that. Just like people, products go through various stages of development—from origination to distribution, when returns start to fail as supply grows, to the final stage of a mass market commodity, when profits may fall. Then innovation becomes the means for continued survival and development. That, coupled with risk taking in new ventures, processes, or equipment, may be the salvation of struggling industries whose products or markets are shrinking, such as steel, shoes, and textiles. During the recent recession, for example, some bold firms invested in computers, robots, automated inventory and packaging, and other innovations. Now their foresight is paying off, for these risk takers are able to hold down prices, capture new markets, and bring on new products.

Societies and their institutions, created by people, also have life cycles—they either adapt to changing times or degen-

Succeeding Through Transformational Management

erate. Thinking managers know this and are very well aware that the industrial way of life is passing. In the past, this was the predominant paradigm or world view that permeated our basic way of thinking, valuing, and acting; but that perspective of reality is passing, and, as a result, leaders are challenged to plan personal, role, and organizational change.

However, these unprecedented social, technological, and economic changes occur at a time when most American businesspeople and executives are narrowly focused and pay too much attention to short-term matters. That is the opinion of Lester B. Korn, CEO of Korn/Ferry International, a leading executive search firm. In a *Los Angeles Times* interview ("Future Executives...," 1982, p. 2) he noted that most executives as we know them will be obsolete by the year 2000: "Tomorrow's executive must possess a broad understanding of history, of culture, of technology, and of human relations." Korn believes that the concept of business leadership must be broadened to include participation in public dialogue and to help solve urgent social problems. Certainly these comments are a fitting capstone to the message delivered in these pages.

Years ago, Lewis Mumford observed that there probably have been no more than a half dozen profound transformations in Western society since the time of primitive man. Now we are in the midst of such a transformation, but instead of being spread over a century or more, it is occurring in decades. This acceleration of social change is causing turbulence, chaos, and confusion for the average person, but for transitional managers it is an opportunity. The very forces propelling us into a new age can stimulate a quantum leap in our growth and maturity. Now is the time to exercise leadership in the metamorphosis. Willis Harman (1984) of the Stanford Research Institute envisions the possibility of a jump to a transindustrial society that transcends mere material concerns and enhances the human spirit and potential.

The thrust of this volume has been on the passage from a disappearing industrial work culture to the metaindustrial work environment. High technology has been viewed as more than something giving manufacturers greater flexibility to perform higher-quality work in less time with fewer people; it has been analyzed as a harbinger of tomorrow's organization. The shift to a global service/information economy drives traditional business and management practices into obsolescence while stimulating more creative, relevant approaches and ventures (Gilder, 1984). Concurrent microelectronics, information, and genetic revolutions contribute mightily to the transformation underway, bringing in their wake new applications of automation, robotics, and other technologies (see Chapters Five and Six). Such forces are the catalysts to the formation of different metaindustrial enterprises and management styles that are more entrepreneurial (see Chapter Three) and more participative (see Chapters Eight and Nine). In the process of creating this new work culture, greater emphasis is placed on the development of human assets and their high performance (see Chapters Four, Seven, and Ten). Finally, personnel need to be prepared by management for change and coached on how to cope with transitional experiences (see Chapter Eleven).

In a 1985 public service television broadcast, populist prophet Alvin Toffler described the main features of the "third wave" civilization coming into being (in essence, summarizing key points in his 1980 book, *The Third Wave*):

1. more individual choice, diversity, and de-massifying in contrast to the industrial age or "second wave" emphasis on conformity and mass consumption;
2. more complexity that requires greater cooperation on a global scale;
3. more information that demands that data processing define our differences and capabilities;
4. more convergence that breaks down traditional separations and distinctions, such as through new communication technology that alters the way we learn;
5. more technology that uses less energy and is less damaging to people and the environment; and
6. more management that is flexible, entrepreneurial, and participative.

Succeeding Through Transformational Management 327

In his latest work on *The Adaptive Corporation* (1985), Toffler asserts that too many leaders explain away their contemporary problems and blame competition, oil prices, government regulations, or even the workers. In fact, they are dramatically underestimating the adaptive changes in themselves, their people, and their organizations—changes that are necessary for survival.

The above six themes confirm the principal message of this book. In Figure 13, Stevenson and Gumpert (1985) illustrate this last point by contrasting the entrepreneurial culture, which increasingly dominates contemporary business, with the administrative focus, which is slowly disappearing in both the public and private sectors.

Leadership in Transformational Management

The new order cries out for transformational management—leaders who not only are open to change and sensitive to people's needs, but who identify accurately trends in the markets and among consumers and who respond quickly and creatively, whether this means restructuring to cut costs, redesigning products and services, retraining workers, or educating them in new knowledge, skills, and attitudes (Kozmetsky, 1985). The transformational leader demonstrates vision and competency in adapting to these new realities:

• The changing nature of the worker—more diverse in terms of race and ethnicity, sex and age, attitudes and expectations, values and motivations; more often a better-educated knowledge worker.

• The changing nature of work—more information processing and service oriented because of production of goods increasingly manufactured through automation or robotics; more application of intelligence and new technologies;

• The changing nature of the economy and market—more global, segmented, volatile, qualitative, and competitive; an information economy characterized by reduction in material and energy consumption with greater emphasis on customization, quality, design, utility, workmanship, and durability, as

Figure 13. The Entrepreneurial Culture Versus the Administrative Culture.

	Entrepreneurial focus			Administrative focus	
	Characteristics	Pressures		Characteristics	Pressures
A Strategic orientation	Driven by perception of opportunity	Diminishing opportunities Rapidly changing technology, consumer economics, social values, and political rules		Driven by controlled resources	Social contracts Performance measurement criteria Planning systems and cycles
B Commitment to seize opportunities	Revolutionary, with short duration	Action orientation Narrow decision windows Acceptance of reasonable risks Few decision constituencies		Evolutionary, with long duration	Acknowledgment of multiple constituencies Negotiation about strategic course Risk reduction Coordination with existing resource base
C Commitment of resources	Many stages, with minimal exposure at each stage	Lack of predictable resource needs Lack of control over the environment Social demands for appropriate use of resources Foreign competition Demands for more efficient resource use		A single stage, with complete commitment out of decision	Need to reduce risk Incentive compensation Turnover in managers Capital budgeting systems Formal planning systems

D Control of resources	Episodic use or rent of required resources	Increased resource specialization Long resource life compared with need Risk of obsolescence Risk inherent in the identified opportunity Inflexibility of permanent commitment to resources	Ownership or employment of required resources	Power, status, and financial rewards Coordination of activity Efficiency measures Inertia and cost of change Industry structures
E Management structure	Flat, with multiple informal networks	Coordination of key noncontrolled resources Challenge to hierarchy Employees' desire for independence	Hierarchy	Need for clearly defined authority and responsibility Organizational culture Reward systems Management theory

Source: Stevenson and Gumpert, 1985, p. 89. Used with permission.

well as more direct interface between producers and consumers. That is the conclusion reached in *The Next Economy* (Hawken, 1983), which suggests that we are remaking our world and that every product, process, and service will have to be completely redesigned or newly constituted.

- The changing nature of organizations—more like energy exchange systems that transform both psychic and physical energy, as well as raw materials, into goods and services. New multidimensional organizational structures and functions provide both decentralization and autonomy while offering some centralization and integration. The metaindustrial organization responds with a combination of increased productivity and quality control; with short-term profitability while engaging in long-range strategic planning and capitalization; and with emphasis on information availability and knowledge assets, as well as human resource development.

- The changing nature of leadership and management—more shared, with concern for utilization of team member talents and increasing productivity through people; more autonomy, entrepreneurship, and risk taking. The new manager leads by example, improves organizational culture, and learns by doing, as well as by fostering both communication and collaboration.

- The changing nature of society—more open and pluralistic as well as more global and interdependent. Economic, social, political, and technological changes are reshaping society so that the only certainty is uncertainty.

A manifesto was published in 1984 under the title, *At the Crossroads* (Communications Era Task Force, Box 3623, Spokane, Wash. 99110). It analyzes the magnitude of these social and cultural changes that alter our perceptions of family, roles, and relationships. It calls for new assumptions that will lead to more and better communication, interconnectedness, and self-reliance. It identifies desirable policy shifts from medicine to health, from courts to mediation, from hierarchy to participation. It points out new directions in lifelong learning, creative living, and local control/global cooperation. The issues in this remarkable document are the issues groups of concerned managers should be discussing. Then we can take a fresh look at the patterns of our lives and make the necessary adjustments.

Among the business leaders to sense these changes early was John Diebold, the computer and information system consultant. For him, the emerging role of business in society demands new management strategies for improved relations with labor, consumers, environmentalists, and government (Diebold, 1982). Yet in the restructuring of society, the most important and relevant services to be provided can become the most profitable for business to deliver (Diebold, 1985).

Some observers of the contemporary scene argue for executives to shed their parochial approaches to problems and programs in the public sector and to lead in private sector participation. For example, environmental safety is one arena for exercising greater corporate social responsibility. Instead of being forced by government to introduce practices and programs that will ensure the public's health and welfare, transformational leaders work with communities and the public sector to initiate plant operations conducive to good health and product safety while planning, together with local neighborhood leaders, strategies for dealing with emergencies. That is the lesson that multinational corporations are learning at home and abroad from such disasters as Three Mile Island and Bhopal, India. In the aftermath of the latter tragedy, Union Carbide's chairman, Warren Anderson, admitted that top management cannot afford to lose control of technology and plant safety, whether the activity occurs domestically or overseas ("Learning from the Bhopal Disaster," 1985, p. 52). In fact, Mitroff and Kilmann (1984) make a case that companies must design mechanisms to cope with unforeseen disasters. They maintain that many executives rely on an obsolete mental map of the industrial age and are not trained to think about tragedies, whether caused by acts of God, terrorists, or corporate failures. They advocate that crises-simulation workshops become part of executive development for systematic strategies to either prevent or cope with major business disasters. Fortunately, some multinational corporations go beyond hygiene needs and express a vision of their global organizations as being concerned for the creation of prosperity and well-being in the communities in which they exist to serve customers, employees, and suppliers.

In these closing decades before entry into the twenty-first century, creative management must not only cope effectively but also transform existing organizational attitudes, roles, policies, processes, and activities. Such progressive corporate governance for better communication and policy making is reflected in the words of C. E. Meyers, then president of Transworld Airlines, on the collective social awareness growing among business leaders: "We have tried to heal divisions, both with insight and effort, resulting in qualitative change in our national attitude, by concern for the environment, job security for the work force, dignity for the handicapped, enhanced purpose for the aged, and higher regard for the consumer" (Ferguson, 1980, p. 340).

Management has new resources to call on in this transformation process. Among them are the National Organization Development (OD) Network (1011 Park Avenue, Plainfield, N.J. 07060), with its membership of over 2,000 professional organization development specialists, and the emerging Organization Transformation (OT) Network (15 Garrison Avenue, Durham, N.H. 03824), with an expanding number of organizational tranformation consultants. Frank Burns, who founded the Delta Force to help renew the United States Army in 1980, described the difference between the two consulting approaches: OD tends to focus on fixing problems here and now, while OT is more concerned with organizational vision and futuring (French and Bell, 1984). As a leading OT practitioner and editor of *Transforming Work* (1984), John Adams indicates that his consultation encourages people to have a vision of what they would like the organization to be. He then helps them personalize this to the point that they will stand up and work for its fulfillment.

A recent *New Age Journal* provided a cameo look at one such organizational transformation in the case of Batterymarch, a Boston investment management firm. In this company, thirty employees manage $11 billion for 137 clients, which range from AT&T to the United Mine Workers. Its president, Dean LeBaron, describes the corporate culture as unstructured and without role assignments; each employee is an entrepreneur who is free to do anything to manage a client account effectively. The management style is creative and innovative, depending heavily on computer use and the free spirit of its human assets. Such organizational transformation concepts are not unlike those suggested in 1969 by UCLA professor Robert Tannenbaum in a seminal article, "Values, Man and Organizations." In that article, he challenged organizations to take on more person-oriented values. Thus, a corporate culture would manifest more trust, cooperation, openness, and wholeness.

The 1980s and 1990s, our vestibule into the life-style of the next century, necessitate transformational leadership if we are to be victors, not victims, of change. Some have described this as supermanaging—allowing managers to take advantage of the changes by seizing the new opportunities being offered (Brown and Weiner, 1984). The question seems to be "What business do we need to be in?" as we break away from conventional wisdom while matching resources with new markets.

Those who aspire to leadership in the transformation of their organizations might begin by seeking answers to the following questions, in addition to others already posed: (1) What existing attitudes, roles, policies, processes, procedures, and activities need to be altered or renewed? (2) What new mechanisms are desirable for improved forecasting, strategic planning, and marketing so as to meet unmet problems? (3) What alternatives are worthy of exploration relative to existing work contracts, schedules, and assignments? (4) What new systems, such as computerized data banks, are required to understand our customers' needs better? (5) How can the organization's resources, human and material, be mobilized for adaptation and flexibility, especially by intelligent use of new technology? The answers to these queries may contribute to development of an ecology of work that results in work systems that optimize both people and business goals.

Coping with Organizational Change

"Sogo Shosha" is the name the Japanese gave to the general trading companies established over a hundred years ago to end self-imposed isolation from the world economy. In 1870,

Mitsubishi was formed to take advantage of these controlled trade channels for acquisition of international raw materials and technologies and to gain access to export markets. In 1954, it was the first of such corporations to be reestablished in America after the war in the Pacific. In a remarkable business research study, *Mitsubishi-USA: The Next Thirty Years—Extinction or Expansion,* New York's St. John's University provided a case study in careful organizational change (Miller and Sugiyama, 1984). The parent company ($65 billion in sales), along with its American subsidiary Mitsubishi International Corporation (MIC, $12 billion in sales), contributed much to making Japan number one in international business. Yet both are at a turning point, faced with transitional decisions to change from trading company to diversified global enterprise. Century-old traditions will have to be dismantled in the process. Obviously, traditions that have governed the selection of employees, their promotion, and their retention will have to be drastically altered (for example, more foreigners will be hired and assigned significant management responsibility). For Mitsubishi, corporate rigidities in management will be replaced by flexibility and fluidity. Innovative strategies will include marketing trading services to other countries, conducting worldwide searches for new raw materials and technologies, seeking fast-growth venture opportunities, restructuring as a transnational global and information network, and granting greater autonomy to subsidiaries. In New York, MIC reflects such planned changes through joint dispersed endeavors with American companies in developing nonferrous metal resources; international commodities (trading materials and handling equipment), oil exportation and refining, and other enterprises unusual for that corporation. Mitsubishi has an association with the Battelle Institute for research and technology transfer. MIC's presidents have been emphasizing human resource development, innovation risk taking, strategic planning, Americanization, and globalization. Thus, because it is willing to change and adopt the practices of excellent companies, Mitsubishi is likely to expand over the decades ahead.

Most human systems today are faced with a transformational challenge to survive and prosper. For those struggling to

Succeeding Through Transformational Management

cope with organization shock, it means changing the corporate or agency or association culture. That is the problem at Bank of America (described in Chapter Eight), which is being rectified with a renewal program called "Visions, Values, and Strategies." Transformational change is the critical issue facing industrial-type manufacturers and industries whose products are too labor intensive or whose processes are simply archaic. It is the reality that confronts the dinosaur corporations whose size, organization, and operations make them sluggish or unresponsive. It is the situation of the enterprise that has viewed its markets as primarily domestic when the whole shift is now regional, global, and even space oriented.

Obviously, only top management can turn around such traditional approaches. Key executives can create an atmosphere to alter the status quo. In an NTL Institute seminar on the new work culture, which I conducted, a brainstorming session was held with participants on how to bring about such organizational change. The results are summarized here in the form of five transformational practices; also cited are illustrations of enlightened management for each guideline:

1. Diagnose the existing work culture through a survey, and provide feedback on results to top management for appropriate actions. In my work with the United States Customs Service, an organizational culture survey instrument was administered to personnel in its Los Angeles Region, and the results were used for strategic planning, as well as in training sessions with employees.

2. Clarify through consensus the contemporary organizational purposes and values. Both General Electric and Atlantic Richfield Company are engaged in such an attempt to assess and redesign their corporate cultures, which so affect performance. These self-examinations are aimed at changing both attitudes and functions.

3. Acquire the tools to reshape the existing work culture, be it acculturation information, automated systems, or training in new technologies, strategic planning, and team building. The Carnegie Foundation for the Advancement of Teaching issued a 1984 report on *Corporate Classrooms: The Learning Business*

(Eurich, 1984), which indicates that big business is spending up to $100 billion a year to teach its workers. The study concludes that these corporate efforts are more than a primary means for improving human resource productivity; they are major centers of adult education for today's society.

4. Focus on human resources and performance—increase span of control, cross-train and provide for succession, eliminate obsolete work procedures and duplication of effort, provide meaningful work and permit decision making at lower levels, reward appropriate and creative behavior. Kimberly Clark Corporation trains its employees to know not only what they are to do but also why they are to do it; not only to operate but also to control a manufacturing process. The purpose of this training is to ensure that their personnel will be both skilled and motivated (Desatnick, 1983).

5. Develop a new work climate that encourages employee input and feedback, skill assessment and training, developmental counseling and lateral transfers or even outplacement, ergonomics and quality-of-life concerns, as well as a project management approach. Many companies, such as IBM and McDonald's, are making provisions for extended job absence; holidays, vacations, and sick leave benefits can be combined. Depending on years of service, these "sabbaticals" can extend from a month to a year without sacrificing income, and most provide a comparable job upon return. To stimulate individual creativity, one out of every ten companies today has such policies to attract and keep competent workers, to deal with stress and burnout, and to provide opportunities for professional or personal growth.

It seems that these managers got the message; we can only hope our readers will, too, and that they will act on it. There are numerous books, films, and courses available to help management with the process for renewing and changing an organization. There is no mystery to increasing the driving forces for change and weakening the opposing forces. Just remember to plan change, to include those in the process who must implement the changes, and to develop and communicate the case for altering the way it has always been done (Lippitt, Langseth, and Mossop, 1985).

Sometimes when talented personnel cannot change an organization in need of it, the best strategy may be for them to get out and start their own enterprises. Many of today's most successful high-technology firms were formed in this manner. For example, two disaffected Hughes Aircraft employees, Simon Ramo and Dean Wooldridge, left the company in 1953 and convinced TRW to put $20 million into their own corporation for manufacturing a new electronics system. These two went on to administer the United States ballistic missile program and a large part of the space program. Eventually, their company was absorbed by TRW, going on to excel in manned spacecraft; it still builds a third of all satellites produced, including Pioneer 10, which is now enroute to another galaxy. Perhaps Ramo and Wooldridge felt comfortable in the well-managed TRW because it is a corporation committed to change, including creative self-destruction of an entity in the process of reshaping. This dynamic capacity to adapt has led TRW to $3.1 billion in assets and $5 billion in sales. It has led them in and out of businesses and into many promising market areas. It is a corporation run by engineers that is technology driven, so it maintains seventeen centers for technology development. How fortunate it is that Simon Ramo was a risk-taking entrepreneur, for he still heads the TRW science and technology committee. Truly, he found a home in an organization that is experimental and exploits opportunity while continually transforming itself and seeking synergy in its new ventures.

In examining high-technology management, Maidique of Stanford and Hays of Harvard (1984) reported on six themes that seem to ensure success in such organizations:

1. business focus—sales occur from a single product or a closely related set of product lines with concentrated R&D and consistent priorities;
2. adaptability—ability to track and exploit rapid shifts and twists in the market and technology, plus organizational agility in frequent realignment of people and responsibilities;
3. cohesion—energy and creativity of the whole company can quickly be translated from new ideas to new products and

processes (that is, able to collaborate in common organizational cause);
4. entrepreneurial culture—innovate with new ventures, programs, and services based on open communication, job rotation, shared decisions, small divisions, risk taking, tolerance of failure, funding variety and investment opportunity;
5. integrity—for long-term relationships with customers, stockholders, employees, and suppliers, there is commitment to ethical values such as honesty, firmness, openness, and even acknowledgment of limitations;
6. "hands-on" top management—direct involvement of key executives in company business by keeping in touch with people at all levels, moving around and asking questions, or sensing.

Maidique and Hays maintain that it is the responsibility of top management to cultivate such an atmosphere so as to make the major changes in organization and resource allocation necessitated by technological transition.

The transformations being manifested in corporations, associations, and government agencies are manifold. A review of some not only will indicate the scope of the changes underway, but also may stimulate change agents to plan for others:

Collaboration Between Big and Little Corporations. IBM, as previously indicated, now owns 12 percent of Intel's shares, has a seat on the latter's board, and has agreed to raise its equity stake above 30 percent; besides providing a capital input, IBM uses an Intel microprocessor as the brain of its PC, and this synergy strengthens the stability of Intel as a supplier.

Working at Home by Computer. Companies are assisting some employees to operate out of their residences and to stay electronically connected with the office. For instance, using a computer at home, a Vermont stockbroker can work for a Philadelphia-based firm and a Palos Verdes executive can run a $10 million software business while going to the office only a few times a month. Almost 30,000 workers are already telecommuting.

Leasing Employees. Renting staff from an independent

company can save time, paper work, taxes, and money. Workers may be separated from their jobs by mutual agreement with their employer and hired by one of more than forty companies, which then reassign them back to their former employer. More than 25,000 workers have such arrangements with organizations including Contract Staffing of America, Inc., and National Employee Leasing Company, Ltd., whose clients are mainly operators of small businesses, such as physicians, dentists, lawyers, and other professionals with staffs of under twenty-five people. Leasing employees not only reduces administrative and cost burdens for the client, but workers often get better fringe benefits under the arrangement. Congressional legislation and Internal Revenue Service rulings presently condone the practice.

Corporate-Sponsored Daycare. Wang Laboratories has leased a former grade school as a center of care for employees' children during work hours. Zale's, a jewelry store chain, has a modern $300,000 daycare center at corporate headquarters for its staff. Some companies charge employees for these services; others offer them as a fringe benefit. Other firms pay tuition for their personnel's children to attend external preschool programs or allow more flexible or shared work schedules so that parents can fulfill these child-rearing responsibilities themselves.

Corporate Venture Capital Funds. Fast-growth companies, such as Analog, have established funds for investment in small-niche firms whose technical research interests them. This new corporate strategy helps ensure a high-tech corporation's survival in the future. Sometimes, the fund is used for start-up enterprises by the company's own employees.

Employee Stock Ownership. A variety of new devices is being created beyond the traditional profit sharing plans so that personnel can become real stakeholders in the business. These mechanisms range from selling the company to the employees to giving stock to workers in place of wage increases to moves such as People's Express giving interest-free loans to employees so they can buy stock in that corporation.

Committees on the Future. For decades, major corporations have established task forces on the future of their business or industry. Now the Communications Workers of America

(CWA) have done the same to assess the implications of changes in their industry and the world of work. In a union report to their 675,000 telecommunications members, a call was made for new initiatives in bargaining, political action, and public relations. The CWA was urged to become strategy driven instead of reactive, making the most of changes in technology, structure, and power; in workers' composition, life-style, needs, and interests; and in emphasizing job security.

Management in Transition. These illustrations of organizational change indicate how institutions of work are being reshaped to be relevant in the emerging culture. The issue is whether the present leadership in human systems will give direction and expansion to such changes. Management in transition should be agents of planned change, particularly as active behavior models of this philosophy through shaping strategy and promoting innovation. Executives demonstrate by example their interest in new directions and ventures, acquisitions and mergers, research and development, strategic planning and coupling of functions. They anticipate human resistance to necessary organizational change and counteract these restraining forces. Transformational managers initiate renewal and reorganization efforts, respond to unique or increased competition, establish new markets, products, and services, adjust to shifts in resources and technology. They provide personnel with the learning and support services necessary to implement change effectively. To stay vibrant, it is management leadership that can take advantage of new technology to aid productivity and maximize strengths. These managers capitalize on information complexity and the ideas produced. While concerned with short-term returns, key management shares with personnel the insights of long-range vision (Charnes and Cooper, 1984). Such attitudes eventually get incorporated into organizational philosophy and often appear in corporate publications.

Thus, a major shift in the work culture through organizational change is being directed toward people, whether in the form of customer or client, supplier or employee. With regard to the latter, the modern work ethic emphasizes *The New Achiever* (Pascarella, 1984). Pascarella, executive editor of *In-*

dustry Week, explains that the new achiever is an employee who is encouraged to grow personally within the work place. The present transition demands a work force of infinite mix, dexterity, and intelligence, regardless of occupational type. Pascarella argues for a concept of fully employed people, not just the obsolete norm of full employment; a transformation in our thinking to concern for quality-of-life interests instead of a more narrow focus on just the quality of product or work. New corporate assets are being discovered in terms of both human and information resources.

Capitalizing on Opportunity

High-tech business developer, Martin Apple, sagely observed that managers do not create successful companies—markets do. If there is truth in that statement, what are some of the markets of opportunity that will further transform both management and organizations? Where can we channel energies for return on investment before and during the twenty-first century? While these topics deserve exploration in the future, I would like to provide three strategies for managers in transition who want to make the most of the transformation now underway. In addition to organizational energies, the new technologies, and a new work culture, focus also on new frontiers of management or marketing. Analyze these in one or more of these contexts—institutional, global, and interplanetary:

Institutional. Those organizations will progress that seek new institutional arrangements and relationships that are synergistic (Corning, 1983). Consider these four illustrations of the point:

1. The economy in the state of Minnesota is experiencing a vigorous rebound because of a unique coalition of public and private interests formed to create jobs. With a cooperative spirit, diverse leaders from business, government, labor, and education have teamed up to back and invest in a number of local ventures, from breeding new high-tech enterprises to trimming state income taxes.

2. A cottage industry of information brokers has

emerged. Currently, the 150 such specialists in the United States combine library research skills with computers to tap 300 data bases. The new service provides information to a variety of organizations and professions but is especially useful to high-tech companies in need of research leads and connections.

3. In Japan, 350 or so robot makers have joined forces to give birth to a new generation of robots that are capable of seeing, teaching, and walking. These "third-generation" robots will be aware of their environment and react to it. They are supposed to be ready in time to take advantage of the projected "fifth-generation" computers expected in 1990 or so.

4. Of the $5 billion spent annually in the United States on university research, less than 5 percent comes from industry, which is one of its major beneficiaries. To improve the balance, universities and industry are forging new relationships to support both academic research and commercial R&D. There are many forms to this new cooperation—joint university/industry research centers, faculty/industry researchers exchanges, corporate donations of equipment to universities, university technology transfer of patents and research to new enterprises. The government sometimes provides seed money for the collaborative undertakings, as when the National Science Foundation gave grants to Stanford's Center for Integrated Systems, to Rutgers's Center for Ceramic Research, and to a consortium of San Diego research institutions, including the University of California and GA Technologies, for supercomputers. Often an industry gives the leadership, as when the Semiconductor Industry Association established a nonprofit subsidiary called Semiconductor Research Collaborative (SRC) to found centers of excellence and research at key universities.

In each of the above examples, the key to opportunity for new business and technological advancement is through some form of synergy or symbiosis—profiting through sharing and combining brain power or economic resources. This is the point of William Ouchi's book, *The M-Form Society* (1984). Ouchi is convinced that America can regain the competitive edge when the industrial pattern of adversarial relations is replaced by interinstitutional teamwork. He believes that the

Succeeding Through Transformational Management 343

metaindustrial situation calls for a multidivisional society in which the business community literally becomes just that, instead of an atomized set of individual actors. That will require changes in our culture, which is very competitive, in legislation, which is anti-trust oriented, and in structures so that new mechanisms are created that are multidisciplinary and cross-industrial. The same concept can be applied to labor, management, stockholder, and consumer relations—that is, with the stakeholders who have more to gain through mutual cooperation than through conflict (Mitroff, 1983).

Global. Those organizations that transform their mind sets from provincialism and ethnocentrism to cosmopolitan and global perspectives will prosper. This applies to markets, information flow, material and human resources, and every aspect of the enterprise's operations. We live now in a "global village" linked by mass communication and transportation, so that all systems are interdependent. That is why companies and business schools are finally emphasizing the concept of the "global manager" (see "The Global Manager Is a Hot Item," 1983). Such corporate leaders understand foreign management, marketing, and cultures and no longer perpetuate the artificial separation between "domestic" and "international."

Coca-Cola was among the first to respond to a universal need by marketing a worldwide brand. Giant enterprises, such as AT&T, are taking off their nationalistic blinders and beginning to adapt products and services for use abroad. With increased offshore operations or twin plants, takeover of native businesses by foreign investors, international joint ventures and mergers, cross-border information exchange, and other such developments, executives now take the management of cultural differences and synergy into consideration. They realize that the world is in transition from old-fashioned conflict situations of military/political/corporate competition for power. Transformational management joins forces to seek answers to common problems, such as global unemployment among unprepared youth or North/South economic exchanges, especially significant for the Third World manufacturing revolution, with its economically poor consumers and high percentage of exports.

However, it is in terms of the world economy that global managers are particularly astute regarding interconnections of their decisions and that reality. They appreciate the international character of financial institutions and take advantage of it. They are aware of the rise of newly industrialized countries (NICs) and how they are meeting the needs in the American market that our own manufacturers neglected. They comprehend that in trying to meet foreign competition, "outsourcing" to the NICs begins with the simple ordering of goods and components but may end up with obtaining sophisticated finished products. In trying to cope with such global economic transformation, we are confronted with such circumstances as a national trade deficit of $120 billion (1984), which is a direct cause of unemployment for three million more Americans while the NICs increase their exports to the United States. South Korea's Daewoo company is a case in point: It began in 1967 with a modest order for clothing from an overseas customer and now is a $4 billion conglomerate that even has a joint venture with General Motors.

Nowhere are new organizational strategies more needed than in the economic and trade shift from the Atlantic to the Pacific. The global manager plans and then optimizes that emerging Pacific Basin market of 1.5 billion potential customers. This new market frontier is marked by dynamic growth in such countries as South Korea, Taiwan, Hong Kong, and Singapore, which have become mini-Japans in their economic revival, and the potential is there for similar action in Malaysia, Indonesia, Australia, China, and other Eastern nations. No wonder United States investment in the area has risen 65 percent in the past five years and companies like General Electric have doubled their trade with the region (to $2 billion in 1983) (Hofheinz and Calder, 1982).

To compete effectively, more industries are becoming global, and multinational corporations are shedding their form and transforming into global enterprises. Universal Medical Supplies is an example; when it promoted the latest technology in disposable syringes and sensed its worldwide application, it had to change its structure to implement its new strategy. Thus, it captured 31 percent of the world syringe market. But this means developing a system that balances high/low coordination and configuration of activities.

Taking advantage of the changing role of the United States in the global economy requires that managers be more versatile in effectively utilizing international resources and opportunities while coping with the disadvantages of export competition. But most of all, it means changing strategies to meet the two major market challenges of the next hundred years—the Pacific and high frontiers.

Interplanetary. John Platt (Criswell, 1985, p. viii) estimates that the areas of greatest growth today are probably molecular genetics, artificial intelligence, and the development of space. He calls all three transformation frontiers in three levels of human organization—the gene, the brain, and the social organism. Some organizations will prosper in the future because they transformed themselves from an Earth-based mentality to a space-based one. For the past thirty years, leaders in the aerospace industry have learned to capitalize on the start-up activities in space developments. Now, thanks to NASA's pioneering efforts, space undertakings are going both international and commercial. Foreign space agencies and consortia, such as in Japan, Europe, and even India, are busily engaged in independent space activities or in ventures with the Americans, such as Skylab. The U.S.S.R. moves steadily ahead on its own and, with Soyuz, has the first space station of sorts; meanwhile, it occasionally enters into agreements with other nations for joint space efforts, such as Cosmos, by which United States biological experiments are flown on Russian spacecraft.

Space has already spawned the new communication satellite business, a growth industry of billions of dollars. But it is the expansion of human presence there that offers the most prospects for management. In 1984, the U.S. Office of Technology Assessment issued a report on competition and cooperation in civilian space activity. It urged development of a national consensus on long-term objectives in space and increased efforts to foster an efficient transition from the current preponderance of government funding for much of the space activities to greater private sector investment in the 1990s. This has already begun, with large corporations like McDonnell-Douglas and Johnson & Johnson entering into joint endeavors with NASA to manufacture pharmaceuticals in the space shuttle's low gravity. The thrust in the protein crystal growth experiments in space has to do with the bioengineering of new drugs for cures for such problems as cancer, high blood pressure, and organ rejection. The effort should result in powerful new medicines with high commercial value. This is but one potential market result from space industrialization. Now 3M Corporation has submitted to NASA a multimillion-dollar space commercialization plan calling for the firm to utilize as many as seventy-two space shuttle flights through 1995 for new product development. With the help of venture capitalists and major brokerage houses, space entrepreneurs have begun enterprises aimed at everything from building private rocket launchers to tourism. Eventually, the operations of both the shuttle system and space station to be built may be handled by private contractors, just as launch facilities are now being contracted by NASA to corporations like Rockwell International.

More and more corporate leaders are beginning to heed the president's message on the fifteenth anniversary of the Apollo 11 lunar landing that the benefits our people can receive from the commercial use of space literally dazzle the imagination. Ronald Reagan enumerated the near-term prospects for space-based factories producing new alloys and manufacturing other products impossible to fabricate on Earth; then he pledged to remove regulatory obstacles while creating unique tax provisions to stimulate space commerce. U.S. Senator John Glenn, himself a former astronaut, offered a vision of a new space infrastructure that is more cost-effective, since it is centered around an orbiting station. That facility, which should be ready in the next decade, would be a lab control center for both public and private operations. The activities there would range from scientific research, global communications, and industrial production to passive defense-related systems, refueling centers for storage and transfer of propellants, and a launch base for sending scientists and workers into higher geosynchronous orbit (O'Leary, 1983).

A 1984 NASA study at the California Space Institute, in which I participated, predicted a new era in space over the next twenty-five years featuring: more complex space activities at multiple locations, involving greater numbers and varieties of people; a space station and lunar outpost, as well as a space transportation system, that would form the basis of further manned and unmanned probes into the universe, beginning with utilization of the resources of near asteroids and Mars; high-risk ventures exposing national prestige and requiring large, up-front capital investment but promising big rewards, both financial and otherwise; large-scale technology projects creating a new type of macromanagement; increasing focus on people in space demanding more sophisticated systems planning, integrated life support and maintenance, new ergonomics and habitats, mining and storing of space resources, and technology that is more generic and can use substitute resources on-site (McKay, 1985).

To make the most of this new "high ground," an infrastructure will have to be created both on Earth and in space that requires a new kind of management (Harris, 1985). In a way, NASA pioneered the new management described in this volume; in conjunction with its partners in the aerospace industry, NASA stimulated both high-technology and matrix organizations. For example, in order for the Apollo mission to land men on the moon successfully, a prodigious large-scale management and technological effort was launched. To renew this planet's infrastructure or to build in space today requires a comparable effort that involves managing complex interfaces. Figure 14 summarizes the multiskills involved in the macromanagement of large-scale enterprises: It provides insight into twenty-first-century management.

Conclusion

Metaindustrial management is more challenging because our times of transition are both more confusing and complex. Transformational managers create the future by taking a comprehensive view of the social, technological, environmental, economic, political, and international changes and then exer-

Figure 14. The Management of Continuing Change and Strategy.

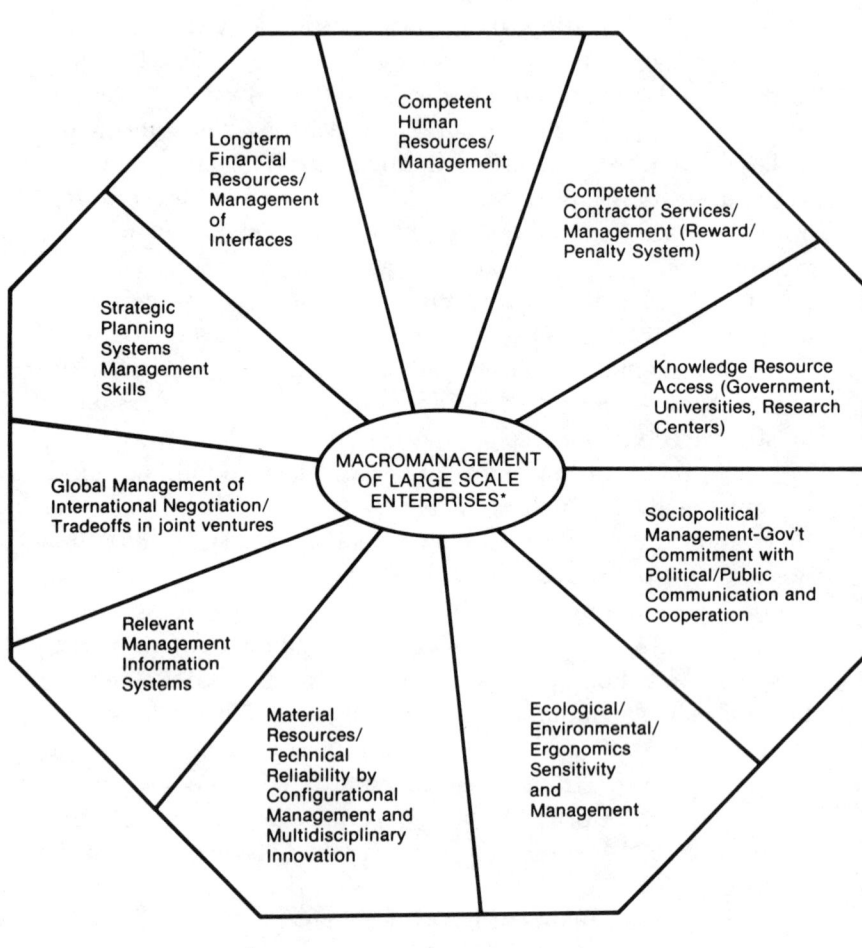

*Long-term projects of $100 million plus, such as, rebuilding American infrastructure and building a Space infrastructure.

Note: Reprinted with permission of aerospace illustrator Dennis M. Davidson of University of California at San Diego Medical School.

cising leverage at critical turning points to move them in the direction of organizational goals. There is no one certain scenario of the future—only opportunities for positive leadership to influence eventual outcomes of issues and events (Diebold, 1985).

As Jesco von Puttkamer (1985) reminds us, ours may be the most dynamic generation since humans began to evolve sociocultural systems three million years ago. This NASA advanced programs manager notes that we are creating a new world for ourselves in decades by changing our biological genetic substance, by interacting with the elementary building blocks of the atoms, by establishing a worldwide communication network, by extending ourselves into the universe. Is there any wonder that there is urgent need for new leaders who can facilitate the adaptation process to reduce social fragmentation and polarization, promote renewal of self and systems, and strive for wholeness and integration in both humanities and sciences? That, then, is the essence of transformational management—that is the challenge of management in transition.

RESOURCES

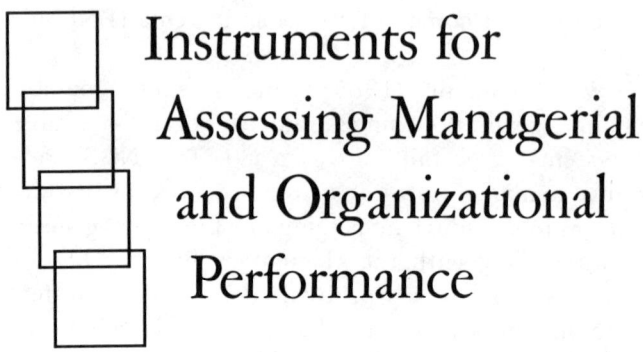

Instruments for Assessing Managerial and Organizational Performance

Creative managers and human resource consultants engage in continuing self- and organizational assessment. They also seek feedback from others on their own or others' performance. They wish to know what is happening in the organization—how people feel about themselves or the organization, its policies and practices. Among the several means for diagnosing organizational climate or culture, instruments offer an easy and helpful way to obtain information from personnel. A data-gathering instrument on human factors may be constructed or purchased commercially. These printed instruments usually require short written answers, although sometimes there is a computerized answer sheet that only requires marking one's choice or punching a hole to indicate a preference. Such instruments may take the form of inventories, questionnaires, checklists, or surveys. As with an opinion poll, the data collected can be statistically analyzed and compared between and among groups of workers. The results provide an individual respondent with self-understanding. For a manager who uses this technique with colleagues and subordinates, insight is gained about the work force. Consultants use such methods for organizational diagnosis of client systems.

This section of *Management in Transition* provides five such instruments:

A. Transformational Management Skills Inventory. This inventory can be used by an individual manager to assess his or her competencies for bringing about planned change and renewal. It also can be administered to a group of managers during a staff meeting or training session as a basis for meaningful discussion of the twenty-five items. It is divided into four parts for self-appraisal of leadership style, change skills, communication skills, and managerial performance. It allows for a five-point rating scale from 1 (lowest) to 5 (highest). The inventory is related to the content of Chapters

Instruments for Assessing Performance 351

One, Eleven, and especially Twelve. When the thirty-one scores possible are tallied, the respondent should seek a total in the range of 120 to 150, the highest. The instrument can be used within a group for team scoring and averaging.

B. Team Synergy Analysis Inventory. This is a short checklist for use by members of a team or work unit. The self-rating is accomplished through twenty-one items in three parts; each offers four options for a single choice—"seldom," "occasionally," "often," and "always." The evaluation concerns critical synergistic skills, such as cooperation and collaboration, feedback, and synthesis. It can be used for project management or in team-building sessions to sensitize participants to key factors of groups' effectiveness and productivity. It should be considered in the context of Chapters Eight and Nine.

C. Group Maturity Analysis Inventory. This inventory is intended for analysis of group performance by its members or external observers. The ten items permit a rating on a five-point scale from 1 (lowest) to 5 (highest). These items deal with such matters as feedback mechanisms, decision making, cohesion, and communication. If desired, a group profile can be drawn up by totaling member scores on each item, and this can provide a basis for useful assessment and learning. It is best used in conjunction with Chapters Seven and Eight.

D. Organizational Roles and Relationships Inventory. This is used to improve the management of responsibility or accountability. It is best to fill it out in triads or small groups of people who work closely together. The eight steps in this process require the use of an attached worksheet for the second item. The matters considered by coworkers through a group exercise are roles, responsibilities, and relationships on the job; resources and obstacles to effective performance; insight exchanges and issue clarification. The final part is devoted to a discussion of strategies for action planning to make changes and progress. By utilizing a flip chart and marking pens for group analysis of responses, the instrument provides a springboard for further learning. This activity is related to the content in Chapters Seven and Eight.

E. Manager's Quality of Life Index. This index is a wellness assessment for managers or professionals. Divided into five sections of thirty total items, it is a self-appraisal in terms of physical self-care as well as psychological, philosophical or spiritual, and social well-being or life-style. The basic assumption of this index is that staying well gives one greater control over one's life and is less costly than getting well after illness. It can be administered individually or in groups, and the data can be analyzed in terms of self-health management. A total score of 100 to 150 would be considered an excellent quality of life index; a rating of between 50 and 99 is average with room for improvement, and a score of 1 to 49 is inadequate and warrants remedial action. The index should be utilized in conjunction with the material in Chapters Ten and Eleven.

These five instruments were created by Philip R. Harris during action research with his own clients. Construct validity was established by the "known group" method. Quantity copies of these and other instruments by the author may be obtained from Management Research Systems, Ltd., P.O. Box 1585, Ponte Vedra Beach, Florida 32082. The reader may wish to write to this source for a catalogue of instruments and to the two recommended below:

• Organizational Tests Ltd., P.O. Box 324, Fredericton, N.B., Canada, E3B 4Y9 or its subsidiary, International Publications, Ltd., Melbourn House, Parliament Street, Hamilton 5-31, Bermuda.

• Teleometrics International, 1755 Woodstead Court, The Woodlands, Texas 77380.

Information on additional publishers can be obtained from the Instrumentation Network, Suite 334, 15612 Highway 7, Minnetonka, Minnesota 55345.

These five instruments may be used by readers in conjunction with this book. Permission is not granted for reproduction. These and other instruments created by the author are available from Management Research Systems, Ltd., P.O. Box 1585, Ponte Vedra Beach, Florida 32082, telephone 904/285-2195. Workshops and lectures by the author on the new work culture theme are available through Harris International, P.O. Box 2321, La Jolla, California 92038, telephone 619/453-2271. In addition, readers interested in obtaining films and learning packages based on the contents of this book for use in management development should contact: McGraw-Hill Training Systems, P.O. Box 641, Del Mar, California 92014, telephone 619/453-5000; attn. James M. Greenway, Marketing Manager, Management/Supervision.

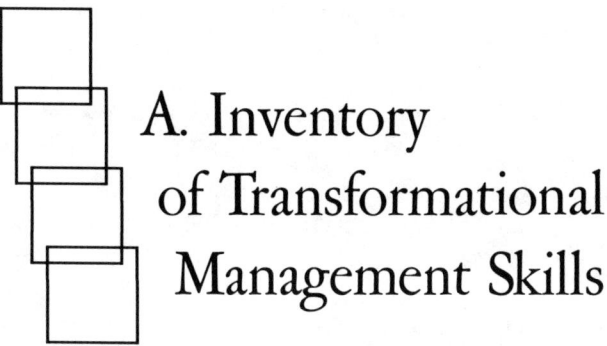

A. Inventory of Transformational Management Skills

This assessment instrument is divided into four parts and can be used for self-appraisal or for evaluation of another person. On each item, please use the scoring scale of 1 to 5. Consider that a rating of 1 would be the lowest score, indicating that the person never or rarely engages in this behavior; 3 would be average or usually; and 5 would be the highest, meaning excellent or always. Please place your number choice in the right-hand column.

Effectiveness rating

Part 1: Leadership Style

This person is:
1. *Open minded*—willing to consider new ideas and approaches, as well as people of different opinions, perspectives, cultures. _____
2. *Flexible*—adaptable to new people, situations, developments, information, or new ways of doing things (processes). _____
3. *Sensitive*—conscious of what is happening to self and others; is person centered and aware of needs and feelings in people; able to respond to others empathetically. _____
4. *Creative*—responds with resourcefulness to new people, situations, and data; exercises initiative, imagination, and innovation. _____

	Effectiveness rating

5. *Synergistic*—given to cooperation and collaboration with colleagues; encourages teamwork and group participation. _____
6. *Facilitative*—exercises coaching, counseling, and negotiating skills; exercises knowledge and skill in group process. _____

   Subtotal (out of possible 30) _____

Part II: Change Skills

This person demonstrates:
7. *Ultrastability*—perceives relativeness of experiences and does not seek absolutes; can cope with change, ambiguity, and uncertainty. _____
8. *Temporariness*—capacity to establish intense, ad hoc relationships that are meaningful; able to deal with transience and mobility. _____
9. *Resiliency*—reevaluates his or her image, values, role, goals, and life-style on the basis of new insights and information; is tentative in responses. _____
10. *Analytical thinking*—capable of perceiving and analyzing the driving and resisting forces for and against a change, the change's effects on the organization's future. _____
11. *Balance*—exercises evenhandedness and understanding regarding the rate or pace of change introduced into the organization so that it is neither too radical nor disruptive; plans for change. _____
12. *Strategic ability*—capable of strengthening the driving forces for a change and overcoming the restraining forces; can communicate the case for change and employ a variety of support strategies. _____

    Subtotal (out of possible 30) _____

Part III: Communication Skills

This person is:
13. *Self-Confident*—projects a positive image of self and role in body language and appearance, as well as verbally and nonverbally; indicates congruence or comfort with self so as to inspire confidence. _____
14. *Understanding*—demonstrates that he or she listens, is trying to enter into the speaker's frame of reference; is respectful and empathetic. _____

Inventory of Transformational Management Skills

                        Effectiveness rating

15. *Mediawise*—uses as many media as feasible to transmit messages effectively, appealing to multiple senses and powers in receiver. _____
16. *Astute*—avoids stereotyping, emotionally loaded words, and communication barriers; strives to ascertain real meanings behind messages and allows for clarification. _____
17. *Authentic*—avoids vagueness and game playing; levels with others as appropriate; usually tells it like it is. _____
18. *An information professional*—demonstrated by
    a. selection of information sources and contact use; _____
    b. use of others for information scanning or to supplement his or her own knowledge; _____
    c. dissemination of information to organization and subordinates appropriately; _____
    d. balance in terms of information collecting and taking actions based on the data; _____
    e. informedness sufficient for passing judgments, making decisions, or giving authorizations; _____
    f. thoroughness in following up on communications to see whether agreements or instructions are carried out. _____
    g. meeting effectiveness in terms of number held and quality of group sessions. _____

Subtotal (out of possible 60) _____

Part IV: Managerial Performance

This person practices:
19. *Relationship Building*—is aware of importance of organizational relations and cultivates them both internally and externally; spends appropriate amount of time linking up with the right persons who affect morale and performance; capable of networking. _____
20. *Action Planning*—translates mental plans into written targets, goals, strategies, and actions; maintains long-term perspectives without neglecting short-term concerns. _____
21. *Time Management*—maintains systematic scheduling for appropriate mix of activities to fulfill role; efficient in use of special times of day or week for particular kinds of work; paces self and balances work load while avoiding fragmentation and excessive interruptions. _____

                                                        Effective-
                                                          ness
                                                          rating

22. *Stress Management*—blends personal rights and needs with duties and obligation; promotes personal wellness through diet, exercise, and healthy life-style; reflects, studies, and reads appropriately.   _____
23. *Personal Involvement*—gets around the organization to find out what people are thinking and to observe activity first-hand rather than being remote and detached; encourages same approach with customers.   _____
24. *Team Management*—functions effectively as a member of a team task force; encourages group participation in problem solving and decision making; shares power.   _____
25. *Accountability Management*—clarifies systematically roles, relationships, and responsibilities; while ensures that expectations are realized and issues confronted so that problems are solved and services rendered. _____

Subtotal (out of possible 35)   _____

Inventory grand total   _____

Scoring Note: the ratings on these thirty-one appraisals can be tallied; for effective managers, the total by individual should be in the range of 120 to 150. To compile results from a group evaluation, total all the individual scores and divide by the number of assessors. For example, if 12 persons were evaluating the manager, then a score of 1440 to 1800 on this instrument would indicate a high-performing manager.

What is a Transformational Manager?

Political scientist James MacGregor Burns maintains that a true leader senses and transforms the needs of followers. He envisions subordinates or followers as having different levels of needs; the leader motivates and mobilizes these persons toward higher needs or consciousness. Transformational managers energize themselves and others, arousing hopes, aspirations, and expectations, as well as translating these into constructive actions. Transformational managers provide a behavior model, then inspire others to achieve something beyond the status quo or present activity. Transformational managers sense the capacity in others and then help these persons actualize their potential. Transformational managers sense when it is time for change and then encourage and support others to accomplish the new and different, the unique and exceptional. Transformational managers have vision and share their dreams with others; they assist people in making the transition to the new work culture.

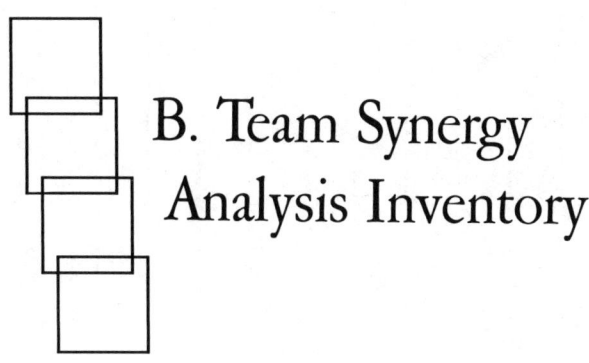

B. Team Synergy Analysis Inventory

	Seldom	Occasion-ally	Often	Always
I. As a management professional in my organization (please check the appropriate category relative to participation in a work unit or team):				
1. I cooperate with my own colleagues at work.				
2. I collaborate, whenever possible, with people from other disciplines, departments, and work units.				
3. I seek variety of input in problem solving and decision making from diverse sources.				
4. I realize the interdependence of technologists with others in the organization or industry outside our field of specialization.				
5. I can function effectively as a member of a team or task force, especially when it is multidisciplinary.				
6. I am willing to consider issues from varied perspectives, even those very different from mine.				
II. With reference to organizational teams and their management:				
7. I can tolerate ambiguity, uncertainty, and seeming lack of structure.				
8. I take an interest in each member's achievement, as well as that of the group as a whole.				
9. I am able to give and receive feedback in an objective, nondefensive manner.				
10. I encourage a team atmosphere that is informal, relaxed, comfortable, and nonjudgmental.				
11. I seek group participation, consensus, and shared decisions.				
12. I clarify roles, relationships, responsibilities, and assignments or expectations.				

13. I have the capacity for establishing temporary, meaningful, and intense relations.
14. I can facilitate group communication on goals, targets, and schedules.
15. I synthesize diverse input, information, insights.

III. *With reference to team-building activities:*

16. I encourage authentic communication enabling members to speak freely and express feelings.
17. I emphasize the constructive channeling of energy caused by disagreements and differences.
18. I seek group support, recognition, and encouragement for individual members.
19. I attempt to draw everyone into discussions, even the silent and insecure.
20. I share the leadership role by fostering others to initiate, clarify, summarize, and decide.
21. I model desirable behavior to the group, such as in the manner of giving/receiving feedback and group process analysis and action planning.

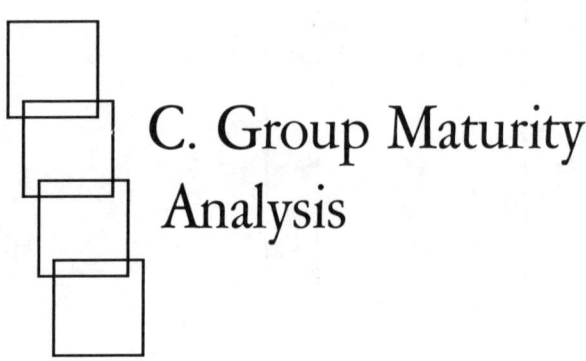

C. Group Maturity Analysis

Instructions: Observe the group at work on its task. When it is completed, consider each category and circle the number that indicates most closely how you think the group acted as a whole.

1. Mechanisms for getting feedback

1	2	3	4	5
Poor feedback mechanisms		Average		Excellent feedback mechanisms

2. Decision-making procedure

1	2	3	4	5
Poor decision-making procedure		Average		Very adequate decision-making procedure

3. Feeling of togetherness

1	2	3	4	5
Low cohesion		Average		Feeling of togetherness

4. Flexibility of organization and procedures

1	2	3	4	5
Very inflexible		Average		Very flexible

5. Use of member resources

1	2	3	4	5
Poor use of resources		Average		Excellent use of resources

Group Maturity Analysis

6. Communication

1	2	3	4	5
Poor communication		Average		Excellent communication

7. Clarity of goals; members' acceptance of goals

1	2	3	4	5
Unclear goals— not accepted		Average		Very clear goals— accepted

8. Feelings of interdependence (feelings that members can disagree) with authority persons

1	2	3	4	5
No interdependence		Average		High interdependence

9. Shared participation in leadership functions

1	2	3	4	5
No shared participation		Average		High shared participation

10. Acceptance of minority views and persons

1	2	3	4	5
No acceptance		Average		High acceptance

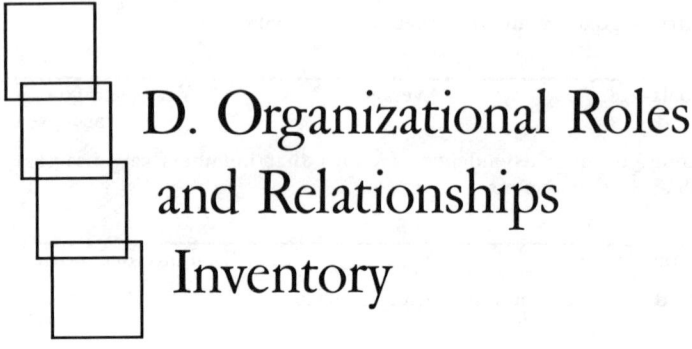

D. Organizational Roles and Relationships Inventory

1. Triads:
Form a triad group by choosing to meet with the two other persons most directly related to the performance of your job.
2. Roles and Responsibilities:
    a. On the accompanying worksheet, individually list all the *functions* you feel should be done by you (not necessarily what is done) to perform your job effectively as you see it. These should be short task statements of job duties. Be as specific and inclusive as possible.
    b. Next to each statement, list the nature of your *responsibility* toward that function. In other words, describe your role relative to the decisions that are to be made with regard to the function and/or actually accomplishing the task. These are questions you may wish to clarify before filling in this section:
    Do you set policy and/or guide the performance of the function? Do you see that it gets done?
    Do you personally execute the performance of the function, or is it necessary that you simply should be consulted, notified, or given approval for someone to accomplish the function?
    c. Finally, note on the third rating column of the accompanying worksheet whether you have a primary (P) or secondary (S) responsibility for this function. Later, when you meet with others in your group, you will want to clarify how they rate themselves on this same function.
3. Relationships:
List the important relationships you must establish with key personnel to perform your job successfully. In the third column, use these terms to describe the relationship: supervisor, colleague (peer), subordinate, con-

Organizational Roles and Relationships Inventory

sultant, other. In the last column, rate the relationship in terms of effectiveness on a five point scale, with 1 being lowest and 5 being highest.

Name	Role	Relationship	Rating

Please go back over the above listing and note in the fourth column whether the individual's role and relationship to you is "C" for clear or "U" for unclear. (Use reverse side of sheet if more space is needed.)

4. Resources:
   As you now perceive your job, what resources are present in the situation that help you perform your job successfully?

5. Obstacles:
   As you see it, list the difficulties or barriers to the successful performance of your job.

6. Exchange:
   One person at a time, exchange your definitions and views with others in the triad. At the same time, others in the group are to identify and clarify points of conflict with their own view of your job. (The triad group of three may wish to list on newsprint sheets the issues that cause conflict or misunderstanding.)

7. Clarification:
   Consolidate key issues identified as sources of friction. Analyze the changes that need to be made in roles and relationships to resolve these sources of friction. (The triad group may also wish to list these changes on newsprint sheets.)

8. Strategies:
   a. What do you propose to do in the next month to clarify your roles and relationships and resolve points of misunderstanding?

   b. What do you plan to do relative to the changes that must be introduced so you can perform your job more effectively?

c. How can you and your division/department/team develop a dynamic procedure for reviewing roles and relationships periodically? _____

_____

_____

The following worksheet is for use with Item #2.

Worksheet for Roles and Relationships Analysis
(Use reverse side of this page if more space is needed)

	Functions	Responsibilities	Rating
1.	_____	1. _____	____
2.	_____	2. _____	____
3.	_____	3. _____	____
4.	_____	4. _____	____
5.	_____	5. _____	____
6.	_____	6. _____	____
7.	_____	7. _____	____
8.	_____	8. _____	____
9.	_____	9. _____	____
10.	_____	10. _____	____

Please review these functions and responsibilities and rate them in the third column as to whether you consider them P for primary (that is, you have the major responsibility) or S for secondary (someone else has the principal responsibility and yours is ancillary). Then target from a final review what roles and relationships need further clarification.

E. Quality-of-Life Index: A Manager's Health and Wellness Inventory

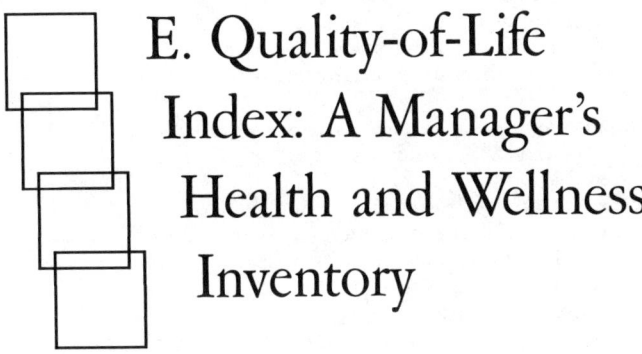

Directions: The underlying concept of this index is that staying well gives one greater control over one's life and is less costly than getting well. This instrument provides the manager with a means for self-assessment of his or her regimen for well-being. It can be filled out individually alone or with a team of managers who work together and are concerned about the quality of their life. It can be analyzed in terms of one's own self-health management or in terms of corporate policy to improve the quality of work life. On each item in the six categories, rate yourself on a scale of 1 (lowest) to 5 (highest).

I. Physical Self-Care

1. I have a thorough examination by a physician annually and act on the results for improved health. _____
   (Note: I get periodic physical check-ups to update both myself and my personal physician as to my conditions/medications.)
2. I seek nourishing food and beverage, trying to control my diet so as to avoid over/underweight conditions. _____
   (Note: Well-balanced diets are usually low in fat, protein, cholesterol, and calories—that is, containing more fruit and vegetables, fewer animal and dairy products.)
3. I exercise daily with a regular routine and try to maintain balance in my physical fitness regimen. _____
   (Note: Ideally, this physical activity is built into one's daily schedule and becomes a part of one's life-style.)

4. I manage to get sufficient and tranquil sleep for maintaining peak performance. _____
   (Note: The number of hours needed for such rest is relative, although six to eight hours a night is recommended, unless supplemented by naps during the day.)
5. I avoid body abuse, whether through overwork, misuse of alcohol or other drugs, cigarettes, or caffeine intake. _____
   (Note: Maintaining body soundness requires positive actions for fitness and avoidance behavior of that which is debilitating.)
6. I project a healthy body image and am able to do what I am capable of doing with energy and intensity. _____
   (Note: This refers to general body appearance from condition of dress and physical cleanliness to body language, as well as physical capacity.)

   Part I subtotal (out of six) _____

II. Psychological Care

7. I strive to keep mentally alert by seeking new and varied input to increase my information/knowledge. _____
   (Note: Mind expansion may occur informally, such as through selected reading, or formally, such as through some means of continuing education.)
8. I try to be creative and open to new ideas. _____
   (Note: This implies an experimental attitude, allowing intuition to be exercised and listening to others.)
9. I cultivate a positive mental attitude and express self-confidence. _____
   (Note: This involves practicing optimism and being comfortable with self versus excess in negativism, depression, or sense of insecurity and inferiority.)
10. I value my independence while not being averse to being interdependent. _____
    (Note: While seeking autonomy of action, one is able to cooperate without becoming overly dependent on people, situations, or substances.)
11. I am able to relax and can "re-create" in diverse ways. _____
    (Note: Leisure is constructively used for both ample and varied activities; one is able to have fun and be interested in many experiences.)
12. I am able to express feeling and experience a full range of human emotions. _____
    (Note: This means one feels and conveys everything from joy to sadness without inhibiting emotions yet can exhibit balance or control in such expressions.)

    Part II subtotal (out of six) _____

Quality-of-Life Index

III. Philosophical/Spiritual Care

13. I have a firm sense of direction and values in my life. ⎯⎯⎯
    (Note: That is, one strives to achieve goals and sets priorities as to what is important.)
14. I can envision my existence in a larger context and have purpose to my actions. ⎯⎯⎯
    (Note: One is able to relate one's life beyond the material to the spiritual side of the human experience.)
15. I cultivate my talents in some intellectual and cultural pursuits. ⎯⎯⎯
    (Note: This means being a multidimensional person who seeks to develop his or her esthetic senses through art, music, books, and so on.)
16. I have a zest for life and am enthusiastic for experiencing its variety and richness. ⎯⎯⎯
    (Note: This implies the pursuit of life-enhancing relationships and activities.)
17. I seek meaning in my life and meaningful associations. ⎯⎯⎯
    (Note: Activities are undertaken with purpose, while relationships are formed with selectivity; escapism is avoided.)
18. I devote time to thinking and contemplating. ⎯⎯⎯
    (Note: I develop quiet times to ponder, meditate, pray, practice yoga, enjoy nature and its beauties.)

Part III subtotal (out of six) ⎯⎯⎯

IV. Social Care

19. I try to stay connected with family, friends, and social contacts. ⎯⎯⎯
    (Note: I avoid social isolation and reach out to others.)
20. I network with professional and business colleagues. ⎯⎯⎯
    (Note: I maintain personal or electronic associations for information and knowledge exchanges.)
21. I am capable of meaningful friendships and intimacy. ⎯⎯⎯
    (Note: I am able to give and share myself at deeper, more personal levels.)
22. I am considerate of others' needs, respect their privacy, and am tolerant of their views or foibles. ⎯⎯⎯
    (Note: I am able to put myself into the other person's perspective or life space without prying or imposing.)
23. I am helpful, trusting, and forgiving with others. ⎯⎯⎯
    (Note: I can provide appropriate assistance as warranted and be loyal to those who trust/depend on me.)

24. I can confront, negotiate, and handle conflict.   _____
    (Note: I am able to say no and level with people, to problem solve and compromise, and to channel energies when people disagree.)

    Part IV subtotal (out of six)   _____

V. *Life-Style*

25. I try to maintain balance in my life and avoid excess.   _____
    (Note: I am able to regulate or moderate activities so as to avoid addiction to work, hobbies, or substances.)
26. I sense the feedback my body gives me and act to preserve good health.   _____
    (Note: I am attuned to my biorhythms, symptoms, and signals of fatigue, illness, or potential "burnout," acting to correct the unhealthy or life-threatening situation.)
27. I develop positive and healthy habits/attitudes.   _____
    (Note: I follow practices that will enhance life quality, such as orderliness, openness, and optimism, as well as nutritional food intake, watching my weight, avoiding salt or smoking, and adequate daily exercise.)
28. I manage stress and tension so that I am not unnerved or overwhelmed.   _____
    (Note: I have attitudes and practices that counteract hypertension, such as playing, using hot tub/steamroom/sauna, taking a nap or deep breathing exercises, listening to music, practicing dance or gymnastics.)
29. I create a life-style that delimits my personal stressors while enhancing the quality of my existence.   _____
    (Note: I am aware of stress, exhaustion, or tension symptoms and inaugurate counteractions for better coping/living.)
30. I seek counsel from professionals, colleagues, or friends whom I regard when I am finding it difficult to cope.   _____
    (Note: I am aware of my limitations and problems and am realistic about obtaining help from others.)

    Part V subtotal (out of six)   _____

    Total Assessment Points   _____

Scoring Interpretation

A total score on these thirty inventory items between:

       100 - 150 = Excellent quality of life-style
        50 - 99 = Average—room for improvement
         1 - 49 = Inadequate—remedial action warranted now.

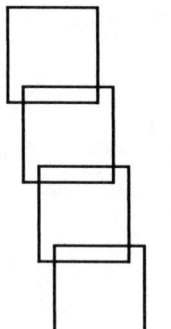

References

"A Question of Balance." *Issues and Observations,* 1984, *4* (1), 1-8.

Abernathy, W., Clark, K. R., and Kantrow, A. M. *Industrial Renaissance.* New York: Basic Books, 1983.

Adams, J. (Ed.). *Transforming Work.* San Diego, Calif.: Miles River Press/University Associates, 1984.

Ainsworth, T., and O'Donnell, M. P. *Health Promotion at the Workplace.* New York: Wiley, 1984.

Albus, J. S. *Brain, Behavior, and Robotics.* Peterborough, N.H.: BYTE Publications, 1981.

American Society of Personnel Administrators. *Work in the 21st Century.* Berea, Ohio: American Society of Personnel Administrators Publications, 1983.

Ansoff, H. I. *Implanting Strategic Management.* Englewood Cliffs, N.J.: Prentice-Hall, 1984.

Antonovsky, A. *Health, Stress and Coping: New Perspectives on Mental and Physical Well-Being.* San Francisco: Jossey-Bass, 1979.

Argote, L., Goodman, P. S., and Schkade, D. "The Human Side of Robotics." *Sloan Management Review,* Spring 1983, *24* (23), 31-41.

Auletta, K. *The Art of Corporate Success.* New York: Putnam, 1984.

Ayres, R. V., and Miller, S. M. *Robotics Applications and Social Implications.* Cambridge, Mass.: Ballinger, 1983.

Bander, D. O., and Giber, D. J. "Competency-Based Project Management." *Data Training,* Jan.-Feb. 1985, pp. 14-15.

Baty, G. B. *Entrepreneurship for the Eighties.* Reston, Va.: Reston, 1981.

Baugh, J. G. "A Study of Decision Making Within Matrix Organizations." Unpublished doctoral dissertation, United States International University, 1981.

Beech, H. R., Burns, L. E., and Sheffield, B. F. *A Behavioral Approach to the Management of Stress.* New York: Wiley, 1984.

"The Bell Breakup: A Year Later." *Los Angeles Times,* Dec. 9, 1984, Part IV, pp. 1-40.

Bennis, W., and Nanus, B. *Leaders.* New York: Harper & Row, 1985.

Best, F. (Ed.). *The Future of Work.* Englewood Cliffs, N.J.: Prentice-Hall, 1973.

"The Best Man for the Job May Be a Woman." *Forbes,* Nov. 21, 1983, p. 1.

Bier, D. "Life of a Yuppie Takes Psychic Toll." *U.S. News & World Report,* Apr. 29, 1985, pp. 73-74.

Blanchard, K., and Johnson, S. *The One Minute Manager.* New York: William Morrow, 1983.

Bolman, L. G., and Deal, T. E. *Modern Approaches to Understanding and Managing Organizations.* San Francisco: Jossey-Bass, 1984.

Bolton, R., and Bolton, D. G. *Social/Management Style.* New York: AMACOM, 1984.

Boorstin, D. *The Discoverers.* New York: Random House, 1984.

Boucher, N. "Transforming the Corporation." *New Age Journal,* Feb. 1985, pp. 36-45.

Boyd, D. P., and Gumpert, D. E. "Coping with Entrepreneurial Stress." *Harvard Business Review,* Mar.-Apr. 1983, pp. 44-64.

Brod, C. *Technostress.* New York: AMACOM, 1983.

Brown, A., and Weiner, E. *Supermanaging.* New York: McGraw-Hill, 1984.

Brown, D. S. *Managing the Large Organization.* Mt. Airy, Md.: Lomond, 1982.
Bry, B. "He Doesn't Sweat Small Things." *Los Angeles Times,* Nov. 1, 1983, p. 21.
Burns, A. *New Information Technology.* New York: Wiley, 1984.
Burns, J. M. *Leadership.* New York: Harper & Row, 1978.
"Business Communications." *Forbes,* advertising supplement, 1983, pp. 1-20.
"Canada's New Capitalists." *World Press Review,* July 1982, p. 50.
Carnevale, A. P. *Human Capital: A High Yield Corporate Investment.* Washington, D.C.: American Society for Training and Development, 1983.
Carnevale, A. P. *Jobs for the Nation.* Washington, D.C.: American Society for Training and Development, 1984.
Charnes, A., and Cooper, W. W. (Eds.). *Creative and Innovative Management.* Cambridge, Mass.: Ballinger, 1984.
Clarke, A. "The Businessman: The Ultimate Artist." *Tarrytown Letter,* May 1983, p. 3. (Available from Tarrytown House, East Sunnyside Lane, Tarrytown, N.Y. 10591.)
Coates, V. T. "The Potential Impact of Robotics." *The Futurist,* Feb. 1983, p. 28.
Cohen, W. A. *The Entrepreneur and Small Business Problem Solver.* New York: Wiley, 1983.
Coleman, E. R. (Ed.). *Labor Issues of the Eighties.* Basking Ridge, N.J.: AT&T Corporate Planning/Emerging Issues Group, 1980.
Condon, M. "Straight Talk About Robots." *Training and Development Journal,* Nov. 1983, pp. 15-22.
Corning, P. A. *The Synergism Hypothesis.* New York: McGraw-Hill, 1983.
Cornish, E. (Ed.). *Careers Tomorrow.* Bethesda, Md.: World Future Society, 1985.
Criswell, D. (Ed.). *Automation and Robotics for the National Space Program.* La Jolla, Calif.: California Space Institute, University of California at San Diego, 1985.
Crumley, D. W. *Concepts for Army Use of Robotic-Artificial Intelligence in the 21st Century.* Carlisle Barracks, Pa.: U.S. Army Futures/Long Range Group, 1982.

Dauphinais, W., and Darnell, L. "Project Management: One Step at a Time." *PC World,* Sept. 1984, pp. 240-250.

Davidson, F. P., and Cox, J. S. *MACRO.* New York: William Morrow, 1983.

Davidson, M. J., and Cooper, C. L. (Eds.). *Working Women.* New York: Wiley, 1985.

Davis, S. A. "Building Talented Teams." *Innovation,* 1970, no. 15, pp. 1-20.

Deal, T. E., and Kennedy, A. A. *Corporate Cultures.* Reading, Mass.: Addison-Wesley, 1982.

Dean, C., and Whitlock, Q. *A Handbook of Computer Based Training.* Washington, D.C.: American Society for Training and Development/Nichols Publishing, 1983.

Derfler, F., and Stallings, W. *A Manager's Guide to Local Networks.* New York: AMACOM, 1983.

Desatnick, R. *The Business of Human Resource Management.* New York: Wiley, 1983.

"Developing a Computer-Assisted Evaluation System." *Personnel Administrator,* Sept. 1983, pp. 43-47.

Didsbury, H. F. (Ed.). *Work Now and in the Future.* Bethesda, Md.: World Future Society, 1983.

Didsbury, H. F. (Ed.). *The Worldly Work.* Bethesda, Md.: World Future Society, 1984.

Diebold, J. *Role of Business in Society.* New York: AMACOM, 1982.

Diebold, J. *World of Computers.* New York: Random House, 1983.

Diebold, J. *Making the Future Work.* New York: Simon & Schuster, 1985.

"Donald Burr: The Perfection Imperative." *Time,* Jan. 7, 1985, p. 70.

Dordick, H. S., Bradley, H. G., and Nanus, B. *The Emerging Network Marketplace.* Norwood, N.J.: Ablex, 1981.

Dorf, R. C. *Robotics and Automated Manufacturing.* Reston, Va.: Reston, 1983.

Drucker, P. E. "Our Entrepreneurial Economy." *Harvard Business Review,* Jan.-Feb. 1984, pp. 58-64.

Drucker, P. E. *Innovation and Entrepreneurship.* New York: Harper & Row, 1985.

Dwyer, C. "Why Many Good Workers Turn Into Bad Bosses." *U.S. News and World Report,* Jan. 23, 1984, p. 71.
Engelberger, J. F. *Robotics in Practice.* New York: AMACOM, 1980.
Eurich, N. *Corporate Classrooms.* New York: The Carnegie Foundation for the Advancement of Teaching, 1984.
"Factories: Flexibility Is the Future." *Los Angeles Times,* July 17, 1983, pp. 1, 16-17.
Feigenbaum, E. A., and McCorduck, P. *The Fifth Generation.* Reading, Mass.: Addison-Wesley, 1983.
Feingold, S. N. "Emerging Careers: Occupations for Post-Industrial Society." *The Futurist,* Feb. 1984, p. 13.
Feingold, S. N., and Miller, N. R. *Emerging Careers.* Bethesda, Md.: World Future Society Book Service/Garrett Press, 1983.
Ferguson, M. *The Aquarian Conspiracy.* Los Angeles: Tarcher, 1980.
"Finding A on the Keyboard." *Time,* May 16, 1983, p. 64.
Finkelstein, J., and Newman, D. "The Third Industrial Revolution: A Special Challenge to Managers." *Organizational Dynamics,* 1984, *13* (1), 53-65.
Flanigan, J. "Robots Won't Take Jobs, Only Research Them." *Los Angeles Times,* Apr. 8, 1984, Part II, p. 1.
Fleming, L. R. "New Hope Seen for Corporate America." *Los Angeles Times,* Feb. 13, 1983, Part IV, pp. 2-3.
Fletcher, J. "High Performance Patterns." *The Bottom Line,* 1983, *3* (1), 4-5.
"For Executives of the 1980s, A Timely Return." *Business Week,* June 1, 1981, pp. 88-91.
Forester, T. (Ed.). *The Microelectronics Revolution—The Complete Guide to the New Technology and Its Impact on Society.* Cambridge: MIT Press, 1985.
Francis, D., and Young, D. *Improving Work Groups.* San Diego, Calif.: University Associates, 1979.
French, W. C., and Bell, C. H. *Organization Development—Behavioral Science Interventions for Organization Improvement.* (3rd ed.) Englewood Cliffs, N.J.: Prentice-Hall, 1984.
"Future Executives: Mix of Technology and History." *Los Angeles Times,* Jan. 20, 1982, Part IV, p. 2.

"General Electric Going with the Winners." *Forbes,* Mar. 26, 1984, pp. 97-106.

Gilder, G. *The Spirit of Free Enterprise.* New York: Simon & Schuster, 1984.

"The Global Manager Is a Hot Item." *Business Week,* Oct. 31, 1983, p. 49.

Goldman, N. *Space Commerce.* Cambridge, Mass.: Ballinger, 1984.

Golembiewski, R. T. *Humanizing Public Organizations.* Mt. Airy, Md.: Lomond, 1985.

Goodman, L. J., and Love, R. N. (Eds.). *Project Planning and Management.* Elmsford, N.Y.: Pergamon Press, 1980.

Goodman, P. S., and Associates. *Change in Organizations: New Perspectives on Theory, Research, and Practice.* San Francisco: Jossey-Bass, 1982.

Grove, A. "Breaking the Chains of Command." *Newsweek,* Oct. 3, 1983.

Grove, A. S. *High Output Management.* New York: Random House, 1983.

Hall, E. T. *Beyond Culture.* Garden City, N.Y.: Anchor Press, 1976.

Harman, W., and Rheingold, H. *Higher Creativity.* Los Angeles: Tarcher, 1984.

Harris, P. R. (Ed.). *Innovations in Global Consultation.* Washington, D.C.: International Consultants Foundation, 1980.

Harris, P. R. *New Worlds, New Ways, New Management.* Ann Arbor, Mich.: Masterco Press/AMACOM, 1983.

Harris, P. R. (Ed.). *Global Strategies for Human Resource Development.* Washington, D.C.: American Society for Training and Development, 1984.

Harris, P. R. "Living on the Moon: Will Humans Develop an Unearthly Culture?" *The Futurist,* Apr. 1985, pp. 30-35.

Harris, P. R. "Management Challenges in a New Space Era." In M. F. McKay (Ed.), *Technological Springboard to the 21st Century.* Houston, Tex.: NASA Publication/Johnson Space Center, forthcoming.

Harris, P. R., and Harris, D. L. "International Human Resource Development Megatrends in the Metaindustrial Work Culture." In P. R. Harris (Ed.), *Global Strategies for Human Re-*

References

source Development. Washington, D.C.: American Society for Training and Development, 1984.

Harris, P. R., and Moran, R. T. *Managing Cultural Differences.* Houston, Texas: Gulf, 1979.

Hawken, P. *The Next Economy.* New York: Holt, Rinehart & Winston, 1983.

Hayes, R. H. *Restoring Our Competitive Edge.* New York: Wiley, 1985.

"Healthy Smokestakes." *Forbes,* Feb. 15, 1983, pp. 58-59.

Hess, K. M. *The Positive Manager.* New York: Wiley, 1983.

"The High-Tech Challenge." *Time,* Dec. 24, 1984, p. 38.

"High-Tech Training Comes of Age." *Successful Meetings,* Sept. 1984, pp. 78-79.

Hiltz, S. R., and Turoff, M. *The Network Nation.* Reading, Mass.: Addison-Wesley, 1978.

Hockey, R. (Ed.). *Stress and Fatigue in Human Performance.* New York: Wiley, 1983.

Hofheinz, R., and Calder, K. R. *The East Asia Edge.* New York: Basic Books, 1982.

Hofstede, G. *Culture's Consequences: International Differences in Work-Related Values.* Beverly Hills, Calif.: Sage, 1980.

"How Do You Feel About Yourself?" *Los Angeles Times,* Apr. 5, 1984, Part I, p. 3.

"How Entrepreneurs Are Changing U.S. Business." *U.S. News & World Report,* Dec. 17, 1984, pp. 68-69.

"How to Integrate New Meeting Technology." *Successful Meetings,* Mar. 1982, pp. 51-59.

"Innovative Unemployment." *The Economist,* Apr. 6, 1985.

"International Banking Survey." *The Economist,* Mar. 24, 1984, p. 28.

"Into Intrapreneurial Britain." *The Economist,* Feb. 16, 1985, pp. 19-25.

"It's About Time." *Forbes,* Apr. 25, 1983, pp. 41-42.

Ivancevich, J. M., Donnelly, J. H., and Gibson, J. L. *Managing for a High Performance.* Plano, Tex.: Business Publications, 1983.

"Japan Invents Robots of the Third Kind." *The Economist,* Aug. 25, 1984, pp. 71-72.

Jay, T. B. "Computerphobia: What to Do Next About It?" *High Technology,* Jan. 1981, pp. 47-48.

Kakabadse, A. *The Politics of Management.* Epping, England: Gower, 1983.

Kakabadse, A., and Mukhi, S. (Eds.). *The Future of Management Education.* Hampshire, England: Gower, 1984.

Kakabadse, A., and Parker, C. (Eds.), *Power, Politics, and Organizations.* New York: Wiley, 1984.

Kanter, R. M. *The Change Masters.* New York: Simon & Schuster, 1983.

Kaplan, R. E., Drath, W. H., and Kofodimos, J. R. *High Hurdles: The Challenge of Executive Self-Development.* Greensboro, N.C.: Center for Creative Leadership, 1985.

Kastens, M. L. *Redefining the Manager's Job.* New York: AMACOM, 1980.

Katzan, H. *Office Automation.* New York: AMACOM, 1983.

Keane, J., Keane, M., and Teagan, M. *Principles of Productivity Management in the Development of Computer Applications.* Englewood Cliffs, N.J.: Prentice-Hall, 1984.

Kemp, S. L. *Women's Entrepreneurial Spirit.* Austin, Tex.: Bard Productions, 1984.

"The Key to Success? It's Drive, Not Talent." *Los Angeles Times,* Feb. 17, 1984, Part I, pp. 3, 31.

Kidder, T. *The Soul of the New Machine.* New York: Avon/Hearst Corp., 1981.

Kilmann, R. H. *Beyond the Quick Fix: Managing Five Tracks to Organizational Success.* San Francisco: Jossey-Bass, 1984.

Kimberly, J. R., Miles, R. H., and Associates. *The Organizational Life Cycle: Issues in the Creation, Transformation, and Decline of Organizations.* San Francisco: Jossey-Bass, 1980.

Kimberly, J. R., and Quinn, R. E. (Eds.). *Managing Organizational Transitions.* Homewood, Ill.: Irwin, 1984.

Kingston, G. "Case Study: Office Automation Impacts on Managers and Professionals." *Seventh Plenary Meeting Summary,* New York: Diebold Office Automation Program, 1981.

Koehn, H. E. (Ed.). "The Tin Collar Worker." *Trends,* 1981, *9,* 1-12.

Koehn, H. E. "The Ultimate Invention." *Trends,* 1983, *14,* 1-7.

Koehn, H. E. "Help Wanted 1990." *Trends,* 1984, *16.*

Koehn, H. E., and Selbert, R. *The Future of Manufacturing.* Los Angeles: Security Pacific National Bank, Futures Research Division, 1984.

Konecci, E. B., Smilor, R. W., and Kozmetsky, G. *Technology Venturing Data Book.* Austin: Institute of Constructive Capitalism, University of Texas, 1984.

Kozmetsky, G. *Perspectives on the Human Potential in Technological Change.* Austin: Institute of Constructive Capitalism, University of Texas, 1981.

Kozmetsky, G. *Transformational Management.* Cambridge, Mass.: Ballinger, 1985.

Kozmetsky, G., Gill, M. D., and Smilor, R. W. *Financing and Managing Fast-Growing Companies.* Lexington, Mass.: Lexington Books, 1985.

Kozmetsky, G., and Kozmetsky, R. *Making It Together.* New York: Free Press, 1981.

Kuhn, R. L. (Ed.). *Commercializing Defense-Related Technology.* New York: Praeger, 1984.

Kuhn, R. L. *To Flourish Among Giants.* New York: Wiley, 1985.

Kuhn, R. L., and Geis, G. T. *The Firm Bond.* New York: Praeger, 1984.

Lawrence, P. R., and Dyer, D. *Renewing American Industry.* New York: Free Press, 1983.

Lazer, E. A., and others. *The Teleconferencing Handbook.* White Plains, N.Y.: Knowledge Industry Publications, 1983.

"Learning from the Bhopal Disaster." *U.S. News & World Report,* Jan. 21, 1985, p. 52.

Levering, R., Moskowitz, M., and Katz, M. *The 100 Best Companies to Work for in America.* Reading, Mass.: Addison-Wesley, 1984.

Levine, A. S. *Managing NASA in the Apollo Era.* Washington, D.C.: U.S. Government Printing Office, 1982.

Levinson, R. E. *The Decentralized Company.* New York: AMACOM, 1983.

Lipnack, J., and Stamps, J. *Networking.* New York: Doubleday, 1982.

Lippitt, G. L., Langseth, P., and Mossop, J. *Implementing Or-*

ganizational Change: A Practical Guide to Managing Change Efforts. San Francisco: Jossey-Bass, 1985.

Livingston, J. S. "New Trends in Applied Management Development." *Training and Development Journal,* Jan. 1983.

London, M. *Developing Managers: A Guide to Motivating and Preparing People for Successful Managerial Careers.* San Francisco: Jossey-Bass, 1985.

McGinnis, T. *More Than a Friend.* Englewood Cliffs, N.J.: Prentice-Hall, 1981.

McKay, M. F. *Space Resources.* Houston, Tex.: NASA Publications/Johnson Space Center, 1985.

McMillon, C. "Automate, Emigrate, or Evaporate." *The Futurist,* Apr. 25, 1985, pp. 45-47.

Maidique, M. A., and Hays, R. H. "The Art of High Technology Management." *Sloan Management Review,* Winter, 1984, pp. 17-31.

"Management: Large-Scale Integration." *The Economist,* July 9, 1983, pp. 70-71.

"Manufacturing Is in Flower." *Time,* Mar. 1984, pp. 50-52.

Marrus, S. K. *Building the Strategic Plan.* New York: Wiley, 1984.

Masuda, Y. *The Information Society as Postindustrial Society.* Bethesda, Md.: World Future Society, 1981.

Matarazzo, J. D., and others (Eds.). *Behavioral Health.* New York: Wiley, 1984.

"Meet America's Number 4 Automaker, Japan, Inc." *U.S. News & World Report,* Dec. 17, 1984, p. 64.

Melkanoff, M. "Automation." *Research and Development,* Apr. 1984, p. 80.

Mensch, G., and Niehaus, R. J. (Eds.). *Work, Organization, and Technological Change.* New York: Plenum, 1982.

Milbrath, M. *Credentials.* Sheboygan, Wis.: Blue River Publishing, 1982.

Miller, B., and Sugiyama, N. *Mitsubishi-USA.* Queens, N.Y.: Business Research Institute, St. John's University, 1984.

Miller, J. G. *Living Systems.* New York: McGraw-Hill, 1978.

Miller, R. J. (Ed.). *Robotics.* Beverly Hills, Calif.: Sage, 1983.

Mintzberg, H. "The Manager's Job: Folklore and Fact." In

E. G. Collins (Ed.), *Executive Success.* New York: Wiley, 1983.

Mitchell, A. *Nine American Lifestyles.* New York: Macmillan, 1984.

Mitroff, I. I. *Stakeholders of the Organizational Mind: Toward a New View of Organizational Policy Making.* San Francisco: Jossey-Bass, 1983.

Mitroff, I. I., and Kilmann, R. H. "Corporate Tragedies: Teaching Cosmopolitans to Cope with Evil." *New Management,* 1984, *1* (4), 48-53.

Moran, R. T., and Harris, P. R. *Managing Cultural Synergy.* Houston, Tex.: Gulf, 1982.

Mottram, R. "Team Skills Management." *Journal of Management Development* (MCB Publications, West Yorkshire, England), 1982, *1,* 22-33.

Mouton, J. S., and Blake, R. R. *Synergogy: A New Strategy for Education, Training, and Development.* San Francisco: Jossey-Bass, 1984.

Nadler, D. A. "Managing Transitions to Uncertain Future States." *Organizational Dynamics,* 1982, *11* (1), 37-42.

Nadler, L. *Corporate Human Resources.* New York: Van Nostrand Reinhold, 1980.

Nadler, L. (Ed.). *Handbook of Human Resource Development.* New York: Wiley, 1984.

Naisbitt, J. *Megatrends.* New York: Warner Books, 1982.

Naisbitt, J. "America Tomorrow." *For Members Only* (American Express card-holders' newsletter), Mar. 1983, pp. 1, 4.

"Nakasone Urges Technology Focus." *Los Angeles Times,* May 20, 1983, p. 2.

Narayanan, K. (Ed.). *The Consultant, Office and Information Systems Quarterly.* Merrimack, N.H.: Digital Equipment Corporation, 1984. (Interview with John Diebold, "Information Technology: Key Questions We Must Face," pp. 8-12; with Joseph Ferreira, "The Personal Computer is a Primitive Product," pp. 13-15.)

National Society for Performance Instruction. *The Performance and Instruction Journal,* May 1983, p. 25.

"The New Corporate Managers." *The Economist,* Dec. 22, 1984, pp. 91-112.
"The New Economy." *Time,* May 30, 1983, pp. 62-70.
"The New Entrepreneurs." *The Economist,* Dec. 24, 1984, pp. 61-73.
"New Era for Management." *Business Week,* Apr. 25, 1983, pp. 50-53.
Newman, D. C. "Oracle of the Computer Age." *McLeans,* Aug. 8, 1983, pp. 34-35.
Norris, M. W. (Ed.). "Networks: A Matrix for Exchange." *J.C. Penney Forum,* Mar. 1983, pp. 1-33.
Odiorne, G. S. *Strategic Management of Human Resources.* San Francisco: Jossey-Bass, 1984.
O'Leary, B. *Space Industrialization,* Vols. 1 and 2. Boca Raton, Fla.: CRC Press, 1983.
O'Neil, G. *The Technology Edge.* New York: Simon & Schuster, 1984.
Osborne, A. *Running Wild.* Berkeley, Calif.: Osborne/McGraw-Hill, 1979.
O'Toole, J. *Declining Innovation.* Los Angeles: Center for Futures Research, University of Southern California, 1982.
O'Toole, J. "Editorial." *New Management,* 1983, *1,* 3.
Ouchi, W. *The M-Form Society.* Reading, Mass.: Addison-Wesley, 1984.
Palmer, B. C., and Palmer, K. P. *The Successful Meeting Master Guide.* New York: AMACOM, 1984.
Pascarella, P. *The New Achiever.* New York: Free Press, 1984.
Peters, T. J. "In Search of Excellence: Companies That Are Willing to Reach Out and Take Risks Have It." *Los Angeles Times,* 1983a; Jan. 30, Part V, p. 3; Jan. 31, Part IV, p. 2; Feb. 1, Part IV, p. 2.
Peters, T. J. "We Underestimated: Excellent Companies Revisited." *New Management,* 1983b, *1,* 6-11.
Peters, T. J. *A Passion for Excellence.* New York: Random House, 1985.
Peters, T. J., and Waterman, R. H. *In Search of Excellence.* New York: Harper & Row, 1982.
Phillips, J. J. *Improving Supervisors' Effectiveness: How Organi-*

zations Can Raise the Performance of Their First-Level Managers. San Francisco: Jossey-Bass, 1985.
Pinchot, G. "Intrapreneurialism for Corporations." *The Futurist*, Feb. 1984a, pp. 82-83.
Pinchot, G. *Intrapreneuring.* New York: Harper & Row, 1984b.
"Planning Meetings With New Meeting Technology." *Successful Meetings*, Mar. 1984, pp. 65-88.
Pope, J. *Business to Business Telemarketing.* New York: AMACOM, 1983.
"The Practicalities of Work at Home." *Seventh Plenary Meeting Summary*, Diebold Automated Office Summary, Aug. 1981, pp. 21-24.
Pratt, S. E., and others. *How to Raise Venture Capital.* New York: Scribner's, 1982.
"Recharting Business and Computing in the Decade Ahead." *The Consultant*, Jan./Feb. 1985, pp. 1-5.
Reich, R. B. *The Next American Frontier.* New York: New York Times Books, 1983.
Riggs, H. E. *Managing High-Tech Companies.* Belmont, Calif.: Wadsworth, 1984.
"Robots: Meet the Future Generation." *Los Angeles Times*, Aug. 14, 1983, Part 2, pp. 1-3.
Ruprecht, M. M., and Wagoner, K. P. *Managing Office Automation.* New York: Wiley, 1984.
Salk, J. *Anatomy of Reality.* New York: Columbia University Press, 1983.
Schein, E. H. "The Role of the Founder in Creating Organizational Culture." *Organizational Dynamics*, 1983, *12*, 13-19.
Schein, E. H. *Organizational Culture and Leadership: A Dynamic View.* San Francisco: Jossey-Bass, 1985.
"Schooling for Survival." *Time*, Feb. 11, 1985, pp. 74-75.
Schreiber, C. T. *Changing Places.* Cambridge: MIT Press, 1985.
Seamans, R. C., and Ordway, F. I. "The Apollo Tradition: An Object Lesson for the Management of Large-Scale Technological Endeavors." *Interdisciplinary Science Reviews*, 1977, *2* (4), 270-303.
Sears, W. H. *Back in Working Order.* Glenview, Ill.: Scott, Foresman, 1983.

Shaevitz, M. *The Superwoman Syndrome.* New York: Warner Communications, 1984.
"Shanghai Composer Works with the Dead." *Los Angeles Times,* May 9, 1984, p. 18.
Sheffield, C., and Rosen, C. *Space Careers.* New York: William Morrow, 1984.
Shonk, J. H. *Working in Teams.* New York: AMACOM, 1983.
Silver, A. D. *The Entrepreneurial Life.* New York: Wiley, 1983.
Sinetar, M. *The Pac-Man Phenomenon and Management Skills.* Englewood Cliffs, N.J.: Prentice-Hall, 1983.
Sleet, D. A., and Hileman, L. *Guide to Health Instruction.* Irvine, Calif.: Human Behavior Resources Group, 1981.
Smilor, R. W. (Ed.). *Small Business and the Entrepreneurial Spirit.* Austin: Institute for Constructive Capitalism, University of Texas, 1982.
Smilor, R. W., and Kuhn, R. L. (Eds.). *Take-off Companies.* New York: Praeger, 1985.
Smith, I. *Diary of a Small Business.* New York: Scribner's, 1982.
Starr, P. *The Social Transformation of American Medicine.* New York: Basic Books, 1982.
Stein, K. "Robo-Shock." *Omni,* 1983, pp. 51, 90.
Stevenson, H. H. "Entrepreneurship: Hunting with Halfalump." *Harvard Business School Bulletin,* June 1983, pp. 50-51.
Stevenson, H. H., and Gumpert, D. E. "The Heart of Entrepreneurship." *Harvard Business Review,* Mar.-Apr. 1985a, pp. 85-94.
Stevenson, H. H., Roberts, M., and Grousbeck, I. *New Business Ventures and the Entrepreneur.* Homewood, Ill.: Richard D. Irwin, 1985b.
Strassman, P. A. *The Information Payoff.* New York: Free Press, 1985.
"Stress! Seeking Cures for Modern Anxieties." *Time,* June 6, 1983, pp. 48-54.
Thompson, P. C. *Quality Circles.* New York: AMACOM, 1983.
"Those People Who Dare to Start a New Business." *U.S. News & World Report,* May 8, 1985, p. 50.
Tichy, N. M. (Ed.). *Human Resource Management.* New York: Wiley, 1984.

References

Toffler, A. *Future Shock.* New York: Random House, 1970.
Toffler, A. *The Third Wave.* New York: William Morrow, 1980.
Toffler, A. *The Adaptive Corporation.* New York: McGraw-Hill, 1985.
"Top Companies in the South East." *Forbes,* July 30, 1984, p. 54.
Treacy, W. R. *Human Resources Development Standards.* New York: AMACOM, 1984.
Tubesing, N. L., and Tubesing, D. A. *Structured Exercises in Wellness Promotion,* Vol. 1. Duluth, Minn.: Whole Person Press, 1983.
"The Ultimate Meritocracy." *Forbes,* Aug. 1, 1983, pp. 106-107.
Vesper, K. H. *Entrepreneurialism and National Policy.* Chicago: Heller Institute for Small Business, 1983.
The Video Age. White Plains, N.Y.: Knowledge Industry Publications, 1982.
Villoldo, A., and Dychtwald, K. *Millenium.* Los Angeles: Tarcher, 1981.
von Puttkamer, J. "Space: The Long-Range Future." *The Futurist,* Feb. 1985, pp. 36-38.
Waite, L. "Women Fill One-Third of Executive Posts." *Los Angeles Times,* Apr. 11, 1984, p. 16.
Wallach, E. "Person-System Match." *Training and Development Journal,* Feb. 1983, pp. 28-38.
"Ways to Control Stress and Make it Work for You." *U.S. News & World Report,* Mar. 12, 1984, pp. 69-70.
Weatherford, J. M. *Tribes on the Hill.* New York: Rawson & Wade, 1981.
Weber, D. "The New American Economy." *Venture,* July 1983, pp. 34-42.
Weisler. "International Banking Survey." *The Economist,* Mar. 24, 1984, p. 28.
Wellin, M. *Behavior Technology at Work.* Epping, England: Gower, 1985.
Welsh, J. A., and White, J. E. *The Entrepreneur's Master Planning Guide.* Englewood Cliffs, N.J.: Prentice-Hall, 1983.
"Westinghouse's Cultural Revolution." *Fortune,* June 15, 1981.

"What Makes Tommy Davis Run?" *Forbes,* Apr. 25, 1983, p. 200.

White, R. A. *The Entrepreneur's Manual.* Radner, Pa.: Chilton, 1977.

"Why They're Jumping Ship at Intel." *Business Week,* Feb. 14, 1983, p. 107.

Woodcock, M. *Team Development Manual.* Epping, England: Gower, 1985.

"World Business." *The Economist,* Apr. 30, 1983, pp. 88.

Zemke, R. "Self-Development 1982: Is There a Junta in Your Future?" *Training,* Sept. 1982, pp. 106-113.

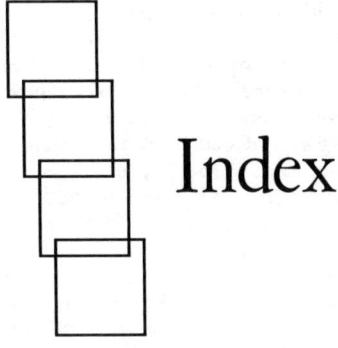

Index

A

A & P, and intrapreneurship, 91-92
ABC, and women's role, 315
Abend, C. J., 320, 321-322
Abernathy, W., 108, 369
Acculturation, concept of, 33
Ad hocracy, and teams, 229
Adams, J., 26, 286, 332, 369
Adams, J. D., 252
Administrative Staff College, and team roles, 245
Adytum, Inc., and university/business forums, 96
Aetna Life & Casualty: and office automation, 156; and videoconferences, 48
Agricultural Extension Service, as dissemination model, 168
Ainsworth, T., 276, 369
Air Florida, and takeovers, 67
Airbus Industry, and joint ventures, 66-67
Albertine, J., 78-79
Albus, J. S., 181, 185, 369
Aldrin, E. E., Jr., 8
All the Good Old Girls, as network, 252

Allied Corporation, and buy-outs, 67
Amara, R., 108
Ambivalence, and wellness, 285
American Assembly of Collegiate Schools of Business, 126
American Association of Entrepreneurs, 72
American Association of Fitness Directors in Business and Industry, 287
American Bar Association, 124
American College Testing Program, and external degrees, 127
American Council on Education (ACE): Commission on Educational Credit and Credentials of, 126; Noncollegiate Sponsored Instruction program of, 127
American Federation of Labor-Congress of Industrial Organizations (AFL-CIO), 137
American General Corporation, communication at, 222
American Law Institute, 124
American Society for Engineering Education, 123
American Society for Training and

Development (ASTD), 103, 104n, 110, 114, 120, 178; International Division (ASID) of, 105
American Society of Personnel Administrators, 142, 369
Analog, and corporate venture funds, 339
Anderson, S. S., 132
Anderson, W., 331
Ansoff, H. I., 22, 116, 369
Antonovsky, A., 274-275, 369
Apple, M., ix-xiii, xxii, 96, 321, 341
Apple Computer, Inc.: and entrepreneurialism, 74; as fast-growth enterprise, 15, 16, 17; and robotics, 196; work as fun at, 212
Argote, L., 188, 369
Armco, Inc., joint venture by, 65-66
Armstrong, N. A., 8
Army War College, Strategic Studies Institute of, 183
ARPANET, 259
Arthur D. Little Company, 107
Artificial intelligence (AI), and robotics, 183, 195, 197, 199-201
ASEA, and robotics, 196
Asimov, I., 178, 180, 190
Association of Southeast Asian Nations (ASEAN), and cultural awareness, 38
AT&T: compensation at, 219, 221; competition from, 57; and corporate break-up, 63-64; diversification by, 2; educational center of, 128; and global opportunity, 343; and metaindustrial management, 8; and personal change, 306; and robotics, 196; teletraining by, 122
Atari: and downsizing, 143; and organizational excellence, 14
Atlantic Richfield Company (ARCO): corporate culture of, 335; and satellite communication, 48; as vanguard corporation, 11
Auletta, K., 63, 369
Australia, and team roles, 245

Automation: analysis of, 135-169; concept of, 172; critical incidents in, 136-139; and downsizing/closing guidance, 142-143; and employee assistance programs (EAP), 142; and human factors management, 164-166; manager's role for, 158-163; new dimensions in managing, 163-168; and occupational transformations, 136-145; office, case study of, 145, 148-158; and organizational culture, 58-60; rates of, 141; and retraining, 143-145; strategic impact of, 160-161; strategies for, 142-145; and supervision of workers at home, 166-168; and two-tiered work force, 140
Autonomy, in work culture, 46-47
Ayres, R. V., 177, 370

B

Baker International, and entrepreneurialism, 53
Bander, D. O., 241, 370
Bank of America, culture of, 228, 335
Barksdale, J., 117
Battelle Memorial Institute; and organizational change, 334; and robotics, 191
Batterymarch, and organizational transformation, 332-333
Baty, G. B., 86, 370
Baugh, J. G., 233, 370
Baxter Technologies Corporation, and robotics, 192-193
Beam Pines Human Resources, and wellness, 279
Beech, H. R., 282, 370
Beecher, R., 180
Behavioral health, and wellness, 279
Bell, A. G., 19
Bell, C. H., 332, 373
Bell Laboratories: culture shock at, 64; and robotics, 196

Bendix, and buy-outs, 67
Bennis, W., 370
Beré, J. F., 214
Berliner, S., 265
Best, F., 44, 370
Bethlehem Steel, and automation, 138, 143
Bier, D., 281-282, 370
Biogenetics/bioagriculture, trends in, 9
BioSearch, woman's role in, 315
Blake, R. R., 379
Blanchard, K., 205, 370
Bloom, B., 208
Blue-collar blues, concept of, 5
Blue Shield, performance at, 204
BMW, and robotics, 196
Boeing Company: and joint ventures, 66; and robotics, 184
Bolman, L. G., 99, 370
Bolton, D. G., 311, 370
Bolton, R., 311, 370
Bonnie Bell Corporation, wellness at, 275
Boone, M., 15
Boorstin, D., 73-74, 370
Borg-Warner Corp., and performance, 214
Borysenko, J., 280
Boston Consulting Group, 200
Boucher, N., 370
Boyd, D. P., 87, 370
Bradley, H. G., 253, 372
Brain hemispheres: and creative performers, 214; and entrepreneurs, 81
Brainstorming, and performance innovations, 213-214
Brod, C., 186, 280, 370
Brown, A., 26, 333, 370
Brown, D. S., 15, 371
Brownstein, B., 191
Brummett, L., 115
Bry, B., 285, 371
Bureau of Indian Affairs (BIA), 88
Bureau of Labor Statistics (BLS), 141
Burns, A., 371
Burns, F., 332

Burns, J. M., 371
Burns, L. E., 282, 370
Burr, D., 211
Bushnell, N., 193
Business Initiative, Global Action Team of, 308
Buy-ins, and organizational cultures, 64-65

C

Cahners Publishing, wellness at, 279
Calder, K. R., 94, 344, 375
Caldwell, P., 217
Califano, J., 279
California: employment training panel in, 113; low-tech network in, 262-263; self-esteem in, 208; social support study in, 294
California at Los Angeles, University of (UCLA), and robotics, 199, 200
California at San Diego, University of: executive training program at, 127-128; Magnetic Recording Research Center at, 94; School of Medicine at, 281; and space culture shock, 302; and supercomputers, 342; and wellness, 291
California Board of Registered Nursing, and wellness, 292
California Space Institute: and robotics, 175-176; and space future, 347
Canada: chief executives studied in, 22; industrialization in, 38-39; network in, 254; robotics in, 175, 192-193; women entrepreneurs in, 80
Cannon Mills, wellness at, 276
Capek, K., 173
Caplan, R. D., 293
CAPS:HITECH, as network, 266
Carnegie Foundation for the Advancement of Teaching, 125, 335-336
Carnegie-Mellon University, and robotics, 192, 199, 201

Carnevale, A. P., 103, 178, 371
Cattabiani, G., 216
CBS, and women's role, 315
Center for Creative Leadership: and management role, 320-321; and wellness, 295-296
Cetus Corporation, and entrepreneurialism, 52
Chandler, A., 61-62
Change: forces of, x, xvi; in organizations, 60-61. *See also* Transformation; Transitions
Charlottesville Institute of Textile Technology, high-tech program of, 128
Charnes, A., 340, 371
Charter Medical, and organizational excellence, 12
Chesney, M., 284
China, People's Republic of, wellness in, 282-283
Cincinnati Milacron, 178
Citibank, and office automation, 156
Citicorp, and robotics, 187-188
Citizen Planners, and personal change, 308-309
Clark, K. R., 108, 369
Clarke, A., 19, 371
Coates, J., 195
Coates, V. T., 194-195, 371
Coca-Cola: and global opportunity, 343; and organizational excellence, 12
Cohen, W. A., 371
Coherence, and wellness, 274-275
Coleman, E. R., 8, 371
Collins, J., 162
Colonial Bank & Trust Company, wellness at, 275
Commodore International, and entrepreneurialism, 74
Communications: consulting level of, 223; individual level of, 222-223; institutional level of, 222; and language, in organizational culture, 59; technologies related to, 58-60; in work culture, 47-48
Communications Era Task Force: manifesto of, 330; as network, 254
Communications Workers of America (CWA), 64, 339-340
Compensation, for high performance, 218-221
Compuserve, 260, 266
Computer-aided design/manufacturing (CAD/CAM), trends in, 9
Computer Assisted Performance Evaluation (CAPE), 208
Computer-based training (CBT), and human resource development, 118, 119, 120-121
Computers: innovations using, 161-163; personal, as discretionary tool, 159; personal, and teams, 236-237; video combinations with, 121-122
Condon, M., 186, 371
Conference Board, 107-108, 221
Conoco, and buy-outs, 67
Conrail, and worker ownership, 219
Consultants' Networks, 264-265
Continental Airlines: compensation at, 219; and corporate breakup, 63; takeover of, 67
Contract Staffing of America, Inc., 339
Contract work, trend toward, 46-47, 225-226, 338-339
Control Data Corporation: and intrapreneurship, 91; and robotics, 199; StayWell program of, 290; as vanguard corporation, 11
Cook, A. S., 241
Cooper, C. L., 313, 372
Cooper, W. W., 340, 371
Corning, P. A., 49, 54, 239, 341, 371
Cornish, E., 53, 144, 371
Corporate break-ups, and organizational cultures, 63-64
Corporate Cup Association, 288
Cosmopolitanism, in management, 15
Coto Research Center, and wellness, 292
Cousins, N., 274

Index

Cox, J. S., 98, 372
Criswell, D., 176, 310, 345, 371
Crocker, M. K., 77
Crumley, D. W., 183, 371
Culture: and adaptation, 34; concepts of, 30, 31, 32; described, 31-38; entrepreneurial versus administrative, 328-329; rationale for awareness of, 35-38; renewing, suggestions for, 13. *See also* Organizational culture; Work culture
Culture shock: characteristics and effects of, 300-301; coping with, 299-305
Cummins, participative management at, 215
Cybernetics, trend toward, 7-8, 172
Cyberphobia and cyberphrenia, 49, 164-165
Cyborgs, concept of, 175

D

Daewoo company, in joint venture, 344
Daimler-Benz, and robotics, 196
Dan River, Inc., compensation at, 219
Darnell, L., 236-237, 272
Data Processing Association, 177
DATAFILE, 264-265
Dauphinais, W., 236-237, 372
Davidson, D. M., 36n, 56n, 348n
Davidson, F. P., 97-98, 372
Davidson, M. J., 313, 372
Davis, S. A., 243, 372
Davis, T., 52, 79
Dayton Hudson, as vanguard corporation, 11
Deal, T. E., 99, 370, 372
Dean, C., 121, 372
Deere, J., 19
Defense Advanced Systems Research Projects Agency, and robotics, 199
Delaney, C., 136
Delphi Group: and electronic middle management, 123; and team development, 237, 238n

Delta Airlines, and organizational excellence, 12
Department of Trade and Industry, Information Technology Centres of, 113
Derfler, F., 267, 372
Desatnick, R., 105, 336, 372
De Sio, T., 93
Diamond International, and performance, 204
Didsbury, H. F., 45, 54, 372
Diebold, J., 158, 331, 349, 372
Diebold Automated Office Program, 157n
Diebold Group, 216n; and automation, 148
Diebold Research Program, and automation, 137, 148
Digital Equipment Corporation: headquarters of, 6; and teams, 230-231
Digital Marketing, team leader software from, 237
Discovery Toys, Inc., woman's role in, 315
Disney, W., 213
Diversification, in organizational cultures, 61-63
Donnelly, J. H., 209, 375
Dordick, H. S., 253, 372
Dorf, R. C., 177, 372
Dorn, J., 97
Dow Chemical Co., compensation at, 219
Drake Beam Morin, and performance, 205
Drath, W. H., 321, 376
Dresser Industries, and diversification, 62-63
Drucker, P. E., xvii-xviii, 12, 70, 71, 178, 317, 372
Duke University, and robotics, 192
DuPont: and buy-outs, 67; diversification by, 61; Medical Care Assistance Program (MEDCAP) of, 278
Durham University, and management development, 129
Dwyer, C., 212, 373

Dychtwald, K., 44, 383
Dyer, D., 23, 377

E

EAN-TECH, and performance, 206
Earth Data, team leader software from, 237
East-West Center, and teams, 241-242
Eastern Air Lines Inc., compensation at, 219
Eastman Kodak: seed money from, 117; as vanguard corporation, 11
Ebasco Services Incorporated, and business certificate program, 126-127
EDUCOM, 128
Electrolux, and robotics, 196
Electronic Data Systems, acquisition of, 180
Engelberger, J. F., 177, 190, 194, 373
Englebart, D., 213
Entrepreneurialism: analysis of, 69-98; case study of, 82-88; concepts of, 69, 72-73, 87; factors leading to, 71-72; grid for, 89-90; and innovation, 88-98; nourishing spirit of, 76-79; procedures in, 75; qualities in, 76, 77-79; and space industries, 97-98; steps in, 82-88; in synergy with venture capital, 75-76; and technology venturing, 96-98; timeliness of, 70-76; and universities, 94-96; and women, 79-82; in work culture, 51-53
Equal opportunity, and organizational culture, 59-60
ETA Systems, and intrapreneurship, 91
Eurich, N., 125, 336, 373
European Economic Community (EEC, Common Market): and contract work, 47; and cultural awareness, 38
European Space Agency, 97
Excellence in organizational structure, trend toward, 12-15

Executives, and wellness, 278-279, 289
Expert systems, and robotics, 199-200

F

F. International, work force of, 225
Fanuc, Ltd., and robotics, 179-180
Farley, P., 52
Fast-growth enterprises, trend toward, 15-18
Fauley, F., 117
Faultless Starch Bon Ami Company, wellness at, 276
Federal Aviation Administration (FAA), and robotics, 184
Federal Express: and adjustable work schedule, 2, 226; and organizational excellence, 12; and videoconferencing, 117
Federal Reserve Bank of Atlanta, and excellent organizations, 12
Feigenbaum, E. A., 121, 197, 373
Feingold, S. N., 144, 147n, 373
Ferguson, M., 332, 373
Ferreira, J., 159
Fiber optics and telecommunications, trends in, 9
Fiero J., 123
Financial astuteness, in management, 14-15
Finkelstein, J., 9, 24, 373
First National Bank of Chicago, teams at, 228
First Travel Corporation, compensation at, 219
Flamholtz, E., 74, 115
Flanigan, J., 178, 373
Fleming, L. R., 10-11, 373
Fletcher, J., 211-212, 373
Flexible manufacturing systems (FMS), and robotics, 197, 200, 201
Flour Corporation, compensation at, 220
Flowers Industries, and organizational excellence, 12
Ford, H., 19
Ford Motor Company: automation

Index

at, 163; and computer-assisted instruction, 120, 121-122; and downsizing, 143; Employee Involvement (EI) at, 49-50, 217-218; participative management at, 215, 217-218; and technology, 58-59; and videoconferences, 48; and worker participation, 47
Forester, T., 7, 373
Forum Corporation, management development programs of, 121
Fox, T., 315
France, and joint ventures, 67
Francis, D., 232, 293, 373
Franklin, B., 250
Freese, K., 96
French, J. R., 293
French, W. C., 332, 373
Fujitsu Fanu, joint venture by, 66
Fuller, B., 322
Future shock: concept of, 300; and work transformation, 5

G

GA Technologies, and supercomputers, 342
Geis, G. T., 377
General Dynamics, and teams, 244
General Electric: corporate culture of, 335; corporate slogan of, 101; and diversification, 62; and entrepreneurialism, 53; and global opportunity, 344; leadership skills at, 55; Learning and Communication Center of, 192; participative management at, 215; and robotics, 23, 179, 192; seed money from, 117
General Motors: compensation at, 220; diversification by, 61-62; joint ventures by, 66, 217, 344; leadership skills at, 55; manufacturing automation protocol (MAP) of, 201; participatory management at, 217; and robotics, 173, 180, 201; seed money from, 117; wellness at, 275
General Motors Institute, degrees from, 126

George Washington University, human resource development degrees from, 115
Germany, Federal Republic of: and joint venture, 67; networks in, 252; and robotics, 196
Giber, D. J., 241, 370
Gibson, J. L., 209, 375
Gilder, G., 326, 374
Gill, M. D., 96-97, 377
Glavin, W., 51
Glenn, J., 346
Global manager, concept of, 343
Glossbrenner, A., 267
Goldman, N., 374
Golembiewski, R. T., 374
Goodacre, M. L., 265
Goodman, L. J., 236, 374
Goodman, P. S., 188, 369, 374
Goodrich & Sherwood, and wellness, 279
Goodyear, and technology, 58-59
Gordon, A., 291
Grayson, C. J., Jr., 259
Grossman, D., 190, 202
Group Maturity Analysis, 351, 360-361
Group Response System (GRS), 132-133
Grousbeck, I., 382
Grove, A. S., 209-211, 256, 319, 374
GTE Corporation, training program of, 112
Gumpert, D. E., 87, 327, 329n, 370, 382

H

Hall, E. T., 33, 374
Hall, J., 218
Harman, W., 44, 325, 374
Harris, D. L., xxi-xxii, 19, 374-375
Harris, P. R., x, xi, 4n, 14, 18, 34, 35, 40, 49, 51, 61, 85, 105-107, 120, 133, 209, 214, 241-242, 264, 300, 302, 307, 316, 347, 351, 374-375, 379
Harris International, and high performance, 51, 209, 352

Harvard Company, team leader software from, 237
Hawken, P., 330, 375
Hawkins, A., 195
Hayes, R. H., 375
Haynes, W., 194
Hays, R. H., 285, 337-338, 378
Health Insurance Association of America, and wellness, 287
Hess, K. M., 207, 375
Hewlett-Packard Co.: compensation at, 220; and robotics, 199
Hileman, L., 382
Hiltz, S. R., 253, 267, 375
Hine, V., 254
Hockey, R., 280, 375
Hoffer, E., 19
Hofheinz, R., 94, 344, 375
Hofstede, G., 375
Holiday Inns, HINET of, 117
Home Depot, and organizational excellence, 12
Honda Motors, and robotics, 181
Honeywell, Inc.: and office automation, 156; and performance, 204; and robotics, 182; as vanguard corporation, 11
Hook, H. S., 222
Hope Reports, 128-129
Horton, T. R., xxx
Hughes Aircraft, and organizational change, 337
Human resource development (HRD): advancing, 99-134; alternative higher education opportunities for, 125-129; assumptions in, 103; concept of, 102; education for, 111-112, 115; educational technologies and strategies for, 116-125; and electronic middle management, 123; and laser disc video training, 123-124; and learning for new work culture, 101-116; megatrends in, 105-107; and performance, 207; and performance-based engineer development, 123; practitioner training for, 115; and productivity, 105; reasons for, 108; and videoconferencing, 117, 124-125; and wellness, 271, 279-280, 286, 290, 297
Human Resource Planning Society, 102-103
Human Resource Wheel, 110

I

IBM: and buy-ins, 64-65, 338; career counseling program of, 129; grants from, 117, 140; job absences at, 336; and networking capabilities, 2; organizational culture of, 57-58; philosophy of, 11; and robotics, 190, 191, 196, 199; supercampus of, 128; and teams, 230; and videoconferences, 48; wellness at, 283
ICI, and contract work, 46
Illinois, Governor's Council on Health and Fitness in, 275
Immerwahr, J., 141-142
India: industrial safety in, 273, 331; and space activities, 345
Informal/synergistic relationships, in work culture, 48-49
Information society: considerations in, 144-145; coping with transition to, 324-327; education for, 112, 140; managers in, 23-24; synergy in, 116; transition to, xvi-xvii, 4
Innovation: and entrepreneurialism, 88-98; stimulation of, 212-214; studies of, 92-94
Institute for Advanced Learning, and wellness, 292
Institute for Labor and Mental Health, 307
Institute for the Information Society, as network, 267
Institute of Electrical and Electronics Engineers (IEEE), and robotics, 193
Institute on Large Scale Problems, 237
Instrumentation Network, 265, 352
Intel Corporation: and matrix or-

Index

ganization, 49; norms of, 50; partial acquisition of, 57, 65, 338; and performance, 210
Intercultural skill, in management, 14
Interfaces, managing, 14
International Consultants Foundation (ICF), as network, 264
International Executive Service Corps, and personal change, 311
International Federation of Training & Development Organizations (IFTDO), 103
International Harvester, performance at, 204
International Labour Office, 24
International Telephone and Telegraph (ITT), Educational Systems of, 116
Intertec Data Systems Corporation, as fast-growth enterprise, 16
Intrapreneurship: characteristics of, 89; concept of, 88-89; innovation through, 88-98
Iowa Foundation for Medical Care, and wellness, 278
Ivancevich, J. M., 209, 375

J

Jaap, T., 222-223
James, J., 62
Japan: artificial intelligence research in, 121; and electronics market, 62; and industrialization, 3, 17-18, 38; joint ventures of, 65-66, 97; networking in, 267; organizational change in, 333-334; participatory management in, 217; robotics in, 172, 179-180, 181, 192, 196, 197, 202, 342; and space activities, 345; statistics teaching in, 15; teams in, 230
Jay, T. B., 376
Jin Miaolin, 282-283
Job Training Partnership Act, 113
Jobs, S., 15, 74
John Deere and Co.: flexible manufacturing process of, 25; as vanguard corporation, 11; wellness at, 277-278
Johnson, S., 205, 370
Johnson & Johnson: and joint venture, 67, 346; Live for Life program of, 277; philosophy of, 11
Joint ventures, international, and organizational cultures, 65-67
Junto, as network, 250

K

Kadushin, C., 255-256
Kahn, H., 28
Kakabadse, A., 131, 319-320, 376
Kanematsu-Gosho, joint venture by, 66
Kanter, R. M., 93-94, 376
Kantrow, A. M., 108, 369
Kaplan, R. E. 321, 376
Kastens, M. L., 20, 376
Kato, I., 196
Katz, M., 224, 377
Katzan, H., 159, 376
Keane, J., 236, 376
Keane, M., 236, 376
Keane, Inc., and teams, 241
Kearney, Inc., A. T., 105
Kemp, S. L., 75, 80, 81, 82, 376
Kennecott Copper Company, wellness at, 275
Kennedy, A. A., 372
Kerr, E., 267
Kidder, T., 17, 376
Kiewit, P., 219-220
Kilmann, R. H., 231, 251, 331, 376, 379
Kimberly, J. R., 18, 376
Kimberly Clark Corporation, human resources at, 336
Kingston, G., 159, 376
Knowledge Industry Publications, 121
Koehn, H. E., 29, 39, 44, 141, 175, 178, 180, 190, 376-377
Kofodimos, J., 295-296, 321, 376
Konecci, E. B., 74-75, 377
Koops, C. E., 294

Korea, Republic of, and joint ventures, 344
Korn, L. B., xvii, 325
Kozmetsky, G., xxii, 53, 96-97, 98, 130-131, 297-298, 327, 377
Kozmetsky, R., 297-298, 377
Kuhn, R. L., 71, 75, 377, 382
Kurtsig, S., 81-82

L

La Jolla Associates, communication at, 222
La Jolla Clinic of Family and Preventive Medicine, 287
Langseth, P., 336, 378
Large Scale Program Institutes, 98
Lasers/holography, trends in, 9-10
Lawrence, P. R., 23, 377
Lazer, E. A., 48, 377
Leadership: issues for, 333; in transformation management, 327-333
LeBaron, D., 332
Lee, J., 87
Lee Data Corporation, and entrepreneurialism, 87
Lehigh University, and robotics, 192
Levering, R., 224, 377
Levine, A. S., 8, 377
Levinson, R. E., 72, 377
Levitt, A., 78-79
Life-styles: types of, 309; and wellness, 287-290
Lincoln National Life Insurance, and telecommunication, 48
Link Consulting Associates, and teams, 230
Lipnack, J., 253, 254, 377
Lippert, D., 125
Lippitt, G. L., 336, 378
Litton Industries, computer use by, 162
Livingston, J. S., 111-112, 378
London, M., 109, 378
Los Alamos National Laboratory (LANL), and entrepreneurialism, 96
Love, R. N., 236, 374
Luckman, C., 251
Lunar Productions, 117

M

McBer and Company, and teams, 241
McCorduck, P., 121, 197, 373
McDonald, F. J., 55
McDonalds, job absences at, 336
McDonnell Douglas, and joint venture, 67, 346
McGullicuddy, J., 319
McGinnis, T., 296, 378
McInnis, N., 267n
McKay, M. F., 34, 347, 378
McMillon, C., 168, 378
Macomb Community College, and robotics, 192
Macroculture, concept of, 31
Macromanagement, aspects of, 14-15
Maidique, M. A., 285, 337-338, 378
Mail Box Etc., and intrapreneurship, 93
Main Event Management (MEM), Model-Netrics of, 222
Man-Machine Interface (MMI), as emerging field, 177
Management: analysis of transformational, 323-349; for automation, 135-169; for big transition, 324-327; conclusion on, 347-349; cross-cultural, 3; development of, for new work culture, 129-133; electronic, 123; and entrepreneurialism, 69-98; global opportunities for, 343-345; for high performance, 203-226; and human resource development, 99-134; in industrial age, 39-40; institutional opportunities in, 341-343; interplanetary opportunity for, 345-347; issues in, 27; leadership in, 327-333; metaindustrial, 8, 14-15, 27-29; by networking, 249-268; new characteristics of, 11-12; new realities for, 327, 330; for office automation, 155-158; opportunities for, 341-347; and organizational change, 333-341; participative, 214-217; priorities and

Index

roles for, 1-202; priorities in development of, 131-132; recommendations for, xi-xii; and robotics, 170-202; as science and art, 19; strategies for, 203-349; for success, 323-349; with teams, 227-248; and transformations, 1-29; in transition, 340-341; transitions in, 299-322; turbulent times for, ix-x; walk-around (WAM), 13, 216; and wellness, 269-298; and work culture, 30-68; of workers at home, 166-168
Management Research Systems, 207, 214, 235, 351-352
Managers: and accountability, 20; and automation, 158-163; choices by, xii-xiii; competencies of, 319-321; cultural awareness by, 35-38; human resource development competencies of, 113-114; human resource development education for, 109-110; in information society, 23-24; issues for, 321-322; networks for, 262-268; options shock for, 158; performance of, 208-209; potential actualized by, 308-309; qualities of, 28, 307-308; reasons for changes by, 317-318; resources for, 332; role changes for, 316-322; roles of, 22; and social responsibility, 331-332; transformational, characteristics of, 20-22; vanguard thinking by, 10-12; wellness resources for, 290-293
Manpower Temporary Services, work force of, 225
Manufacturers Hanover Trust (MHT): and computer use, 131-132; and management role, 319
Marietta, and buy-outs, 67
Marks & Spencer: contracting by, 2; and walk-around management, 216
Marrus, S. K., 378
Maslow, A., 206n
Massachusetts Institute of Technology (M.I.T.): and National Technological University, 116-117; and robotics, 192, 199; and wellness, 292-293
Masuda, Y., 17, 44, 378
Matarazzo, J. D., 271, 274, 279, 294, 378
Matsushita Electric Industrial Company, robotics in, 172
Matthews, D., 117
Mayfield Funds, and entrepreneurialism, 79
MEDIASENSE, 124
Meehan, J., 53
Meetings: international, 133; technology for, 132-133; and videoconferencing, 117, 124-125
Melkanoff, M., 200, 378
Mensch, G., 130, 378
Merrill Lynch, and videoconferencing, 124
Metasystems Design Group, as network, 267
Meyers, C. E., 332
Michigan, robot manufacturing in, 137
Michigan, University of, ERIC Clearinghouse on Counseling and Personnel Services at, 266
Microcomputer Information Support Tools (MIST), 267
Microculture, concept of, 31
Microelectronic and Computer Technology Corporation (MCC): as fast-growth enterprise, 17; and intrapreneurship, 91, 94; and robotics, 199
Microprocessors, trends in, 9
Mid-America, University of (UMA), technologies of, 127
Middle States Association of Colleges and Schools, 125
Milbrath, M., 126, 378
Miles, R. H., 18, 376
Miller, B., 334, 378
Miller, J. G., 128, 378
Miller, N. R., 373
Miller, R. J., 378
Miller, R. W., 105
Miller, S. M., 177, 570

Million Dollar Roundtable (MDRT), as insurance network, 251-252
Ministry of International Trade, 202
Minkin, B., 213
Minnesota, job creation in, 341
Mintzberg, H., 22, 379
Miraflores Designs, woman's role in, 314-315
Mitchell, A., 309, 379
Mitroff, I. I., 251, 331, 343, 379
Mitsubishi International Corporation (MIC), and organizational change, 334
Mitsubishi Rayon Co.: joint venture by, 65-66; and organizational change, 334
Moran, R. T., 18, 35, 40, 49, 61, 107, 133, 241-242, 300, 307, 374, 379
Morgan Guarantee Trust, wellness at, 283
Moskowitz, M., 224, 377
Mossop, J., 336, 378
Motorola: Training and Education Center of, 123; as vanguard corporation, 11
Mottram, R., 245-248, 379
Mouton, J. S., 379
Mukhi, S., 131, 376
Mumford, L., 325
Murphy, J. J., 62-63

N

Nadler, D. A., 379
Nadler, L., xxii, 58, 102, 115, 379
Nadler, Z., xxii
Naisbitt, J., 7, 132, 254, 379
Nakasone, Y., 18
Nanus, B., 253, 370, 372
Narayanan, K., 158, 159, 379
National Academy of Engineering, 54
National Academy of Sciences, 166
National Aeronautics and Space Administration (NASA): and culture shock, 302; and entrepreneurialism, 97; and management opportunity, 345-347; management systems of, 8; and robotics, 194, 196-197; and strategic planning, 34-35; and teams, 243
National Council on Employee Ownership, 47
National Employee Leasing Company, Ltd., 339
National Fitness Foundation, 288
National Institute of Education, 138
National Organization Development (OD) Network, 332
National Science Foundation, 342
National Service Industries (NSI), and management role, 318-319
National Society for Performance Instruction (NSPI), 266, 379
National Technological University, as electronic university, 117
National Training Laboratories (NTL) Institute: new work culture seminars of, xvii, 335; and wellness, 292
National University, as fast-growth, 125
NBC, and women's roles, 315
Netword, woman's role in, 315
Network Builders International, 265-266
Network Institute, 262, 267
Networking: analysis of, 249-268; concept of, 249, 253-254; electronic, 257-262; for entrepreneurs, 77; facilitating, 250-253; guidelines for, 255-256, 263-264; management and consultant, 262-268; personal, 253-257; resources on, 267; for wellness, 291, 295
New United Motor Manufacturing (NUMM), participatory management at, 217
New York, University of the State of, 127
New York Telephone Company, wellness at, 275
New York University, Center for Research on Information Systems of, 166
Newman, D., 9, 24, 373

Index

Newman, D. C., 118, 380
Niehaus, R. J., 130, 378
Nissan Motor Manufacturing Corporation, and robotics, 181
Nolan, R. L., 148, 156
Nomura Research Institute, and robotics, 181
Norms: and organizational culture, 60; and teams, 235; in work culture, 50-51
Norris, M. W., 255-256, 380
Norris Industries, and corporate breakup, 63
North America Mica, team leader software from, 237
Northrup University, degree program of, 126
Nozette, S., 98
Nucor, and organizational excellence, 12

O

Occupations: and automation, 136-145; future titles of, 146-147; robotics transformations of, 172-173
Odetics, Inc., and robotics, 174
Odiorne, G. S., 102, 380
O'Donnell, M. P., 276, 369
Office automation (OA): case study of, 145, 148-158; conception stage of, 148-149; conclusions on, 154-158; consolidation stage of, 153-154; contagion stage of, 151-153; creative evolution stage of, 154; initiation stage of, 149-151; integrated, 157; management development for, 155-158
Office for Open Network Resources, 254, 267
O'Leary, B., 97, 346, 380
Olson, M. H., 166-167
Omaha Wellness Council, 276
Omicron, team leader software from, 237
Omnet, Inc., 259
O'Neil, G., 380
Opel, J., 57, 140, 201
Opinion Research Corporation (ORC), Center for Management Research of, 107
Ordway, F. I., 8, 381
Organization development (OD), and team building, 243
Organization for Economic Cooperative Development, 225
Organization shock: concept of, 301-302; and work transformation, 5
Organization Transformation (OT) Network, 332
Organizational culture: and automation, 58-60; and buy-ins, 64-65; concept of, 85-86; and corporate break-ups, 63-64; diversification in, 61-63; future, 55-60; and international joint ventures, 65-67; and performance, 214-215; synergistic alterations of, 60-68; and wellness, 296-297. *See also* Work culture
Organizational Roles and Relationships Inventory, 351, 362-364
Organizational Tests Ltd., 352
Organizational transformation, emerging field of, 332-333
Organizations: and attitudinal changes, 25-27; change guidelines for, 335-336; change in, and management, 333-341; concept of, 55; cultures of, 55-68; as energy exchange system, 18, 55; excellent structures of, 12-15; fast-growth, characteristics of, 16-17; and market changes, 24; matrix, 49, 233; and structural changes, 24-25; transformation of, 18-22; transition strategies for, 22-27
Osborne, A., 97, 380
Osborne, Adam, 15
Osborne, Alex, 213
Osborne Computers: and entrepreneurialism, 74; as fast-growth enterprise, 15
Oshman, K., 65
O'Toole, J., 10, 11, 12, 13, 92, 380
Ouchi, W., 229-230, 342-343, 380
Owens-Illinois, wellness at, 277

P

Pace University, and business certificate program, 126-127
Pacific Basin: and cultural awareness, 38; and entrepreneurialism, 94; and global management, 344-345
Palevsky, M., 52
Palmer, B. C., 380
Palmer, K. P., 380
Panzer, S., 264
Parker, C., 320, 376
Participation, in work culture, 47
Pascarella, P., 217, 340-341, 380
Payn, R., 123
Peace Corps, and transitions, 300, 311
Penney Company, J. C., and networking, 252, 258n
People Express: and human resource development, 99, 339; and performance, 211, 219
PepsiCo, wellness at, 279
Performance, high: analysis of managing for, 203-226; and communications, 221-223; compensation for, 218-221; and competence, 217-218; and cultural match, 214-215; and diversified work force, 223-226; innovation stimulated for, 212-214; instruments for assessing, 350-368; interviews for, 211-212; leveraging, 209-210; maintaining, 211-223; motivators for, 206-207; and participative management, 214-217; strategies for improving, 204-211; and wellness, 272; and work as fun, 212; in work culture, 51, 205
Peter Kiewit Sons, Inc., compensation at, 219-220
Peters, T. J., 12-13, 14, 216, 323, 380
Pfizer Pharmaceuticals, computer use by, 161
Phillips, J. J., 207, 380-381
Piedmont Technical College, 192

Pierce, C. J., 255
Pinchot, G., III, 53, 88-89, 90n, 381
Pioneer Electronics Corporation, and robotics, 196
Pitney Bowes Corporation, and performance, 204
PLATO: as network, 266; and wellness, 290
Platt, J., 345
Polaroid, wellness at, 278
Political savvy, in management, 14
Pope, J., 48, 381
Post-managerial society, 98
Pratt, S. E., 83, 381
Primavera Systems, team leaders software from, 237
Processes, in organizational culture, 60
Procter & Gamble, wellness at, 283
Productivity, maintaining, 207
Professional Services Industries, woman's role in, 315
Professional Writers network, 262
Professionals, reeducation for, 116
Project on Technology, Work, and Character, 282

Q

Quaker Oats, and wellness, 278
Quality of Life Index, 351, 365-368
Quality of work life, in work culture, 49-50
Quinn, R. E., 376

R

Ramo, S., 337
Rank-Xerox, and contract work, 46, 225-226
RCA Services Company, and networking, 265
Reagan, R., 71, 97, 346
Reddy, R., 195
Reed, C., 222
Reentry shock, concept of, 303
Reich, R. B., 25, 381
Rensselaer Polytechnic Institute

(RPI): and entrepreneurialism, 95; and robotics, 192
Research and development orientation, in work culture, 54
Revenue Canada, 80
Rewards and recognition, in organizational culture, 59
Reynolds, A., 120
Rheingold, H., 374
Richards, R., 263-264
Richmond, J., 273
Riggs, H. E., 94, 381
Roberts, M., 382
Robo-shock: as culture shock, 301; impact of, 171, 173, 186
Robot Institute of America, 173
Robotics: advantages and disadvantages for, 176-177; analysis of, 170-202; for arc welding, 184; and artificial intelligence, 183, 195, 197, 199-201; case examples for, 179-180, 187-189; concepts of, 173-177; distinguished from automated devices, 174-175; economic and technical issues of, 185; education and training for, 191-194; examples of, 172-173; human factor in, 190-191; insights about, 189-190; in integrated manufacturing systems, 197-198; for jet flying, 184; and jobs, 177-186; jobs needed in, 182; and manufacturing, future of, 194-202; occupations transformed by, 172-173; in office, 187-188; and people, 186-194; personal, 193; in plant, 188-189; psychological implications of, 186-190; research on, 196-197; self-regulating, 184; stages in introducing, 183-184; types of robots for, 174; and universities, 192-193, 199, 200-201
Rock, A., 52
Rockwell International, and space facilities, 346
Rolm Corporation, partial acquisition of, 2, 57, 65

Rosato, P., 191
Rosen, C., 144, 382
Ross, S. J., 215-216
Round Table Foundation, 251
Ruprecht, M. M., 145, 381
Rutgers University, Center for Ceramic Research at, 342
Ryan, R. S., 293

S

Salk, J., 6, 381
Salk Institute, 281
San Diego State University: Center for Health Games and Simulations at, 290; and robotics, 193
San Diego Technology Executives Network (SDTEN), 77, 257
Sandeman, H., xvi
Sara Lee Bakeries, and cybernation, 25, 139
Say, J. B., 87
Schein, E. H., 55, 85-86, 381
Scherer Brothers Lumber, wellness at, 275-276
Schkade, D., 188, 369
Schlafman, I., 123
Schlumbergers, Ltd.: market share of, 63; and robotics, 199; synergistic strategy of, 61
Schreiber, C. T., 381
Schrieber, J. J. S., 118
Science Net, 259
Scientific Data Systems, and entrepreneurialism, 52, 79
Scitor, team leader software from, 237
Scripps Memorial Hospital Foundation, health education center of, 291-292
Seagram, and buy-outs, 67
Seamans, R. C., 8, 381
Sears, W. H., 23, 74, 381
Sears, Roebuck, personal services from, 2
Seattle, entrepreneur network in, 77
Security Pacific Bank, Futures Research Division of, 310

Selbert, R., 29, 39, 377
Selye, H., 44, 280-281
Semiconductor Industry Association, 342
Semiconductor Research Collaborative (SRC), 342
Service Corps of Retired Executives (SCORE), and personal change, 311
Shaevitz, M., 297, 382
Shaiken, H., 186
Shakespeare, W., 166
Shaw, P., 285
Shea, G., 122
Sheffield, B. F., 282, 370
Sheffield, C., 144, 382
Sherwin-Williams Co., compensation at, 219
Shneour, E., 84
Shonk, J. H., 239, 382
Shugart Corporation, and intrapreneurship, 89, 91
Sieff, Lord, 216
Signetics, participative management at, 215
Silver, A. D., 77, 382
Sinetar, M., 63, 382
Sinetar & Associates, and corporate break-ups, 63
Singer, H., 286
Singer, I. M., 19
Sizzler Restaurants, laser training programs of, 124
Slater, P., 251
Sleet, D. A., 288-289, 382
Small Business Administration, 71, 80
Small Business Innovation Research (SBIR), 54
Smilor, R. W., 75, 77, 81, 96-97, 377, 382
Smith, I., 84, 382
Smith, R. B., 180
Smoking, consequences of, 294-295
Social support, and wellness, 293-298
Society of Manufacturing Engineers, 192
Sonoco Products, and organizational excellence, 12

Source, The, 260, 266
Southern California, University of: Center for Futures Research at, 92-93, 129-130, 160-161; Graduate School of Business at, xv, 11-12; and National Technological University, 116-117
Southern California Technology Executives Network, 77, 264
Space: and culture shock, 302; and entrepreneurialism, 97-98; future of, 347; opportunities in, 345-347; and robotics, 175-176, 194, 196-197; and team building, 243-244; and technological trends, 8-10
Spain, and joint venture, 67
Speedball Corporation, wellness at, 275
Spencer, Stuart & Associates, 67
Stallings, W., 267, 372
Stamps, J., 253, 254, 377
Stanford Research Institute (SRI) International: and automation, 137; and innovation, 213; and wellness, 270
Stanford University: automation study by, 138-139; Center for Integrated Systems at, 342; and National Technological University, 116-117; and robotics, 199
Starr, P., 276, 382
Starr, R., 163
Stein, K., 187, 190, 191, 382
Sterling Institute: computer and video training by, 121, 239; and office automation, 145; and team building, 239
Stevenson, H. H., 72-73, 327, 329n, 382
Strassman, P. A., xvi, 382
Strategy, concept of, 22
Stress: analysis of managing, 280-287; concepts of, 280, 281; controlling, help with, 285-287; management of, 282-285; mechanism for, 280-282
Success: future, profile of, x-xi; themes in, 337-338; tracks to,

231; transformational management for, 323-349
Sugiyama, N., 334, 378
Sullivan, D., 314-315
Super Fresh chain, and intrapreneurship, 91-92
Sweden: robotics in, 196; worker participation in, 47
Swift, diversification by, 61
Symbiosis, in robotics, 194
Syme, L., 294
Synergy: concept of, 61; from entrepreneurialism and venture capital, 75-76; in management, 14; in organizational cultures, 60-68; in teams, 232, 239; in university/industry research, 342; in worker relationships, 48-49
Syte Information Technology, and wellness, 285

T

Tandem Corporation, and wellness, 296-297
Tannenbaum, R., 333
Taylor, F., 26
Taylor Hitech, and robotics, 173
Teagan, M., 236, 376
Team Synergy Analysis Inventory, 351, 357-359
Teams: analysis of, 227-248; building of, 231-232, 243-245; characteristics of, 232, 242-243; concept of, 229; guidelines for, 240; issues in building, 243-244; maintenance orientation in, 234-235; management with, 228-231; and norms, 235; process of, 231-235; roles on, 245-248; skills on, 237-243; task activities of, 235-237; task orientation in, 234
Technologies: and communication/information, 58-60; and human resource development, 99-134; issues of, 119-120; for meetings, 132-133; transfer of, concept of, 3; trend toward new, 7-10; trends in, 117-118; in work culture, 53-54

Technology Diffusion Model, 194-195
Technology Transfer Society, 193, 198n
Technology venturing, and entrepreneurialism, 96-98
Technostress, concept of, 186, 280
Teleometrics International, 352; and participatory management, 218
Telespan Publishing Corporation, 262
Teleworking, trend toward, 53
Texas at Austin, University of: and entrepreneurialism, 94; Institute of Constructive Capitalism at, 71, 98; and robotics, 199
Texas Instruments: and matrix organization, 49; and robotics, 199
Texas International, takeover by, 67
The Executive Committee (TEC), 77, 230, 262-263
Thomas, C., 294
Thomas Riddell firm, 80
Thompson, P. C., 382
3M Corporation, and space commerce, 346
Thurow, L., 6
Thurston, W., 27
Tichy, N. M., 382
Time: and culture shock, 304-305; in organizational culture, 59
Time Inc., wellness at, 279
Toffler, A., 24, 166, 293, 299-300, 326-327, 383
Toyota Motor Company: joint venture by, 66, 217; participatory management at, 217; and robotics, 181
Transformation: analysis of, 1-29; examples of, 338-339; guidelines for, 335-336; occupational, and automation, 136-145; occupational, and robotics, 172-173; of organizations and management, 18-22; strategies for, 22-27; of work, 1-18
Transformational management. See Management

Transformational Management Skills Inventory, 350-351, 353-356
Transitions: analysis of, 299-322; concept of, 22; coping with, 324-327; personal, 305-312; in roles, 312-322; in work, 299-305
Transnational Network for Appropriate/Alternative Technologies (TRANET), 254, 267
Travis, J. W., 293
Treacy, W. R., 383
TRW Systems: and organizational change, 337; and robotics, 185; and teams, 243
Tubesing, D. A., 286, 290-291, 383
Tubesing, N. L., 286, 290-291, 383
Turoff, M., 253, 375
24-Carat Club, as network, 254
Tyler Corporation, and wellness, 291
Tymshare, innovation at, 213
Type A personalities, and stress management, 283-284

U

Ueberroth, P., 219
Ultrastability, and teams, 229
Union Carbide, and industrial safety, 273, 331
Union of Soviet Socialist Republics, and space activities, 176, 196, 345
Unions: and automation, 137, 139; culture shock for, 42-43; and organizational change, 340; and performance, 204, 217; and robotics, 180-181, 186, 191-192
United Airlines: and computer-based learning, 120; and corporate breakup, 63
United Auto Workers, 49, 180-181, 186, 204
United Food and Commercial Workers (UFCW), 91
United Kingdom: contract work in, 46-47, 225-226; human resource development in, 113, 129; industrialization in, 2, 17, 39; and joint venture, 67; robotics in, 173; transformation of work in, 4; walk-around management in, 216
United Nations Educational, Scientific, and Cultural Organization (UNESCO), and cultural awareness, 38
U.S. Air Force, computer use by, 162
U.S. Army, Delta Task Force in, 253, 332
U.S. Bureau of Labor Statistics, and women's role, 316
U.S. Bureau of the Census, robots counted by, 171
United States Chamber of Commerce, 221
U.S. Customs Service, organizational culture survey for, 335
U.S. Department of Agriculture, forecasting by, 2
U.S. Department of Defense: cooperative research by, 230; and culture shock, 302; seed money from, 117
U.S. Department of Transportation: Commercial Space Transportation Office of, 97; and seat belts, 288; and worker ownership, 219
U.S. Office of Technology Assessment, 345
United Technologies, and executive training, 113-114
Universal Medical Supplies, and global opportunity, 344-345
Universities: consortia of, 116-117, 126, 127; and entrepreneurialism, 94-96; and human resource development training, 115, 125-129; research partnerships of, 342; and robotics, 192-193, 199, 200-201; and wellness, 291, 292-293

V

Van Harrison, R., 293

Index

Vanguard management thinking and planning, trend toward, 10-12
Vasconcellos, J., 208
Vedax Sciences Corporation, and entrepreneur network, 77, 262
Velsor, E. N., 268
Venture capital, in synergy with entrepreneurialism, 75-76
Very high speed integrated circuits (VHSIC), and team research, 230
Very large scale integrated circuits (VLSIC), and robotics, 197
Vesper, K. H., 71, 383
Victor Technologies, and entrepreneurialism, 74
Video age, 121
Videoconferencing, and human resource development, 117, 124-125
VIDEONET, 124
Villoldo, A., 44, 383
VisiCorp, team leader software from, 237
von Puttkamer, J., 349, 383

W

Wagoner, K. P., 145, 381
Waite, L., 313, 383
Wallach, E., 214, 215n, 383
Wang Institute, graduate programs of, 126
Wang Laboratories, daycare at, 339
Warner Communications, participative management at, 215-216
Warner-Lambert, wellness at, 279
Waterman, R. H., 12-13, 14, 323, 380
Watson, T., 57
Weatherford, J. M., 383
Weber, D., 16, 383
Weiner, E., 26, 333, 370
Weingarten, N., 119
Weirtown Steel Company, employee buy out of, 46, 219
Weisler, J., 228, 383
Welch, J. E., Jr., 55

Wellin, M., 235, 383
Wellness: and ambivalence, 285; analysis of, 269-298; categories of, 271; concept of, 287; and corporate behavioral health, 270-272; and entrepreneurs, 86-87; and executives, 278-279, 289; and family and friends, 293-298; and health care, 275-280; historical view of, 272-275; and lifestyle, 287-290; networking for, 291, 295; resources of, 290-293; and social support, 293-298; and stress management, 280-287; and work culture, 271, 275-280, 284-285
Welsh, J. A., 75, 383
Western Airlines: compensation at, 219; and takeover, 67
Western Association of Schools and Colleges, 125
Western Behavioral Science Institute (WBSI), School of Management and Strategic Studies of, 123
Westinghouse, G., 19
Westinghouse Electric Corp.: participative management at, 216; Unimation robot of, 178, 191-192
Westminster, team leader software from, 237
Weyerhaeuser: and technology, 58-59; as vanguard corporation, 11
White, J. E., 75, 383
White, R. A., 77-78, 384
White House Commission on Industrial Competitiveness, 220
Whitehead, A. N., 107
Whitlock, Q., 121, 372
Wiener, N., 8, 172
Wisconsin, University of, and entrepreneurialism, 95
Wisconsin Alumni Research Foundation, 95
Wisconsin at Stevens Point, University of, and wellness, 291
Women: and culture shock, 303; and entrepreneurialism, 79-82;

and networking, 252, 254; and personal change in work, 311; role changes for, 312-316; and wellness, 296, 297
Woodcock, M., 229, 293, 384
Wooldridge, D., 337
Worcester Polytechnic Institute, and robotics, 192
Work: concepts of, 41-42, 43-45; contract, 338-339; critical incidents in, 1-2; energy related to, 42; fast-growth enterprises for, 15-18; at home by computer, 166-168, 338; implications for, 6-7; industrial stage of, 3-4; new technologies in, 7-10; personal changes related to, 310-311; problems in transforming, 5-6; transformation of, 1-18; transitions in, 299-305; trends in, 7-18, 45
Work culture: analysis of, 30-68; aspects of, 55-56; autonomy in, 46-47; characteristics of future, 45-55; communications/information orientation in, 47-48; dimensions of, 59-60; entrepreneurialism in, 51-53; future of, 41-55; and guide to culture, 31-38; industrial, 38-39; informal/synergistic relationships in, 48-49; insights for future, 55-60; learning for, 101-116; management development for, 129-133; norms in, 50-51; participation in, 47; past, 38-41; performance and productivity in, 51, 205; personal computers and, 159; quality of work life in, 49-50; research and development orientation in, 54; shapers of, 108; synergistic alterations of, 60-68; technological, research areas on, 130; technological orientation in, 53-54; and wellness, 271, 275-280, 284-285
Work force: contract and part-time members of, 46-47, 225-226, 338-339; core professionals in, 224-225; executives in, 226; two-tiered, 140
Work in America Institute, 206
World, University of the, technologies of, 128
World Future Society, 45, 53-54, 259

X

Xerox Corporation: educational complex of, 128; and entrepreneurialism, 52; norms of, 50-51; Office Systems research by, 159-160; and robotics, 199; self-learning courses from, 132

Y

Yale University, and robotics, 199
Yankelovich, D., 141-142
Young, D., 232, 373
Young, J. F., 201, 220

Z

Zaban, E., 318
Zachary, W., 177
Zale's, daycare at, 339
Zemke, R., 218, 250, 384
Zickelfoose, R. D., 51
Zuboff, S., 137-138
Zysman, J., 10

will find Harris's advice and suggestions of great use.

"OUTSTANDING . . . A ROADMAP FOR PLANNING"

"*Management in Transition* describes the various dimensions of the new work culture, offers new management leadership strategies which focus on human resource development and high performance management, and contains an extensive list of resources and instruments for the new-age manager. . . .

"Dr. Harris has done an outstanding job of researching a variety of fast-moving subject areas, selecting data and examples which indicate future trends, synthesizing the information, and organizing it in a manner which has high impact on the reader. Dr. Harris's writing is clear, easy to read, and carries the reader forward from one idea to the next in such a way that the reader is reluctant to put the book down . . . a roadmap for planning"—*Bobette Williamson and Robert P. McManus, management consultants and faculty members of U.C. San Diego Extension's Department of Business and Management.*

THE AUTHOR

PHILIP R. HARRIS is president of Harris International Ltd., a management consulting firm. Harris has been a consultant to a wide range of multinational corporations, government agencies, educational systems, and professional associations—and has carried out numerous workshops on management in transition. He is the author of 29 books including *New Worlds, New Ways, New Management.*